Research and Development in
Intelligent Systems XXV

Max Bramer Frans Coenen Miltos Petridis
Editors

Research and Development in Intelligent Systems XXV

Proceedings of AI-2008, the Twenty-eighth SGAI
International Conference on Innovative Techniques
and Applications of Artificial Intelligence

 Springer

Max Bramer, BSc, PhD, CEng, CITP,
FBCS, FIET, FRSA, FHEA
Faculty of Technology
University of Portsmouth, Portsmouth, UK

Frans Coenen, BSc, PhD
Department of Computer Science,
University of Liverpool, Liverpool, UK

Miltos Petridis, DipEng, MBA, PhD,
MBCS, AMBA
University of Greenwich, UK

British Library Cataloguing in Publication Data
A catalogue record for this book is available from the British Library

ISBN 978-1-84882-170-5   e-ISBN 978-1-84882-171-2

Printed on acid-free paper

Springer Science+Business Media
springer.com

TECHNICAL PROGRAMME CHAIR'S INTRODUCTION

M.A.BRAMER
University of Portsmouth, UK

This volume comprises the refereed technical papers presented at AI-2008, the Twenty-eighth SGAI International Conference on Innovative Techniques and Applications of Artificial Intelligence, held in Cambridge in December 2008. The conference was organised by SGAI, the British Computer Society Specialist Group on Artificial Intelligence.

The papers in this volume present new and innovative developments in the field, divided into sections on CBR and Classification, AI Techniques, Argumentation and Negotiation, Intelligent Systems, From Machine Learning to E-Learning and Decision Making. The volume also includes the text of short papers presented as posters at the conference.

This year's prize for the best refereed technical paper was won by a paper entitled 'On the Classification Performance of TAN and General Bayesian Networks' by Michael G. Madden (College of Engineering & Informatics, National University of Ireland, Galway, Ireland). SGAI gratefully acknowledges the long-term sponsorship of Hewlett-Packard Laboratories (Bristol) for this prize, which goes back to the 1980s.

This is the twenty-fifth volume in the *Research and Development* series. The Application Stream papers are published as a companion volume under the title *Applications and Innovations in Intelligent Systems XVI*.

On behalf of the conference organising committee I should like to thank all those who contributed to the organisation of this year's technical programme, in particular the programme committee members, the executive programme committee and our administrators Rachel Browning and Bryony Bramer.

Max Bramer
Technical Programme Chair, AI-2008

ACKNOWLEDGEMENTS

AI-2008 CONFERENCE COMMITTEE

Dr. Miltos Petridis   (Conference Chair and UK CBR Organiser)
University of Greenwich

Dr Frans Coenen   (Deputy Conference Chair, Local Arrangements
University of Liverpool   and Deputy Technical Programme Chair)

Prof. Adrian Hopgood   (Workshop Organiser)
De Montfort University

Rosemary Gilligan   (Treasurer)

Dr Nirmalie Wiratunga   (Poster Session Organiser)
The Robert Gordon University

Professor Max Bramer   (Technical Programme Chair)
University of Portsmouth

Dr. Tony Allen   (Application Programme Chair)
Nottingham Trent University

Richard Ellis   (Deputy Application Program Chair)
Stratum Management Ltd

Alice Kerly   (Research Student Liaison)
University of Birmingham

Dr. Kirsty Bradbrook   (Research Student Liaison)

Prof. Alun Preece   (Committee Member)
University of Cardiff

Rachel Browning   (Conference Administrator)
BCS

Bryony Bramer   (Paper Administrator)

TECHNICAL EXECUTIVE PROGRAMME COMMITTEE

Prof. Max Bramer, University of Portsmouth (Chair)

Dr. Frans Coenen, University of Liverpool (Vice-Chair)

Dr. John Kingston, University of Edinburgh

Dr. Peter Lucas, University of Nijmegen, The Netherlands

Dr. Miltos Petridis, University of Greenwich

Prof. Alun Preece, University of Cardiff

Dr. Nirmalie Wiratunga, The Robert Gordon University, Aberdeen

TECHNICAL PROGRAMME COMMITTEE

Alia Abdelmoty (Cardiff University)

Andreas A Albrecht (Queen's University Belfast)

Roman Belavkin (Middlesex University)

Yaxin Bi (University of Ulster)

Mirko Boettcher (University of Magdeburg, Germany)

Max Bramer (University of Portsmouth)

Krysia Broda (Imperial College, University of London)

Ken Brown (University College Cork)

Frans Coenen (University of Liverpool)

Bruno Cremilleux (University of Caen)

Madalina Croitoru (University of Southampton)

Ireneusz Czarnowski (Gdynia Maritime University, Poland)

Richard Dapoigny (University of Savoie)

Marina De Vos (University of Bath)

John Debenham (University of Technology; Sydney)

Stefan Diaconescu (Softwin, Romania)

Nicolas Durand (University of Aix-Marseille 2)

Anneli Edman (University of Upsala)

Virginia Francisco (Universidad Complutense de Madrid)

Adriana Giret (Universidad Politécnica de Valencia)

Nadim Haque (Temenos UK)

Joana Hois (University of Bremen)

Arjen Hommersom (University of Nijmegen, The Netherlands)

Piotr Jedrzejowicz (Gdynia Maritime University; Poland)

Rasa Jurgelenaite (Radboud University, The Netherlands)

John Kingston (University of Edinburgh)

Konstantinos Kotis (University of the Aegean)

Ivan Koychev (Bulgarian Academy of Science)

T. K. Satish Kumar (Institute for Human and Machine Cognition, USA)

Peter Lucas (University of Nijmegen)

Daniel Manrique Gamo (University of Madrid)

Roberto Micalizio (Universita' di Torino)

Alfonsas Misevicius (Kaunas University of Technology)

Lars Nolle (Nottingham Trent University)

Tomas Eric Nordlander (SINTEF ICT, Norway)

Dan O'Leary (University of Southern California)

Nir Oren (Kings College London)

Filipo Perotto (II / UFRGS (Porto Alegre - Brazil))

Alun Preece (University of Cardiff)

Juan Jose Rodriguez (University of Burgos)

Maria Dolores Rodriguez-Moreno (Universidad de Alcala)

Fernando Saenz Perez (Universidad Complutense de Madrid)

Miguel A. Salido (Universidad Politécnica de Valencia)

Rainer Schmidt (University of Rostock, Germany)

Simon Thompson (BT)

Jon Timmis (University of York)

Gianluca Torta (Università di Torino)

Andrew Tuson (City University)

M.R.C. van Dongen (University College Cork)

Carl Vogel (Trinity College Dublin, Ireland)

Graham Winstanley (University of Brighton)

Nirmalie Wiratunga (Robert Gordon University)

Fei Ling Woon (SDG Consulting UK)

CONTENTS

BEST TECHNICAL PAPER

On the Classification Performance of TAN and General Bayesian Networks

Michael G. Madden[1]

Abstract. Over a decade ago, Friedman *et al.* introduced the Tree Augmented Naïve Bayes (TAN) classifier, with experiments indicating that it significantly outperformed Naïve Bayes (NB) in terms of classification accuracy, whereas general Bayesian network (GBN) classifiers performed no better than NB. This paper challenges those claims, using a careful experimental analysis to show that GBN classifiers significantly outperform NB on datasets analyzed, and are comparable to TAN performance. It is found that the poor performance reported by Friedman *et al.* are not attributable to the GBN per se, but rather to their use of simple empirical frequencies to estimate GBN parameters, whereas basic parameter smoothing (used in their TAN analyses but not their GBN analyses) improves GBN performance significantly. It is concluded that, while GBN classifiers may have some limitations, they deserve greater attention, particularly in domains where insight into classification decisions, as well as good accuracy, is required.

1   Introduction

This paper examines the performance of Bayesian networks as classifiers, comparing their performance to that of the Naïve Bayes (NB) classifier and the Tree-Augmented Naïve Bayes (TAN) classifier, both of which make strong assumptions about interactions between domain variables.

In the experiments performed for this work, described below in Section 3, standard Bayesian networks (referred to as General Bayesian Networks, GBNs, to distinguish them from NB and TAN) are compared with NB and TAN classifiers on 28 standard benchmark datasets. Our experiments indicate that the GBN classifier is substantially better than NB, with performance closer to that of TAN. This contrasts with the conclusions drawn in the landmark paper on Bayesian network classifiers by Friedman *et al.* (1997). That paper presented results on many of the same datasets, showing that GBNs constructed using the minimum description length (MDL) score tend to perform no better than NB. That result has been widely noted by other authors (e.g. Grossman & Domingos, 2004; Keogh &

---

[1] College of Engineering & Informatics, National University of Ireland, Galway, Ireland.
Email: michael.madden@nuigalway.ie

Pazzani, 2002); in one case the result was interpreted as indicating that NB "easily outperforms" GBN.

Our contention is that it has become 'accepted wisdom' that GBN classification performance is no better than that of NB, and significantly worse than TAN (ignoring other considerations such as computational complexity or interpretability). Our results indicate that GBN's classification performance is superior to that of NB and much closer to that of TAN, when the same parameter estimation procedure is used for all.

It turns out that Friedman *et al.* used simple frequency counts for parameter estimation in constructing GBN classifiers, whereas they used parameter smoothing in constructing TAN classifiers (see Sec. 2.3 for details). Our experiments show that if frequency counts are used for both GBN and TAN, neither is much better than NB (Sec. 3.3, Figure 5), but if parameter smoothing is used for both, they both perform similarly well (Figure 4). Furthermore, since GBN classifiers are commonly constructed through heuristic search, it is possible for improved GBN construction algorithms to lead to improved performance.

The structure of the paper is as follows. Section 2 reviews Bayesian networks and the algorithms for constructing GBN and TAN classifiers that are used in this paper. Section 3 presents experiments applying NB, TAN and two GBN algorithms to classification problems on 28 standard datasets, and identifies why the results of this paper are at odds with those of Friedman *et al.* as mentioned above. Finally, Section 4 draws general conclusions about the suitability of GBNs as classifiers.

2   Bayesian Networks and Classification

As is well known, a Bayesian network is composed of the network structure and its conditional probabilities. The structure B_S is a directed acyclic graph where the nodes correspond to domain variables x_1, ..., x_n and the arcs between nodes represent direct dependencies between the variables. Likewise, the absence of an arc between two nodes x_1 and x_2 represents that x_2 is independent of x_1 given its parents in B_S. Using the notation of Cooper & Herskovits (1992), the set of parents of a node x_i in B_S is denoted π_i. The structure is annotated with a set of conditional probabilities, B_P, containing a term $P(X_i \mid \Pi_i)$ for each possible value X_i of x_i and each possible instantiation Π_i of π_i

2.1 Inductive Learning of Bayesian Networks

Several algorithms have been proposed since the late 1980s for inductive learning of general Bayesian networks. Recent developments include the global optimization approach of Silander and Myllymäki (2006), the Greedy Equivalence Search algorithm (Chickering, 2002), and the Three-Phase Dependency Analysis algorithm (Cheng *et al.,* 2002), though this latter algorithm has subsequently been shown to be incorrect (Chickering & Meek, 2006). We evaluate two approaches to GBN construction, described in the following subsections, both of which have relatively low computational complexity:

1. The K2 search procedure (Cooper & Herskovits, 1992) in conjunction with the Bayesian BDeu scoring metric (Buntine, 1991), which is a refinement of the K2 metric
2. The approach used by Friedman *et al.* (1997), which combines hill-climbing search with the MDL score.

These are both search-and-score methods for construction of GBNs; a search heuristic is used to propose candidate networks, and a scoring function is used to assess, for any two candidates, which one is more likely given the training data.

The scoring functions and search procedures are described in greater detail in the following sub-sections. Rather can constructing general BN structures, restrictions may be placed on the structures; this is described in Section 2.2. Typically, the conditional probabilities (parameters) associated with a network are not computed from the data until after the structure has been found; parameter estimation is described in Section 2.3.

2.1.1 K2 Search with BDeu Scoring Approach

If D is a database of training cases, Z is the set of variables in each case in D, and B_{S_i} and B_{S_j} are two belief-network structures containing exactly those variables that are in Z, then the comparison amounts to calculating $P(B_{S_i}|D)/P(B_{S_j}|D)$, which in turn reduces to calculating $P(B_{S_i},D)/P(B_{S_j},D)$.

Assume that Z is a set of n discrete variables, where a variable x_i in Z has r_i possible value assignments, $(v_{i1}, ..., v_{ir_i})$, and that D has N cases, each with a value assignment for each variable in Z. A network structure B_S is assumed to contain just the variables in Z. Each variable x_i in B_S has zero or more parents, represented as a list π_i. Let w_{ij} denote the jth unique instantiation of π_i relative to D, and assume that there are q_i such unique instantiations of π_i. Let N_{ijk} be defined as the number of cases in D in which variable x_i has the value v_{ik} and π_i is instantiated as w_{ij}. Let N'_{ijk} denote a Dirichlet parameter. Let N_{ij} and N'_{ij} be defined as:

$$N_{ij} = \sum_{k=1}^{r_i} N_{ijk} \quad N'_{ij} \equiv \sum_{k=1}^{r_i} N'_{ijk} \tag{1}$$

With these definitions, the BD metric (Heckerman *et al.,* 1995) is defined as:

$$P(B_S, D) =$$

$$P(B_S)\prod_{i=1}^{n} \prod_{j=1}^{q_i} \frac{\Gamma(N'_{ij})}{\Gamma(N'_{ij} + N_{ij})}\prod_{k=1}^{r_i} \frac{\Gamma(N'_{ijk} + N_{ijk})}{\Gamma(N'_{ijk})} \tag{2}$$

Note that Γ is the gamma function, defined as $\Gamma(x+1) = x\Gamma(x)$, which is closely related to the factorial function but defined for real numbers, not just integers. In a practical implementation, the logs of terms in Eq. 2 are computed.

The K2 metric (Cooper & Herskovits, 1992) corresponds to Eq. 2 with all Dirichlet exponents set to 'uninformative' values of $N'_{ijk} = 1$. Alternative uninformative values are proposed by Buntine (1991):

$$N'_{ijk} = \frac{N'}{r_i q_i} \tag{3}$$

Using Buntine's values, Eq. 2 becomes what Heckerman *et al.* (1995) term the BDeu metric, which has the additional property of being structure-equivalent. This is the metric used in the current work. Assuming that all structures are equally likely *a priori*, $P(B_S)$ is constant, so to maximize $P(B_S,D)$ just requires finding the set of parents for each node that maximizes the second inner product of Eq. 2.

The K2 search procedure requires a node ordering. It operates by initially assuming that a node has no parents, and then adding incrementally that parent whose addition most increases the probability of the resulting network. Parents are added greedily to a node until the addition of no one parent can increase the structure probability. This is repeated for all nodes in the sequence specified by the node ordering.

In the experiments of Section 3, the node ordering in each dataset is arbitrarily taken to be the order of attributes in the input files, except that the class node is always placed first in the order. In addition, the maximum number of parents a node may have is limited to 4.

2.1.2   MDL Scoring Approach

In constructing GBNs, Friedman *et al.* (1997) use a scoring function based on the minimum description length (MDL) principle. The MDL score of a network B given a database of training cases D is:

$$MDL(B \mid D) = \frac{1}{2} \log N|B| - LL(B \mid D) \tag{4}$$

where $|B|$ is the number of parameters in the network and $LL(B \mid D)$ denotes the log-likelihood of B given D. To calculate $LL(B \mid D)$, let $\hat{P}_D(\cdot)$ be the empirical probability measure defined by frequencies of events in D. Then:

$$LL(B \mid D) = N \sum_i \sum_{X_i,\Pi_i} \hat{P}_D(X_i,\Pi_i) \log(\hat{P}_D(X_i|\Pi_i)) \tag{5}$$

The search procedure used by Friedman *et al.* is to start with the empty network and successively apply local operations that greedily reduce the MDL score maximally until a local minimum is found. The local operations applied are arc insertion, arc deletion and arc reversal.

2.1.3   Classification using a GBN

A Bayesian network may be used for classification as follows. Firstly, any nodes outside of the Markov blanket of the classification node x_c may be deleted. Then, assume that the value of x_c is unknown and the values of all other nodes are known. Then, for every possible instantiation of x_c, calculate the joint probability of that instantiation of all variables in the network given the database D. By the definition of a Bayesian network, the joint probability of a particular instantiation of all n variables is calculated as:

$$P(x_1 = X_1,...,x_n = X_n) = \prod_{i=1}^{n} P(x_i = X_i | \pi_i = \Pi_i) \qquad (6)$$

By normalizing the resulting set of joint probabilities of all possible instantiations of x_c, an estimate of the relative probability of each is found. The vector of class probabilities may be multiplied by a misclassification cost matrix, if available. Note that the classification node is not considered 'special' when building the GBN, and in Eq. 6, x_c is just one of the variables $x_1...x_n$.

Although arbitrary inference in a GBN with discrete variables is NP-hard (Cooper, 1990), the classification procedure just described just requires Eq. 6 to be evaluated once for each possible instantiation of x_c; thus its time complexity is $O(n_m r_c)$, where n_m is the number of nodes in x_c's Markov blanket; $n_m \leq n$.

2.2 Restricted Bayesian Classifiers

Figure 1 schematically illustrates the structure of the Bayesian classifiers considered in this paper. The simplest form of Bayesian classifier is Naïve Bayes. When represented as a Bayesian network, a Naïve Bayes (NB) classifier has a simple structure whereby there is an arc from the classification node to each other node, and there are no arcs between other nodes, as illustrated in Figure 1(a). Since NB has a fixed structure, learning simply involves estimating the parameters according to one of the procedures discussed below in Section 2.3.

Several researchers have examined ways of achieving better performance than NB. Friedman *et al.* (1997) in particular consider (among other structures) *Tree Augmented Naïve Bayes* (TAN), which allows arcs between the children of the classification node x_c as shown in Figure 1(b), thereby relaxing the assumption of conditional independence. In their approach, each node has x_c and at most one other node as a parent, so that the nodes excluding x_c form a tree structure. Optimal TAN structures are constructed by finding the maximum weighted spanning tree within a complete graph connecting the nodes, where arcs are annotated by the conditional mutual information between all pairs of non-class nodes, conditioned on the class node, according to Eq. 7.

$$I(x_i, x_j | c) = \sum_{X_i, X_j, C} P(X_i, X_j, C) \log \frac{P(X_i, X_j | C)}{P(X_i | C) P(X_j | C)} \tag{7}$$

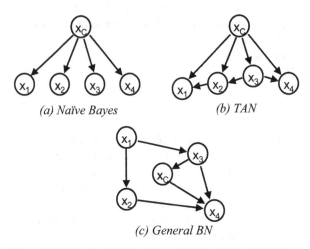

(a) Naïve Bayes   *(b) TAN*

(c) General BN

Figure 1: Illustration of Naive Bayes, TAN and General BN Structures.

2.3 Parameter Estimation

Let θ_{ijk} denote the conditional probability that a variable x_i in B_S has the value v_{ik}, for some k from 1 to r_i, given that the parents of x_i, represented by π_i, are instantiated as w_{ij}. Then $\theta_{ijk} = P(x_i{=}k | \pi_i{=}w_{ij})$ is termed a network conditional probability. The simplest form of parameter estimation is based on frequency counts (referred to as *unsmoothed* estimates by Friedman *et al.*):

$$\theta_{ijk}^f = \frac{N_{ijk}}{N_{ij}} \tag{8}$$

A problem with using Eq. 8 is that it can result in zero estimates for some parameters if not all combinations of variables are well represented in the training data, resulting in a probability of 0 being computed for some instantiations of all variables. One solution is to replace zero estimates by a small positive value.

As well as using unsmoothed estimates, Friedman *et al.* use technique based on Dirichlet priors that they term *parameter smoothing,* which boils down to the following calculation:

$$\theta_{ijk}^{s} = \frac{N_{ijk} + N_0\, N_i/N}{N_{ij} + N_0} \tag{9}$$

where $N_i/N = \hat{P}(x_i)$ is the frequency of the given value of x_i observed in the dataset. (Friedman *et al.* report that, after experimentation, a value of $N_0 = 5$ was chosen.)

As part of our controlled comparisons, the same parameter smoothing is used for all classifiers in the analyses presented below in Section 3.

To avoid any ambiguity, it should be pointed out that smoothed parameter estimates are used only to estimate the conditional probabilities, B_P, after the network structure, B_S, has been determined. TAN and GBN structure learning uses simple frequency counts (Eq. 8).

3 Experiments

3.1 *Methodology*

For this work, the Naïve Bayes, TAN and two general BN algorithms were compared using 26 datasets from the UCI repository of Machine Learning datasets (Asuncion & Newman 2007). For consistency with previous work in this domain (Cheng & Greiner, 2001; Friedman *et al.*, 1977; Keogh & Pazzani, 2002; Madden, 2003), continuous variables were discretized using the discretization utility of MLC++ (Kohavi *et al.*, 1977) with its default entropy-based setting (*Dougherty et al.*, 1995) and any cases with missing values were removed. The two general BN algorithms are those listed earlier:

1. GBN-K2: K2 search procedure with the Bayesian BDeu scoring metric
2. GBN-HC: hill-climbing search with MDL score, following Friedman *et al.*

The GBN-HC implementation used in this work is that in WEKA (Bouckaert, 2004a). The NB, TAN and GBN-K2 algorithms were implemented for this work in Common Lisp (code available by email on request).

Previous comparisons of similar classifiers (Cheng & Greiner, 2001; Friedman *et al.*, 1977; Madden, 2003) have estimated classifier accuracy using holdout sets for the larger datasets and 5-fold cross validation for smaller datasets. However, it has been shown that such analyses may suffer from high sensitivity to the specific divisions used (Bouckaert, 2004a). Also, previous analyses have compared accuracy figures by simply considering the magnitude of the estimated accuracy without performing statistical significance tests (Cheng & Greiner, 2001; Friedman *et al.*, 1977), or using t-tests that are not corrected to account for the overlap in folds from a multi-fold cross-validation run (Madden, 2003). This latter approach has been shown to have a high Type I error (Nadeau & Bengio, 2000).

To avoid such problems, the experimental methodology used in this work follows the 10 x 10 fold sorted cross-validation approach proposed by Bouckaert (2004b), with associated t-tests to measure significance. This has been shown to have good replicablility, thereby facilitating future comparisons, and because by applying it consistently across all datasets and algorithms, coherent comparisons can be drawn.

3.2 Results

Table 1 lists the accuracy (and standard deviation of accuracy) of each of the four classification algorithms being considered, as measured from 10 runs of 10-fold cross-validation on each dataset. In each row, the best of the four classifier results are displayed in bold. Specifically, for each dataset, the classifier with the highest performance is highlighted in bold and compared with that of the other two classifiers, using a paired t-test at the 5% significance level based on the 10x10 fold sorted cross-validation results. If another's performance is not significantly different from the best, it is also highlighted, but if the differences between all four classifiers are not statistically significant, then none of them are highlighted.

As these results show, there are no statistical differences between the algorithms on 10 of the 26 datasets, at the 5% significance level. In just 2 other cases, NB is best (including joint best), in 13 cases TAN is best, in 10 cases GBN-K2 is best and in 7 cases GBN-HC is best.

Figure 2 shows two scatter-plots comparing TAN with NB and with GBN-HC. Figure 2(a) shows that TAN generally outperforms NB, as was also demonstrated in the experiments of Friedman *et al.* (1997). Figure 2(b) also shows TAN outperforming GBN-HC, though the difference in performance is not as marked as in the results of Friedman et al.

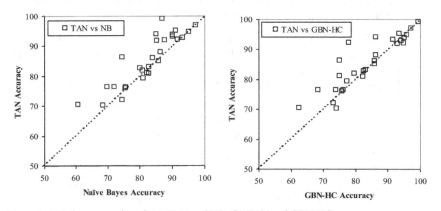

Figure 2: Relative accuracies of: (a) TAN and NB; (b) TAN and GBN-HC.

Table 1: Classification performance (accuracy ± std dev) of four algorithms as measured on 28 datasets; results in bold are best or joint best, as described in text.

No.	Dataset	Naïve Bayes	TAN	GBN-K2	GBN-HC
1	Adult	84.03 ± 0.53	**86.15 ± 0.35**	**86.16 ± 0.33**	**86.02 ± 0.48**
2	Australian	85.80 ± 4.03	85.06 ± 3.90	86.22 ± 3.83	85.93 ± 4.06
3	Breast Cancer	97.38 ± 1.84	96.99 ± 1.88	97.32 ± 1.81	97.15 ± 1.83
4	Car	85.15 ± 2.74	**93.96 ± 1.90**	89.61 ± 2.20	86.36 ± 3.15
5	Chess	87.85 ± 1.70	92.09 ± 1.39	**94.45 ± 1.41**	**94.95 ± 1.47**
6	Cleve	82.87 ± 6.20	81.04 ± 6.77	81.07 ± 6.22	82.33 ± 6.27
7	Connect-4	72.11 ± 0.63	76.43 ± 0.40	**79.08 ± 0.66**	73.88 ± 0.70
8	Corral	87.05 ± 9.46	**99.23 ± 3.19**	99.62 ± 2.53	99.38 ± 2.37
9	DNA Splice	95.26 ± 0.98	94.92 ± 1.10	**95.93 ± 1.05**	95.81 ± 1.02
10	Flare	80.12 ± 3.47	82.65 ± 3.47	82.24 ± 3.39	82.56 ± 3.48
11	German	74.61 ± 4.31	72.07 ± 4.04	74.20 ± 3.97	73.25 ± 4.07
12	Glass2	81.16 ± 8.68	79.37 ± 8.95	79.00 ± 9.35	77.29 ± 9.86
13	Heart	82.74 ± 6.70	83.11 ± 7.30	82.30 ± 7.49	83.04 ± 7.32
14	Hepatitis	86.38 ± 10.97	88.00 ± 11.64	87.00 ± 13.29	86.38 ± 14.22
15	Letter	74.67 ± 1.05	**86.28 ± 0.61**	81.76 ± 0.73	75.12 ± 0.72
16	Lymphography	82.16 ± 10.61	81.07 ± 9.57	77.46 ± 9.47	75.06 ± 10.98
17	Mofn-3-7-10	85.34 ± 3.43	**91.96 ± 2.63**	86.85 ± 3.56	**93.04 ± 2.86**
18	Nursery	90.29 ± 0.77	**93.30 ± 0.81**	91.18 ± 0.89	91.68 ± 0.82
19	Pima	75.69 ± 4.42	76.37 ± 3.94	76.33 ± 4.26	76.18 ± 4.27
20	Segment	91.27 ± 1.70	**95.27 ± 1.49**	**94.64 ± 1.56**	93.45 ± 1.48
21	Soybean-Large	**91.83 ± 3.50**	**92.35 ± 3.08**	89.22 ± 4.22	78.02 ± 6.45
22	Spect	68.53 ± 9.14	**70.29 ± 8.99**	**68.98 ± 8.50**	**74.19 ± 8.89**
23	Tic Tac Toe	69.76 ± 4.45	**76.32 ± 3.82**	69.26 ± 4.74	68.38 ± 4.83
24	Vehicle	60.62 ± 4.88	**70.36 ± 4.58**	**67.30 ± 5.18**	62.50 ± 5.46
25	Vote	90.27 ± 4.30	**93.84 ± 3.26**	93.57 ± 3.53	**95.11 ± 3.03**
26	Waveform-21	**80.90 ± 1.64**	**81.96 ± 1.70**	**81.67 ± 1.56**	79.73 ± 1.96

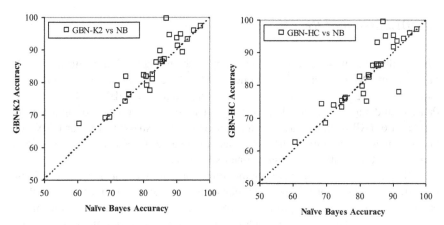

Figure 3: Relative accuracies of: (a) GBN-K2 and NB; (b) GBN-HC and NB.

But what about the claim that GBNs perform as badly as, or even worse than, NB? Figure 3 shows two scatter-plots comparing GBN-K2 and GBN-HC with NB. In this and subsequent graphs, "A vs B" indicates that A is plotted on the vertical axis and B is plotted on the horizontal axis. Visually, points above the diagonal are those where classifier A has higher accuracy. Our results do not provide evidence for that claim. They show that the classification performance of both GBN algorithms is good relative to NB, although the performance of GBN-K2 is a little better than that of GBN-HC. On the basis of paired t-tests, it is found that GBN-K2 is better than NB on 11 datasets whereas NB is better than it on just 1; likewise, GBN-HC is better than BN on 9 datasets whereas NB is better on 1.

Furthermore, when GBN-K2, rather than GBN-HC, is compared with TAN, the differences between them are not at all pronounced, as shown in Figure 4.

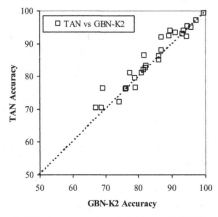

Figure 4: Relative accuracies of TAN and GBN-K2.

3.3 Discussion of Results

The results presented in Table 2 and illustrated in Figure 3 indicate that GBN outperforms NB overall. This conclusion is clearly at variance with the experimental results of Friedman et al., who compared GBN and NB on 25 datasets and reported that GBN was significantly better on 6 and significantly worse on 6. (All of those datasets are included in this study except for CRX and Glass, which are variants of the Australian and Glass2 datasets that are included.) Our GBN-HC algorithm is the same one that they used.

Differences in experimental methodology might account for some of the disparities in conclusions drawn from our work and that of Friedman et al, as their experiments may be more prone to Type I errors and have lower replicability. However, we believe that parameter estimation has a much more significant effect. For the TAN and NB algorithms, they present results using unsmoothed (Eq. 8) and smoothed (Eq. 9) parameter estimates. As would be expected, parameter smoothing has little effect on the performance of NB, but it improves the performance of TAN since zero probability estimates are more likely to arise in more complex structures. However, Friedman et al. present results for GBN without smoothing only; they do not present corresponding smoothed GBN results, even though one would expect parameter smoothing to improve the performance of GBN also. In contrast, the results presented above in Table 2 and Figures 2-4 use parameter smoothing for all classifiers.

To explore this further, we repeated our analyses using unsmoothed parameter estimates. Figure 5(a) presents a plot comparing Unsmoothed GBN with Unsmoothed NB. These results are qualitatively similar to those of *Friedman et al.*; Unsmoothed GBN is not much better than Unsmoothed NB. However, the comparison in Figure 5(b) is also interesting, as it shows that Unsmoothed TAN is also no better than Unsmoothed NB.

In a further set of experiments, we used unsmoothed parameter estimates but replaced zero probabilities with small epsilon values. When we did so, the results were quite close to the smoothed result of Table 1. We therefore conclude that the essential cause of the poor performance of the TAN and GBN classifiers relative to NB in Figure 5 may be attributed to the zero probabilities in the computations.

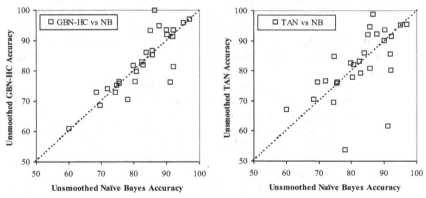

Figure 5: Relative Accuracies of: (a) Unsmoothed GBN-HC vs Unsmoothed NB; (b) Unsmoothed TAN vs Unsmoothed NB.

4 Conclusions: Suitability of GBN as a Classifier

The results of the preceding section have shown that, when TAN and GBN-K2 classifiers are compared under careful experimental procedures and using the same parameter estimation procedure for both, there is little to distinguish between them in terms of classification accuracy.

An advantage of TAN is its low computational complexity, which is $O(n^2 N)$. However, for a fixed maximum number of parents per node, to complexity of the

GBN-K2 algorithm is $O(n^3 N r)$, which is just a factor $(n r)$ worse. (Here, r is the maximum number of different values any node may have.)

Nonetheless, if GBN classifiers are more expensive to construct than TAN classifiers and do not offer greater classification accuracy, why use them? There are other possible drawbacks of GBNs as classifiers:

1. It is often observed in Machine Learning that we should not solve a more general problem than required, so why build a full GBN if all that is required is a classifier?

2. GBNs are in general more complex than TAN classifiers, though not necessarily; in fact, as discussed below, A GBN classifier may end up with fewer arcs than a TAN classifier on the same domain, since not all nodes might be within the Markov blanket.

3. The GBN that best describes the domain as a whole does not necessarily correspond to the one that best discriminates between classes, and the classification node might potentially be unconnected from the network.

While aware of these drawbacks, we propose three reasons for their use:

1. *Insightful analysis:* In many practical domains, particularly where it is required to convince end-users such as scientists or engineers that classification decisions are reasonable and logical, it is as important to gain insight into the problem as it is to achieve high classification accuracy. GBN classifiers support this by modelling the distribution, allowing more complex interactions between nodes to be represented than with TAN and also potentially identifying nodes that are outside the classification node's Markov blanket. They also aid in identifying conditional independencies in the data, which may also be useful for domain insight.

2. *Representational power:* Zhang & Ling (2001) have examined the representational power of discrete BNs and have concluded that, if each node has at most u parents, a BN can represent parity functions of maximum order u. This implies, as would be expected, that GBN has greater representational power than TAN which in turn has greater representational power than NB.

3. *Appropriate complexity:* As noted above, a GBN classifier may have fewer arcs than a TAN classifier for the same domain. In TAN, nodes are must have the class node as a parent, and a full tree of arcs between non-class nodes, so all but two nodes have exactly two parents each. In GBN, there are no such constraints; a node may have no parents or several. On the Adult dataset for example, the typical GBN had 13 arcs with 0-3 parents per node, which is the same number of arcs as Naïve Bayes for the dataset, which has exactly one parent per node. The TAN classifier for the Adult dataset was more complex, with 25 arcs. On the Connect 4 dataset, Naïve Bayes has 13 arcs, TAN has 83 arcs and GBN has a median of 74 arcs.

GBN approaches are not as widely used for classification tasks as TAN. Notable exceptions include the work of Cheng & Greiner (2001), the application by Baesens *et al.* (2002) of Monte Carlo Markov Chain search to constructing GBN classifiers, and Grossman & Domingos' (2004) algorithm for learning GBNs that maximize conditional likelihood.

However, a larger number of researchers have analysed TAN and proposed improvements. Examples include the work of Keogh and Pazzani (2002) who proposed the use of classification accuracy rather than conditional mutual information in building TAN-style classifiers; Zhang & Ling (2001), who extended Keogh & Pazzani's work by using AUC measures; Cerquides and de Mántaras (2005), who identified theoretical weaknesses in the TAN approach and proposed corrections for them; and Garg & Roth (2001) who addressed the question of why classifiers such as TAN that make often inaccurate assumptions tend to perform well.

Although the experiments here have shown that the GBN-K2 algorithm has quite good classification performance, it is likely that other algorithms would perform even better. Given the relative complexity of GBN construction compared to TAN construction, improving the performance of GBN classifiers would appear to be a topic with some potential for research. A limitation of GBN-K2 is that it requires an ordering on nodes. In specific applications it may be possible to determine a reasonable node ordering from domain knowledge, but it would be interesting to analyse the performance of other algorithms that do not require node ordering. That being said, GBN-HC does not require node ordering and its performance on the test datasets was slightly weaker than that of GBN-K2, but its simple hill-climbing search without restarts is quite limited.

In the future, it is hoped to analyse more sophisticated algorithms, particularly the algorithm of Silander and Myllymäki (2006), which searches for a globally optimal network. In order to address the issue noted earlier in this section that the optimal GBN for a domain is not necessarily the optimal one for classification, it would be necessary to develop an approach that constructs a Markov blanket around the classification node.

Overall, we believe that GBNs may deserve greater attention as classifiers, particularly in problem domains where data is plentiful and insight into the domain, as well as high accuracy, is required, although work remains to be done to optimize them for classification tasks.

Acknowledgements

This research has been supported by a Marie Curie Transfer of Knowledge Fellowship of the EU 6th Framework Programme, contract CT-2005-029611.

References

1.   Baesens, B., Egmont-Petersen, M., Castelo, R. and Vanthienen, J. (2002) Learning Bayesian network classifiers for credit scoring using Markov Chain Monte Carlo search. *Proc. 2002 International Congress on Pattern Recognition,* IEEE Computer Society.

2. Asuncion, A. & Newman, D.J. (2007). *UCI Machine Learning Repository.* http://www.ics.uci.edu/ ~mlearn/MLRepository.html. University of California, Irvine.
3. Bouckaert, R.R. (2004): Bayesian networks in Weka. *Technical Report 14/2004.* Computer Science Department. University of Waikato.
4. Bouckaert, R.R. (2004): Estimating Replicability of Classifier Learning Experiments. *Proc. 21st International Conference on Machine Learning.*
5. Buntine, W. (1991). Theory Refinement on Bayesian Networks. *Proc. 7th International Conference on Uncertainty in Artificial Intelligence.*
6. Cerquides, J. and de Mántaras, R. (2005). TAN Classifiers Based on Decomposable Distributions. *Machine Learning* Vol. 59, pp 323-354.
7. Cheng, J. and Greiner, R. (2001). Learning Bayesian Belief Network Classifiers: Algorithms and System. *Proc. 14th Canadian Conference on Artificial Intelligence.*
8. Cheng, J., Greiner, R., Kelly, J., Bell, D. and Liu, W. (2002). Learning Belief Networks from Data: An Information Theory Based Approach. *Artificial Intelligence,* Vol. 137, pp 43-90.
9. Chickering, D.M. (2002). Optimal Structure Identification with Greedy Search. *Journal of Machine Learning Research,* Vol. 3, pp 507-554.
10. Chickering, D.M. and Meek, C. (2006). On the Incompatibility of Faithfulness and Monotone DAG Faithfulness. *Artificial Intelligence,* Vol. 170, pp 653-666.
11. Cooper, G.F. (1990). The Computational Complexity of Probabilistic Inference Using Bayesian Belief Networks. *Artificial Intelligence,* Vol. 42, pp 393-405.
12. Cooper, G.F. and Herskovits, E. (1992). A Bayesian Method for the Induction of Probabilistic Networks from Data. *Machine Learning,* Vol. 9, pp 309-347. Kluwer Academic Publishers.
13. Domingos, P. & Pazzani, M. (1996). Beyond Independence: Conditions for the Optimality of the Simple Bayesian Classifier. *Proc. 13th International Conference on Machine Learning.*
14. Domingos, P. & Pazzani, M. (1997). On the Optimality of the Simple Bayesian Classifier under Zero-One Loss. *Machine Learning,* Vol. 29. Kluwer Academic Publishers.
15. Dougherty, J., Kohavi, R. and Sahami, M. (1995). Supervised and Unsupervised Discretization of Continuous Features. *Proc. 12th International Conference on Machine Learning.*
16. Friedman, N., Geiger, D. and Goldszmidt, M. (1997). Bayesian Network Classifiers. *Machine Learning,* Vol. 29, pp 131-163. Kluwer Academic Publishers, Boston.
17. Garg, A. and Roth, D. (2001) Understanding Probabilistic Classifiers. *Proc. 12th European Conference on Machine Learning.*
18. Grossman, D. and Domingos, P. (2004). Learning Bayesian Network Classifiers by Maximizing Conditional Likelihood. *Proc. 21st International Conference on Machine Learning.*
19. Heckerman, D., Geiger, D. and Chickering, D.M. (1995). Learning Bayesian Networks: The Combination of Knowledge and Statistical Data. *Machine Learning,* Vol. 20, pp 197-243.
20. Keogh, E. and Pazzani, M.J. (2002). Learning the Structure of Augmented Bayesian Classifiers. *International Journal on Artificial Intelligence Tools,* Vol. 11, No. 4, pp 587-601.
21. Kohavi, R., Sommerfield, D. and Dougherty, J. (1997). Data Mining using MLC++. *International Journal on Artificial Intelligence Tools,* Vol. 6, No. 4, pp 537-566.
22. Ling, C.X. and Zhang, H. (2002). The Representational Power of Discrete Bayesian Networks. *Journal of Machine Learning Research,* Vol. 3.
23. Madden, M.G. (2003). The Performance of Bayesian Network Classifiers Constructed using Different Techniques. *Proc. European Conference on Machine Learning,* Workshop on Probabilistic Graphical Models for Classification.
24. Nadeau, C. and Bengio, Y. (2000). Inference for the generalization error. *Advances in Neural Information Processing Systems 12,* MIT Press.
25. Pearl, J. (1988). Probabilistic Reasoning in Intelligent Systems: Networks of Plausible Inference. Morgan Kaufmann, San Francisco.
26. Silander, T. and Myllymäki, P. (2006). A Simple Approach for Finding the Globally Optimal Bayesian Network Structure. *Proc. 22nd Conference on Uncertainty in Artificial Intelligence.*
27. Zhang, H. and Ling, C.X. (2001) An improved learning algorithm for augmented Naive Bayes. *Proc. Fifth Pacific-Asia Conference on Knowledge Discovery in Databases.*

CBR AND CLASSIFICATION

Code Tagging and Similarity-based Retrieval with myCBR

Thomas R. Roth-Berghofer and Daniel Bahls

Abstract This paper describes the code tagging plug-in *coTag*, which allows annotating code snippets in the integrated development environment eclipse. *coTag* offers an easy-to-use interface for tagging and searching. Using the similarity-based search engine of the open-source tool *myCBR*, the user can search not only for exactly the same tags as offered by other code tagging extensions, but also for similar tags and, thus, for similar code snippets. *coTag* provides means for context-based adding of new as well as changing of existing similarity links between tags, supported by *myCBR*'s explanation component.

1 A Programmer's Dilemma

During their professional life developers work in many projects, use many APIs and programming languages. Thereby, they re-encounter many tasks and problems that they have already solved in the past. But especially in the domain of programming, the accurate way of using a specific API, coding in a certain language or a certain algorithm can be hard to remember. One often remembers the fact that a similar situation has already been solved, but the respective piece of code cannot be found or is not even available on the file system anymore.

Not only one's own experience may contain the solution to a difficult situation. There is also the possibility to share experience with other developers. With the

Thomas R. Roth-Berghofer · Daniel Bahls
Knowledge Management Department, German Research Center for Artificial Intelligence DFKI GmbH, 67663 Kaiserslautern, Germany, and Knowledge-based Systems Group, Department of Computer Science, University of Kaiserslautern,
e-mail: thomas.roth-berghofer|daniel.bahls@dfki.de

advance of technologies, a developer has to become acquainted to more and more new programming techniques and modules in everyday life. The introduction to an unfamiliar technology requires a lot of time and money. Since the own experience does not contain the required knowledge, other resources must be used.

Many portals with tutorials, introductions, and best practices regarding API's and programming languages exist on the Web. But even though their quality is often good, finding them costs time, since it is awkward to retrieve via small text boxes on web pages that are neither meant for complex developer questions nor for code insertion. Anyway, the used search tool is a web browser in this case, which is not aware of your working context.

Yet another reason to share code references can be given by the need for documentation. New members of a large project team get lost quickly if they are not somehow familiar with the project. In order to understand the structure of the code, they have to pose many questions to others, or at least to themselves. Thereby, it may be helpful to have a system that is capable of providing guidance.

Delivering the right information at the right place at the right time is the main goal of knowledge management. As soon as there is a tool that helps formulating the problem quickly and easily, finds the desired piece of code reliably, and presents it after a few seconds right inside the developers working place, i.e., in his or her integrated development environment (IDE), then the requirements of good knowledge management are met.

With the evolution of the Web towards Web 2.0, one technique for information description called tagging has become very popular. Even though, tagging often lacks semantical foundations, its acceptance in social domains such as bookmark sharing[1] or photo exchange[2] among many others proves its practical usefulness. Easy-to-use interfaces allow annotating digital resources with concepts drawn from ones own personal information model (8) and intuitive navigation, due to their simple search and find algorithms.

In this paper, we strive for the goal to bring these capabilities also to the domain of programming, starting out with personal re-use of code by providing means for marking and finding relevant knowledge via tagging of code snippets and similarity-based search.

The plug-in *coTag*[3] allows annotating code snippets in the open source IDE eclipse[4]. Using the similarity-based search engine of the open-source tool *myCBR*[5] (9), the user can search not only for exactly the same tags as offered by other code tagging extensions, but also for similar tags and, thus, for similar code snippets. *coTag* offers an easy-to-use interface for tagging, searching, and context-based adding of new as well as changing of existing similarity links between existing tags.

---

[1] http://del.icio.us

[2] http://flickr.com

[3] http://cotag.opendfki.de

[4] http://eclipse.org

[5] http://mycbr-project.net

The rest of the paper is structured as follows: Section 2 gives an introduction to other approaches supporting code reuse. The details to our approach including case structure and similarity measures are elaborated in Section 3. All implementation issues such as the integration into eclipse, the integration of the CBR tool *myCBR*, and the design of the user interfaces are presented in Section 4. First evaluation results are presented in Section 5. The paper concludes with an outlook to further development plans in Section 6.

2 Related Work

Many approaches to support documentation, navigation, and reuse of software arte-facts have been developed over the years. Each of them varies slightly regarding motivation and purpose. We want to introduce some related ideas in the following and make clear how they differ from our approach.

An interesting concept has been followed by (4) who built a suggestion system for the domain of software design. It applies a company's own development experience as a case base of a CBR system. Therefore, it has been integrated into the commercial UML tool Enterprise Architect[6] and assists every software designer of the belonging company in generating new UML diagrams. Although, it covers a bunch of questions respective software design, it cannot answer language specific ones, since it doesn't comprise coding details. Also, the practical usage of a foreign API cannot be explained, because its UML diagrams are not available ad hoc.

A similar approach was followed with CIAO-SI (6). This tool also is based on CBR techniques. At the beginning of a new development project CIAO-SI suggests software artefacts (models, documents, source code) that have been used in past projects. Therefore, the developer must formulate a query that consists of the respective application domain and additional software characteristics. With the use of CASE[7] tools, the resulting artefacts can be adapted to the requirements of the new project. CIAO-SI assists developers in the complete application design phase. It considers the outlines of the planned project in a macroscopic level of detail. In contrast to this, our intention is to show small code snippets or passages of source code documents in a much smaller context and to provide light-weight assistance for individual developers in day-to-day use.

Quite complementary to the above is the following approach (10). With Tag-SEA[8] Storey et al. aim at a better documentation and navigation of source code by enriching bookmarks with meta-data such as provenance and social tags.[9] TagSEA allows sharing of these among project teams. But their goal was to provide a more sophisticated use of bookmarks within source code, not to answer questions about

---

[6] http://www.sparxsystems.de/

[7] Computer Aided Software Engineering

[8] http://tagsea.sourceforge.net

[9] Their bookmarks are called *waypoints* following the metaphor used in navigation systems.

the usage of API's or programming languages. Hence, it provides only a quite simple user interface to find the desired bookmarks based on exact match filters rather than on information retrieval techniques. Further, it restricts browsing to workspace files only, which means that no foreign code can be taken to answer a question. TagSEA has been implemented as a plug-in for the eclipse IDE.

eclipse already comes with a snippet view that allows storing pieces of code as a template with a name and a description under an arbitrary category. The snippets are organised in a folder structure known from file systems, i.e., the snippet can only belong to one category. The plug-in probably is not meant for large amounts of snippets, hence there is also no retrieval support. This means that categories must be well arranged in order to still get the full picture. Finding a certain snippet means browsing and navigating the categories, i.e., finding the right path in this structure. This binds the user to a single pattern of thought and makes categorising a hard and effortful issue. As a consequence, the user is held back from archiving all interesting snippets of his workspace, which in turn results in an even sparser usage of the functionality at all.

Another very powerful tool to search for pieces of code is provided by google codesearch[10]. Queries can be formulated by regular expressions and other google specific patterns. The very fast search engine returns syntactically suitable results from a huge collection of source code. Although the knowledge base is very large, it does not contain a user's personal experience knowledge, of course. Hence, any queries concerning private modules cannot be covered. Public portals and search engines force also the subordination to common public terminology and understanding of relevance. They just do not support the user's personal information model.

3 Tag Retrieval from a CBR Perspective

Case-Based Reasoning (CBR) is a reasoning paradigm that uses experiences in the form of cases to perform inferences (1). CBR is very well suited for problem domains where similar problems have similar solutions (CBR assumption) and where knowledge in form of cases is easily acquired. The relevance or utility of cases is estimated by similarity measures (cf. (5)). The result of such a similarity-based retrieval is an ordered list of cases. In the context of this paper cases are code snippets with their respective tags, where the tags are linked via similarities. It is our opinion that CBR is a methodology very well suited for building tagging systems that can act like an intelligent support assistant in software development.

The task at hand is a typical CBR task. Similarly tagged code snippets are deemed similar with respect to the personal view, i.e., mental model, of the user. In the domain of programming, there is a lot of special knowledge that cannot or only with great effort be formalised. Something a programmer is neither willing nor able to do in his daily work.

---

[10] http://www.google.de/codesearch

The vocabulary, one of the knowledge containers of a CBR system (7), must be powerful enough to enable users to describe their situation significantly. It must provide means to refer to the API's in use, such as to refer to the used programming language. In order to support project internal search functionality, the name of the project must also be considered.

Table 1 Case attributes

Attribute	Value type	Category
Tags	String (multiple)	Problem description
Code snippet	String	Solution
Project name	String	Context
File path	String	Context
Document type	String	Context
Author ID	String	Context
Creation date	String	Maintenance
Quality feedback	Float	Maintenance

Table 1 lists the case attributes with their value type and main purpose. The main search attribute is *tags*. Since the number of libraries, modules and key words is not fix the tags attribute is of set type. Users need to be totally free in formulating their tags and in the number of tags they want to associate with a code snippet. The *code snippet* forms the solution part of the case and contains the section of code associated with the given tags; it is not yet used for searching. *Document type*, *author ID* and *project name* work as filter attributes to constrain the context of search. *File path* maintains a link to the original source file. *Creation date* enables filtering cases from a certain time and provides provenance information. Finally, *quality feedback* allows for maintaining additional quality related information about the case.

The tags' similarity measure is used for determining a case's global similarity value. The context attributes are used for filtering functionality to constrain the search space. Although, it could be reasonable to define similarities between different projects, languages or maybe even authors, the user interface would inevitably become more complicated. But it may be of higher importance in future work (see Section 6). *coTag* uses standard similarity calculations of *myCBR* (9). The similarity measure comprises two parts: the similarity of two single tags and the similarity of two sets of tags.

Tag similarity calculation In order to support semantical relations between tags, we view tags as symbols (instead of strings) having their very own meaning. Accordingly, the similarity value of two tags is looked up in a symbol table which is filled by the user (see Section 4.2.4). The main scenarios are illustrated in Table 2. However, as the tags can be entered freely, they will not be found in the table in many cases and especially not in the beginning. In such a situation, when the similarity obviously cannot be determined semantically, *coTag* determines the similarity in a syntactical way, i.e., by applying trigram matching.

Table 2 Examples: similarity between two tags

Tag 1	Tag 2	Similarity
SWING	*AWT*	Syntactically very different, but semantically similar $\Rightarrow$ customise this similarity
Logger	*LoggingHandler*	Syntactically and semantically similar $\Rightarrow$ no customisation necessary
SWING	*XING*	Syntactically very similar, but semantically different $\Rightarrow$ customise this similarity

Tag set similarity calculation Having defined the similarity assessment for two tags, we now define the similarity assessment for two sets of tags. For each query tag, the most similar case tag is determined as its partner. Thereby, the case tags can be reused, which means that two query tags may have the same partner. Unused case tags are ignored. Eventually, the arithmetic mean of all partner similarities is returned for the final similarity value. Mathematically, it formulates as follows:

$$\text{sim}_{Set}(\mathbf{q}, \mathbf{c}) = \frac{1}{N_q} \sum_{i=1}^{N_q} \max_{j=1,\cdots,N_c} \text{sim}_{Single}(q_i, c_j)$$

where $\mathbf{q}$ and $\mathbf{c}$ represent the tag vectors of query and case, sim_{Set} and sim_{Single} are the two parts of the similarity measure, and N_q, N_c are the respective numbers of tags in query and case.

4 coTag Architecture

As a plug-in, *coTag* is integrated into eclipse, a widely used and freely available IDE for a multitude of programming languages, especially for Java development. Because of its well structured open source plug-in framework, context information such as used programming language, current development project, used APIs and the developer's name are easy to acquire.

Further, the retrieved code snippets can be shown directly in an editor of the IDE without containing inappropriate characters that result often from a copy-&-paste action from other applications[11]. Another advantage is the large quantity of plug-ins that are available for this platform. One of them is TagSEA which was already mentioned in Section 2 and which is considered as a potential candidate for extension with similarity-based search functionality as it already offers powerful tagging and sharing capabilities.

An overview of the system architecture is illustrated in Figure 1. The front end of *coTag* consists of three different UI elements using the standard widget toolkit (SWT) of eclipse. The query view can be opened via the eclipse menu. The same

---

[11] e.g., comments, line or page numbers within HTML or PDF documents

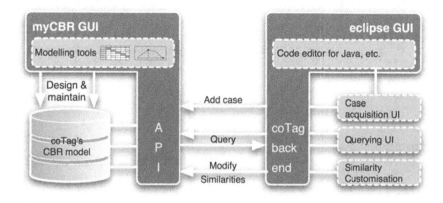

Fig. 1 System architecture

view displays also the results after retrieval. The Case acquisition UI is accessible via the context menu of a text selection.

The back end of *coTag* uses *myCBR*, an open source tool for modelling and maintaining structural CBR projects, which is available as a plug-in for the open source ontology editor Protégé[12]. Since our CBR model, as introduced in Section 3, was designed with *myCBR*, *coTag*'s task is reduced to load the project via *myCBR*'s API and operate it to add cases, submit queries, obtain their results, and modify the provided similarity measure.

4.1 Back End: Accessing myCBR

The CBR model introduced in Section 3 was implemented as a *myCBR* project. The editors of *myCBR* (shown in Figure 2) allowed a quick realisation and give us the ability to maintain the project efficiently. However, *myCBR* manages the case base and similarity measures, performs similarity calculation, and delivers the results. Additionally, it provides detailed explanations how the similarities were found. Please note that the *coTag* users are not intended to work with *myCBR* directly at any time.

Operating *myCBR*'s API is the task of *coTag*'s back end. *coTag* is a light-weight application. It shuts down *myCBR* as often as possible. Actually, it loads the CBR project only when a query is posed and closes it immediately thereafter. Even newly acquired cases and similarity modifications are cached first and are submitted shortly before the next retrieval or when *coTag* respectively the IDE is shutting down.

---

[12] http://protege.stanford.edu

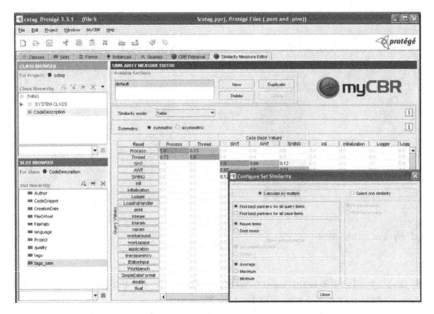

Fig. 2 *myCBR*'s similarity editors for tags attribute

4.2 Front End: Tagging, Searching, and Similarity Modelling

Providing intuitive, nice-looking, simple, but not less powerful user interfaces is a
main concern in *coTag*'s development. The user must be given the ability to specify his query precisely, to understand the outcome of the retrieval, and to take full
advantage of the results.

There must also be a convenient way to modify the similarity measure as described in Section 3. Especially this part is critical, because the eclipse user is in the
mode of programming and therefore not willing to be distracted from her main task,
especially if the interaction process is complex and needs the full attention.

4.2.1 Case Acquisition

As soon as a developer encounters a code passage that he considers worth remem-
bering, he selects the respective code fragment in the code editor and right-clicks
to find the menu item in the context menu[13], which in turn opens *coTag*'s capture
window (Figure 3).

As most meta information about the piece of code is gained automatically, the
form contains only a few components. The text area for the tags is completely empty
at the beginning. The user is free to enter any keywords, but there are also tag pro-

---

[13] or simply by pressing the key combination *CTRL + ALT + ENTER*

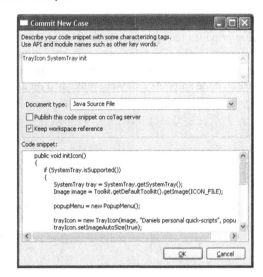

Fig. 3 Case acquisition

posals provided by an eclipse-style content assistance, which can be triggered by the key combination *CTRL + SPACE*. Although the document type of the source file is already known, a drop-down box is presented enabling the user to define it explicitly.

Sometimes it can be interesting to see how a piece of code is embedded in the source file. By keeping the workspace reference *coTag* is able to provide context for the codes snippet, i.e., by showing the exact position of the snippet in the source file. The eclipse marker framework was used in order to avoid modifying source files. But sometimes, e.g., if the snippet is of very generic nature, it might suffice to only store the code snippet and cut the link to the source file.

Since we are also supporting the exchange of cases with other users of work group, there is also the option to publish the snippet on a *coTag* server. But this is not discussed any further in this paper.

The text area at the bottom of the frame is meant for minor changes of the chosen code snippet, i.e., for further annotating the code fragment. A click on the OK button[14] completes the acquisition. The new case is stored in *myCBR*'s case base.

4.2.2 Query Specification

Queries are formulated using the *coTag* view.[15] The upper part of Figure 4 shows a query form. It contains a text box for entering tags and a section for constraining the search space.

---

[14] or by pressing the capture case key combination again

[15] An eclipse view is a widget that can be placed anywhere inside the IDE, which does not bother a user and is available as soon as needed.

The search scope of a query is defined in two dimensions. The technical dimension provides the options to include either all available snippets, only those snippets having a workspace reference, only the snippets coming from a certain project or snippets of a particular document type. The social dimension offers the option to search code snippets that were published on a *coTag* server.

Fig. 4 *coTag*'s query view showing an example query and its results

4.2.3 Retrieval Results

A ranking of the retrieved cases is listed at the bottom of Figure 4. Each row displays a case's document type, tags and similarity to the query. Case tags matching query tags are emphasized. A click on the tags rendered in a web link style causes *coTag* to present the respective code snippet in the default editor of eclipse. If a workspace reference is available for this snippet, the original document is opened and the respective code passage is highlighted inside the editor.

There is an inherent problem due to the evolution of the code. If the code passage has not changed at all but moved to another line, it can still be found reliably with the help of the eclipse marker. But if the content of this code passage has changed, a comparison to the originally tagged snippet is necessary. The point is that the user must be informed if the original document does not contain the tagged snippet anymore as is. We utilise the default parser of eclipse to determine whether both pieces of code are still semantically equal, else comparison viewer illustrates their differences.

4.2.4 Similarity Explanation and Customisation

This is surely the most tricky part of the user interface as here new knowledge is introduced, i.e., in the form of new or changed similarity relations between tags.

Looking again at *coTag*'s query view (Figure 4) one can see two arrows at the right of each row in the result list. They indicate that there is additional retrieval information available. If the user clicks on them the accordeon list reveals an explanation panel below the selected row (Figure 5). It illustrates the result of the partner

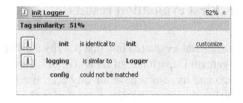

Fig. 5 Explanation of set similarity between two sets of tags

matching described in Section 3. Furthermore, the buttons on the left open an explanation for the respective single similarity (Figure 6). This information is available due to the explanation support of *myCBR* (2; 3).

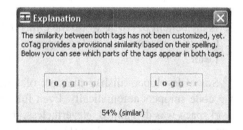

Fig. 6 Explanation of similarity between two single tags

Given this explanation, the user may disagree with *coTag*'s similarity understanding. The customisation button on the right of the explanation panel gives the opportunity to edit the tag similarities as shown in Figure 7. Not only the degree of similarity for the already matched tags can be modified, also new relations between query and case tags can be introduced with the help of a general similarity editor (not shown here).

Another advantage of this kind of similarity editing is to know the context in which the similarity was edited. An adjustment of a similarity value does not only provide the information that a similarity relation between two tags is set to a new value. Available is also the information which query and which case are currently

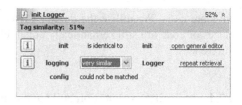

Fig. 7 Customisation of tag
similarities involved in a
particular result

given. Under this aspect, similarity editing can be seen as feedback to the shown
results of a certain query. One finds out why a suggested case fits or fits not to the
query. But this additional information is not yet explored any further regarding its
utility for the application.

5 First evaluation results

coTag was evaluated in a first pass by a group of developers at the Knowledge Management Department of DFKI GmbH. This evaluation was carried out some months
ago and its results have already been used to improve the tool. Especially the con-
fusing design of the first user interface had caused complications.

The task of the developers was to annotate pieces of code in their workspace with
tags and submit a few queries. Thereby, they should answer the following questions:

1. How intuitive is the handling?
2. How much effort involves the acquisition of new cases?
3. Does the result of a similarity-based retrieval answer the query satisfyingly?
4. Is the customization of similarities useful?
5. Is the benefit of *coTag* worth the effort of tagging?
6. Can you imagine that *coTag* supports you to achieve your programming goals
   faster?

Some developers dislike the task of tagging and were missing the option to
tag code snippets automatically. Even fully automatic acquisition of cases from a
workspace was demanded. Nevertheless, the effort of manual case acquisition was
perceived as surprisingly low (Question 2). Those developers clearly were not the
right target group for *coTag*.

The results of a query were considered reasonable (Question 3), although the
search was mostly syntax-based, since the option of similarity customization was
only used sparsely (Question 4). One reason was probably the visual design at that
time. Another one could be attributed to the fact that most search interfaces only
present results, but don't allow any interaction.

All in all, the CBR approach to mark and find personal programming experience
was considered as very interesting and holding a lot of potential, and the benefit was
assessed to be high (Question 5). But due to the aversion to tagging and the fact that
tag proposition was not yet available, *coTag* did not meet the demands of usability

for those developers. The software was in an early stage and needed to be developed further to be applicable for every-day usage (Question 6). We are optimistic that the newly designed user interface and the implemented tag proposition will lead to better results. However, it is also to mention that the evaluation time was too short to let users get accustomed to the new features.

6 Looking Forward

So far, users are enabled to reference and archive pieces of code within their workspaces and attach tags they deem relevant. The semi-semantic retrieval functionality of *coTag*—combining syntactical trigram-based search with semantical similarity-based retrieval—provides smarter access to them. Semantics can be added easily when analysing retrieval results of a specific query, supported by explanations. Hence, users are able to organise their tag archive with respect to their personal information models and understanding of similarity, i.e., their preferences. A direct integration into the IDE improves the usability of the system.

Current development focuses on sharing similarity and case knowledge. The freely available *coTag* server[16] supports communities/workgroups in sharing their coding knowledge. So, every developer can check in those cases he decides to publish and again take advantage from the global case base. In a similar way, the semantically improved similarity measures will be sharable.

This purpose raises the necessity of more detailed provenance information. For more transparency and better administration, it must be traceable who adjusted a certain similarity relation. There must be also a way to measure the quality of a case. A simple star rating system as known from youtube[17] or iTunes[18], which allows quick and easy quality feedback, could provide information about the value of a case's code snippet and the appropriateness of its tags. These concepts would also provide a good starting point for maintaining similarity measures and case base.

Another improvement possibility is to introduce similarity measures for the attributes author, project name and language. Until now, one can apply filters on these attributes, which exclude all cases that differ from the query in the respective attribute. On the one hand, filters are often too strong, since projects for instance may be related semantically or technically. On the other hand, such a feature would also demand the user interface to support weighting of the query attributes, which most likely reduces simplicity.

Compared to this, supporting tag proposition is less controversial. The idea is to propose API names and maybe other keywords when acquiring a new case. This could be implemented quite easily as eclipse provides means to access (program-

---

[16] http://cotag.opendfki.de
[17] http://youtube.com
[18] http://www.apple.com/itunes/

ming) language specific knowledge. By suggesting tags from a selected code passage, usability of query specification could also benefit.

Acknowledgements The authors thank Ralf Biedert for his valuable comments during the writing of this paper.

References

[1] Aamodt, A., Plaza, E.: Case-Based Reasoning: Foundational issues, methodological variations, and system approaches. AI Communications **7**(1), 39–59 (1994)

[2] Bahls, D.: Explanation support for the case-based reasoning tool myCBR. Project thesis, University of Kaiserslautern (2008)

[3] Bahls, D., Roth-Berghofer, T.: Explanation support for the case-based reasoning tool myCBR. In: Proceedings of the Twenty-Second AAAI Conference on Artificial Intelligence. July 22–26, 2007, Vancouver, British Columbia, Canada., pp. 1844–1845. The AAAI Press, Menlo Park, California (2007)

[4] Gomes, P., Leitão, A.: A tool for management and reuse of software design knowledge. In: E. Motta, F. van Harmelen, V. Uren, D. Sleeman (eds.) Managing Knowledge in a World of Networks 15th International Conference, EKAW 2006, Podebrady, Czech Republic, October 2-6, 2006., vol. 4248, pp. 381–388. Springer Verlag (2006)

[5] Lenz, M., Bartsch-Spörl, B., Burkhard, H.D., Wess, S. (eds.): Case-Based Reasoning Technology: From Foundations to Applications, *Lecture Notes in Artificial Intelligence*, vol. LNAI 1400. Springer-Verlag, Berlin (1998)

[6] Nkambou, R.: Capitalizing software development skills using cbr: The ciaosi system. In: Innovations in Applied Artificial Intelligence, *Lecture Notes in Computer Science*, vol. 3029, pp. 483–491. Springer Verlag (2004)

[7] Richter, M.M.: The knowledge contained in similarity measures. Invited Talk at the First International Conference on Case-Based Reasoning, ICCBR'95, Sesimbra, Portugal (1995)

[8] Sauermann, L., Grimnes, G., Roth-Berghofer, T.: The semantic desktop as a foundation for pim research. In: J. Teevan, W. Jones (eds.) Proceedings of the Personal Information Management Workshop at the CHI 2008 (2008)

[9] Stahl, A., Roth-Berghofer, T.R.: Rapid prototyping of CBR applications with the open source tool myCBR. In: R. Bergmann, K.D. Althoff (eds.) Advances in Case-Based Reasoning. Springer Verlag (2008)

[10] Storey, M.A., Cheng, L.T., Bull, I., Rigby, P.: Shared waypoints and social tagging to support collaboration in software development. In: P. Hinds, D. Martin (eds.) CSCW '06: Proceedings of the 20th anniversary conference on Computer supported cooperative work, pp. 195–198. ACM, New York, NY, USA (2006). http://doi.acm.org/10.1145/1180875.1180906

Sparse Representations for Pattern Classification using Learned Dictionaries

Jayaraman J. Thiagarajan, Karthikeyan N. Ramamurthy and Andreas Spanias

Abstract Sparse representations have been often used for inverse problems in signal and image processing. Furthermore, frameworks for signal classification using sparse and overcomplete representations have been developed. Data-dependent representations using learned dictionaries have been significant in applications such as feature extraction and denoising. In this paper, our goal is to perform pattern classification in a domain referred to as the data representation domain, where data from different classes are sparsely represented using an overcomplete dictionary. We propose a source model to characterize the data in each class and present an algorithm to infer the dictionary from the training data of all the classes. We estimate statistical templates in the data representation domain for each class of data, and perform classification using a likelihood measure. Simulation results show that, in the case of highly sparse signals, the proposed classifier provides a consistently good performance even under noisy conditions.

1 Introduction

Sparse approximations of signals over an overcomplete dictionary aim to find a low cost solution in terms of coefficient sparsity with a constraint on the reconstruction error. Redundant representations have proven to be more robust in presence of noise, and provide flexibility in representing the signals using an overcomplete set of basis functions [4]. Sparse representations have been used in a variety of signal and image processing applications such as denoising, image inpainting and signal classification

Jayaraman J. Thiagarajan
Department of Electrical Engineering, Arizona State University, USA, e-mail: jjayaram@asu.edu

Karthikeyan N. Ramamurthy
Department of Electrical Engineering, Arizona State University, USA, e-mail: knatesan@asu.edu

Andreas Spanias
Department of Electrical Engineering, Arizona State University, USA, e-mail: spanias@asu.edu

[3]. The problem of computing a sparse representation can be solved using greedy pursuit methods such as the Matching Pursuit (MP) and the Orthogonal Matching Pursuit (OMP) or using a convex relaxation method like the Basis Pursuit (BP) [10]. Although these algorithms are effective in rendering sparse representations, choosing a dictionary that efficiently captures the significant features in the given set of data is difficult. Dictionary learning algorithms address this problem by adapting the dictionary elements to the features in the training data, thereby providing an efficient approximation. Some of the developments in this direction involve the idea of relating the K-Means clustering procedure to the problem of sparse representation and designing dictionary update algorithms based on this connection [1]. K-SVD is an iterative algorithm that generalizes the K-Means clustering procedure and alternates between obtaining a sparse code for the input observation, and updating the dictionary to better fit the data. This has been proven to be highly successful for image denoising and shown to produce state-of-the art results [2].

1.1 Sparse Coding of Signals

The strategy proposed by Olshausen and Field [4] to reduce higher-order redundancy in images is based on using a probabilistic model to capture the image structures. In this model, images are described as a linear superposition of basis functions and these functions are adapted in terms of a collection of statistically independent events. The appropriate form for the probability distribution of these events is proposed to be highly peaked around zero with a heavy tail. This is because most of the elements in a sparse code are close to 0. The primary motivation for considering sparse representations is the fact that natural images can be sparsely decomposed into a set of elementary features [5] such as edges, lines and other features. However, it is very important to note that sparse coding is not a general principle to find statistically independent components in data; it only applies if the data actually has a sparse structure.

Sparse representation problems aim to approximate a target signal using a linear combination of elementary signals drawn from a large collection. In this paper, we work in finite dimensional, real inner-product space $\mathbb{R}^N$, which is referred to as the *signal space* and the signals we deal with, are elements drawn from this space. The notation $\|.\|_p$ refers to the l^p norm and since we are interested in an inner-product space, distance between two signals is the Euclidean norm of their difference. A *dictionary* for the signal space, Φ, is a finite collection of unit-norm elementary functions. Each elementary function of the dictionary is referred to as an *atom*. The *representation* of a signal is the linear combination of selected atoms that approximate the signal. It is parameterized by a *coefficient vector*, $a \in \mathbb{R}^K$. This indicates the amount of contribution of each of the dictionary atoms to reconstruct the target signal. The coefficient value a_k denotes the contribution of the kth dictionary atom and hence the length of the coefficient vector equals the total number of atoms in Φ. This process is also referred to as *atomic decomposition*.

Given a signal $y \in \mathbb{R}^n$ and the basis functions $\phi_k \in \mathbb{R}^n$, the generating model that represents the coding of an input signal in a linear framework can be expressed as,

$$y = \sum_{k=1}^{K} a_k \phi_k, \tag{1}$$

where a_k is the coefficient associated with the basis function ϕ_k. If the dictionary is overcomplete (i.e.) the number of basis functions exceeds the input signal dimensionality, there exist multiple solutions for the code a_k. The collection of basis functions ϕ_k is denoted by the dictionary $\Phi \in \mathbb{R}^{n \times K}$, where K is the number of basis functions. Similarly, $a \in \mathbb{R}^K$ is a vector comprising the coefficients a_k. The sparsest solution for (1) can be determined by solving one of the following optimization problems,

$$\min_{a} \|a\|_0 \quad \text{subject to} \quad \|y - \Phi a\|_2 \le \varepsilon, \tag{2}$$

$$\min_{a} \|a\|_1 \quad \text{subject to} \quad \|y - \Phi a\|_2 \le \varepsilon, \tag{3}$$

where $\|.\|_0$, $\|.\|_1$ and $\|.\|_2$ refer to the l^0 norm, l^1 norm and l^2 norm respectively. The constrained optimizations problems in (2) and (3) are *error-constrained* (i.e.) the constraint is placed on the approximation error. It can be clearly seen that, if the support of the coefficient vector obtained with this approximation indexes a linearly independent collection of atoms, we can increase the sparsity of the solution. Otherwise, we can even discard some atoms to increase the sparsity, if linear dependencies could be exploited. It has been found that each minimizer of these error-constrained problems will have the same level of sparsity but different approximation errors. On the other hand, approximations can also be carried out by formulating them as *sparsity-constrained* optimization problems. Greedy pursuit methods [7], [8] are used to solve (2) and convex optimization algorithms [9] are used to solve (3).

To obtain a more robust approximation, when presented with multiple signals, simultaneous sparse approximations can been used [11]. In this case, the goal is to obtain a good approximation of several signals at once, using different linear combinations of the same elementary signals. Numerical methods to solve this problem, based on greedy pursuit and convex relaxation have also been proposed [11], [12]. Simultaneous approximations have been successfully used to recover elementary signals from a set of noisy training observations, where the recovery becomes better as the number of observations increase. This motivates the use of simultaneous approximation in a pattern inference problem, where we need to learn a template pattern from the set of noisy observations.

1.2 Template Matching

Template matching is one of the earliest approaches used in classification problems. In this approach, a template or a prototype of the pattern is generated and compared to the test pattern to be recognized, taking into account the random transformations that might have occurred in the test pattern. The metric for similarity is often a correlation measure, but if the template is modeled statistically, a likelihood measure can be used. A statistical model using wavelet transforms has been used to obtain a sparse representation template and the generated template has been used for pattern classification [6].

Consider the problem where we need to classify a test signal as belonging to one of the predetermined classes. A very simple approach to this problem is to design a mask or a *template* for each class and scan it systematically across the entire signal. This is because the test signal may be randomly translated with respect to the template. In most practical applications, we do not expect a perfect template match. Instead, we define some measure to quantify how well the test signal matched the template. Given a signal y and a template x_p, a measure that can be used for template matching is

$$M_p(m) = \sum_j |y(j) - x_p(j-m)|, \ \forall j \text{ such that } (j-m) \text{ is in } D, \tag{4}$$

where D denotes the domain of definition of the template, m indicates the amount of translation provided to the template and p identifies the class. In effect, we wish to compute M_p for all template translations and note those translations for which it is small. It can be easily seen that the metric in (4) is based on the l^1 norm. The class to which the signal belongs is identified as,

$$c = \underset{p}{\operatorname{argmin}} \left[\min_m M_p(m) \right] \tag{5}$$

The other distance metric commonly used in template matching is the standard Euclidean distance.

$$E_p(m) = \left[\sum_j [y(j) - x_p(j-m)]^2 \right]^{1/2} . \tag{6}$$

To examine (6) in detail, we remove the square root,

$$E_p^2(m) = \left[\sum_j [y^2(j) - 2y(j)x_p(j-m) + x_p^2(j-m)] \right] . \tag{7}$$

It can be easily seen from this expression that the last term is unchanged for any value of m. The first term, indicating energy of the signal, varies with m since the range of j depends on the amount of translation. For now, consider that the variation in the first term is small and can be ignored. Thus, we are left with the second term, which we will refer to as the cross-correlation between the two signals,

$$R_p(m) = \left[\sum_j y(j)x_p(j-m) \right] . \tag{8}$$

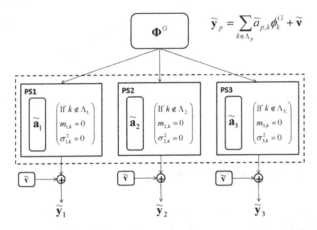

Fig. 1 The probability source model. PS1, PS2 and PS3 are the sources and each source represents a class that uses a fixed set of dictionary atoms from the generating dictionary.

It can be easily seen that the measure $E_p^2(m)$ becomes small when the cross-correlation increases. Classification using the Euclidean and cross-correlation measures are done similar to (5), except that the objective function is maximized when the cross-correlation measure is used. An important aspect of template matching is that, the operation makes use of only local information. This local aspect is the reason for both the appealing simplicity and the limitations of this technique [16].

1.3 Proposed Classification Framework

The major contribution of this paper is to develop a template based statistical classification framework in the data representation domain, where an unlabeled training data set is sparsely represented using an overcomplete dictionary. We assume a source model, where we have a number of sources and each source uses a set of dictionary elements chosen from a large dictionary, called the generating dictionary. Each source represents a class and generates a set of training observations by linearly combining its own set of dictionary elements with random weights. The source model is illustrated in Figure 1 and the details are provided in Section 4.1. We are presented with only the unlabeled training data set from all sources and our problem is to infer the generating dictionary, find the representation for each class of training data and estimate a statistical template for each class of data. We use the Simultaneous Orthogonal Matching Pursuit (S-OMP) algorithm [11] to compute representations for the training data set from each source. To infer the generating dictionary, we take the observations from all the sources into consideration and generalize the K-SVD algorithm. We estimate a statistical template in the data representation domain for each source, using the coefficients of the observations generated by the source. The coefficients for a set of observations are computed using the S-OMP algorithm over the adapted dictionary. We propose a classifier in the data representation domain that associates test data to a specific source based on a likelihood measure. The likelihood measure for each class (source) is computed using the representation coefficients of the test data and the estimated statistical template of a source. The results of our simulations show that, in the case of highly sparse signals, the proposed classifier provides a consistently good performance even under noisy conditions.

2 Simultaneous Approximations

In a general sparse approximation problem, a signal is approximated using a linear combination of atoms from a large dictionary. Consider the scenario where we have several observations of the same signal, that has a sparse representation. Each observation is assumed to be corrupted by noise, which need not be statistically independent. This generalization of a simple approximation to the case of several input signals is referred to as simultaneous sparse approximation. Given several input signals, we wish to approximate all the signals at once using different linear combinations of the same set of elementary signals. In this process, we need to minimize the error in approximating the data against the elementary signals used [11]. Some of the important applications that have used simultaneous sparse approximation include magnetoencephalography [13], equalization of sparse communication channels [14] and blind source separation [15].

Considering a set of T observations from a single source, we form the signal matrix $Y = [y_1 y_2 ... y_T]$. The problem is to find a representation such that all the signals in Y use the same set of dictionary atoms from Φ with different coefficients, minimizing the error given by $\|Y - \Phi A\|_F^2$. Here $A \in \mathbb{R}^{K \times T}$ indicates the coefficient matrix, where each column corresponds to the coefficients for a single observation and $\|.\|_F$ refers to the Frobenius norm. This problem can be solved using the S-OMP algorithm, which is an extension of the OMP algorithm, for the case of multiple signal observations. The details of this algorithm can be found in [11]. In the greedy selection procedure of S-OMP, we select an atom from the dictionary that has the maximum sum of absolute correlations with all the columns in the signal matrix. The reason behind this approach is that the atom that has the maximum sum of correlations will contribute a lot of energy to every column in the signal matrix [11]. This can be exploited in a pattern learning scenario, where the dictionary atoms selected represent the key features in the set of observations belonging to a source.

3 K-SVD Algorithm

The underlying relation between clustering and the problem of sparse approximation has been studied and the connections have been identified [10]. In clustering, each sample is represented by a vector, selected from a set of basis functions or a codebook based on distance measures. This is analogous a sparse approximation problem with sparsity equal to 1 and a fixed coefficient of value 1. As sparse coding involves representation using a linear combination of basis atoms, it can be regarded as a generalization of the clustering problem. The K-SVD algorithm is a generalization of the K-Means clustering procedure, where a two-step process is used to adapt a dictionary based on the the training data set. The first step involves, finding a representation for the given signal assuming that the dictionary is fixed. The next step updates the dictionary, with the assumption that the coefficients are fixed [1]. When K-SVD is forced to work with one atom per signal, it behaves exactly similar to a vector quantization. It involves a sparse coding step, realized using a greedy pursuit method or a convex optimization algorithm. This is followed by a dictionary update step, that computes the Singular Value Decomposition (SVD) of the residual data matrices, to update the dictionary columns. This algorithm uses a dictionary of small and a fixed size and hence new dictionary atoms cannot be added to improve the approximation.

Considering the set of P training signals $Y = [y_1...y_P]$, the goal of the K-SVD algorithm is to adapt a dictionary Φ such that $\|Y - \Phi A\|_F^2$ is minimized, with sparsity constraints on the coefficient matrix A. As mentioned earlier, this involves a sparse coding step and a dictionary update step. In the sparse coding step, we use a greedy pursuit algorithm to compute the coefficient vectors a_p, $p = 1,...,P$, by minimizing $\|y_p - \Phi a_p\|_2^2$ with constraints on the coefficient sparsity. In the dictionary update step, each column ϕ_k, $k = 1,...,K$, of the dictionary is updated separately. The representation error matrix, E_k, is the matrix obtained by removing the contribution of the dictionary element, ϕ_k, from the matrix of training signals, Y. The restricted error matrix, E_k^R, is the matrix containing only the columns of E_k corresponding to the training signals that use ϕ_k. The algorithm updates the dictionary in an accelerated manner by computing the coefficients for the updated dictionary element while adapting it [1]. In our proposed framework, we generalize this algorithm to the case of multiple training observations from multiple sources. This enables us to infer the generating dictionary that is a representative of the basic patterns in the signals generated by all the sources.

4 Proposed Algorithm for Template Generation

In this section, we propose a framework for estimating a statistical template in the representation domain for each source. Simultaneous approximation procedure will be used to compute representation for the multiple observations from every source, using the adapted dictionary. Dictionary update will be performed using the K-SVD algorithm generalized to work with multiple observations of the signal from every source. We now describe a probability source model that we assume for the multiple observations of the signal generated from a source.

4.1 Probability Source Model

The observation vectors are assumed to be the output of a probability source that linearly combines a fixed set of basis functions with random weights, that belong to a Gaussian distribution. For the source p, this is expressed as

$$\tilde{y}_p = \sum_{k \in \Lambda_p} \tilde{a}_{p,k} \phi_k^G + \tilde{v}, \tag{9}$$

where $\tilde{y}_p$ is the random observation vector, $\tilde{a}_{p,k}$ are the random weights, ϕ_k^G are the fixed basis elements chosen from the generating dictionary Φ^G (with K elements) and $\tilde{v}$ is the Additive White Gaussian Noise (AWGN) vector. $\tilde{a}_p \sim N(m_p, \Sigma_p)$ is the random vector with mean m_p and covariance Σ_p, and has $\tilde{a}_{p,k}$ as its elements. In our case, we assume the random weights to be independent and hence Σ_p is a diagonal matrix. The weight vectors are realizations of $\tilde{a}_p$ and they linearly combine the dictionary elements to generate the observations for the source p. Λ_p contains the indices of a subset of dictionary atoms from Φ^G, that were used in the generation of $\tilde{y}$ for source p. Therefore, Λ_p indexes the elements in $\tilde{a}_p$ that have a non-zero variance. The other elements of $\tilde{a}_p$ have the value zero. Note that we are dealing with sparsely representable signals, so typically $|\Lambda_p| \ll K$. An illustration of the source model is given in Figure 1 for the case with 3 sources.

Assuming that we have P such probability sources, there are P random vectors $\tilde{y}_1, ..., \tilde{y}_P$. The T observations of the source p are the realizations of the random vector $\tilde{y}_p$, and are denoted by $y_{p,1}, ..., y_{p,T}$. The observation matrix for source p is given by $Y_p = [y_{p,1}...y_{p,T}]$. The matrix of the observations of all the sources can be denoted by $Y = [Y_1...Y_P]$.

We want to find the representation matrix $A_p = [a_{p,1}...a_{p,T}]$ for each Y_p using the adapted dictionary Φ, where $a_{p,t}$ is the coefficient vector for the observation t from the source p. Note that for each of the vectors in a given Y_p, the same dictionary elements are used, but in different linear combinations. In the meanwhile, we also desire to build a dictionary Φ that is adapted to the data matrix Y. This is solved as an iterative representation and dictionary update procedure.

4.2 Representation Step

S-OMP is the greedy method used to solve the optimization problem of minimizing $\|Y_p - \Phi A_p\|_F^2$ with constraints on coefficient sparsity. All the columns in Y_p use the same dictionary elements from Φ and the indices of the dictionary elements used is stored in the set Γ_p. The maximum number of dictionary atoms that can be used in the approximation for each source is indicated by the sparsity, $S = |\Gamma_p|$. It follows that the rows of A_p indexed by the set Γ_p are non-zero. Computing the representation by S-OMP is repeated for all the observation matrices indexed by $1, ..., P$. The final coefficient matrix is given by $A = [A_1...A_P]$.

4.3 Dictionary Update Step

In the dictionary update step, we consider the training data $Y = [Y_1...Y_P]$ and seek to update the dictionary element ϕ_k with the rank-1 approximation of the restricted error matrix E_k^R. Updating the dictionary element by SVD also leads to updating the coefficients for each of the training data associated with that dictionary element. The iterative adaptation finally results in the the dictionary elements representing key features in the set of training observations. It also reduces the representation error for a fixed sparsity. Here, we have generalized the K-SVD algorithm by considering multiple training observations for each source.

The steps involved in the proposed algorithm for inferring Φ are outlined below.

Task: Find the best dictionary that represents the data samples from all the P probability sources as sparse linear combinations.

Initialization: Set initial dictionary $\Phi^{(0)}$ with K randomly chosen normalized columns from Y. Set iteration counter $J = 0$.

while convergence not reached
  Representation Step: For each source p,
    - Given Y_p and $\Phi^{(J)}$, find the $A_p^{(J)}$ using S-OMP, with sparsity S.
    - Update the index set of dictionary atoms used by each source, $\Gamma_p^{(J)}$.
    - Compute the overall coefficient matrix for all sources,
    $A^{(J)} = \left[A_1^{(J)} A_2^{(J)} ... A_P^{(J)} \right].$

  Dictionary Update Step: For each column $k = 1, ..., K$ in $\Phi^{(J)}$,
    - Identify the indices of observation vectors, ω_k, that use $\phi_k^{(J)}$.
    - Compute the representation error matrix, E_k, by removing the contribution of $\phi_k^{(J)}$ from Y.
    - Restrict the error matrix, E_k to E_k^R, considering only the columns indexed by ω_k.
    - Update the dictionary atom with the first singular vector of E_k^R and update the corresponding coefficients.
  $J = J + 1.$
end

4.4 Statistical Template Generation and Classification

In order to extend this framework to a pattern learning application, we need to estimate a statistical template in the data representation domain, for each source. As we have already assumed, the observation matrix Y_p consists of T training vectors from the source p. Each training vector is an independent observation from the probability source. Each column of A_p, $a_{p,t}$, is a realizations of the random vector $\tilde{a}_p$. Since we have assumed a Gaussian distribution for $\tilde{a}_p$, we can estimate its mean and variance as follows,

$$\hat{m}_p = \frac{1}{T} \sum_{t=1}^{T} a_{p,t}, \tag{10}$$

$$\hat{\Sigma}_p = \frac{1}{T-1} \sum_{t=1}^{T} (a_{p,t} - \hat{m}_p)(a_{p,t} - \hat{m}_p)^T, \tag{11}$$

where $\hat{m}_p$ is the mean estimate and $\hat{\Sigma}_p$ is the estimate of covariance for the probability source p parameterized by the statistical template, $\Theta_p = \{m_p, \Sigma_p\}$. Note that, we need to estimate only the diagonal elements in the covariance matrix, because of our independence assumption on the elements of $\tilde{a}_p$. We denote the vector containing the diagonal elements in the covariance matrix by $\hat{\Sigma}_p^d = diag(\hat{\Sigma}_p)$. As we described earlier, only the rows of A_p indexed by the set, Γ_p, will be non-zero. So, the means and variances in the remaining rows will be zero. To avoid numerical issues, we fix the variance to be a very small value, if it falls below a threshold.

We have P sets of mean and covariance matrices that characterize each of the probability sources. Given a test vector, z, the classification problem is to identify the probability source that could have generated it, in the Maximum Likelihood (ML) sense. Let w be the coefficient vector of z using the dictionary Φ. The likelihood function used is,

$$L(w|\hat{\Theta}_p) = \sum_{k=1}^{K} \left(-\frac{1}{2} \ln(2\pi\hat{\sigma}_{p,k}^2) - \frac{1}{2} \frac{(w_k - \hat{m}_{p,k})^2}{\hat{\sigma}_{p,k}^2} \right), \tag{12}$$

where $\hat{m}_{p,k}$, $\hat{\sigma}_{p,k}^2$ and w_k are the elements of the vectors $\hat{m}_p$, $\hat{\Sigma}_p^d$ and w respectively. The index p for which the likelihood is maximized, is the probability source that generated z in the ML sense.

5 Simulations

In this section, we perform simulations to analyze the dictionary learning ability and the classification power of the proposed algorithm, using synthetic signals. We fix the dimension, N, of the signals to be 16 and the number of dictionary atoms to be 64. The synthetic signals are generated using the source model in (9), with the additive noise adjusted according to the target SNR. The dictionary Φ^G consists of Gaussian random vectors with zero mean and unit variance. We fix the number of probability sources, $P = 1500$. For each source, we generate $T = 25$ training observations. For a particular source, the observations are generated by linearly combining S randomly picked dictionary elements. In our simulations, the sparsity S is fixed at 2,3 or 4. The same sparsity is used as the constraint while adapting the dictionary and computing the atomic representation. The weights of the linear combination are realized from independent Gaussian PDFs with different non-zero means and unit variance.

The aim of the dictionary learning stage in our algorithm is to infer the generating dictionary from training vectors of all the sources. An estimate of the statistical template, $\hat{\Theta}_p$, is computed for each of the P sources, once the dictionary is adapted and the representation is computed. We seek to minimize the distance in terms of correlation between the elements of Φ^G and the adapted dictionary Φ. If the correlation between an atom in Φ and an atom in Φ^G is greater than 0.99, then we consider that atom in Φ^G to be recovered.

For the purpose of classification, we generate 1500 test observations from randomly picked sources. We corrupt the test observations with noise corresponding to the target SNR. The coefficients are computed using the adapted dictionary, for each of the test vectors. Classification is performed by computing the likelihood measure for the representation of each test vector, using the statistical template as in (12). Figure (2) illustrates the classification rate as a function of the target SNR, for different values of sparsity. The ratio of the number of recovered atoms to the actual number of atoms in Φ^G is shown in Figure 3 for $S = 4$.

The classification rate for a given sparsity is the best under near no-noise conditions as seen in Figure 2. When only 2 dictionary atoms are used per source, the maximum classification rate of 95.5% is obtained for a SNR of 500dB. Increasing the number of dictionary atoms used per source has two effects. The classification rate drops and the classifier becomes less robust with noise (i.e.) the rate drops faster with decrease in SNR. Therefore, it could be understood that the performance of the classifier will be maximum when the signals are highly sparse with respect to the generating basis functions. On the other hand, the number of dictionary atoms recovered is more or less independent of the additive noise as shown in Figure 3.

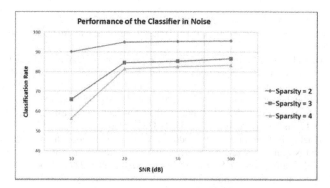

Fig. 2 Performance of the proposed classifier in noise. Near no-noise condition is simulated with SNR of 500 dB.

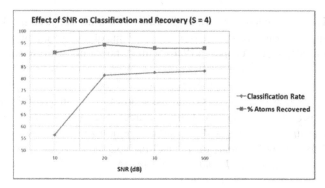

Fig. 3 Comparison of recovery and classification rate when each source uses 4 atoms from the dictionary.

6 Conclusions

In this paper, we presented a framework for template learning and pattern classi-fication based on sparse representations. The ability of the algorithm to adapt the dictionary to the training vectors is a key factor in this classification setup. The sim-ulation results show that the proposed algorithm with assumptions on the source model achieves good signal recovery and classification rate. The flexibility of this novel framework allows for extension to signals of higher dimensions like images, where additional constraints such as translational and rotational invariance should be considered.

References

1. Aharon, M., Elad, M. and Bruckstein, A.: K-SVD: An algorithm for designing overcomplete dictionaries for sparse representation. IEEE Transactions on Signal Processing. **54**(11), 4311–4322 (2006).
2. Aharon, M. and Elad, M.: Image denoising via sparse and redundant representations over learned dictionaries. IEEE Transactions on Image Processing. **15**(12), 3736–3745 (2006).
3. Huang, K. and Aviyente, S.: Sparse Representation for Signal Classification. Proceedings of Advances in Neural Information Processing Systems 19. MIT Press (2006).
4. Olshausen, A. and Field, J.: Sparse Coding with an Overcomplete Basis Set: A Strategy Em-ployed by V1? Vision Research. **37**(23), 3311–3325 (1996).
5. Field, J.: What is the Goal of Sensory Coding?. Neural Computation. **6**, 559–601 (1994).
6. Scott, C. and Nowak, R.: TEMPLAR: a wavelet-based framework for pattern learning and analysis. IEEE Transactions on Signal Processing. **52**(8), 2264–2274 (2000).
7. Mallat, S. and Zhang, Z.: Matching Pursuits with Time-Frequency Dictionaries. IEEE Trans-actions on Signal Processing. **41**(12), 3397–3415 (1999).
8. Tropp, J. A.: Greed is good: Algorithmic Results for Sparse Approximation. IEEE Transac-tions on Information Theory. **50**(10), 2231–2242 (2004).
9. Chen, S. S. and Donoho, D. L. and Saunders, M. A.: Atomic decomposition by basis pursuit. SIAM Review. **43**(1), 129-159 (2001).

10. Tropp, J. A.: Topics in Sparse Approximation. PhD thesis. University of Texas (2004).
11. Tropp, J. A.: Algorithms for simultaneous sparse approximation. Part I: Greedy pursuit. Signal Processing. **86**, 572–588 (2006).
12. Tropp, J. A.: Algorithms for simultaneous sparse approximation Part II: Convex relaxation. Signal Processing. **86**, 589–602 (2006).
13. Gorodnitsky, I. F. and George, J. S. and Rao, B. D.: Neuromagnetic source imaging with focuss: a recursive weighted minimum norm algorithm. Journal of Electroencephalogr Clin Neurophysiol. **95**(4), 231-251 (1995).
14. Cotter, S. and Rao, B. D.: Sparse channel estimation via matching pursuit with application to equalization. Journal of Electroencephalogr Clin Neurophysiol. **50**(3), 374–377, March (2002).
15. Gribonval, R.: Sparse decomposition of stereo signals with matching pursuit and application to blind source separation of more than two sources from a stereo mixture. Proceedings of the 2002 IEEE International Conference on Acoustics, Speech, and Signal Processing. Orlando, Florida, May (2002).
16. Duda, R. and Hart, P. and Stork D.: Pattern Classification (2nd edition). Wiley-Interscience (2000).

Qualitative Hidden Markov Models for Classifying Gene Expression Data

Zina M. Ibrahim and Ahmed Y. Tawfik and Alioune Ngom

Abstract Hidden Markov Models (HMMs) have been successfully used in tasks involving prediction and recognition of patterns in sequence data, with applications in areas such as speech recognition and bioinformatics. While variations of traditional HMMs proved to be practical in applications where it is feasible to obtain the numerical probabilities required for the specification of the parameters of the model and the probabilities available are descriptive of the underlying uncertainty, the capabilities of HMMs remain unexplored in applications where this convenience is not available. Motivated by such applications, we present a HMM that uses qualitative probabilities instead of quantitative ones. More specifically, the HMM presented here captures the order of magnitude of the probabilities involved instead of numerical probability values. We analyze the resulting model by using it to perform classification tasks on gene expression data.

1 Introduction and Motivation

Hidden Markov Models (HMMs) [16] are probabilistic graphical models that capture the dependencies between random variables in time-series data. They have been successfully applied to several areas of artificial intelligence such as speech recognition (e.g. [18]), robotics (e.g. [3]), pattern recognition [12] and several areas of bioinformatics, such as transmembrane protein classification (e.g. [10]) to perform predictive and recognitive tasks.

The power of HMMs stems from the provision of efficient and intuitive algorithms that grant HMMs their predictive and recognitive capabilities by computing quantities of interest described by the model [16]. For example, given the specifications of the model, there exist efficient algorithms for computing the probability of observed events [20].

University of Windsor, 401 Sunset Avenue, Windsor, Ontario, Canada N9B 3P4, e-mail: {ibrahim,atawfik,angom}@uwindsor.ca

HMMs however, remain unexplored in application domains where they can be useful, by virtue of the unavailability of the statistical data necessary for the specification of the parameters of the model. Although overcoming the lack of real data by means of approximation [17] or synthesis [6] is possible for some applications, it is not an option for many types of applications. For example, epidemiological data describing factors influencing the occurrence of illnesses cannot be approximated or synthesized when not sufficient. Another example is the problem of predicting the topological structure of proteins, where the topology of very few proteins are currently known, and available data is in general incomplete and uncertain, and HMMs have only been successfully used in the prediction of a special class of proteins called transmembrane proteins [10].

In response to this problem, formalisms of qualitative probability [22, 5, 15] have been proposed as alternatives where numerical probabilities are difficult to obtain. These formalisms aim at capturing the likelihood of events in a way which mimics that of probability theory without resorting to numerical values. Indeed, there exist evidence in the literature for the use of qualitative probabilities in complex problems, such as the protein topology prediction problem [14] and image interpretation [9].

Moreover, qualitative methods for dealing with uncertainty are not only an alternative for when data is not available, but are also useful where quantitative approaches have been proposed. For example, in bioinformatics, a heap of high-throughput data is available. The large amount of data has made formulating mechanisms to provide some biological insight work in progress [4]. We believe that qualitative equivalents of the quantitative methods available can serve as a guide for a better analysis for the mechanisms available. In other words, they can be used to perform an initial analysis to filter the data available, which aids in reducing the complexity of the full analysis performed by the quantitative methods .

In this paper, we present a *Qualitative* HMM, that is a HMM that trades traditional probabilities with the qualitative framework found in [5], which captures the order of magnitude of probabilities instead of their numerical values. We use the resulting model to conduct a qualitative analysis of gene expression data.

Traditional HMMs have been used to cluster time-series of gene expression data in the aim of finding the correlations among different genes (e.g. [19], [23]). The qualitative HMM we propose here are applied to the same problem, and serve to create pre-clusters that the existing quantitative HMMs can use as a guide for a better analysis. This is of special interest to the pharmaceutical industry, for which any new insight about the dynamics of genes can have a great impact on designing drugs for currently hard-to analyze diseases [13].

On a side note, it is essential that the reader keeps in mind that the provision of better qualitative knowledge about massive data is not only of use for health-care applications, but to applications in various domains (e.g. economics [7]).

We have previously formulated a model of a qualitative equivalent of HMMs [8] that was specifically tailored to use qualitative probability values in spatio-temporal applications. Other works in this regard is that of [17] which uses estimates of the parameters of HMM. However, there does not exist a general model which uses a qualitative abstraction of probability theory to formulate a qualitative equivalent to HMMs.

In the remainder of the paper, we present the qualitative model along with its application to the analysis of gene expression data. In the first section, we present an overview of the main constituents of standard HMMs and follow by outlining the qualitative theory of probabilities representing their order of magnitude in the second section. We then present the building blocks of the qualitative HMM and build the qualitative algorithm used to solve one of the canonical problems associated with HMMs. Then, we shift our attention to using the devised model to cluster time-series gene expression data and provide an analysis of the results.

2 Hidden Markov Models

Hidden Markov Models (HMMs) [16] are probabilistic graphical models used to represent the behavior of a system which is known to possess a number of states. The states of the model are hidden, in the sense that their operations can only be studied through discrete time series of the observed output produced by the states.

Formally, a HMM=$\{S,V,\pi,A,B\}$ is defined by the following parameters:

1. A finite set of n unobservable (hidden) states S=$\{s_1,...,s_n\}$
2. A finite set of m observable outputs, or the alphabet of the model: $V = \{v_1,...,v_m\}$ that may be produced by the states given in S at any time t.
3. The vector π of the the initial state probability distribution, i.e. the probability of the system being at state s_i at time 0: $P(q_0=s_i)$, $\forall s_i \in S$ ($1 \leq i \leq n$).
4. The matrix $A = [a_{ij}]_{1\leq i\leq n}$ which describes the transition probability distribution among associated states. For each entry a_{ij} in A, $a_{ij} = P(q_t = s_i|q_{t-1} = s_j)$, $\forall$ $1\leq i, j \leq n$, which describes the probability of the system being in state s_i at time t given that it was in state s_j at time $t - 1$. This formulation reflects the Markov property which dictates that the next state is only dependent on the current state, and is independent of previous states. This property also implies that the transition probabilities must satisfy:

$$\sum_{i=0}^{n} \sum_{j=0}^{n} P(q_t = s_i|q_{t-1} = s_j) = 1$$

5. The matrix $B = \{b_j(o_t), 1 \leq j \leq n\}$ of the emission probabilities of the observable output at a given state $P(o_t = v_i|q_t = s_j)$, which describes the probability of the system producing output v_i at time t given that it is in state s_j ($1 \leq i \leq m$). This information reflects the assumption that the output at a given time is only dependent on the state that produced it and is independent of previous output. In other words:

$$\sum_{i=0}^{m} P(o_t = v_i|q_t = s_j) = 1$$

Hence, a HMM can be described by a doubly stochastic structure. The first stochastic process provides a high-level view of the system and is operated by a Markov chain (described by the transition matrix A) governing the transitions among the hidden states. The second stochastic process, on the other hand, is the one governing the production of observable output independently by each state (described by the emission matrix B). This structure provides HMMs with a high degree of flexibility, which makes them attractive for sequential data analysis.

In this paper, we redefine the semantics of HMMs to accept qualitative abstractions of probability values for the emissions and transitions. We do this by using the qualitative probability model described in the next section.

3 Order of Magnitude of Probabilities: the Kappa Calculus

The kappa calculus [1, 5] is a system that abstracts probability theory by using order of magnitude of probabilities as an approximation of probability values. It does so by capturing the degree of disbelief in a proposition ω, or the degree of incremental surprise or abnormality associated with finding ω to be true [5], labeled $\kappa(\omega)$. The value of $\kappa(\omega)$ is assigned so that probabilities having the same order of magnitude belong to the same κ class, and that $\kappa(\omega)$ grows inversely to the order of magnitude of the probability value $P(\omega)$.

The abstraction is achieved via a procedure which begins by representing the probability of a proposition ω, $P(\omega)$, by a polynomial function of one unknown, ε, an infinitesimally small positive number ($0 < \varepsilon < 1$). The rank κ of a proposition ω is represented by the power of the most significant ε-term in the polynomial representing $P(\omega)$ (the lowest power of ε in the polynomial). Accordingly, the relation between probability and κ values is that $P(\omega)$ is of the same order as ε^n, where $n = \kappa(\omega)$ [21], that is:

$$\varepsilon < \frac{P(\omega)}{\varepsilon^n} \leq 1 \text{ or equivalently: } \varepsilon^{n+1} < P(\omega) \leq \varepsilon^n$$

Where ε^n is the most significant ε-term of the polynomial representing $P(\omega)$.

The κ-calculus is useful because it provides an abstraction which only requires specifying the κ values of propositions, which is an easier task than specifying the exact probabilities associated with the occurrence of a proposition. The κ values are in turn representative of the interval into which the probability falls [5].

3.1 Properties

The degree of surprise, κ, obeys the following properties:

$$\kappa(true) = 0 \tag{1}$$
$$\kappa(\psi + \phi) = \min(\kappa(\psi), \kappa(\phi)) \tag{2}$$

Property (1) above states that there is no degree of surprise associated with finding a world where a true belief is true.

Property 2 describes the disjunction (modeled by +) of two propositions ψ and ϕ as the minimum degree of surprise associated with them. Hence, the choice of which proposition to augment depends on the propositions relative strengths.

The above two properties are easily extended to give the general properties of ranking functions given below, which reflect the usual properties of probability functions (given in the right-hand side), with minimum replacing addition, and addition replacing multiplication [5].

$$\kappa(\phi) = \min_{\omega \models \phi} \qquad P(\phi) = \sum_{\omega \models \phi} P(\omega) \tag{3}$$
$$\kappa(\phi) = 0 \vee \kappa(\neg\phi) = 0 \qquad P(\phi) + P(\neg\phi) = 1 \tag{4}$$
$$\kappa(\psi \wedge \phi) = \kappa(\psi|\phi) + \kappa(\phi) \qquad P(\psi \wedge \phi) = P(\psi|\phi) \times P(\phi) \tag{5}$$

4 A Qualitative HMM

In this section, we introduce HMM_κ, a HMM which uses the κ ranking function as a measure of the order of magnitude of probabilities for the specification of its transitions. For the rest of the paper, we will assume the existence of $\lambda = (S,V,\pi,A,B)$, a HMM_κ with n possible hidden states and m observable outputs, and whose structure and parameters are specified, and use it to define the semantics.

4.1 Semantics

Introducing κ values to the transitions of λ gives the models the following semantics:

1. $\forall \pi_i \in \pi, 1 \leq i \leq n$, π_i represents the degree of surprise associated with having state i to be true at time 0:

$$\pi_i = \kappa(q_0 = s_i)$$

2. $\forall a_{ij} \in A$, where $1 \leq i, j \leq n$, a_{ij} represents the degree of surprise associated with state s_i holding at time t given that state s_j was true at time $t - 1$. The resulting matrix A is called the transition κ matrix.

$$a_{ij} = \kappa(s_t = q_i|s_{t-1} = q_j)$$

3. $\forall b_j(o_t = v_i) \in B$, where $1 \leq i \leq m$ and $1 \leq j \leq n$, b_{ij} represents the degree of surprise associated with state s_j being responsible for producing observable output v_i at time t. The resulting matrix B is called the emission κ matrix.

$$b_j(v_i) = \kappa(o_t = v_i | q_t = s_j)$$

4.2 Independence Assumptions

Property 3 of the κ calculus is used to reformulate the independence assumptions to go along with the semantics of λ. The reformulations are presented below.

1. The limited memory assumption: states that the degree of surprise associated with observing output v_i at time t being generated by state s_j is only dependent on the degree of surprise associated with state s_j, with any other state or output being irrelevant. This is represented as:

$$\kappa(o_t = v_i | q_t = s_j, q_{t-1} = s_k, ..., q_1 = s_l,$$
$$v_{t-1} = o_m, ..., v_1 = o_n) = \kappa(o_t = v_i | q_t = s_j). \tag{6}$$

Accordingly, and due to property 3, the emission κ matrix should satisfy:

$$\min_{i=0}^{m} \kappa(o_t = v_i | q_t = s_j) = 0^1 \tag{7}$$

2. The Markov assumption: dictates that the degree of surprise associated with observing state s_i at time t is only dependent on the degree of surprise associated with the previous state, i.e. state s_j at time $t-1$, with all other states and output being irrelevant. This is represented as:

$$\kappa(s_t = s_i | q_{t-1} = s_j, q_{t-2} = s_k, ..., q_1 = s_l,$$
$$v_t = o_m, ..., v_1 = o_n) = \kappa(q_t = s_i | q_{t-1} = s_j) \tag{8}$$

Again, having this assumption in conjunction with property 3 yields the following:

$$\min_{i=1}^{n} \kappa(q_t = s_i | q_{t-1} = s_j) = 0 \tag{9}$$

---

[1] Although the above equation is a direct reformulation of the HMM property to accommodate κ values, it makes visible an inherent problem in the kappa calculus, which is that small κ-values do not accumulate into a strong argument (as in the lottery paradox [11]). However, [5] defends that in applications where the reasoning chains are somewhat shallow, this deviation is considered a reasonable price to pay for achieving deductive closure and is tolerable in general. Part of our current research is to ammend the above problem.

4.3 Additional Properties

Two interesting concepts arise from the introduction of the semantics of λ. They are:

1. Output generator: A state s_i, $1 \le i \le n$ is the generator of output v_j, $1 \le j \le m$ at time t *iff* s_i is the state associated with the minimum degree of surprise of having produced v_j

$$\kappa(o_t = v_j, q_t = s_i | \lambda) = \min_{i=1}^{n} \kappa(o_t = v_j, q_t = s_i | \lambda) \tag{10}$$

2. State generator: A state s_i, $1 \le i \le n$ at time t is the generator of state s_j, $1 \le j \le n$ at time $t+1$ *iff* s_i is the state holding at time t which is associated with the minimum degree of surprise of having preceded state s_j at time $t+1$

$$\kappa(q_{t+1} = s_j, q_t = s_i | \lambda) = \min_{i=1}^{n} \kappa(q_{t+1} = s_j, q_t = s_i | \lambda) \tag{11}$$

5 Evaluating Observed Output

Having constructed the semantics of HMM_κ, we shift our attention to formulating the qualitative equivalent of one of the algorithms associated with HMMs to perform recognition and prediction tasks. In what follows, we present the evaluation problem; one of the canonical problems associated with HMMs, along with its reformulation to accept κ values, and construct the corresponding algorithm to provide a solution to the problem for HMM_κ.

5.1 The Evaluation Problem

The traditional evaluation problem can be stated as follows: Given a HMM_κ, λ, and a sequence of observed output O, the task is to determine the likelihood of O being a valid sequence produced by λ.

An efficient algorithm, the *forward algorithm* [16] finds a solution to the evaluation problem by performing induction on the length of the output sequence $O = o_1, o_2, ..., o_t$ as follows.

An inductive variable, called the *forward variable* is defined to capture the likelihood of observing the output sequence O of length t and having state s_i ($1 \le i \le n$) to be the state that produced the last output of the sequence, o_t. Hence the *forward variable* captures the probability $P(O, q_t = s_i | \lambda)$. Induction is then used to derive the probability associated with increasing the length of the output sequence by one (i.e. observing one more letter, o_{t+1} at time $t+1$), and calculating the resulting probability, i.e. $P(O, o_{t+1}, q_t = s_i, q_{t+1} = s_j | \lambda)$.

5.2 Problem Reformulation

The evaluation problem for HMM_κ can be formulated as follows. Given the structure and parameters of a HMM_κ, λ, and an output sequence O of length t, the task is to find the likelihood of the sequence O being produced by λ by computing the degree of surprise associated with O given λ.

We redefine the *forward variable* $f_t(i)$ to be the inductive variable capturing the degree of surprise associated with observing the output sequence O of length t and having state s_i ($1 \leq i \leq n$) to be the state that produced the last output of the sequence, o_t at time t, i.e. $\kappa(O, q_t = s_i | \lambda)$.

$$f_t(i) = \kappa(O, q_1, q_2, ..., q_{t-1}, q_t = s_i | \lambda) \tag{12}$$

If o_t is indeed a valid output generated by state s_i of λ, then state s_i is the output generator of o_t. This enables writing equation (12) as a variation of (10), which amounts to the following:

$$f_t(i) = \min_{i=1}^{n} \kappa(o_1, ..., o_t, q_1, ..., q_{t-1}, q_t = s_i | \lambda) \tag{13}$$

5.3 The Qualitative Forward Algorithm

The algorithm finds the solution by solving for $f_t(i)$ inductively as follows:

1. Initialization:

$$f_1(i) = \kappa(o_1, q_1 = s_i | \lambda) \tag{14}$$
$$= \kappa(o_1 | q_1 = s_i, \lambda) + \kappa(q_1 = s_i, \lambda) \tag{15}$$
$$= b_i(o_1) + \pi_i \tag{16}$$

The initialization step applies the inductive variable to the base case for which the length of the output sequence is 1. Property (5) of the κ calculus transforms the variable $f_1(i)$ given in (14) to the expression given in (15). In (15), $\kappa(o_1 | q_1 = s_i, \lambda)$ is the emission κ value associated with the only output o_1 being produced (by state s_i) at time 0 and $\kappa(s_i, \lambda)$ is the initial degree of surprise associated with state s_i, which amounts to the expression given in (16).

2. Induction:

The inductive step applies the inductive variable to the case where the sequence O is of length $t + 1$ and where state s_j is responsible for producing the output o_{t+1}. We hence devise a new variable $f_{(t+1)}(j)$ which represents the degree of surprise associated with observing an output sequence of length $t + 1$ with state s_j

being the one that produced $o_{(t+1)}$, given that $f_t(i)$ holds at time t. The inductive variable $f_{(t+1)}(j)$ is given in equation (17) and is derived below.

Starting with the forward variable obtained in equation (13), and using property (5) of the κ-calculus, $f_{t+1}(j)$ can be rewritten by assigning ψ the values of $o_1, ..., o_t, q_1, ..., q_t$ and ϕ those of $o_{(t+1)}, q_{(t+1)} = s_j, \lambda$ as given below.

$$f_{t+1}(j) = \min_{j=1}^{n}[\kappa(o_1, ..., o_t, o_{(t+1)}, q_1, ..., q_t, q_{(t+1)} = s_j | \lambda))$$

$$= \min_{j=1}^{n}[\kappa(o_1, ..., o_t, q_1, ..., q_t \,|\, o_{(t+1)}, q_{(t+1)} = s_j, \lambda) +$$
$$\kappa(o_{(t+1)}, q_{(t+1)} = s_j, \lambda)]$$

The above equation is further rewritten using two properties, one is property (6) of HMM_κ, making the term $\kappa(o_1, ..., o_t, q_1, ..., q_t | o_{(t+1)}, q_{(t+1)} = s_j, \lambda)$ simply $\kappa(o_1, ..., o_t, q_1, ..., q_t | \lambda)$ because the elements of $o_1, ..., o_t, q_1, ..., q_t$ are independent of $o_{(t+1)}$ and $q_{(t+1)}$ according to the memoryless independence assumption. The second property is property (5) of the κ-calculus, with ψ being $o_{(t+1)}$ and ϕ being $q_{(t+1)} = s_j$.

$$f_{t+1}(j) = \min_{j=1}^{n}[\kappa(o_1, ..., o_t, q_1, ..., q_t | \lambda) + \kappa(o_{(t+1)} \,|\, q_{(t+1)} = s_j, \lambda) +$$
$$\kappa(q_{(t+1)} = s_j, \lambda)]$$

The inductive hypothesis dictates that in order for $f_{t+1}(j)$ to be true, $f_t(i)$ must have been true. This makes the state that held at time t to be s_i, and the resulting equation is shown below.

$$f_{t+1}(j) = \min_{j=1}^{n}[\kappa(o_1, ..., o_t, q_1, ..., q_t = s_i | \lambda) + \kappa(o_{(t+1)} | q_{(t+1)} = s_j, \lambda) +$$
$$\kappa(q_{(t+1)} = s_j | q_{(t)} = s_i \lambda)]$$

In the above equation, it can be clearly seen that the first term is the inductive variable $f_t(i)$, the second term is a_{ij}, while the third is $b_j(o_{(t+1)})$, which is only one value, and hence is taken out of the sum to give equation (17) given below, which is the final form of the inductive step.

$$f_{t+1}(j) = \min_{i=1}^{n}[f_t(i) + a_{ij}] + b_j(o_{(t+1)}) \tag{17}$$

As made clear in the derivation, the inductive step of equation (17), which computes $f_{t+1}(j)$, is only executed if at time t, the degree of surprise of having state s_i producing output o_t, given output sequence O and the complete specification of the structure and parameters of λ has been computed by $f_t(i)$.

3. Termination:
   Given that the inductive step computes the forward variable at every time step
   until t, starting with the base case at time 1, the inductive algorithm correctly
   terminates at step t, by calculating $f_t(i)$, $\forall\ 1 \leq i \leq n$, and consequently finding
   the degree of surprise associated with observing the last output o_t of the sequence
   O.

$$\kappa(O|\lambda) = \min_{i=1}^{n} f_t(i) \tag{18}$$

6 A Qualitative HMM for Gene Expression Data

6.1 The Problem

The human genome contains an estimated 30,000 genes that regulate most of the
biological process required for the cells to live and function. These genes function
by interacting with each other and controlling each other's behavior in ways that
are not yet fully understood. One of the fundamental questions to computational
biologists is to determine how genes interact to regulate biological process [19].

Genes are present in the cell's nucleus in the form of long DNA sequences. A
gene remains idle, in DNA form, until it is activated by a stimulus. Once a gene
is activated, it undergoes a process that transforms it into a functional product (in
the form of a protein) that is capable of performing the tasks required by the gene.
The process of transforming an idle gene lying on the DNA sequence to a protein
functional product is called gene expression [2]

The stimulus that activates a gene, forcing it to undergo expression can be an
external stimulus (e.g. change in the cell's PH level, light, etc..) or an internal one.
An internal stimulus is usually the expression levels of other genes. In other words,
the expression of certain genes causes the expression (or inhibition) of other genes.
Discovering the network of interaction among genes causing their expression and
inhibition is the challenge in analyzing gene expression data.

Discovering the patterns that govern the expression of genes and their interactive
behavior is made possible by the availability of time-series microarray gene expression data. An intuitive way of looking at gene expression data is by regarding it
as a two-dimensional array, where each row corresponds to one gene's expression
levels during incremental t time steps. Hence, a 1000×10 time-series microarray
models the expression of 1000 genes for 10 time steps. It is obvious that microarray
technology allows the simultaneous measurement of the expression levels of tens of
thousands of genes at different times.

From the above, it can be seen that related genes will behave similarly at different
times. In other words, their expression levels will be similar or related. This makes
it only logical to use clustering methods to classify genes based on their expression
profiles and group them in logical groups in order to gain some biological insight,
which in turn can help in the discovery of their general behavior and the identifica-

tion of abnormal behavior to understand diseases and formulate drugs accordingly [13].

Traditional HMMs have been good in this regard. They have been used to cluster and classify time-series gene expression data [23]. In this section, we present the building blocks for using HMM_κ to classify microarray expression data. Our aim here is not to produce better results than those obtained using traditional HMMs, however, we believe that qualitative HMMs can be useful in the following ways:

1. HMM_κ can be used as a pre-clustering medium that guides the initial stages of clustering using quantitative HMMs for very large time-series gene expression data.
2. HMM_κ will not suffer from the assumption that the actual numbers labeled in expression levels (which are basically the concentration levels of proteins expressed from genes under study) are dealt with as the probability of expression of a certain gene. With HMM_κ, the expression level merely measures the degree of surprise of a gene being expressed; a less strict statement than that made by the probability-based assumption.

6.2 Aim

The aim of the experiments conducted in this section is to demonstrate the capability of HMM_κ and its associated qualitative forward algorithm of producing results that can at least be used as a pre-clustering model that may be used to obtain useful insight about the data without having deal with the numerical aspects of the expression process.

6.3 The Structure of the HMM

Given a matrix $M < n, m >$ corresponding to a time-series microarray data set, construct a HMM to model the stochastic behavior of the matrix M as follows:

- Construct the set of states $S = \{s_1, ..., s_n\}$, where $\forall s_i \in S : s_i$ represents the hidden behavior of gene i $(1 \leq i \leq n)$, i.e. the behavior governing the time-series for gene i.
- Construct the set of observation variables $O = \{o_1, ..., o_m\}$, where $\forall o_t \in O : o_t$ represents the expression level of some gene at time t $(1 \leq t \leq m)$. Hence, the matrix $B = \{b_j(o_t), 1 \leq j \leq n\}$ represents the observed expression level of gene j at time t.

6.4 Data Set

For the purpose of the initial examination of the performance of HMM_κ embodied in this paper, we use two data sets. The first is a set of simulated data describing the expression levels of 550 genes for a 5-step time series, and for which the correct clustering of the gene time-series is known. The second is the *E.Coli* data set, for which we evaluate our algorithm by comparing our results with the literature.

6.5 Obtaining HMMκ

Ideally, we would like the HMM to be trained with kappa values instead of numerical probabilities. This, however, requires a qualitative version of the learning algorithms, which is currently under development. Therefore, the HMM was trained with the well-known Baum-Welch algorithm [16], which iteratively searches for the HMM parameters by maximizing the likelihood of the observations given the model, $P(O|\lambda)$. We use the Baum-Welch to obtain a HMM = (S,V,π,A,B) that uses regular probabilities. The κ values of the corresponding HMM_κ are then obtained from the probability values of the π vector, the A and B matrices by mapping the probability values using the notion introduced in section 3 as follows:

$$\varepsilon < \frac{P(\omega)}{\varepsilon^n} \leq 1 \text{ or equivalently: } \varepsilon^{n+1} < P(\omega) \leq \varepsilon^n$$

6.6 Experiment and Analysis

The classification capability of the qualitative forward algorithm presented in this paper is tested on two data sets. The first is that of simulated data for which the correct classification is known, while the second is the *E.coli* data set. The experiments are performed by running the qualitative algorithm on each data set using different values of ε (and hence varying the level of abstraction of the probability values).

The results are summarized in the tables given below. In both tables, the rows correspond to the size of the data set, while the columns are the different ε values for which our qualitative algorithm is tested. Each cell in the table represents the percentage of correctly-classified sequences for the given ε value for the data set of the specific size using our qualitative algorithms. It can be seen that increasing the level of abstraction (higher ε value) influences the accuracy of evaluation. Moreover, the results are comparable to those obtained with standard non-qualitative methods.

Table 1 Using Simulated Data: Percentages of correct classification for different sizes of data using incremental values of ε

Data Size	$\varepsilon = 0.025$	$\varepsilon = 0.05$	$\varepsilon = 0.075$	$\varepsilon = 0.1$
100	0.900	0.912	1.000	1.000
250	0.877	0.879	0.912	0.921
350	0.854	0.852	0.904	0.905
500	0.820	0.988	0.870	0.891

Table 2 Using the *E.Coli* dataset: Percentages of correct classification for different sizes of data using incremental values of ε

Data Size	$\varepsilon = 0.025$	$\varepsilon = 0.05$	$\varepsilon = 0.075$	$\varepsilon = 0.1$
289	0.87	0.891	.954	1.000
631	0.834	0.854	0.917	0.911
1790	0.791	0.834	0.903	0.901
2975	0.762	0.811	0.865	0.879

7 Conclusion and Future Work

We presented HMM_κ, which is a HMM that uses κ values to capture the degree of surprise of associated events by reformulating the π vector, A and B matrices to accept κ values instead of probabilities. We have also presented an algorithm, which uses HMM_κ to evaluate the likelihood of output sequences observed by an external agent.

We have used the resulting HMM_κ to classify time-series gene expression profiles and found the results obtained to be compatible by those generated by traditional quantitative HMMs.

We are currently working on formulating qualitative learning algorithms to train HMM_κ and test the model and its associated algorithms with real gene expression data available in databases instead of the simulated data used in this paper.

References

1. A. Darwiche and M. Goldszmidt. On the relation between kappa calculus and probabilistic reasoning. In *Proceedings of the Tenth Annual Conference on Uncertainty in Artificial Intelligence (UAI)*, pages 145–153, 1994.
2. P. D'haeseleer, S. Liang, and R. Somogyi. Gene expression data analysis and modeling. Tutorial, University of New Mexico, 1999.
3. M. Fox, M. Ghallab, G. Infantes, and D. Long. Robot introspection through learned Hidden Markov Models. *Artificial Intelligence*, 170(2):59–113, 2006.
4. N. Friedman. Inferring cellular networks using probabilistic graphical Models. *Science*, 303:799–805, 2004.
5. M. Goldszmidt and J. Pearl. Qualitative probabilities for default reasoning, belief revision, and causal modeling. *Artif. Intell.*, 84(1-2):57–112, 1996.

6. D. Hand. Protection or privacy? data mining and personal data. In *Proceedings of the 10th Pacific-Asia Conference, Advances in Knowledge Discovery and Data Mining (PAKDD)*, pages 1–10, 2006.

7. X. Huang, A. Acero, and H.W. Hon. *Spoken Language Processing: A Guide to Theory, Algorithm and System Development*. Prentice Hall PTR, 2001.

8. A. Ibrahim, A. Tawfik, and A. Ngom. A qualitative Hidden Markov Model for spatio-temporal reasoning. In *Proceedings of the 9th European Conference on Symbolic and Quantitative Approaches to Reasoning with Uncertainty, (ECSQARU)*, pages 707–718, 2007.

9. A. Jepson and R. Mann. Qualitative probabilities for image interpretation. In *Proceedings of the International Conference on Computer Vision-Volume 2 (ICCV)*, pages 1123–1130, 1999.

10. R. Kahsay, G. Gao, and L. Liao. An improved Hidden Markov Model for transmembrane protein detection and topology prediction and its applications to complete genomes. *Bioinformatics*, 21(9):853–1858, 2005.

11. H. Kyburg. Probabiliity and the logic of rational belief. Technical report, Wesleyan Universit Press, 1961.

12. B. Lovell. Hidden Markov Models for spatio-temporal pattern recognition and image segmentation, 2001.

13. Z. Lubovac, B. Olsson, P. Jonsson, K. Laurio, and M.L. Andersson. Biological and statistical evaluation of gene expression profiles. In *Proceedings of Mathematics and Computers in Biology and Chemistry*, pages 149–155, 2001.

14. S. Parsons. Hybrid models of uncertainty in protein topology prediction. *Applied Artificial Intelligence*, 9(3):335–351, 1995.

15. S. Parsons. Qualitative probability and order of magnitude reasoning. *International Journal of Uncertainty, Fuzziness and Knowledge-Based Systems*, 11(3):373–390, 2003.

16. Rabiner. A tutorial on Hidden Markov Models and selected applications in speech recognition. *Proceedings of the IEEE*, 77(2):257–289, 1989.

17. V. Ramezani and S. Marcus. Estimation of Hidden Markov Models: risk-sensitive filter banks and qualitative analysis of their sample paths. *IEEE Transactios on Automatic Control*, 47(12):1000–2009, 2002.

18. A. Rosti and M. Gales. Factor analysed Hidden Markov Models for speech recognition. Technical Report 453, Cambridge University Engineering Department, 2003.

19. A. Schliep, A. Schonhuth, and C. Steinhoff. Using Hidden Markov Models to analyse gene expression time course data. *Bioinformatics*, 19(1):i255–i263, 2003.

20. P Smyth. Belief Networks, Hidden Markov Models, and Markov Random Fields: A unifying view. *Pattern Recognition Letters*, 18(11-13):1261–1268, 1997.

21. W. Spohn. Ordinal conditional functions: A dynamic theory of epistemic states. *Causation in Decision, Belief Change, and Statistics*, 2:105–134, 1987.

22. M. Wellman. Some varieties of qualitative probability. In *Proceedings of th e5th International Conference on Processing and Management of Uncertainty in Knowledge-Based Systems (IPMU)*, pages 171–179, 1994.

23. Y. Zeng and J. Garcia-Frias. A novel HMM-based clustering algorithm for the analysis of gene expression time-course data. *Computational Statistics & Data Analysis*, 50:2472–2494, 2006.

Description Identification and the Consistency Problem

E.N. Smirnov and N.Y. Nikolaev and G.I. Nalbantov

Abstract The description-identification problem is to find a description from train-ing specializations and generalizations of that description. The set of all consistent solutions for the problem forms a version space. This paper shows that the problem of version-space classification is equivalent to the consistency problem: determining the existence of a description consistent with the data. In this context we propose here the first efficient consistency algorithms for description identification.

1 Introduction

The description-identification problem is to find a description in a description space D from the training specializations and generalizations of that description [1, 7, 9]. The set of all the descriptions in D consistent with the training data form a version space [8]. The version space is represented by boundary sets proposed in [8].

Although the boundary sets are a useful version-space representation, for some description spaces we can have one of the following two problems:

- the boundary-set size is exponential in the size of the training data,
- the boundary sets are infinite.

The two boundary-set problems were first observed in concept learning[1] [3, 5]. To avoid them, the concept-learning research concentrated on alternative version-space representations [4, 6, 10, 11, 12]. Then, it was shown in [5] that the problem

E.N. Smirnov
MICC, Maastricht University, Maastricht, The Netherlands, e-mail: smirnov@micc.unimaas.nl

N.Y. Nikolaev
Goldsmiths College, London University, London, United Kingdom, e-mail: n.nikolaev@gold.ac.uk

G.I. Nalbantov
MICC, Maastricht University, Maastricht, The Netherlands, e-mail: g.nalbantov@micc.unimaas.nl

[1] We note that in concept learning only training specializations are available.

of version-space classification is equivalent to the consistency problem: determining the existence of a description consistent with the data. Hence, efficient consistent algorithms were proposed in [5] resulting in efficient version-space classification.

This paper studies how to avoid the boundary-set problems for description identification. Our task is non-trivial since the description-identification problem is computationally more difficult than the concept-learning problem [7]. Following [5] we first prove that for description identification the problem of version-space classification is equivalent to the consistency problem. Then, we provide our main contribution - the first efficient consistency algorithms for description identification applicable for lower-bounded and upper-bounded description spaces.

2 The Description-Identification Problem

The description-identification problem assumes a universe O of objects [7]. Any concept c is defined as a subset of O. The set of all the concepts in O is the power set 2^O. To represent concepts from 2^O we introduce a description space D as a countable set of descriptions. The descriptions in D are ordered by a relation *subsumption* ($\geq$). Description $d_i \in D$ subsumes description $d_j \in D$, denoted by $d_i \geq d_j$, if and only if any object $o \in O$ represented by d_j is represented by d_i. Hence, the subsumption relation is a partially-ordered relation.

The description space D includes set $D_s \subseteq D$ of possible specializations and set $D_g \subseteq D$ of possible generalizations such that $D_s \cap D_g = \emptyset$. The specializations and generalizations can be positive and negative relatively to a description $d \in D$.

Definition 1. Given a description $d \in D$ we say that:

- a specialization $d_i \in D_s$ is a positive specialization for d if and only if $d \geq d_i$,
- a specialization $d_i \in D_s$ is a negative specialization for d if and only if $\neg(d \geq d_i)$,
- a generalization $d_i \in D_g$ is a positive generalization for d if and only if $d_i \geq d$,
- a generalization $d_i \in D_g$ is a negative generalization for d if and only if $\neg(d_i \geq d)$.

Notation 1 *Positive and negative specializations are labeled by "1" and "$\bar{1}$", respectively. The set $\{1,\bar{1}\}$ is denoted by* Ls. *Positive and negative generalizations are labeled by "$\mathbf{u}$" and "$\bar{\mathbf{u}}$", respectively. The set $\{\mathbf{u},\bar{\mathbf{u}}\}$ is denoted by* Lg.

To determine the label set for $d \in D_s \cup D_g$ a label-set function is needed. The function returns the label set Ls (Lg) if d is a specialization (generalization).

Definition 2. (Function Label-Set (L))

$L : D_s \cup D_g \rightarrow \{\text{Ls}, \text{Lg}\}$
defined by:
$$L(d) = \begin{cases} \text{Ls if } d \in D_s, \\ \text{Lg if } d \in D_g. \end{cases}$$

To determine the label of a specialization/generalization $d_j \in D_s \cup D_g$ with respect to a description $d_i \in D$ we introduce a label function.

Definition 3. (Function Label (l))

$l : D \times (D_s \cup D_g) \to \mathrm{Ls}$
defined by:

$$l(d_i, d_j) = \begin{cases} \mathbf{l} & \text{if } d_j \in D_s \text{ and } d_i \geq d_j, \\ \overline{\mathbf{l}} & \text{if } d_j \in D_s \text{ and } \neg(d_i \geq d_j), \\ \mathbf{u} & \text{if } d_j \in D_g \text{ and } d_j \geq d_i, \\ \overline{\mathbf{u}} & \text{if } d_j \in D_g \text{ and } \neg(d_j \geq d_i). \end{cases}$$

Any unknown description in D can be characterized by a set of labeled specializations and generalizations $(d_1, l_1), (d_2, l_2), \ldots, (d_n, l_n)$ where $d_i \in D_s \cup D_g$ and $l_i \in \mathrm{Ls} \cup \mathrm{Lg}$. We assume that there is no label noise.

Notation 2 *Sets of positive and negative specializations are denoted by* L *and* $\overline{\mathrm{L}}$, *respectively. Sets of positive and negative generalizations are denoted by* U *and* $\overline{\mathrm{U}}$, *respectively. Union of any sets is denoted by the concatenation of the set symbols[2].*

Problem Formulation: *Given a description space D, a subsumption relation "$\geq$", and a training set* $\mathrm{L}\overline{\mathrm{L}}\mathrm{U}\overline{\mathrm{U}}$ *for a target description, the description-identification problem is to find descriptions $d \in D$ with respect to* $\mathrm{L}\overline{\mathrm{L}}\mathrm{U}\overline{\mathrm{U}}$.

The description-identification problem can be considered as a search problem in the partially-ordered space D [7]. By theorem 3 the specializations and generalizations are either **monotonic** or **anti-monotonic** constraints for the target descriptions.

Theorem 3. *For any descriptions $d_i, d_j, d_k \in D$ s.t. $d_i \geq d_j$[3]:*

(**a**) *if $d_j \geq d_k$, then $d_i \geq d_k$,*
(**m**) *if $d_k \geq d_i$, then $d_k \geq d_j$,*
(**m**) *if $\neg(d_i \geq d_k)$, then $\neg(d_j \geq d_k)$,*
(**a**) *if $\neg(d_k \geq d_j)$, then $\neg(d_k \geq d_i)$.*

To search in the description space D we use search operators defined below [7].

Definition 4. (Search Operators) For any descriptions $d_i, d_j \in D$:

(1) $\mathbf{uu}(d_i, d_j) = MIN(\{d \in D | (d \geq d_i) \wedge (d \geq d_j)\}))$,
(2) $\mathbf{l\overline{u}}(d_i, d_j) = MAX(\{d \in D | (d_i \geq d) \wedge \neg(d \geq d_j)\})$,
(3) $\mathbf{ll}(d_i, d_j) = MAX(\{d \in D | (d_i \geq d) \wedge (d_j \geq d)\})$,
(4) $\mathbf{u\overline{u}}(d_i, d_j) = MIN(\{d \in D | (d \geq d_i) \wedge \neg(d_j \geq d)\})$.

where $MIN(S)$ and $MAX(S)$ are the sets of minimal and maximal elements of a set $S \subseteq D$, respectively[4].

The operator $\mathbf{uu}(d_i, d_j)$ computes the set of the minimal elements of the set of descriptions subsuming $d_i, d_j \in D$. The operator $\mathbf{l\overline{u}}(d_i, d_j)$ computes the set of the maximal elements of the set of descriptions subsumed by $d_i \in D$ that do not subsume

---

[2] For example, the union of all the sets is denoted by $\mathrm{L}\overline{\mathrm{L}}\mathrm{U}\overline{\mathrm{U}}$.

[3] Theorems are given without proofs if they were formulated in one of the references [1-12].

[4] Element m in a poset S is a minimal element for S if and only if $(\forall d \in S)(m \geq d \to m = d)$ [2]. The maximal elements are defined by duality.

$d_j \in D$. The operator $\mathbf{ll}(d_i, d_j)$ computes the set of the maximal elements of the set of descriptions subsumed by $d_i, d_j \in D$. The operator $\mathbf{u\overline{u}}(d_i, d_j)$ computes the set of the minimal elements of the set of descriptions subsuming $d_i \in D$ that are not subsumed by $d_j \in D$.

Notation 4 *The maximal set size of any search operator is denoted by B. The maximal time complexity of any search operator is denoted by T_s. The maximal time complexity to test $d_i \geq d_j$ for any descriptions $d_i, d_j \in D$ is denoted by T_t.*

3 Version Spaces

Since we assumed no label noise, any description $d \in D$ can be a solution for a description-identification problem if d is consistent with the training set $L\overline{L}U\overline{U}$ [7].

Definition 5. A description $d \in D$ is consistent with a training set $L\overline{L}U\overline{U}$, denoted by $cons(d, L\overline{L}U\overline{U})$, if and only if $(\forall (d_i, l_i) \in L\overline{L}U\overline{U}) l(d, d_i) = l_i$.

The consistency of a description $d \in D$ for the training set $L\overline{L}U\overline{U}$ can be viewed through the consistency of d for the training sets $L, U, \overline{L}$, and $\overline{U}$.

Corollary 1. *For any description $d \in D$ and set $L\overline{L}U\overline{U}$ $cons(d, L\overline{L}U\overline{U})$ if and only if*

$$((\forall(d_i, l_i) \in L)(d \geq d_i) \wedge (\forall(d_i, l_i) \in \overline{L})\neg(d \geq d_i) \wedge$$
$$(\forall(d_i, l_i) \in U)(d_i \geq d) \wedge (\forall(d_i, l_i) \in \overline{U})\neg(d_i \geq d)).$$

The set of all the descriptions in D consistent with $L\overline{L}U\overline{U}$ is a version space [7, 8].

Definition 6. (Version Spaces) Given a description space D and a training set $L\overline{L}U\overline{U}$, the version space $VS(L\overline{L}U\overline{U})$ equals the set $\{d \in D | cons(d, L\overline{L}U\overline{U})\}$.

By definition 6 version spaces are sets. Theorem 5 given below determines when two version spaces $VS(L_i\overline{L}_iU_i\overline{U}_i)$ and $VS(L_j\overline{L}_jU_j\overline{U}_j)$ are in the subset relationship.

Theorem 5. $VS(L_i\overline{L}_iU_i\overline{U}_i)$ *is a subset of* $VS(L_j\overline{L}_jU_j\overline{U}_j)$ *if and only if any description $d_i \in VS(L_i\overline{L}_iU_i\overline{U}_i)$ is consistent with $L_j\overline{L}_jU_j\overline{U}_j$.*

The version-space classification rule assigns label $l \in Ls \cup Lg$ to a specialization/generalization $d \in D_s \cup D_g$ if and only if all descriptions in a non-empty version space $VS(L\overline{L}U\overline{U})$ agrees with l; otherwise, d is not labeled (indicated by "?").

Definition 7. Non-empty version space $VS(L\overline{L}U\overline{U})$ assigns label $VS(L\overline{L}U\overline{U})(d) \in Ls \cup Lg \cup \{?\}$ to a specialization/generalization $d \in D_s \cup D_g$ as follows:

$$VS(L\overline{L}U\overline{U})(d) = \begin{cases} l & (\forall d_i \in VS(L\overline{L}U\overline{U})) l(d, d_i) = l, \\ ? & \text{otherwise.} \end{cases}$$

To implement the version-space classification rule we need a classification algorithm. Below we formalize the conditions when such an algorithm is efficient.

Definition 8. A classification algorithm is efficient if in the worst case it outputs label $VS(L\overline{L}U\overline{U})(d)$ in time polynomial in $|L|$, $|\overline{L}|$, $|U|$, $|\overline{U}|$, B, T_s, and T_l.

There are two approaches to version-space classification. The first one is the boundary-set approach [7]. The second approach is the consistency-test approach.

4 The Boundary-Set Approach

The boundary-set approach is a standard approach for version spaces [7, 8]. It was proposed for the class of admissible description spaces. A partially-ordered description space D is admissible if and only if each subset of D is bounded [2].

Definition 9. (Admissible Description Spaces) A description space D is admissible if and only if for any non-empty sub-set $S \subseteq D$:

$$S \subseteq \{d \in D | (\exists s \in MIN(S))(d \geq s) \wedge (\exists g \in MAX(S))(g \geq d)\}.$$

The boundary-set approach is based on the minimal and maximal boundary sets.

Definition 10. (Boundary Sets) If the description space D is admissible, then:

- the minimal boundary set $S(L\overline{L}U\overline{U})$ of $VS(L\overline{L}U\overline{U})$ equals $MIN(VS(L\overline{L}U\overline{U}))$,
- the maximal boundary set $G(L\overline{L}U\overline{U})$ of $VS(L\overline{L}U\overline{U})$ equals $MAX(VS(L\overline{L}U\overline{U}))$.

By theorem 6 the boundary sets represent correctly version spaces.

Theorem 6. *If the description space D is admissible, then for any description $d \in D$:*

$$d \in VS(L\overline{L}U\overline{U}) \leftrightarrow (\exists s \in S(L\overline{L}U\overline{U}))(\exists g \in G(L\overline{L}U\overline{U}))(d \geq s \wedge g \geq d).$$

The boundary sets are formed by a learning algorithm defined in theorem 7 [7].

Theorem 7. (Boundary-Set Learning Algorithm) *Given an admissible description space D, a training set $L\overline{L}U\overline{U}$, and a description $d \in D$:*

- *if d is a specialization with label l, then:*

  $S(L\overline{L}U\overline{U} \cup \{(d,l)\}) = MIN(\{s \in S | (\exists g \in G(L\overline{L}U\overline{U}))(g \geq s)\})$,
  $G(L\overline{L}U\overline{U} \cup \{(d,l)\}) = \{g \in G(L\overline{L}U\overline{U}) | (g \geq d)\}$,
  where $S = MIN(\bigcup_{s \in S(L\overline{L}U\overline{U})} \mathbf{uu}(s,d))$.

- *if d is a specialization with label* $\bar{\mathbf{l}}$, *then:*

$$S(L\overline{L}U\overline{U} \cup \{(d,\bar{\mathbf{l}})\}) = \{s \in S(L\overline{L}U\overline{U})| \neg (s \geq d)\},$$
$$G(L\overline{L}U\overline{U} \cup \{(d,\bar{\mathbf{l}})\}) = MAX(\{g \in G|(\exists s \in S(L\overline{L}U\overline{U}))(d \geq s)\}),$$
where $G = MAX(\bigcup_{g \in G(L\overline{L}U\overline{U})} \mathbf{l}\overline{\mathbf{u}}(g,d))$.

- *if d is a generalization with label* **u**, *then:*

$$S(L\overline{L}U\overline{U} \cup \{(d,\mathbf{u})\}) = \{s \in S(L\overline{L}U\overline{U})|(d \geq s)\},$$
$$G(L\overline{L}U\overline{U} \cup \{(d,\mathbf{u})\}) = MAX(\{g \in G|(\exists s \in S(L\overline{L}U\overline{U}))(g \geq s)\}),$$
where $G = MAX(\bigcup_{g \in G(L\overline{L}U\overline{U})} \mathbf{l}\mathbf{l}(g,d))$.

- *if d is a generalization with label* $\bar{\mathbf{u}}$, *then:*

$$S(L\overline{L}U\overline{U} \cup \{(d,\bar{\mathbf{u}})\}) = MIN(\{s \in S|(\exists g \in G(L\overline{L}U\overline{U}))(g \geq s)\}),$$
$$G(L\overline{L}U\overline{U} \cup \{(d,\mathbf{l})\}) = \{g \in G(L\overline{L}U\overline{U})| \neg (d \geq g)\},$$
where $S = MIN(\bigcup_{s \in S(L\overline{L}U\overline{U})} \mathbf{u}\overline{\mathbf{u}}(s,d))$.

The learning algorithm handles positive specialization $(d,\mathbf{l})$ by first computing the minimal set S of the union of sets $\mathbf{u}\mathbf{u}(d,s)$ over all $s \in S(L\overline{L}U\overline{U})$. Then, the minimal boundary set $S(L\overline{L}U\overline{U} \cup \{(d,\mathbf{l})\})$ is formed by the elements of S subsumed by some $g \in G(L\overline{L}U\overline{U})$. The maximal boundary set $G(L\overline{L}U\overline{U} \cup \{(d,\mathbf{l})\})$ is formed by the elements of $G(L\overline{L}U\overline{U})$ subsuming d. The algorithm performance for labels $\bar{\mathbf{l}}, \mathbf{u}$, and $\bar{\mathbf{u}}$ is analogous. Thus, the algorithm worst-case space complexity of the boundary sets equals to $O(B^{|L|+|\overline{U}|} + B^{|\overline{L}|+|U|})$ (see notation 4); i.e., it is exponential in the size of the training data.

Theorem 8 given below provides the boundary-set classification algorithm.

Theorem 8. (Boundary-Set Classification Algorithm) *Consider an admissible description space D and a non-empty version space* $VS(L\overline{L}U\overline{U})$. *Then:*

- $VS(L\overline{L}U\overline{U})$ *assigns to a specialization* $d \in D_s$ *a label* $l \in Ls$ *equal to:*

    $\mathbf{l}$ *if and only if* $(\forall s \in S(L\overline{L}U\overline{U}))(s \geq d)$,
    $\bar{\mathbf{l}}$ *if and only if* $(\forall g \in G(L\overline{L}U\overline{U})) \neg (g \geq d)$.

- $VS(L\overline{L}U\overline{U})$ *assigns to a generalization* $d \in D_g$ *a label* $l \in Lg$ *equal to:*

    $\mathbf{u}$ *if and only if* $(\forall g \in G(L\overline{L}U\overline{U}))(d \geq g)$,
    $\bar{\mathbf{u}}$ *if and only if* $(\forall s \in S(L\overline{L}U\overline{U})) \neg (d \geq s)$.

The worst-case time complexity of the boundary-set classification algorithm is $O((B^{|L|+|\overline{U}|} + B^{|\overline{L}|+|U|})T_i)$ since all the elements of the boundary sets $S(L\overline{L}U\overline{U})$ and $G(L\overline{L}U\overline{U})$ have to be visited (see notation 4). Thus, it is exponential in the size of the training data and by definition 8 we conclude that the algorithm is not efficient.

5 The Consistency-Test Approach

This section introduces our consistency-test approach to version-space classification. First we prove that the version-space classification can be realized if we can test whether version spaces are empty (collapsed) (see theorem 9). Then, we show that testing version spaces for collapse is the consistency problem. Hence, the version-space classification can be implemented by any consistency algorithm.

Theorem 9 given below states that all the descriptions $d_i \in \mathrm{VS}(\overline{LLUU})$ assign label $l \in L(d)$ to a specialization/generalization $d \in D_s \cup D_g$ if and only if the version space $\mathrm{VS}(\overline{LLUU} \cup \{(d, l_j)\})$ for label $l_j \in L(d) \setminus \{l\}$ is empty.

Theorem 9 uses lemmas 1 and 2. Lemma 1 states that for any specialization/generalization $d \in D_s \cup D_g$ the union of the version spaces $\mathrm{VS}(\overline{LLUU} \cup \{(d, l)\})$ for all the labels $l \in L(d)$ equals to the version space $\mathrm{VS}(\overline{LLUU})$.

Lemma 1. $(\forall d \in D_s \cup D_g)(\bigcup_{l \in L(d)} VS(\overline{LLUU} \cup \{(d, l)\}) = \mathrm{VS}(\overline{LLUU}))$.

Proof. ($\subseteq$) Consider arbitrary $d \in D_s \cup D_g$ and $d_i \in \bigcup_{l \in L(d)} \mathrm{VS}(\overline{LLUU} \cup \{(d, l)\})$. By theorem 5 $(\forall l \in L(d)) \mathrm{VS}(\overline{LLUU} \cup \{(d, l)\}) \subseteq \mathrm{VS}(\overline{LLUU})$. Thus, $d_i \in \mathrm{VS}(\overline{LLUU})$. ($\supseteq$) Consider arbitrary $d \in D_s \cup D_g$ and $d_i \in \mathrm{VS}(\overline{LLUU})$; i.e., $cons(d_i, \overline{LLUU})$. Since $l(d_i, d)$ equals some $l \in L(d)$, we have $cons(d_i, \overline{LLUU} \cup \{(d, l)\})$. Thus, by definition 6 $d_i \in \mathrm{VS}(\overline{LLUU} \cup \{(d, l)\})$; i.e., $d_i \in \bigcup_{l \in L(d)} VS(\overline{LLUU} \cup \{(d, l)\})$. □

Lemma 2 states that for any specialization/generalization $d \in D_s \cup D_g$ the intersection of $\mathrm{VS}(\overline{LLUU} \cup \{(d, l)\})$ for all $l \in L(d)$ equals $\emptyset$.

Lemma 2. $(\forall d \in D_s \cup D_g)(\bigcap_{l \in L(d)} VS(\overline{LLUU} \cup \{(d, l)\}) = \emptyset)$.

Proof. The proof is by contradiction. We assume that for arbitrary $d \in D_s \cup D_g$ there exists description $d_i \in \bigcap_{l \in L(d)} \mathrm{VS}(\overline{LLUU} \cup \{(d, l)\})$. By definition 6 $(\forall l \in L(d)) cons(d_i, \overline{LLUU} \cup \{(d, l)\})$. This implies by definition 5 $(\forall l \in L(d)) l(d_i, d) = l$. Since $|L(d)| > 1$, the latter contradicts with the fact that l is a function. □

Theorem 9. *For any specialization/generalization $d \in D_s \cup D_g$ and label $l \in L(d)$:*

$$(\forall d_i \in \mathrm{VS}(\overline{LLUU})) l(d_i, d) = l \leftrightarrow (\forall l_j \in L(d) \setminus \{l\}) \mathrm{VS}(\overline{LLUU} \cup \{(d, l_j)\}) = \emptyset.$$

Proof. For any $d \in D_s \cup D_g$ and $l \in L(d)$:

$(\forall d_i \in \mathrm{VS}(\overline{LLUU})) l(d_i, d) = l$ **iff** [by definition 6]
$(\forall d_i \in \mathrm{VS}(\overline{LLUU}))(cons(d_i, \overline{LLUU}) \wedge l(d_i, d) = l)$ **iff**
$(\forall d_i \in \mathrm{VS}(\overline{LLUU})) cons(d_i, \overline{LLUU} \cup \{(d, l)\})$ **iff** [by definition 6]
$(\forall d_i \in \mathrm{VS}(\overline{LLUU}))(d_i \in \mathrm{VS}(\overline{LLUU} \cup \{(d, l)\}))$ **iff**
$\mathrm{VS}(\overline{LLUU}) \subseteq \mathrm{VS}(\overline{LLUU} \cup \{(d, l)\})$ **iff** [by thm 5 $\mathrm{VS}(\overline{LLUU}) \supseteq \mathrm{VS}(\overline{LLUU} \cup \{(d, l)\})$]
$\mathrm{VS}(\overline{LLUU}) = \mathrm{VS}(\overline{LLUU} \cup \{(d, l)\})$ **iff**
$\mathrm{VS}(\overline{LLUU}) \setminus \mathrm{VS}(\overline{LLUU} \cup \{(d, l)\}) = \emptyset$ **iff** [by lemma 1]

Algorithm *CACT*:

Input: $d \in D$ - description to be labeled.
Output: $l \in L(d)$ - label for d.

Initialize a label variable l equal to "?".
for each label $l_i \in L(d)$ **do**
  if $CA(L\overline{L}U\overline{U} \cup \{(d, l_i)\})$ **then**
    if $l = $"?" **then** $l = l_i$;
    else return "?";
return l.

Fig. 1 Classification algorithm based on the consistency test (*CACT*).

$\bigcup_{l_j \in L(d) \setminus \{l\}} \mathrm{VS}(L\overline{L}U\overline{U} \cup \{(d, l_j)\}) \setminus$
$\bigcup_{l_j \in L(d) \setminus \{l\}} (\mathrm{VS}(L\overline{L}U\overline{U} \cup \{(d, l_j)\}) \cap \mathrm{VS}(L\overline{L}U\overline{U} \cup \{(d, l)\})) = \emptyset$ **iff** [by lemma 2]
$\bigcup_{l_j \in L(d) \setminus \{l\}} \mathrm{VS}(L\overline{L}U\overline{U} \cup \{(d, l_j)\}) = \emptyset$ **iff**
$(\forall l_j \in L(d) \setminus \{l\}) \mathrm{VS}(L\overline{L}U\overline{U} \cup \{(d, l_j)\}) = \emptyset.\square$

By definition 6 to test whether the version space $\mathrm{VS}(L\overline{L}U\overline{U})$ is collapsed we test whether there exists any description $d \in D$ consistent with the training set $L\overline{L}U\overline{U}$. The latter test is essentially the consistency problem [5]. Thus, by theorem 9 *the problem of version-space classification is equivalent to the consistency problem*. So, the version-space classification can be realized using any consistency algorithm (*CA*). We assume that a *CA* algorithm has one parameter, set $S \subseteq D \times (\mathrm{Ls} \cup \mathrm{Lg})$, and returns true if and only if consistent descriptions for S exist in D.

The version-space classification algorithm based on the consistency test (*CACT*) labels a description $d \in D_s \cup D_g$ by running the *CA* algorithm with set $L\overline{L}U\overline{U} \cup \{(d, l_i)\}$ for each label $l_i \in L(d)$ (see Figure 1). By theorem 9 it returns label $l_i \in L(d)$ if *CA* returns true only for one set $L\overline{L}U\overline{U} \cup \{(d, l_i)\}$. Otherwise, "?" is returned.

We note that for any specialization/generalization $d \in D_s \cup D_g$ the size of the set of possible labels $|L(d)|$ is two. Thus, the time complexity of *CACT* is two times the time complexity of *CA*.

6 Consistency Algorithms for Lower-Bounded Description Spaces

This section proposes the first two efficient consistency algorithms for description identification. The algorithms are valid for the class of lower-bounded description spaces, a sub-class of the admissible description spaces.

6.1 Definition of Lower-Bounded Description Spaces

The lower-bounded description spaces form a broad class of admissible description spaces [5]. They are introduced formally in the definition given below.

Definition 11. (Lower-Bounded Description Spaces) An admissible description space D is said to be lower-bounded if and only if for each nonempty set $S \subseteq D$ there exists greatest lower bound $glb(S) \in D$.

The lower-bounded description spaces reduce the space needed for the boundary sets. By theorems 10 and 11 given below the space reduction is as follows:

- the size of $S(L\bar{L}U)$ of any version space $VS(L\bar{L}U)$ equals one,
- the size of $G(LU\bar{U})$ of any version space $VS(LU\bar{U})$ equals one.

Theorem 10. *If the description space D is lower-bounded, then* $|S(L\bar{L}U)| = 1$.

Proof. By definition 6 $(\forall d \in VS(L\bar{L}U))cons(d, L\bar{L}U)$ which by corollary 1 implies:

$$(\forall d \in VS(L\bar{L}U))(\forall (d_i, l_i) \in \bar{L})\neg(d \geq d_i), \qquad (1)$$
$$(\forall d \in VS(L\bar{L}U))(\forall (d_i, l_i) \in U)(d_i \geq d). \qquad (2)$$

Since $(\forall d \in VS(L\bar{L}U))(d \geq glb(VS(L\bar{L}U))$, by theorem 3 formulas (1) and (2) imply:

$$(\forall (d_i, l_i) \in \bar{L})\neg(glb(VS(L\bar{L}U)) \geq d_i), \qquad (3)$$
$$(\forall (d_i, l_i) \in U)(d_i \geq glb(VS(L\bar{L}U))). \qquad (4)$$

The set $VS(L\bar{L}U)^l$ of all the lower bounds of $VS(L\bar{L}U)$ includes L. Thus, since $glb(VS(L\bar{L}U))$ is the greatest element of $VS(L\bar{L}U)^l$:

$$(\forall (d_i, l_i) \in L)(glb(VS(L\bar{L}U)) \geq d_i). \qquad (5)$$

By corollary 1 formulas (3), (4), and (5) imply $cons(glb(VS(L\bar{L}U)), L\bar{L}U)$. By definition 11 $glb(VS(L\bar{L}U)) \in D$. Thus, by definition 6 $glb(VS(L\bar{L}U)) \in VS(L\bar{L}U)$. Since $glb(VS(L\bar{L}U))$ is a lower bound of $VS(L\bar{L}U)$ and $glb(VS(L\bar{L}U)) \in VS(L\bar{L}U)$, $glb(VS(L\bar{L}U))$ is the least element of $VS(L\bar{L}U)$. Thus, $|S(L\bar{L}U)| = 1.\square$

Theorem 11. *If the description space D is lower bounded, then* $|G(LU\bar{U})| = 1$.

---

[5] For example they include the 1-CNF discrete-attribute languages.

Proof. Since D is lower-bounded, $glb(U)$ is the greatest lower bound of the set U^l of all the lower bounds of the set U that includes $VS(L\overline{U})$. Thus,

$$(\forall(d_i, l_i) \in U)(d_i \geq glb(U)), \tag{6}$$
$$(\forall d \in VS(L\overline{U}))(glb(U) \geq d). \tag{7}$$

By definition 6 $(\forall d \in VS(L\overline{U}))cons(d, L\overline{U})$ which implies by corollary 1:

$$(\forall d \in VS(L\overline{U}))(\forall(d_i, l_i) \in L)(d \geq d_i), \tag{8}$$
$$(\forall d \in VS(L\overline{U}))(\forall(d_i, l_i) \in \overline{U})\neg(d_i \geq d). \tag{9}$$

Since formula (7), by theorem 3 formulas (8) and (9) imply:

$$(\forall(d_i, l_i) \in L)(glb(U) \geq d_i), \tag{10}$$
$$(\forall(d_i, l_i) \in \overline{U})\neg(d_i \geq glb(U)). \tag{11}$$

By corollary 1 formulas (6), (10), and (11) imply $cons(glb(U), L\overline{U})$. By definition 11 $glb(U) \in D$. Thus, by definition 6 $glb(U) \in VS(L\overline{U})$. Thus, since $glb(U) \in VS(L\overline{U})$ and formula (7), $glb(U)$ is the greatest element of $VS(L\overline{U})$. Thus, $|G(L\overline{U})| = 1.\square$

6.2 Applicability Conditions of the Consistency Algorithms

We propose consistency algorithms of lower-bounded description spaces applicable for two cases defined below:

- *the case of the eliminated set* $\overline{U}$ *(e$\overline{U}$):* for each negative generalization $(d_i, l_i) \in \overline{U}$ there exists a positive specialization $(d_j, l_j) \in L$ so that d_j is not subsumed by d_i;
- *the case of the eliminated set* $\overline{L}$ *(e$\overline{L}$):* for each negative specialization $(d_i, l_i) \in \overline{L}$ there exists a positive generalization $(d_j, l_j) \in U$ so that d_j does not subsume d_i.

For case (e$\overline{U}$) theorem 12 states that the version spaces $VS(L\overline{L}U)$ and $VS(L\overline{L}U\overline{U})$ are equal. Similarly, for case (e$\overline{L}$) theorem 13 states that the version spaces $VS(LU\overline{U})$ and $VS(L\overline{L}U\overline{U})$ are equal.

Theorem 12. *For case (e$\overline{U}$):* $VS(L\overline{L}U) = VS(L\overline{L}U\overline{U})$.

Proof. ($\subseteq$) Consider arbitrary $d_i \in VS(L\overline{L}U)$ and $d_j \in \overline{U}$ so that there exists $d_k \in L$ with $\neg(d_j \geq d_k)$. Since $d_i \geq d_k$ and $\neg(d_j \geq d_k)$, by theorem 3 $\neg(d_j \geq d_i)$. Thus, $(\forall d_j \in \overline{U})\neg(d_j \geq d_i)$ and by definition 5 $cons(d_i, L\overline{L}U\overline{U})$. Thus, by definition 6 $d_i \in VS(L\overline{L}U\overline{U})$.

Algorithm $CA_{e\overline{U}}$:

Input: $L\overline{L}U\overline{U}$ - data set.

Output: *true* iff $(\exists d \in D)cons(d, L\overline{L}U\overline{U})$.

Take the first positive specialization $(d,\mathbf{l}) \in L$;

$L' = \{d\}, \overline{L}' = \emptyset, U' = \emptyset$;

$S(L') = \{d\}$;

for each new positive specialization $(d,\mathbf{l}) \in L$ **do**

$\quad S(L' \cup \{(d,\mathbf{l})\}) = MIN(\bigcup_{s \in S(L')} \mathbf{uu}(s,d))$;

$\quad L' = L' \cup \{(d,\mathbf{l})\}$;

if $S(L') = \emptyset$ **then return** false;

$S(L'\overline{L}') = S(L')$;

for each new negative specialization $(d,\bar{\mathbf{l}}) \in \overline{L}$ **do**

$\quad S(L'\overline{L}' \cup \{(d_i, \bar{\mathbf{l}})\}) = \{s \in S(L'\overline{L}') | \neg(s \geq d)\}$;

$\quad \overline{L}' = \overline{L}' \cup \{(d,\bar{\mathbf{l}})\}$;

if $S(L'\overline{L}') = \emptyset$ **then return** false;

$S(L'\overline{L}'U') = S(L'\overline{L}')$;

for each new positive generalization $(d,\mathbf{u}) \in U$ **do**

$\quad S(L'\overline{L}'U' \cup \{(d,\mathbf{u})\}) = \{s \in S(L'\overline{L}'U') | (d \geq s)\}$;

$\quad U' = U' \cup \{(d,\mathbf{u})\}$;

if $S(L'\overline{L}'U') = \emptyset$ **then return** false;

return true.

Fig. 2 Consistency algorithm $CA_{e\overline{U}}$ for case $(e\overline{U})$.

($\supseteq$) This part of the theorem follows from theorem 5. $\square$

Theorem 13. *For case $(e\overline{L})$:* $VS(LU\overline{U}) = VS(L\overline{L}U\overline{U})$.

Proof. Consider arbitrary $d_i \in VS(LU\overline{U})$ and $d_j \in \overline{L}$ so that there exists $d_k \in U$ with $\neg(d_k \geq d_j)$. Since $d_k \geq d_i$ and $\neg(d_k \geq d_j)$, by theorem 3 $\neg(d_i \geq d_j)$. Thus,$(\forall d_j \in \overline{L})\neg(d_i \geq d_j)$ and by definition 5 $cons(d_i, L\overline{L}U\overline{U})$. Thus, by definition 6 $d_i \in VS(L\overline{L}U\overline{U})$.

($\supseteq$) This part of the theorem follows from theorem 5. $\square$

6.3 Consistency Algorithms

The consistency algorithm $CA_{e\overline{U}}$ for case $(e\overline{U})$ is given in Figure 2. It first takes the first positive specialization $(d,\mathbf{l}) \in L$ and initializes the auxiliary data sets $L', \overline{L}'$ and U', and the auxiliary minimal boundary set $S(L')$: L' and $S(L')$ are set to $\{d\}$, $\overline{L}'$ and U' are set to $\emptyset$. Then, $S(L')$ is updated for each new positive specialization $(d,\mathbf{l}) \in L$ by theorem 7 using the search operator $\mathbf{uu}$. Once L' becomes equal to L, $S(L')$ equals the real minimal boundary set $S(L)$ and it is tested for collapse. If

---

Algorithm $CA_{e\overline{L}}$:

Input: $L\overline{L}U\overline{U}$ - data set.

Output: *true* iff $(\exists d \in D)cons(d, L\overline{L}U\overline{U})$.

Take the first positive generalization $(d, \mathbf{u}) \in U$;
$U' = \{d\}, L' = \emptyset, \overline{U}' = \emptyset$;
$G(U') = \{d\}$;
for each new positive generalization $(d, \mathbf{u}) \in U$ **do**
  $G(U' \cup \{(d, \mathbf{u})\}) = MAX(\bigcup_{g \in G(L\overline{L}U\overline{U})} \mathrm{ll}(g, d))$;
  $U' = U' \cup \{(d, \mathbf{u})\}$;
if $G(U') = \emptyset$ **then return** false;
$G(L'U') = G(U')$;
for each new positive specialization $(d, \mathbf{l}) \in L$ **do**
  $G(L'U' \cup \{(d_i, \mathbf{l})\}) = \{g \in G(L'U') | (g \ge d)\}$;
  $L' = L' \cup \{(d, \mathbf{l})\}$;
if $G(L'U') = \emptyset$ **then return** false;
$G(L'U'\overline{U}') = G(L'U')$;
for each new negative generalization $(d, \overline{\mathbf{u}}) \in \overline{U}$ **do**
  $G(L'U'\overline{U}') \cup \{(d, \overline{\mathbf{u}})\}) = \{g \in G(L'U'\overline{U}')) | \neg(d \ge g)\}$;
  $\overline{U}' = \overline{U}' \cup \{(d, \overline{\mathbf{u}})\}$;
if $G(L'U'\overline{U}') = \emptyset$ **then return** false;
return true.

Fig. 3 Consistency algorithm $CA_{e\overline{L}}$ for case $(e\overline{L})$.

$S(L') = \emptyset$, by definition 9 $VS(L) = \emptyset$. By theorem 5 $VS(L) \supseteq VS(L\overline{L}U\overline{U})$. Thus, the version space $VS(L\overline{L}U\overline{U})$ is empty. This means by definition 6 that there is no $d \in D$ consistent with $L\overline{L}U\overline{U}$, and "false" is returned.

If $S(L') \neq \emptyset$, a new auxiliary minimal boundary set $S(L'\overline{L}')$ is set equal to $S(L')$. Then, $S(L'\overline{L}')$ is updated for each negative specialization $(d, \overline{\mathbf{l}}) \in \overline{L}$ by theorem 7: a minimal element s is kept if $\neg(s \ge d)$. Once $\overline{L}'$ becomes equal to $\overline{L}$, $S(L'\overline{L}')$ equals the real minimal boundary set $S(L\overline{L})$ and it is tested for collapse. If $S(L'\overline{L}') = \emptyset$, by definition 9 $VS(L\overline{L}) = \emptyset$. By theorem 5 $VS(L\overline{L}) \supseteq VS(L\overline{L}U\overline{U})$. Thus, the version space $VS(L\overline{L}U\overline{U})$ is empty. This means by definition 6 that there is no $d \in D$ consistent with $L\overline{L}U\overline{U}$, and "false" is returned.

If $S(L'\overline{L}') \neq \emptyset$, a new auxiliary minimal boundary set $S(L'\overline{L}'U')$ is set equal to $S(L'\overline{L}')$. Then, set $S(L'\overline{L}'U')$ is updated for each positive generalization $(d, \mathbf{u}) \in U$ by theorem 7: a minimal element s is kept if $d \ge s$. Once U' becomes equal to U, $S(L'\overline{L}'U')$ equals the real minimal boundary set $S(L\overline{L}U)$ and it is tested for collapse. If $S(L'\overline{L}'U') = \emptyset$ by definition 9 $VS(L\overline{L}U) = \emptyset$. By theorem 5 $VS(L\overline{L}U) \supseteq VS(L\overline{L}U\overline{U})$. Thus, the version space $VS(L\overline{L}U\overline{U})$ is empty. This means by definition 6 that there is no $d \in D$ consistent with $L\overline{L}U\overline{U}$, and "false" is returned.

If $S(L'\overline{L}'U') \neq \emptyset$, $VS(L\overline{L}U) \neq \emptyset$. By theorem 12 $VS(L\overline{L}U) = VS(L\overline{L}U\overline{U})$, since case $(e\overline{U})$ holds. Thus, $VS(L\overline{L}U\overline{U})$ is non-empty. This implies by definition 6 that there is description $d \in D$ consistent with $L\overline{L}U\overline{U}$, and "true" is returned.

The consistency algorithm $CA_{e\overline{L}}$ for case $(e\overline{L})$ is presented in Figure 3. It can be explained analogously.

6.4 Complexity Analysis

By theorem 10 the size of the minimal boundary set on each step of the consistency algorithm $CA_{e\overline{U}}$ is one. Thus, the worst-case time complexity of $CA_{e\overline{U}}$ equals $O(|L|T_s + (|\overline{L}| + |U|)T_t)$ (see notation 4). If $CA_{e\overline{U}}$ is used for the consistency test in the version-space classification algorithm $CACT$, the worst-case time complexity of $CACT$ equals $O(|L|T_s + (|\overline{L}| + |U|)T_t)$ (see section 5). Thus, by definition 8 the version-space classification algorithm $CACT$ based on $CA_{e\overline{U}}$ is efficient for lower-bounded description spaces when case $(e\overline{U})$ holds.

We note that the boundary-set learning algorithm can be used for the consistency test as well: first, it computes both boundary sets, and then tests them for collapse. If the description space is lower-bounded and case $(e\overline{U})$ holds, the worst-case space complexity of the minimal boundary set $S(L\overline{L}U\overline{U})$ is $O(1)$ and that of the maximal boundary set $G(L\overline{L}U\overline{U})$ is $O(B^{|\overline{L}|})^6$. Thus, the worst-case time complexity of the boundary-set consistency algorithm equals $O(B^{|\overline{L}|}(T_s + |L|T_t))$. If the boundary-set consistency algorithm is used for the consistency test in the version-space classification algorithm $CACT$, the worst-case time complexity of $CACT$ becomes $O(B^{|\overline{L}|}(T_s + |L|T_t))$. Thus, by definition 8 the version-space classification algorithm $CACT$ based on the boundary-set consistency algorithm is not efficient for lower-bounded description spaces when case $(e\overline{U})$ holds.

The worst-case time complexity of the consistency algorithm $CA_{e\overline{L}}$ for case $(e\overline{L})$ is derived analogously and equals $O(|U|T_s + (|L| + |\overline{U}|)T_t)$. If $CA_{e\overline{L}}$ is used by the algorithm $CACT$, the worst-case time complexity of $CACT$ is $O(|U|T_s + (|L| + |\overline{U}|)T_t)$. Thus, the version-space classification algorithm $CACT$ based on $CA_{e\overline{L}}$ is efficient for lower-bounded description spaces when case $(e\overline{L})$ holds. In this context, we note that the worst-case time complexity of the boundary-set consistency algorithm is $O(B^{|L|+|\overline{U}|}(T_s + (|U|)T_t))$ in this case. Thus, the version-space classification algorithm $CACT$ based on the boundary-set consistency algorithm is not efficient for lower-bounded description spaces when case $(e\overline{L})$ holds.

6.5 Consistency Algorithms for Upper-Bounded Description Spaces

The upper-bounded description spaces and their consistency algorithms are obtained by duality from subsection 6.1. To avoid repetitions we leave out their description.

---

[6] In general the worst-case space complexity of $G(L\overline{L}U\overline{U})$ is $O(B^{|\overline{L}|+|U|})$. Since D is lower-bounded, U does not have a branching impact on $G(L\overline{L}U\overline{U})$. Thus, the factor $|U|$ is eliminated.

7 Conclusion

This paper showed two important results for the description-identification problem. First, we proved that the problem of version-space classification is equivalent to the consistency problem. Second, we introduced the first efficient consistency algorithms for the description-identification problem applicable for lower-bounded and upper-bounded description spaces. As a result we can classify with version spaces in polynomial time when the size of the boundary sets is exponential or when they are infinite. Of course we note that the consistency algorithms proposed are applicable when one type of specializations or generalizations is eliminated; i.e., the applicability is restricted. This is due to the fact that the description-identification problem is harder than the concept-learning problem. So, our future research will focus on finding new consistency algorithms for the description identification with less applicability restrictions, a research direction not studied in machine learning so far.

References

1. J.-F. Boulicaut, L. De Raedt, and H. Mannila. *Constraint-Based Mining and Inductive Data-bases*. Springer, 2006.
2. B.A. Davey and H.A. Priestly. *Introduction to lattices and order*. Cambridge University Press, Cambridge, 1990.
3. D. Haussler. Quantifying inductive bias: AI learning algorithms and valiant's learning framework. *Artificial Intelligence*, 36(2):177–221, 1988.
4. H. Hirsh. Polynomial-time learning with version spaces. In *Proceedings of the Tenth National Conference on Artificial Intelligence (AAAI-92)*, pages 117–122, Menlo Park, CA, 1992. AAAI Press.
5. H. Hirsh, N. Mishra, and L. Pitt. Version spaces and the consistency problem. *Artificial Intelligence*, 156(2):115–138, 2004.
6. P. Idemstam-Almquist. Demand networks: an alternative representation of version spaces. Master's thesis, Department of Computer Science and Systems Sciences, Stockholm University, Stockholm, Sweden, 1990.
7. C. Mellish. The description identification problem. *Artificial Intelligence*, 52(2):151–167, 1991.
8. T.M. Mitchell. *Machine learning*. McGraw-Hill, New York, NY, 1997.
9. L. De Raedt. *From Inductive Logic Programming to Multi-Relational Data Mining*. Springer, 2006.
10. M. Sebag and C. Rouveirol. Tractable induction and classification in first order logic via stochastic matching. In *Proceedings of the Fifteenth International Joint Conference on Artificial Intelligence (IJCAI-97)*, pages 888–893, San Francisco, CA, 1997. Morgan Kaufmann.
11. E.N. Smirnov, J. van den Herik, and I.G. Sprinkhuizen-Kuyper. A unifying version-space representation. *Ann. Math. Artif. Intell.*, 41(1):47–76, 2004.
12. B.D. Smith and P.S. Rosenbloom. Incremental non-backtracking focusing: a polynomially bounded algorithm for version spaces. In *Proceedings of the Eight National Conference on Artificial Intelligence (AAAI-90)*, pages 848–853. MIT Press, 1990.

AI TECHNIQUES

Analysing the Effect of Demand Uncertainty in Dynamic Pricing with EAs

Siddhartha Shakya, Fernando Oliveira, and Gilbert Owusu

Abstract Dynamic pricing is a pricing strategy where a firm adjust the price for their products and services as a function of its perceived demand at different times. In this paper, we show how Evolutionary algorithms (EA) can be used to analyse the effect of demand uncertainty in dynamic pricing. The experiments are conducted in a range of dynamic pricing problems considering a number of different stochastic scenarios with a number of different EAs. The results are analysed, which suggest that higher demand fluctuation may not have adverse effect to the profit in comparison to the lower demand fluctuation, and that the reliability of EA for finding accurate policy could be higher when there is higher fluctuation then when there is lower fluctuation.

1 Introduction

Pricing is one of the most important decisions that a firm needs to make in order to survive in a competitive marketplace. If done carefully, it can be a valuable tool for the firm to achieve a number of different business goals, such as profit maximisation, demand management, value creation, etc. Conversely, a poor pricing policy could lead to a loss, and consequently extinction of the firm. Dynamic pricing [27] [15][3] is a pricing strategy where a firm adjust the price for their products and services as a function of its perceived demand at different times. Traditionally, it has been

Siddhartha Shakya
Intelligent Systems Research Centre, BT Group Chief Technology Office, Adastral Park, Ipswich, IP5 3RE, UK,e-mail: sid.shakya@bt.com

Fernando Oliveira
Warwick Business School, University of Warwick, Coventry, CV4 7AL, UK, e-mail: fernando.oliveira@wbs.ac.uk

Gilbert Owusu
Intelligent Systems Research Centre, BT Group Chief Technology Office, Adastral Park, Ipswich, IP5 3RE, UK,e-mail: gilbert.owusu@bt.com

applied in service industries, such as airlines, hotels and rentals [16]. For example, in airlines, the price for a seat changes according to the time remaining prior to the flight and number of available seats. Recent developments in information technology and eCommerce have led the dynamic pricing to spread over a wide range of other industries such as retail [11][6][1], wholesale [23] and auctions [24].

In this paper we show how the evolutionary models can be used for dynamic pricing in a stochastic setting where the demand is uncertain. Our motivation is to use such pricing approach to control demand and manage resources in a service industry [28][18]. In the type of problems we are analyzing, resource management is the effective workforce utilization for a given calendarised work demand profile, while meeting a set of constraints such as quality of service targets, conflict resolution schemes, such as overtime and borrowing additional workforce [17]. The system described in [18] integrates various Artificial Intelligence and Operational Research techniques in order to forecast demand for specific products and services at regional level, and to optimize the allocation of resources to each one of the region. Our aim is to use evolutionary algorithms as an alternative technique to manage resources by means of effective pricing. In particular, we extend the model presented in [26] and implement several evolutionary algorithms (EA) [7] for solving them. We analyse the performance of these algorithms in finding optimal profit, and also analyse the effect of demand uncertainty have on total profit and on the reliability of these algorithms.

EAs have been successfully applied in wide range of search and optimization problems. They are inspired by Darwin's theory of evolution where *selection* and *variation* work together to evolve a better solution. Different EA has been proposed using different approaches to selection and variation. In this paper we investigate two EAs to solve dynamic pricing problems, namely the genetic algorithm (GA) [7][12] and the estimation of distribution algorithms (EDA) [10],[14]. GA and EDA differ in the way they implement the variation operator. In particular, GA uses *crossover* and *mutation* approach to variation. In contrast, EDA uses probabilistic approach to variation, where a probabilistic model is built and sampled to generate new solutions. EDA is a relatively new area in evolutionary computation field and are being increasingly applied to real-world optimization problems. They are often reported to perform better than the traditional GAs [8] [22]. It is, therefore, interesting to see the performance of both EDA and GA with regards to dynamic pricing.

The objectives of this paper are to: a) analyze the performance of evolutionary algorithms as tools to approximate optimal behaviour in dynamic pricing; b) compare the algorithms under different scenarios with different levels of demand uncertainty; and c) analyse the effect of demand uncertainty have on the profit.

The paper is structured as follows. Section 2 presents the mathematical model of uncertainty for dynamic pricing. Section 3 describes a way to representing the dynamic pricing problem for solving them using EA, and also gives an overview of the implemented EAs. Section 4 describes the experimental results and presents the analysis of the results. Finally, section 5 concludes the paper.

2 A Mathematical Model of Dynamic Pricing

Depending on the nature of the product (or service), and the expected demand behaviour, a company has to choose between short-term or long-term profits. Short-term profit is to take advantage of the dynamics of demand throughout a week, or even during a day. Long-term profit is to model the long-term implications of short-term pricing and investment policies with the goal of maximising the long-term, for example months or years, profit. This section describes a dynamic pricing model that can be used for analyzing both short-term and long-term profits.

The total profit, (Π), earned from a product during the planning horizon can be modelled as

$$\Pi = \sum_{t=1}^{N} (P_t Q_t - C_t Q_t) \tag{1}$$

Here, N is the number of periods in planning horizon, Q_t is the total sales (or the production) of the product (which is equal to, or less than, the demand for the product), P_t is the average price of the product, and C_t is the cost of producing one extra product in period t, $P_t Q_t$ is the total revenue at period t, and $C_t Q_t$ is the variable cost at period t. In the situations where the demand is uncertain, the sales can be given by the sum of expected sales $E(Q_t)$ and a stochastic term modelling the fluctuation in demand as

$$Q_t = E(Q_t) + \varepsilon_t \tag{2}$$

Here, ε_t represents the fluctuation in demand. We give it as a normal random variable, upper and lower bounded by the positive and negative expected sales respectively. This can be written as

$$\varepsilon_t = \begin{cases} max\{-E(Q_t), N(0, \sigma E(Q_t))\} & \text{if} \quad N(0, \sigma E(Q_t)) < 0 \\ min\{E(Q_t), N(0, \sigma E(Q_t))\} & \text{if} \quad N(0, \sigma E(Q_t)) > 0 \end{cases} \tag{3}$$

where, $\sigma \geq 0$ is the fraction of $E(Q_t)$ representing the strength of the fluctuation. Higher σ represents high fluctuation in demand and lower σ represents lower fluctuation in demand. From (1) and (2), the total profit can be written as

$$\Pi = \sum_{t=1}^{N} (E(Q_t) + \varepsilon_t)(P_t - C_t) \tag{4}$$

Therefore, the expected profit can be written as

$$E(\Pi) = \sum_{t=1}^{N} E(Q_t)(P_t - C_t) \tag{5}$$

Also, the expected sales $E(Q_t)$ in a period t depends on the price for the product in that period and the price for the product in other periods in the planning horizon. For example, in airlines (or hotels), sales for seats (or rooms) in a given day depend on their price on that day and on other days within the planning horizon, which are visible to customers. We represent this price-demand relationship linearly [1] as

$$E(Q_t) = b_{0t} + b_{1t}P_1 + b_{2t}P_2 + \ldots + b_{tt}P_t + \ldots + b_{Nt}P_N \tag{6}$$

where, b_{0t} is the intercept of the linear model representing the customer base (total customers willing to buy the product in period t), and b_{jt} are the parameters known as slopes which represent the impact of price at time j have on the demand at time t. Note that, in general, the parameter b_{tt} is negative, since higher price for the product in a period is likely to decrease the demand for that product in that period.

Inversely, the price for the product P_t in a period can be written in terms of the expected sales for the product in that period and the expected sales in other periods in the planning horizon as

$$P_t = a_{0t} + a_{1t}E(Q_1) + a_{2t}E(Q_2) + \ldots + a_{tt}E(Q_t) + \ldots + a_{Nt}E(Q_N) \tag{7}$$

where, a_{0t} is the intercept and a_{jt} are the parameters representing the impact of sales at time j have on the price at time t. Note that, in general, the parameter a_{tt} is negative, since higher sales for the product in a period is likely to be due to the lower price for that product in that period.

From (4) and (7) we get the general model for the total profit with stochastic demand as

$$\Pi = \sum_{t=1}^{N} (E(Q_t) + \varepsilon_t) \left(a_{0t} + \sum_{j=1}^{N} a_{jt}E(Q_j) - C_t \right) \tag{8}$$

The model of stochastic dynamic pricing presented here is different than the model presented in [26]. Here, rather than applying the single stochastic term to total profit, we apply stochastic term to each individual periods in order to accurately model individual demand fluctuations in different selling periods.

Now let us define some additional constraints a firm needs to impose when defining its policy for pricing a given product.

a. Capacity constraints - These are the number of products available in a given period, and have the lower and upper bounds, represented for all $t = 1..N$ as

$$M_t \leq Q_t - \text{Lower bound for the capacity constraint}$$
$$K_t \geq Q_t - \text{Upper bound for the capacity constraint} \tag{9}$$

b. Price caps - These are the selling price of a product in a given period, and also have lower and upper bounds, represented for all $t = 1..N$ as

$$\overline{P}_t \leq P_t - \text{Lower bound for the price cap}$$
$$\underline{P}_t \geq P_t - \text{Upper bound for the price cap} \tag{10}$$

---

[1] Linear models are widely used for representing the price and demand relationship, both in research and in practice. There are, however, other models, such as *exponential* and *multinomial logit* [27][23], that could be similarly used to represent this relationship. Testing these models is out of the scope of this paper and could be the part of the future work.

Given the parameters a_{jt}, the upper bound and lower bound to both the capacity constraint and the price cap, and also the σ for ε representing the fluctuation in demand, our goal is to find a policy $E(Q_t)$ (from which, using 7, we get the P_t) for all $t = \{1..N\}$ that maximize the total profit, i.e. maximize Π in the equation (8). Since equation (8) is nonlinear and requires to satisfy constraints defined in (9) and (10), this problem is a nonlinear constrained optimization problem.

3 Optimising Stochastic DP models using EAs

A general constrained optimization problem can be defined as $max_x f(x)$, $x \in S \subset \mathbb{R}^n$ subject to the linear or nonlinear constraints $g_i(x) \leq 0$, $i = 1,...,m$. Here m is the total number of constraints. One of the most popular ways to solving constrained optimization problems with EAs is by using a *penalty function*. The idea is to construct a function that penalizes the original objective function for violating the constraints in the model. In order to avoid the penalty, the algorithm tries to focus its search on the feasible part of the search space. Here we use one such technique adopted from [19] and also implemented by [26], and define the penalty function as

$$F(x) = f(x) - h(k)H(x), \quad x \in S \subset \mathbb{R}^n \tag{11}$$

where, $f(x)$ is the original objective function (in our case it is defined by Π in equation (8)). $h(k)H(x)$ is the penalising part of the function, where $H(x)$ is the main penalty factor (equals to 0 when no constraints are violated) and $h(k)$ is known as the dynamically modified penalty value that intensifies the level of penalty according to the algorithm's current iteration k. Due to the limited space, we do not describe these factors in detail, interested readers are referred to [19] [26].

Solution representation for EA: A solution, x, is represented as a set $E(Q) = \{E(Q_1), E(Q_2),...,E(Q_N)\}$, where each $E(Q_t)$ is represented by a bit-string of length l. The total length of a bit-string solution, $x = \{x_1, x_2,..., x_n\}$, where $x_i \in \{0, 1\}$, is therefore, equal to $n = l \times N$. The goal of an algorithm is to maximize the modified objective function defined in (11).

Overview of the used EAs: We adopt the approach presented in [26] and implement two EDAs and a GA for solving this problem. They include Population Based Incremental Learning (PBIL) algorithm [2]), Distribution Estimation using Markov Random Field with direct sampling (DEUM$_d$) algorithm [25] and a GA [7]. We also find it interesting to use a non-population based algorithm known as Simulated Annealing (SA) [9] for this problem. Let us describe the workflow of these algorithms.

PBIL

---

1. Initialize a probability vector $p = \{p_1, p_2,..., p_n\}$ with each $p_i = 0.5$. Here, p_i represents the probability of x_i taking value 1 in the solution
2. Generate a population P consisting of M solutions by sampling probabilities in p

3. Select set D from P consisting of N best solutions
4. Estimate probabilities of $x_i = 1$, for each x_i, as

$$p(x_i = 1) = \frac{\sum_{x \in D, x_i = 1} x_i}{N}$$

5. Update each p_i in p using $p_i = p_i + \lambda (p(x_i = 1) - p_i)$. Here, $0 \leq \lambda \leq 1$ is a parameter of the algorithm known as the learning rate
6. Go to step 2 until termination criteria are meet

DEUM$_d$

1. Generate a population, P, consisting of M solutions
2. Select a set D from P consisting of N best solutions, where $N \leq M$.
3. For each solution, x, in D, build a linear equation of the form

$$\eta(F(x)) = \alpha_0 + \alpha_1 x_1 + \alpha_2 x_2 + \ldots + \alpha_n x_n$$

Where, function $\eta(F(x)) < 0$ is set to $-ln(F(x))$, for which $F(x)$, the fitness of the solution x, should be ≥ 1; $\alpha = \{\alpha_0, \alpha_1, \alpha_2, \ldots, \alpha_n\}$ are equation parameters.
4. Solve the build system of N equations to estimate α
5. Use α to estimate the distribution $p(x) = \prod_{i=1}^{n} p(x_i)$, where

$$p(x_i = 1) = \frac{1}{1 + e^{\beta \alpha_i}}, \quad p(x_i = -1) = \frac{1}{1 + e^{-\beta \alpha_i}}$$

Here, β (inverse temperature coefficient) is set to $\beta = g \cdot \tau$; g is current iteration of the algorithm and τ is the parameter known as the cooling rate
6. Generate M new solution by sampling $p(x)$ to replace P and go to step 2 until termination criteria are meet

GA

1. Generate a population P consisting of M solutions
2. Build a breeding pool by selecting N promising solutions from P using a selection strategy
3. Perform crossover on the breeding pool to generate the population of new solutions
4. Perform mutation on new solutions
5. Replace P by new solutions and go to step 2 until termination criteria are meet

SA

1. Randomly generate a solutions $x = \{x_1, x_2, ..., x_n\}$
2. For $i = 1$ to r do

   a. Randomly mutate a variable in x to get x'
   b. Set $\Delta F = F(x') - F(x)$
   c. Set $x = x'$ with probability

$$p(x') = \begin{cases} 1 & \text{if } \Delta F \leq 0 \\ e^{-\Delta F/T} & \text{if } \Delta F > 0 \end{cases}$$

   Where, temperature coefficient T was set to $T = 1/i \cdot \tau$; here, i is the current iteration and τ is the parameter of the algorithm called the cooling rate

3. Terminate with answer x.

The two implemented EDAs, PBIL and DEUM$_d$, both fall in the category of univariate EDAs, and assume that the variables in the solutions are independent. Other categories of EDA include, bivariate EDA [4][21], assuming at most pair-wise interaction between variables, and multivariate EDA [20][13][5], assuming interaction between multiple variables. Our motivation behind using univariate EDAs is two fold. Firstly, they are simple, and, therefore, often quickly converge to the optima, resulting in higher efficiency. This is particularly important in dynamic environment, where the pricing decisions have to be frequently changed. Secondly, the number of problems that has been shown to be solved by them is surprisingly large.

4 Experiments and Results

We perform three sets of experiments for both sort-term and long-term analysis, where each set modelled different scenarios.

For short-term analysis, we assume that the production for a given day is a negative function of the price on that day and a positive function of the prices on other days of the week. More specifically, we assume that at any given time t: a) Production decreases by one unit for each unit increase in price; b) an increase in sales in a given day reduces the sales during other days of the week. Further, the cost of an additional unit of production was assumed to be zero (all costs are fixed, i.e. no incremental cost) and the minimum production for each day was also assumed to be zero. Moreover, it was assumed that demand is higher during the first few days of the week [2]. These are reflected in table 1 showing the setup for all a_{jt}. Also, for experiment 1, maximum production capacity, M_t, was set to 1000 units and maximum price, $\overline{P_t}$, was set to 250/unit (i.e., higher production flexibility and lower pricing flexibility), for experiment 2, M_t was set to 1000 units and $\overline{P_t}$ was set to 1000/unit (i.e., higher production flexibility and higher pricing flexibility), and for experiment 3, M_t was set to 300 units and $\overline{P_t}$ was set to 1000/unit during all seven days of the week (i.e., lower production flexibility and higher pricing flexibility).

Table 1 a_{jt} for all three short-term experiments

t	a_{0t}	a_{1t}	a_{2t}	a_{3t}	a_{4t}	a_{5t}	a_{6t}	a_{7t}
1	900	-1.0	0.1	0.1	0.1	0.1	0.1	0.1
2	800	0.0	-1.0	0.1	0.1	0.1	0.1	0.1
3	800	0.0	0.0	-1.0	0.1	0.1	0.1	0.1
4	700	0.0	0.0	0.0	-1.0	0.1	0.1	0.1
5	600	0.0	0.0	0.0	0.0	-1.0	0.1	0.1
6	500	0.0	0.0	0.0	0.0	0.0	-1.0	0.1
7	400	0.0	0.0	0.0	0.0	0.0	0.0	-1.0

Table 2 a_{jt} for long-term experiments no 1

t	a_{0t}	a_{1t}	a_{2t}	a_{3t}	a_{4t}	a_{5t}	a_{6t}	a_{7t}
1	3000	-1.0	0.0	0.0	0.0	0.0	0.0	0.0
2	3000	0.5	-1.0	0.0	0.0	0.0	0.0	0.0
3	3000	0.0	0.5	-1.0	0.0	0.0	0.0	0.0
4	3000	0.0	0.0	0.5	-1.0	0.0	0.0	0.0
5	3000	0.0	0.0	0.0	0.5	-1.0	0.0	0.0
6	3000	0.0	0.0	0.0	0.0	0.5	-1.0	0.0
7	3000	0.0	0.0	0.0	0.0	0.0	0.5	-1.0

Table 3 a_{jt} for long-term experiments no 2 and 3

t	a_{0t}	a_{1t}	a_{2t}	a_{3t}	a_{4t}	a_{5t}	a_{6t}	a_{7t}
1	3000	-1.0	0.0	0.0	0.0	0.0	0.0	0.0
2	3000	0.9	-1.0	0.0	0.0	0.0	0.0	0.0
3	3000	0.0	0.9	-1.0	0.0	0.0	0.0	0.0
4	3000	0.0	0.0	0.9	-1.0	0.0	0.0	0.0
5	3000	0.0	0.0	0.0	0.9	-1.0	0.0	0.0
6	3000	0.0	0.0	0.0	0.0	0.9	-1.0	0.0
7	3000	0.0	0.0	0.0	0.0	0.0	0.9	-1.0

For long-term analysis, we assumed that the production in a year is a negative function of the average price in that year and positive function of the production during previous year. More specifically, we assumed that at any given time t: a) production decreases by one unit for each pound increase in price; b) the company keeps a given proportion of its customers from the previous year. These are reflected in table 2 and 3 showing the setup for all a_{jt}. Further, in all three experiments, the cost of an additional unit production was assumed to be zero. For experiment 1, the maximum production capacity, M_t, was set to 3000 units during the first 4 years and set to 6000 units during the last 3 years, no maximum price, $\overline{P_t}$, was set and it was assumed that the company keeps 50% of its customers from the previous year. For experiment 2, the M_t was set to 3000 units during the first 4 years and set to 6000 units during the last 3 years, no maximum price was set and it was assumed that the

---

[2] This is a typical scenario for products, or services, whose demand is higher during working days of the week, such as airline seats, mobile phone use, and even restaurant lunch hour sales

company keeps 90% of its customers from the previous year. For experiment 3, the M_t was set to 3000 units during all 7 years, no maximum price was set and it was assumed that the company keeps 90% of its customers from the previous year.

Also, for each of these three scenarios in both short-term and long-term environment, we experiment with eleven different setups for demand fluctuation ranging from $\sigma = 0$ (i.e. no fluctuation) to $\sigma = 1$ (i.e. very high fluctuation).

In terms of the algorithms, we set the size of the bit string representing each $E(Q_t)$ to $l = 12$. Therefore the solution length, n, was equal to $l \times N = 84$. Since, there were a very high number of simulations involved, using moderate size of $l = 12$ significantly reduced the simulation time. Also, in order to parameterise the algorithms, we conduct a range of experiments using wide range of parameter setups for each algorithm and choose the setup that had the best performance. Such an empirical approach to parameterisation is typical in EA research. Following were the setups used for each of the algorithm: In each execution, the algorithm was allowed to do a fixed number of fitness evaluations. This was equal to 400000 for PBIL, DEUM$_d$ and GA, and 600000 for SA [3]. The number of fitness evaluation for PBIL, DEUM$_d$ and GA was calculated as the product of their population size, $PS = 400$, and the maximum number of generations, $MG = 1000$. For all experiments, the learning rate for PBIL was set to 0.02 and cooling rate for DEUM$_d$ was set to 0.02. For SA a very small cooling rate of 0.00001 was used. 10 best solutions were selected in PBIL and DEUM$_d$ for estimating the marginal probabilities. For GA, one-point crossover was used with crossover probability set to 0.7 and the mutation probability set to 0.01.

4.1 Results

A total of 100 executions of each algorithm were done for each experiment and the best policy together with the total profit found in each execution was recorded. The average total profit (Mean), the standard deviation of total profit (Stdev), and the best total profit (Max) out of all 100 executions for each of the algorithms are shown in Table 4 for short-term experiment 1, in Table 5 for short-term experiment 2 and in Table 6 for short-term experiment 3 for five different setups of σ [4]. Similarly, Table 7, 8 and 9 shows the results for long-term experiments 1, 2 and 3 respectively.

Also, a reliability factor (RL) measuring the reliability of the policy found by the algorithm is shown in the tables along with the other three metrics. For each algorithm, the reliability factor is the total percentage of runs where the *final population* of the algorithm converged to a feasible policy, i.e. the one satisfying all the constraints. If the final population in all of the runs converged to the feasible solution, the RL of the suggested policy is very high, since this indicates the high probability

---

[3] Since SA was not performing well in comparison to other algorithms, we allowed it to do more evaluation, in order to see whether its performance will be improved

[4] Although we perform experiment with 11 different setups of σ, due to the space limitation, we only present the tables with 5 different setups

Table 4 Short-term 1

σ	metric	SA	PBIL	DEUM$_d$	GA
0.0	Mean	N/A	924938	923564	**942937**
	Stdev	N/A	3188	4176	**5998**
	Max	N/A	927935	938937	**949922**
	RL	0%	100%	100%	**100%**
0.2	Mean	N/A	907226	904476	**914536**
	Stdev	N/A	8454	10579	**10167**
	Max	N/A	928237	934521	**937266**
	RL	0%	46%	46%	**48%**
0.5	Mean	N/A	899672	**898091**	N/A
	Stdev	N/A	13946	**14223**	N/A
	Max	N/A	925939	931484	N/A
	RL	0%	26%	**28%**	2%
0.8	Mean	N/A	**886883**	890867	N/A
	Stdev	N/A	**1452**	16913	N/A
	Max	N/A	**917616**	934883	N/A
	RL	0%	**19%**	15%	0%
1.0	Mean	N/A	**878393**	884754	N/A
	Stdev	N/A	**17150**	17642	N/A
	Max	N/A	**911962**	926150	N/A
	RL	0%	**12%**	11%	0%

Table 5 Short-term 2

σ	metric	SA	PBIL	DEUM$_d$	GA
0.0	Mean	1160467	**1173280**	1173251	1173243
	Stdev	7524	**165**	233	283
	Max	1173253	**1173299**	1173299	1173299
	RL	100%	**100%**	100%	100%
0.2	Mean	1129388	**1166115**	1161622	1163458
	Stdev	22396	**4313**	6453	5829
	Max	1167782	**1172747**	1172320	1171941
	RL	91%	**100%**	100%	100%
0.5	Mean	1086776	**1149881**	1138054	1136587
	Stdev	40797	**5965**	12182	12827
	Max	1155558	**1159827**	1163172	1156967
	RL	69%	**100%**	98%	100%
0.8	Mean	1085741	**1151703**	1140924	1139230
	Stdev	31044	**5526**	9257	10383
	Max	1144442	**1160956**	1157105	1159019
	RL	55%	**100%**	98%	100%
1.0	Mean	1084185	**1153184**	1141891	1140133
	Stdev	28600	**4160**	8779	8746
	Max	1154238	**1160043**	1158329	1156692
	RL	60%	**100%**	98%	100%

Table 6 Short-term 3

σ	metric	SA	PBIL	DEUM$_d$	GA
0.0	Mean	968970	968970	968970	**968970**
	Stdev	0.00	0.01	0.00	**0.21**
	Max	968970	968970	968970	**968970**
	RL	100%	100%	100%	**100%**
0.2	Mean	803924	847691	849495	**786725**
	Stdev	33489	10418	17122	**14848**
	Max	883369	869569	888038	**840326**
	RL	66%	47%	27%	**84%**
0.5	Mean	690419	695022	710566	**593640**
	Stdev	51689	23680	31968	**26811**
	Max	811061	764219	793566	**674953**
	RL	38%	49%	39%	**86%**
0.8	Mean	627084	**582653**	597541	571215
	Stdev	53243	**7547**	25650	13810
	Max	774356	**610820**	713464	646189
	RL	36%	**99%**	63%	98%
1.0	Mean	607560	**582401**	577594	570692
	Stdev	60597	**3837**	18248	13769
	Max	807870	**591077**	661086	655611
	RL	37%	**100%**	72%	95%

of achieving at least the suggested profit with such demand. Obviously, this is the case when there is no demand fluctuation ($\sigma = 0$). However, when uncertainty is introduced, for some tightly constrained problems, most of the policy could be out of the boundary of the constraints due to the higher fluctuation in demand. The algorithm would then converge to a non feasible region of the solution space. However, even in these scenarios, few random policies could be sampled with lower fluctuation that satisfies the constraints, simply due to the random error. Although, such a policy is not likely to achieve suggested profit, the algorithm would keep it as the best policy, even though its final population would converge to a non feasible policy. In these scenarios, *RL* allows us to identify the probability of obtaining such a false result by examining whether both the best policy found during entire iteration of the algorithm and the final population of the algorithm converged to a feasible solution. We, therefore, take *RL* as the main measure to test the performance of the

Table 7 Long-term 1

σ	metric	SA	PBIL	DEUM$_d$	GA
0.0	Mean	27821948	**28206184**	28205996	28205951
	Stdev	345156	**7**	672	814
	Max	28205221	**28206185**	28206185	28206185
	RL	100%	**100%**	100%	100%
0.2	Mean	26372470	27198936	27193683	**26876389**
	Stdev	706535	229150	274612	**208255**
	Max	27516273	27880747	27814142	**27486350**
	RL	79%	78%	78%	**91%**
0.5	Mean	24173310	25526098	25593119	**23866124**
	Stdev	1261215	407533	570856	**501397**
	Max	26969345	26788111	26964174	**25128428**
	RL	52%	77%	72%	**95%**
0.8	Mean	23404411	**24098148**	24216003	23585299
	Stdev	1059765	**396234**	553567	356613
	Max	25950583	**25215353**	26031802	24663332
	RL	42%	**99%**	74%	99%
1.0	Mean	23018437	**24010452**	23889324	23639083
	Stdev	1257847	**140554**	438312	268953
	Max	25709590	**24281190**	25256155	24170419
	RL	35%	**100%**	77%	99%

Table 8 Long-term 2

σ	metric	SA	PBIL	DEUM$_d$	GA
0.0	Mean	52203789	**54779449**	54779309	54779247
	Stdev	2201309	**34**	237	1130
	Max	54777957	54779471	54779471	54779470
	RL	100%	100%	100%	100%
0.2	Mean	46971642	50236548	50426208	**46345442**
	Stdev	1928960	686963	1099312	**1026420**
	Max	51136540	52412106	52589577	**49887769**
	RL	61%	43%	29%	**86%**
0.5	Mean	40631344	44166229	43926709	**35766901**
	Stdev	2900701	1512555	1842733	**1595034**
	Max	50084429	48960669	48251958	**41688039**
	RL	50%	29%	34%	**85%**
0.8	Mean	37252169	38197104	38735770	**34775462**
	Stdev	3133699	399310	1640259	**1399360**
	Max	46234840	38886057	43009539	**38414691**
	RL	45%	47%	43%	**95%**
1.0	Mean	36380548	38315131	37495900	**34631043**
	Stdev	3026899	380666	1579632	**1495657**
	Max	46097274	40576934	41897947	**40827152**
	RL	46%	57%	48%	**97%**

Table 9 Long-term 3

σ	metric	SA	PBIL	DEUM$_d$	GA
0.0	Mean	48635382	**48636408**	48636394	48636406
	Stdev	843	**0.00**	144	2.45
	Max	48636408	48636408	48636408	48636408
	RL	100%	100%	100%	100%
0.2	Mean	40051377	42674286	42917395	**38312603**
	Stdev	1808341	843943	1028819	**891778**
	Max	44852209	45048582	45973335	**40744748**
	RL	60%	40%	26%	**79%**
0.5	Mean	33785719	34590258	35346913	**28040236**
	Stdev	3308233	1530366	1755677	**1076736**
	Max	43427472	40296346	39909935	**30777018**
	RL	46%	43%	39%	**86%**
0.8	Mean	29884971	27536913	29387154	**26901891**
	Stdev	2994800	706814	1763762	**803103**
	Max	41867831	30598589	35041308	**30141010**
	RL	48%	96%	45%	**96%**
1.0	Mean	28830505	27362045	27753364	**26741629**
	Stdev	3187659	168031	1216581	**553008**
	Max	37370691	27687168	31542620	**29126642**
	RL	44%	100%	57%	**98%**

algorithms. If two algorithms had similar *RL*, the mean profit was taken as the next measurer of the performance. Also note that, the profits presented in the table represent the expected profit, $E(\Pi)$ (5) i.e., the one without the error term included. The value for the best performing algorithm is plotted in bold. Following are the analysis of the results.

a. Performance of the algorithms in different scenarios: As we can see from the tables, for all of the experiments, SA has the worst performance compared to other three algorithms with lowest value for *RL*. The performance of DEUM$_d$ and PBIL was somewhat comparable for all four metrics, with occasionally one outperforming another. In terms of mean profit, PBIL and DEUM$_d$ has the best performance. Finally, GA has the highest value for *RL* and therefore has the overall best performance. It can be noticed that, when there is no uncertainty in demand, the reliability of all three EAs are similar, though in terms of mean total profit two EDAs, PBIL and DEUM$_d$, were better than GA (similar to [26]). However, when demand uncertainty is introduced our results show that GA, in most cases, retained its reliability, whereas the reliability of two EDAs decreased.

b. Impact of demand uncertainty on total profit: It can be observed from the tables that, in general, demand uncertainty reduces the total profit, and is true for all the tested algorithms. In order to show this, a graph showing the best average total profit found by the algorithms for long-term experiment 1 with 11 different setups of σ is plotted in Figure (1) [5]. Note that the total profit is mapped to the ratio between 1 and 0. It can be seen that the total profit reduces as demand fluctuation gets higher, till it reaches to the mark of 50% ($\sigma = 0.5$). However, the decrement in

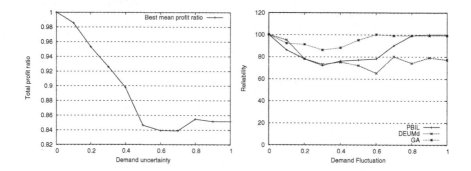

Fig. 1 Fluctuation Vs Profit   **Fig. 2** Fluctuation Vs Reliability

profit slows as the fluctuation in demand gets very high, from 0.5 onwards till 1.0. Interestingly, the high fluctuation in demand results in slight increment in the total profit. This indicates that, in some cases, higher fluctuation in demand may not have extremely adverse effect to the profit in comparison to the low fluctuation.

c. Algorithm reliability vs. uncertainty: Another interesting observation that we make is the effect of fluctuation in demand have on the reliability of the results found by each algorithms. A typical illustration is given in Figure (2), which plots the *RL* found by each algorithm for long-term experiment 1 (the curves were similar for rest of the instances). It can be noticed that the *RL*. for the algorithms are very high (equal to 100%) when there is no fluctuation in the demand. Once the fluctuation is introduced the reliability decreases. However, interestingly, once the fluctuation gets very high, the reliability of the results starts increasing back to 100%. As can be seen from the figure, this is true for all three tested algorithms. This suggests that, when there is some fluctuation in demand, it is difficult to find a reliable policy that guarantees the profit, however if there is very high fluctuation in demand the found profit could be guaranteed. These results also supplement the

---

[5] Due to limited space we do not plot this graph for rest of the instances, though we note that the shape of the curves were similar

results on the impact of uncertainty on total profit where the profit slightly increases once demand fluctuation is very high. The explanation for this is as follows: when there is extreme fluctuation in demand with σ closer to 1, the fluctuating term Q_t in equation (2) is either twice the expected sales $E(Q_t)$ or equal to zero (from equation (3)).It is therefore easier for the algorithm to solve the problem with only two values for Q_t than when there are higher number of possible values for Q_t (in case of lower σ). This therefore increases the reliability of the algorithm.

5 Conclusion

In this paper, we used evolutionary algorithms for solving dynamic pricing problem in a stochastic setup. The model used in this paper is more realistic than the one used in [26] since different uncertainty is imposed to each individual periods. Our results show that GA is the most reliable algorithm for solving dynamic pricing in stochastic setup with implemented model, although similar to [26] we found that EDAs were better when there was no demand fluctuation. We also found that higher fluctuation in demand may not have adverse effect in comparison to lower fluctuation, and could result in increased reliability of the found pricing policy.

We note that the results found in this paper apply to the binary EAs. It would be interesting to see the performance of the real valued version of these algorithms on this problem. Also, further work should be done to theoretically justify these empirical results. This work is under way and interesting results are expected in the near future.

References

1. Baker, W., Marn, M.V., Zawada, C.: Price smarter on the net. Harvard Business Review **79** (2001)
2. Baluja, S.: Population-based incremental learning: A method for integrating genetic search based function optimization and competitive learning,. Tech. Rep. CMU-CS-94-163, Pittsburgh, PA (1994). URL citeseer.nj.nec.com/baluja94population.html
3. Bichler, M., Kalagnanam, J., Katircioglu, K., King, A.J., Lawrence, R.D., Lee, H.S., Lin, G.Y., Lu., Y.: Applications of flexible pricing in business-to-business electronic commerce. IBM Systems Journal **41(2)**, 287–302 (2002)
4. de Bonet, J.S., Isbell Jr., C.L., Viola, P.: MIMIC: Finding optima by estimating probability densities. In: M.C. Mozer, M.I. Jordan, T. Petsche (eds.) Advances in Neural Information Processing Systems, vol. 9. The MIT Press (1997). URL citeseer.nj.nec.com/debonet96mimic.html
5. Etxeberria, R., Larrañaga, P.: Global optimization using Bayesian networks. In: A. Ochoa, M.R. Soto, R. Santana (eds.) Proceedings of the Second Symposium on Artificial Intelligence (CIMAF-99), pp. 151–173. Havana, Cuba (1999)
6. Ferdows, K., Lewis, M.A., Machura, J.A.M.: Rapid-fire fulfilment. Harvard Business Review **82**, 104–110 (2004)
7. Goldberg, D.: Genetic Algorithms in Search, Optimization, and Machine Learning. Addison-Wesley (1989)

8. Inza, I., Merino, M., Larrañaga, P., Quiroga, J., Sierra, B., Girala, M.: Feature subset selection by population-based incremental learning. A case study in the survival of cirrhotic patients with TIPS. Artificial Intelligence in Medicine (2001)
9. Kirkpatrick, S., Gelatt, C.D., Vecchi, M.P.: Optimization by simulated annealing. Science, Number 4598, 13 May 1983 **220, 4598**, 671–680 (1983). URL citeseer.ist.psu.edu/kirkpatrick83optimization.html
10. Larrañaga, P., Lozano, J.A.: Estimation of Distribution Algorithms: A New Tool for Evolutionary Computation. Kluwer Academic Publishers (2002)
11. McWilliams, G.: Lean machine: How dell fine-tunes its pc pricing to gain edge in slow market. Wall Street Journal (June 8, 2001)
12. Mitchell, M.: An Introduction To Genetic Algorithms. MIT Press, Cambridge, Massachusetts (1997)
13. Mühlenbein, H., Mahnig, T.: FDA - A scalable evolutionary algorithm for the optimization of additively decomposed functions. Evolutionary Computation **7**(4), 353–376 (1999). URL citeseer.nj.nec.com/uhlenbein99fda.html
14. Mühlenbein, H., Paaß, G.: From recombination of genes to the estimation of distributions: I. binary parameters. In: H.M. Voigt, W. Ebeling, I. Rechenberg, H.P. Schwefel (eds.) Parallel Problem Solving from Nature – PPSN IV, pp. 178–187. Springer, Berlin (1996). URL citeseer.nj.nec.com/uehlenbein96from.html
15. Narahari, Y., Raju, C.V., Ravikumar, K., Shah, S.: Dynamic pricing models for electronic business. Sadhana **30**(part 2,3), 231–256 (April/June 2005)
16. Netessine, S., Shumsky, R.: Introduction to the theory and practice of yield management. INFORMS Transactions on Education **3**(1) (2002)
17. Owusu, G., Dorne, R., Voudouris, C., Lesaint, D.: Dynamic planner: A decision support tool for resource planning, applications and innovations in intelligent systems x. In: Proceedings of ES 2002, pp. 19–31 (2002)
18. Owusu, G., Voudouris, C., Kern, M., Garyfalos, A., Anim-Ansah, G., Virginas, B.: On Optimising Resource Planning in BT with FOS. In: Proceedings International Conference on Service Systems and Service Management (2006)
19. Parsopoulos, K., Vrahatis, M.: Particle swarm optimization method for constrained optimization problems. Intelligent Technologies–Theory and Application: New Trends in Intelligent Technologies, volume 76 of Frontiers in Artificial Intelligence and Applications pp. 214–220 (2002)
20. Pelikan, M., Goldberg, D.E., Cantú-Paz, E.: BOA: The Bayesian Optimization Algorithm. In: W. Banzhaf et al. (ed.) Proceedings of the Genetic and Evolutionary Computation Conference GECCO99, vol. I, pp. 525–532. Morgan Kaufmann Publishers, San Fransisco, CA (1999)
21. Pelikan, M., Mühlenbein, H.: The bivariate marginal distribution algorithm. In: R. Roy, T. Furuhashi, P.K. Chawdhry (eds.) Advances in Soft Computing - Engineering Design and Manufacturing, pp. 521–535. Springer-Verlag, London (1999)
22. Petrovski, A., Shakya, S., McCall, J.: Optimising cancer chemotherapy using an estimation of distribution algorithm and genetic algorithms. In: proceedings of Genetic and Evolutionary Computation COnference (GECCO 2006). ACM, seattle, USA (2006)
23. Phillips, R.: Pricing and revenue optimization. Stanford University Press (2005)
24. Sahay, A.: How to reap higher profits with dynamic pricing. MIT Sloan management review **48**, 53–60 (2007)
25. Shakya, S.: Deum: A framework for an estimation of distribution algorithm based on markov random fields. Ph.D. thesis, The Robert Gordon University, Aberdeen, UK (April 2006)
26. Shakya, S., Oliveira, F., Owusu, G.: An Application of EDA and GA to Dynamic Pricing. In: proceedings of Genetic and Evolutionary Computation COnference (GECCO2007), pp. 585–592. ACM, London, UK (2007)
27. Talluri, K., van Ryzin, G.: The Theory and Practice of Revenue Management. Springer, Berlin Heidelberg, New York (2004)
28. Voudouris, C., Owusu, G., Dorne, R., Ladde, C., Virginas, B.: Arms: An automated resource management system for british telecommunications plc. European Journal for Operational Research **171**, 951–961 (2006)

Restart-Based Genetic Algorithm for the Quadratic Assignment Problem

Alfonsas Misevicius

Abstract The power of genetic algorithms (GAs) has been demonstrated for various domains of the computer science, including combinatorial optimization. In this paper, we propose a new conceptual modification of the genetic algorithm entitled a "restart-based genetic algorithm" (RGA). An effective implementation of RGA for a well-known combinatorial optimization problem, the quadratic assignment problem (QAP), is discussed. The results obtained from the computational experiments on the QAP instances from the publicly available library QAPLIB show excellent performance of RGA. This is especially true for the real-life like QAPs.

1 Introduction

The quadratic assignment problem (QAP) can be stated as follows. Given two matrices $A = (a_{ij})_{n \times n}$, $B = (b_{kl})_{n \times n}$, and the set Π of all possible permutations of the integers from 1 to n, find a permutation $\pi = (\pi(1), \pi(2), ..., \pi(n)) \in \Pi$ that minimizes the following function:

$$z(\pi) = \sum_{i=1}^{n} \sum_{j=1}^{n} a_{ij} b_{\pi(i)\pi(j)} . \tag{1}$$

The QAP is a classical combinatorial optimization problem, where solutions are represented by permutations and the objective function is defined according to the above formula. In the location theory, the QAP formulation is used to model the problem of allocating n facilities to n locations with the objective to minimize the cost associated with the flow and distance between the facilities [9]. The matrices A and B correspond to the flow and distance matrices, respectively. Usually, the distance matrix is symmetric. This is just the case of the current paper.

It has been proved that the QAP belongs to the class NP-hard [19] and it is believed that this problem cannot be solved exactly within polynomial computation

Alfonsas Misevicius, Kaunas University of Technology
Studentu st. 50-400a/416a, LT-51368 Kaunas, Lithuania, alfonsas.misevicius@ktu.lt

time. Overall, the quadratic assignment problem seems to be one of the extremely difficult combinatorial optimization problems and poses a real challenge for the scientists in this field. In particular, the attention of the researchers has been concentrated on the design of heuristic approaches like ant colony optimization [6], greedy randomized adaptive search procedures (GRASP) [10], iterated local search [20], scatter search [3], simulated annealing [1], tabu search [13,21]. Also, the genetic algorithms (GAs) have been applied to the QAP with a high degree of success (see, for example, [4,5,11,12,18]).

In this paper, a new modification of the genetic algorithm for the QAP (called a "*restart-based genetic algorithm*") is proposed. The remaining part of this paper is organized as follows. Firstly, some preliminaries are given and the main philosophy of the restart-based genetic algorithm is outlined. The results of the computational experiments with RGA are presented as well. The paper is completed with concluding remarks.

2 Preliminaries and General Aspects

The early principles of genetic algorithms were formulated by Holland [8]. GAs are based on imitation of the biological process in populations of live organisms. Over generations, less fitted species fail to have offspring and disappear from the population, while more fitted individuals tend to predominate, eventually evolving into a super-individual.

Suppose that an optimization problem is defined by a pair (S, f), where $S = \{s_1, s_2, ..., s_i, ...\}$ is a finite (or possibly countable infinite) set of feasible solutions (a search space) and $f: S \rightarrow R^1$ is a real-valued objective (cost) function (we assume that f seeks a global minimum). Without a significant loss of generality, we also assume that solutions are represented by permutations of integers from 1 to n. Then, the genetic algorithm operates with a finite group P of solutions $s_1, ..., s_i, ..., s_{|P|}$ from S, where the solutions are equivalent to individuals of a population of biological system, and the cost of a solution (the objective function value $- f(s_i)$) is equivalent to the fitness of an individual. The solution (permutation) s_i may be also be thought of as a chromosome of an individual; then, the single element $s_i(j)$ corresponds to a gene occupying the jth locus of the chromosome.

Selection, crossover/reproduction, mutation, and replacement (culling) are the main genetic operations, which are applied in an iterative way to seek super-quality solutions[1].

The genetic process in its canonical form faces severe barriers such as slow or premature convergence. This is mainly conditioned by the fact that the standard genetic operations are of the explorative character, rather than the improving operators. To accelerate the convergence speed, local improvement (post-

---

[1] For a more thorough description of the principles of GAs, see [17].

crossover) procedures are usually incorporated [16]. These GAs are commonly known as hybrid genetic (or memetic) algorithms (HGAs) [15]. Applying hybrid GAs (especially when time-consuming improving procedures are used) still does not necessarily mean that good solutions are reached at reasonable computation time. Indeed, using the powerful improving algorithms causes the loss of a genetic variability quite rapidly. Of course, there is always also a risk of quick falling into a local optimum, without easy ways to escape from it.

To try to overcome these difficulties, we propose a new conceptual modification of GA entitled as a "restart-based genetic algorithm" (RGA). The main philosophy of RGA is to increase the efficiency of the evolution process by involving an additional diversification tool and thus withstanding the premature convergence and stagnation.

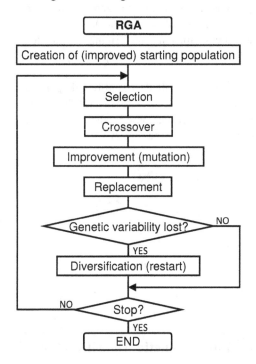

Fig. 1 Generalized flowchart of a restart-based genetic algorithm

There are only a surprisingly few formal requirements for the restart-based genetic algorithm. In particular, we need a quantitative measure of the genetic variability to identify the actual loss of diversity of individuals within a population[2]. Naturally, we also require a diversification mechanism to increase diversity and enable exploring the search space for new promising regions. We then have to test

---

[2] The entropy of a population may be used as a quantitative measure of the individuals' diversity.

whether the actual quantity of the genetic variability is below a certain a priori value (threshold), τ. If it is (this just indicates less or more loss of diversity), a diversification (restart) procedure is applied to the current population; the obtained changed population serves as a "starting point" for the next generation. Otherwise, the search process is continued with the unchanged population.

The general flowchart of RGA is shown in Fig. 1.

It is recommended that the restart process consist of the following main phases: a) mutation (perturbation) of the members of the population, b) improvement of the mutated solutions.

Mutation enables to maintain a sufficient degree of diversity of individuals. It may be accomplished in a variety of ways; for example, one can apply some kind of a gentle "shaking" of the individuals, or try much more aggressive transformation of the members of a population (including the generation of an entirely new population — something like "invasion" of new species).

The improvement phase of the restart process aims at transforming the mutated solutions again into the optimized solutions to ensure the superiority of the restarted population.

The restart-based GAs slightly resemble so-called island-based genetic algorithms (IGAs) [7]. The difference is that IGA deals with several "parallel" populations (sub-populations), while, in the restart-based algorithms, the populations are processed rather in a "sequential" way (see Fig. 2).

(a)   (b)

Fig. 2 Restart-based GA (a) vs. island-based GA (b)

3 Implementation of the Restart-Based Genetic Algorithm for the QAP

RGA is a general-purpose optimization method, but not a pure heuristic. A specific problem knowledge should be involved and all the components of the algorithm must be carefully designed and properly tuned for the particular problem to achieve the best joint advantage. An effective problem-oriented implementation of the re-start-based GA for the quadratic assignment problem is presented in this section.

RGA is initiated by creation of a fixed-size starting population. Further, the selection, crossover, improvement, replacement and (conditional) restart are applied iteratively until a pre-defined number of generations have been performed. The high-level description of RGA for the QAP in a programming language-like form is shown in Fig. 3.

```
procedure RestartBasedGeneticAlgorithm;
//input: n − problem size, A,B − flow and distance matrices,
//       PS − population size, N_gen − # of generations, N_offspr − # of offspring per generation,
//       Q − # of improving iterations, W − tabu search depth, ρ − mutation rate, τ − variability threshold
//output: π* − best solution found (resulting solution)
begin
    create the initial population P ⊂ Π such that |P| = PS;
    π* := argmin z(π) ;   // π* denotes the best so far solution
          π ∈ P
    for i := 1 to N_gen do begin //main cycle of RGA
        P* := ∅;
        for j := 1 to N_offspr do begin  //creation of the offspring
            select parents π', π'' ∈ P;
            apply crossover to π' and π', get the offspring π'';
            π* := IteratedTabuSearch(π'', Q, W, ρ);  //improving the offspring
            P* := P* ∪ { π* };
            if z(π*) < z(π*) then π* := π*  //saving the best so far solution
        endfor;
        remove N_offspr individuals from P ∪ P*,
            get the updated population P such that |P| = PS;
        if Entropy(P) < τ then begin  //apply restart in two steps
            (1) mutate all the members of P, except the best one;
            (2) improve each mutated solution by using the procedure
                IteratedTabuSearch;
            if z(argmin z(π)) < z(π*) then π* := argmin z(π)
                  π ∈ P                              π ∈ P
        endif
    endfor
end.
```

Note. The entropy of the population P is calculated according to the following formulas [5]:

$$\text{Entropy}(P) = \sum_{i=1}^{n}\sum_{j=1}^{n} e_{ij} \Big/ n \log_2 n \,, \quad e_{ij} = \begin{cases} 0, \kappa_{ij} = 0 \\ -\frac{\kappa_{ij}}{|P|}\log_2 \frac{\kappa_{ij}}{|P|}, \text{otherwise} \end{cases}, \text{ where } \kappa_{ij} \text{ is the number of times that}$$

the gene i occupies the locus j in the current population P. (Entropy(P) takes values between 0 and 1.)

Fig.3 High-level pseudo-code of the restart-based genetic algorithm for the QAP

To obtain a high-quality initial population, we use an iterated tabu search (ITS) algorithm, which, in turn, is based on an improved robust tabu search (IRoTS) procedure and a special mutation procedure called a controlled chained mutation (CCM) [14] (see below).

For the parents selection, a rank based selection rule is applied (more details can be found in [23]).

The offspring is produced by a so-called cohesive crossover (COHX) [4]. The key principle of COHX is based on maintaining a set of special distance vectors. In [4], it is proposed to maintain n vectors $\mathbf{d}^{(1)}$, $\mathbf{d}^{(2)}$, ..., $\mathbf{d}^{(i)}$, ..., $\mathbf{d}^{(n)}$ such that $d_j^{(i)} = b_{ij}$, $i = 1, 2, ..., n$, $j = 1, 2, ..., n$, where b_{ij} is the "real distance", i.e. the corresponding entry of the matrix $\boldsymbol{B}$.

The ith recombined solution (child) $\pi^{(i)}$ ($i = 1, 2, ..., n$) is then created in the following four steps:

— the median, ω, of $\mathbf{d}^{(i)}$ is calculated;

— the positions which are closer than the median to the ith (pivot) position are assigned the genes from the first (better) parent, i.e. $\pi^{(i)}(j) = \pi_{\text{better}}(j)$ if $d_j^{(i)} < \omega$, $j = 1, 2, ..., n$, $\pi_{\text{better}} = \operatorname{argmin}\{z(\pi'), z(\pi'')\}$;

— all other positions are assigned the genes from the second (worse) parent, i.e. $\pi^{(i)}(j) = \pi_{\text{worse}}(j)$ if $d_j^{(i)} \geq \omega$, $j = 1, 2, ..., n$, $\pi_{\text{worse}} = \operatorname{argmax}\{z(\pi'), z(\pi'')\}$;

— it is possible that some genes are assigned twice and some are not assigned at all; so, a list of unassigned genes is created and all genes from the second parent that are assigned twice are replaced with the genes from the list.

The illustrative example of producing a child is shown in Fig. 4. Note that there are in all n different children. Only the best child (the child that has the smallest objective function value) is returned by COHX.

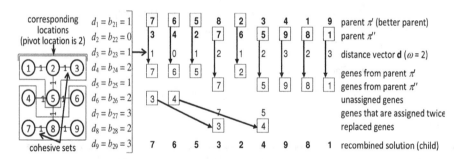

Fig. 4 Example of producing a child in the cohesive crossover

Every produced offspring is optimized to ensure that each population consists solely of the super-quality individuals. For this purpose, we apply the above-mentioned iterated tabu search algorithm — ITS. The ITS algorithm it is based on a so-called $(Q, W, 1, \rho)$-scheme. In this scheme, the number of improving itera-tions (cycles) is equal to Q, whereas W is the tabu search depth. (Q may also be thought of as a measure of the search breadth (extensity), while W can be viewed as the search intensity.) A single execution of the mutation procedure takes place every W iterations, and the mutation strength is defined by the parameter ρ.

Regarding the candidate selection for the mutation procedure, we apply a so-called "where you are" (WYA) strategy. In this case, every new local optimum (no matter its quality) is accepted for mutation. This strategy is capable of exploring a wider area of the search space — the last fact is very important in the presence of the huge number of local optima, which is exactly the case of the QAP.

The pseudo-code of the iterated tabu search algorithm is given in Fig. 5. The main components of this algorithm are discussed below.

```
function IteratedTabuSearch(π, Q, W, ρ);
//input: π − current solution, Q − number of iterations, W − tabu search depth, ρ − mutation rate
//output: π* − improved solution (best solution found)
begin
    π* := ImprovedRobustTabuSearch(π, W);   //preliminary improvement of the current solution
    π* := π*;
    for q := 1 to Q do begin   //main cycle of ITS
        π := π*;   //candidate acceptance according to a "where you are" strategy
        π~ := ControlledChainedMutation(π, ρ);   //applying mutation to the accepted solution
        π* := ImprovedRobustTabuSearch(π~, W);   //applying tabu search to the mutated solution
        if z(π*) < z(π*) then π* := π*   //saving the best so far solution (local optimum)
    endfor;
    return π*
end.
```

Fig. 5 Pseudo-code of the iterated tabu search algorithm

3.1 Tabu search procedure

Our tabu search procedure is entitled as an improved robust tabu search — IRoTS. It is similar the robust tabu search (RoTS) algorithm due to Taillard [21], but has also several significant differences. (Recall that the RoTS procedure explores, in an iterative way, neighbouring solutions[3] of the current solution and chooses the move[4] that improves most the objective function value. During exploration, the moves that are not forbidden or aspired are only taken into consideration. The tabu list is then updated and the current solution is replaced by the new one, which is used as a starting point for the next iteration. The tabu tenure (tabu list size) is maintained in a random way. The process continues until the given number of iterations have been performed (see also [21]).)

The most important new features of our improved tabu search procedure are as follows.

---

[3] The neighbouring solutions are determined using a neighbourhood function $\Theta: \Pi \to 2^{\Pi}$ which assigns for each $\pi \in \Pi$ its neighbourhood $\Theta(\pi) \subset \Pi$.

[4] A move from the current solution, π, to the neighbouring one, $\pi' \in \Theta(\pi)$, can formally be defined, for example, by an operator $\phi: \Pi \to \Pi$, which swaps some elements of the given solution (permutation).

```
function ImprovedRobustTabuSearch(π, W);
```
// input: π – current solution, W – tabu search depth; parameters: h_{min}, h_{max}, α, inter_intensification_interval
// output: π^* – best solution found
```
begin
```
   tabu := 0; $\pi^* := \pi$; NeighbourhoodSize := $n(n-1)/2$; h := h_{min}; w' := 1; i := 1; j := 1;
   calculate differences in the objective function values $\Delta_z(\pi, k, l)$,
   $k = 1,...,n-1$, $l = k+1,...,n$;
   for w := 1 **to** W **do begin** // main cycle of IRoTS
      Δ_{min} := ∞;
      for current_iteration_number := 1 **to** NeighbourhoodSize **do begin**
         $i := \text{IIF}(j < n, i, \text{IIF}(i < n-1, i+1, 1))$; $j := \text{IIF}(j < n, j+1, i+1)$;
         tabu_criterion := $\text{IIF}(tabu_{ij} \geq$ current_iteration_number **and** RANDOM(0,1) $\geq \alpha$,
                           TRUE, FALSE);
         aspiration_criterion := $\text{IIF}(z(\pi) + \Delta_z(\pi, i, j) < z(\pi^*)$ **and** tabu_criterion = TRUE,
                           TRUE, FALSE);
         if ($\Delta_z(\pi, i, j) < \Delta_{min}$ **and** tabu_criterion $\neq$ TRUE) **or** aspiration_criterion = TRUE
            then begin $\Delta_{min} := \Delta_z(\pi, i, j)$; u := i; v := j **endif**
      endfor;
      if $\Delta_{min} < \infty$ **then begin**
         $\pi' := \pi \oplus \phi_{uv}$;
         update differences $\Delta_z(\pi', k, l)$, $k = 1,...,n-1$, $l = k+1,...,n$;
         $tabu_{uv}$:= w + h; h := $\text{MAX}(h_{min}, (h \bmod h_{max})+1)$; //prohibiting the move ϕ_{uv}
         if $\Delta_{min} < 0$ **and** $w - w' >$ inter_intensification_interval **then begin**
            apply deterministic steepest descent to π'; w' := w
         endif;
         $\pi := \pi'$; **if** $z(\pi) < z(\pi^*)$ **then** $\pi^* := \pi$ //saving the best so far solution
      endif;
   endfor;
   return π^*
end.

Notes. 1. The difference $\Delta_z(\pi, k, l)$ is calculated by the formula: $\Delta_z(\pi,k,l) = \sum_{m=1, m \neq k, l}^{n} a''_{klm} b''_{\pi(l)\pi(k)\pi(m)}$, where

$a''_{ijk} = a'_{ik} - a'_{jk}$, $b''_{ijk} = b_{ik} - b_{jk}$, $i, j, k = 1, ..., n$, $a'_{ij} = a_{ij} + a_{ji}$, $i, j = 1, ..., n$, $i \neq j$, $a'_{ii} = a_{ii}$, $i = 1, ..., n$ (the

entries a''_{ijk}, b''_{ijk}, a'_{ij} are calculated only once before starting RGA). 2. The function IIF returns one value
if the given condition is met, and another value if the condition is not met. 3. The function RANDOM(0,1)
generates a pseudo-random real number from the interval [0,1). 4. $\pi \oplus \phi_{uv}$ denotes the move which swaps
the u-th and v-th element in the permutation π. 5. The difference $\Delta_z(\pi', k, l)$ is updated by the formula:
$\Delta_z(\pi',k,l) = \Delta_z(\pi,k,l) + (a''_{klu} - a''_{klv})(b''_{\pi(l)\pi(k)\pi(v)} - b''_{\pi(l)\pi(k)\pi(u)})$ (if $k = u$ or $k = v$ or $l = u$ or $l = v$, then

the formula $\Delta_z(\pi',k,l) = \sum_{m=1, m \neq k, l}^{n} a''_{klm} b''_{\pi'(l)\pi'(k)\pi'(m)}$ is applied). 6. The steepest descent procedure is quite
similar to the current IRoTS procedure, except the using of the tabu and aspiration criteria.

Fig. 6 Pseudo-code of the improved robust tabu search procedure

In the IRoTS procedure, the tabu tenure, h, is maintained in a deterministic
way; in particular, h varies in a cyclic manner, that is, h is dropped to a lower
```
```

value h_{min} each time the higher value h_{max} has been reached (here, h_{min}, h_{max} are a priori parameters). We use $h_{min} = 0.2n$, $h_{max} = 0.4n$ for smaller n's ($n \leq 50$) and $h_{min} = 0.1n$, $h_{max} = 0.2n$ for larger n's ($n > 50$). These tabu tenures are much more smaller than those used in Taillard's algorithm ($0.9n$ and $1.1n$, respectively), thus allowing more aggressive exploration of the search space.

To bring even more robustness to the search process, a randomized tabu criterion is applied. So, we ignore the tabu status with a small probability, α, even if the aspiration criterion does not hold (we used $\alpha = 0.05$). Doing so increases the number of accepted moves and helps avoiding potential stagnation (especially when long-term prohibitions often take place). The above approach may be thought of as some kind of "intra-intensification".

The other intensification strategy ("inter-intensification") is based on a combination of the tabu search and deterministic descent search. Each time the neighbourhood of the current solution is explored, we check if the solution found is better than the current one. If it is, the tabu search procedure is temporally interrupted in order to apply a steepest descent (SD) based procedure — this is with an intention of exploring the neighbourhood of the current solution more accurately. Note that the SD procedure is omitted if it already took place within the last I iterations, where I is an inter-intensification interval (we used $I = 0.5n$).

It should also be noted that, in our procedure, the neighbourhood exploration time is reduced considerably by using the enhanced data structures and refined formulas for the calculation of the differences in the objective function values.

A more thorough description of the IRoTS algorithm can be found in [14]. The pseudo-code of the IRoTS procedure is shown in Fig. 6.

3.2 Mutation procedure

The mutation procedure is based on random pairwise interchanges of the elements (genes) of a solution (individual). This mutation can be seen as a series of chained elementary moves $\phi_{\xi(1)\xi(2)}, \phi_{\xi(2)\xi(3)}, ..., \phi_{\xi(\rho-1)\xi(\rho)}$, where $\xi(1)$, $\xi(2)$, ..., $\xi(\rho)$ is a sequence of random integer numbers between 1 and n such that $\xi(i) \neq \xi(j)$, $i, j = 1, 2, ..., \rho$, $i \neq j$, $1 < \rho \leq n$ (note that the move ϕ_{ij} interchanges the ith and jth element of the current solution). The mutated solution $\tilde{\pi}$ can thus be represented as a composition $((((\pi \oplus \phi_{\xi(1)\xi(2)}) \oplus \phi_{\xi(2)\xi(3)}) \oplus ...) \oplus \phi_{\xi(i)\xi(i+1)}) \oplus ...) \oplus \phi_{\xi(\rho-1)\xi(\rho)}$, where π is the current solution (here, notation $\pi \oplus \phi_{ij}$ means that the move ϕ_{ij} is applied to the solution π). The parameter ρ is called a mutation rate.

The mutation procedure should be disruptive enough to allow to escape from the current local optimum and discover new unvisited regions of the search space. Disruptiveness can be easily increased by enlarging the value of the mutation rate ρ.

On the other hand, the mutation process should be quite delicate to keep characteristics of good solutions since parts of these solutions may be close to the ones of the optimal or near-optimal solution. Taking this point into consideration, we produce some number of different mutated solutions. We disregard the solutions with large values of the objective function; in fact, only the best mutated solution (i.e. the solution with the smallest value of the objective function) is accepted for the subsequent tabu search procedure. We call the resulting mutation process a controlled chained mutation (CCM). The pseudo-code of the CCM procedure is presented in Fig. 7.

```
function ControlledChainedMutation(π, ρ);
//input: π – current solution, ρ – actual mutation rate; parameters: η – number of trials
//output: π̃ – mutated solution
begin
    π° := π;  z̆ := ∞;  η° := 0.3·n;
    for k := 1 to η do begin
        for i := 1 to n do ξ(i) := i;   //producing a starting sequence of integer numbers
        for i := 1 to ρ do begin   //generation of a random sequence ξ=(ξ(1),ξ(2),..., ξ(ρ))
            generate j, randomly, uniformly, i ≤ j ≤ n;
            if i ≠ j then swap ith and jth element of the current sequence ξ
        endfor;
        π := π°;
        for i := 1 to ρ-1 do π := π ⊕ φ_{ξ(i)ξ(i+1)} ;   //applying chained mutation to π
        if z(π) < z̆ then begin   //choosing the best mutated solution
            π̃ := π;  z̆ := z(π) endif
    endfor;
    return π̃
end.
```

Fig. 7 Pseudo-code of the controlled chained mutation procedure

After improving the offspring by the ITS algorithm, the replacement of the population takes place to determine which individuals survive to the next generation. In the actual version of RGA, the replacement is done according to a well-known "μ, λ" strategy, where μ is the size of a population (*PS*) and λ denotes the number of newly created individuals (N_{offspr}). Thus, the new individuals simply replace the corresponding members of the current population (every child replaces its worse parent). This strategy may be viewed as a "random replacement", since the fitness of the children is not taken into consideration.

Naturally, the genetic variability test must be periodically performed — according to our new proposed methodology. It is convenient that this test is accomplished each time before moving to the next generation. In our algorithm, in particular, we check whether the entropy of the current population is less than the pre-defined variability threshold τ. If it is (this is a symptom of the loss of genetic variance), then the restart mechanism is activated; otherwise, the algorithm is simply continued with the current population.

Obviously, the behaviour of RGA is very much influenced by the entropy threshold τ. The best suitable value of τ for every particular case can be found empirically. Fig. 8 illustrates the entropy dynamics for two cases: a) $\tau = 0$ (note that this is the case of the straightforward GA) and b) $\tau = 0.25$ (this is the case of the restart-based GA). In our implementation, we used quite negligible value of τ ($\tau = 0.1$) for smaller n's ($n < 50$) and enlarged value ($\tau = 0.25$) for larger n's ($n \geq 50$).

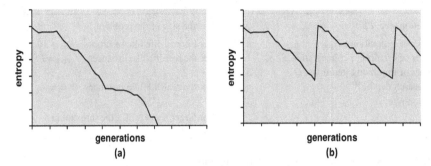

Fig. 8 Entropy dynamics for the straightforward (a) and restart-based (b) genetic process

There are two main steps of the restart process, as mentioned above.

During the first step, we apply the controlled chained mutation procedure with the maximally available mutation rate $\rho = n$ (mutation is applied to all individuals but the best). This results in a very drastic restructuring of the genotype of the population; at the same time, it helps much by preventing falling back into the previous (visited) local optima.

The goal of the second step is to guarantee the local optimality of all the members of the obtained population. For this purpose, we use the ITS algorithm. To achieve even more effect, we substantially increase (more than double) the number of improving iterations during this restart phase.

After restart, the algorithm proceeds in the ordinary way. The overall process is continued until a given number of generations, N_{gen}, have been performed.

4 Computational Experiments

A number of computational experiments were carried out in order to investigate the performance of the proposed algorithm. The experiments were performed on a 1.8 GHz computer. The following types of the QAP instances taken from the publicly available electronic library QAPLIB [2] were used:

a) random instances (these instances are randomly generated according to a uniform distribution; in QAPLIB, they are denoted by tai20a, tai25a, tai30a, tai35a, tai40a, tai50a, tai60a, tai80a, tai100a);

b) real-life like instances (they are generated in such a way that the entries of the matrices A, B resemble a distribution from real-world problems; the instances are denoted by tai20b, tai25b, tai30b, tai35b, tai40b, tai50b, tai60b, tai80b, tai100b, tai150b).

The values of the main control parameters of RGA used in the experiments are collected in Table 1.

Table 1 Main control parameters of RGA

Parameter	Value	Remarks
Population size, PS	$2 \cdot \lfloor \sqrt{n} \rfloor$	n is the size of the problem
Number of generations, N_{gen}	n	For the real-life like instances, $N_{gen} = 10n$
Number of offspring per generation, $N_{offsprn}$	1	For the real-life like instances, $N_{offsprn} = PS/2$
Number of improving iterations, Q	5	
Tabu search depth, W	n^2	For the real-life like instances, $W = n$
Mutation rate, ρ	$\lfloor 0.4n \rfloor$	
Variability threshold, τ	0.1	For larger n's ($n \geq 50$), the threshold is increased to 0.25

Table 2 Results of the comparison of different algorithms

Instance	n	BKV	$\bar{\delta}$					Time[‡] (sec.)
			RoTS	FANT	GLS	IHGA	RGA	
tai20a	20	703482	0.061	0.857	0.157	**0.000**	**0.000**	*1.2*
tai20b	20	122455319	**0.000**	0.091	0.009	**0.000**	**0.000**	*0.05*
tai25a	25	1167256	0.125	1.100	0.356	0.007	**0.000**	*2.8*
tai25b	25	344355646	0.044	0.007	0.061	**0.000**	**0.000**	*0.3*
tai30a	30	1818146	0.058	0.940	0.886	**0.000**	**0.000**	*7.5*
tai30b	30	637117113	0.408	0.029	0.401	**0.000**	**0.000**	*0.6*
tai35a	35	2422002	0.184	1.279	1.154	0.005	**0.000**	*17*
tai35b	35	283315445	0.233	0.198	0.256	**0.000**	**0.000**	*1.2*
tai40a	40	3139370	0.436	1.394	1.345	0.209	**0.193**	*42*
tai40b	40	637250948	0.204	**0.000**	0.188	**0.000**	**0.000**	*2.4*
tai50a	50	4938796	0.786	1.695	1.488	0.474	**0.328**	*150*
tai50b	50	458821517	0.239	0.222	0.359	0.008	**0.000**	*8.5*
tai60a	60	7205962	0.866	1.646	1.690	0.597	**0.330**	*360*
tai60b	60	608215054	0.291	0.179	0.411	0.009	**0.000**	*12*
tai80a	80	13515450	0.711	1.349	1.056	0.420	**0.334**	*1600*
tai80b	80	818415043	0.270	0.312	0.399	0.019	**0.000**	*63*
tai100a	100	21054656	0.682	1.260	1.233	0.389	**0.258**	*5000*
tai100b	100	1185996137	0.186	0.096	0.180	0.010	**0.000**	*190*
tai150b	150	498896643	0.392	0.514	0.393	0.050	**0.045**	*1000*

[‡] average time per one run is given

In the experimentation, we examined the following algorithms: robust tabu search (RoTS) [21], fast ant system (FANT) [22], genetic-local search (GLS) [11], improved hybrid genetic algorithm (IHGA) [12], and the current algorithm (RGA). As a performance criterion for the algorithms, we use the average relative deviation ($\bar{\delta}$) of the solutions from the best known (pseudo-optimal) solution (BKS). It is defined by the following formula: $\bar{\delta} = 100(\bar{z} - z^{\diamond})/z^{\diamond}$ [%], where $\bar{z}$ is the average objective function value over 10 runs of the algorithm and $z^{\diamond}$ denotes the best known value (BKV) of the objective function. (BKVs are from QAPLIB.)

The computations were organized in such a way that all the algorithms utilize approximately similar CPU times. The results of these experiments are summarized in Table 2.

The results from Table 2 confirm the excellent performance of our restart-based genetic algorithm. It can be seen that RGA is clearly superior to other heuristic algorithms used in the experimentation. Of course, the results may be improved even more by a careful tuning of the control parameters (like the population size, number of improving iterations, mutation rate, variability threshold). More extensive experiments with these parameters could be one of the future research directions.

5 Concluding Remarks

In this paper, we introduce a restart-based genetic algorithm for solving the difficult combinatorial optimization problem, the quadratic assignment problem. In contrast to the standard GAs that are based on principles of natural evolution in a quite straightforward manner, the hybridized restart-based GA rather imitates a more complex, cultural reality, where the lifetime transformations, adaptations and the interactions between individuals and the environment are at least as much important as the transmission of the parents' genotype.

The central idea of RGA is to increase the efficacy of the genetic search by incorporating a proper restart-based diversification mechanism. One of the main advantages of RGA is that the high degree of individuals' diversity is maintained. This appears to be extremely important in prevention of the premature convergence and stagnation of the evolution process. The other positive feature is that very compact populations are enabled; thus, a huge amount of time can be saved — this fact is probably the most crucial when designing the competitive intelligent optimization algorithms.

The results from the experiments demonstrate that the new proposed genetic algorithm is among the best heuristic approaches for the quadratic assignment problem. The further investigations and enhancements of the restart-based genetic algorithm still would be worthwhile. It may also be worthy to apply this type of algorithms to other (combinatorial) optimization problems.

References

1. Bölte, A., Thonemann, U.W.: Optimizing simulated annealing schedules with genetic programming. Eur. J. Oper. Res. **92**, 402–416 (1996)

2. Burkard, R.E., Karisch, S., Rendl, F.: QAPLIB – a quadratic assignment problem library. J. Glob. Optim. **10**, 391–403 (1997) http://www.seas.upenn.edu/qaplib. Cited 30 May 2008
3. Davendra, D., Onwubolu, G.C.: Enhanced differential evolution hybrid scatter search for discrete optimization. In: Tan, K.C. et al. (eds.) Proceedings of the IEEE Congress on Evolutionary Computation (CEC 2007), pp. 1156–1162. IEEE Press, Piscataway (2007)
4. Drezner, Z.: A new genetic algorithm for the quadratic assignment problem. INFORMS J. Comput. **15**, 320–330 (2003)
5. Fleurent, C., Ferland, J.A.: Genetic hybrids for the quadratic assignment problem. In: Pardalos, P.M., Wolkowicz, H. (eds.) Quadratic Assignment and Related Problems. DIMACS Series in Discrete Mathematics and Theoretical Computer Science, Vol.16, pp. 173–188. AMS, Providence (1994)
6. Gambardella, L.M., Taillard, E.D., Dorigo, M.: Ant colonies for the quadratic assignment problems. J. Oper. Res. Soc. **50**, 167–176 (1999)
7. Gordon, V., Whitley, L.D.: Serial and parallel genetic algorithms as function optimizers. In: Forrest, S. (ed.) Proceedings of the 5th International Conference on Genetic Algorithms (ICGA-93), pp. 177–183. Morgan Kaufmann, San Mateo (1993)
8. Holland, J.H.: Adaptation in Natural and Artificial Systems. University of Michigan Press, Ann Arbor, MI (1975)
9. Koopmans, T., Beckmann, M.: Assignment problems and the location of economic activities. Econometrica **25**, 53–76 (1957)
10. Li, Y., Pardalos, P.M., Resende, M.G.C.: A greedy randomized adaptive search procedure for the quadratic assignment problem. In: Pardalos, P.M., Wolkowicz, H. (eds.) Quadratic Assignment and Related Problems. DIMACS Series in Discrete Mathematics and Theoretical Computer Science, Vol.16, pp. 237–261. AMS, Providence (1994)
11. Lim, M.H., Yuan, Y., Omatu, S.: Efficient genetic algorithms using simple genes exchange local search policy for the quadratic assignment problem. Comput. Optim. Appl. **15**, 249–268 (2000)
12. Misevicius, A.: An improved hybrid genetic algorithm: new results for the quadratic assignment problem. Knowl. Based Syst. **17**, 65–73 (2004)
13. Misevicius, A.: A tabu search algorithm for the quadratic assignment problem. Comput. Optim. Appl. **30**, 95–111 (2005)
14. Misevicius, A.: An implementation of the iterated tabu search algorithm for the quadratic assignment problem. Working Paper, Kaunas University of Technology, Lithuania (2008) under review
15. Moscato, P.: Memetic algorithms. In: Pardalos, P.M., Resende, M.G.C. (eds.) Handbook of Applied Optimization, pp. 157–167. Oxford University Press, New York (2002)
16. Reeves, C.R., Höhn, C.: Integrating local search into genetic algorithms. In: Rayward-Smith, V.J., Osman, I.H., Reeves, C.R., Smith, G.D. (eds.) Modern Heuristic Search Methods, pp. 99–115. Wiley, Chichester (1996)
17. Reeves, C.R., Rowe, J.E.: Genetic Algorithms: Principles and Perspectives. Kluwer, Norwell (2001)
18. Rodriguez, J.M., Macphee, F.C., Bonham, D.J., Bhavsar, V.C. Solving the quadratic assignment and dynamic plant layout problems using a new hybrid meta-heuristic approach. In: Eskicioglu, M.R. (ed.) Proceedings of the 18th Annual International Symposium on High Performance Computing Systems and Aplications (HPCS), pp. 9–16. Department of Computer Science, Winnipeg, Canada (2004)
19. Sahni, S., Gonzalez, T.: P-complete approximation problems. J. ACM **23**, 555–565 (1976)
20. Stützle, T.: Iterated local search for the quadratic assignment problem. Eur. J. Oper. Res. **174**, 1519–1539 (2006)
21. Taillard, E.D.: Robust taboo search for the QAP. Parallel Comput. **17**, 443–455 (1991)
22. Taillard, E.: FANT: fast ant system. Tech. Report IDSIA-46-98, Lugano, Switzerland (1998)
23. Tate, D.M., Smith, A.E. A genetic approach to the quadratic assignment problem. Comput. Oper. Res. **1**, 73–83 (1995)

CONSTRAINT SATISFACTION AND FIXES: REVISITING SISYPHUS VT

Trevor Runcie, Peter Gray and Derek Sleeman

Abstract This paper explores the solution of the VT Sisyphus II challenge using a Constraint Satisfaction Problem (CSP) paradigm and is an extension of the ExtrAKTor work presented at EKAW 2006. ExtrAKTor takes a Protégé KB describing a propose and-revise (PnR) problem, including both constraints & fixes. Subsequently, it extracts and transforms these components so that they are directly usable by the ECLiPSe CSP toolkit to solve a range of configuration tasks. It was encouraging to note that (a) the solver coped very well with constraints involving real variables even when using a generalised propagation technique and (b) the techniques needed no "fix" information, yet successfully dealt with the "antagonistic constraints" and the associated "thrashing" problem that had been a key issue in the original Marcus, Stout & McDermott VT paper. Consequently, we believe this is a widely useable technique for automatically generating and then solving this class of constraint problems, when they are expressed as Protégé ontologies.

1 Introduction

In a previous paper presented at EKAW2006 [7] we explored the reuse of knowledge bases through semi-automated extraction of knowledge and code generation of new KBs. The approach was explored in the context of the Sisyphus II VT (Vertical Transport) challenge and the related class of problems, and the "propose and revise" (P&R) algorithm. In this paper we extend that work by investigating how Constraint Logic Programming (CLP) techniques [12] can be used to find solutions to "Parametric Design" or "Configuration Tasks" such as VT, by working directly from the

Trevor Runcie
Department of Computing Science, University of Aberdeen,
Aberdeen, AB24 3FX, Scotland, UK e-mail: t.runcie@abdn.ac.uk

Peter Gray e-mail: p.gray@abdn.ac.uk · Derek Sleeman e-mail: d.sleeman@abdn.ac.uk acquired knowledge so that one format both documents the knowledge and is also directly executable.

With the P&R PSM, as we have noted, each constraint is associated with a set of ordered fixes. When a "proposed" solution does not satisfy all the constraints, the first violated constraint is identified, and the associated fixes are applied in the order specified to change the initial value for a specified variable until that constraint is satisfied or the list of fixes is exhausted.

However, a crucial issue with P&R is that "thrashing" can occur. We report results using a CLP package where we use the CLP solver itself to search for consistent variable values which overcomes the "thrashing" problem, without needing any explicit fixes from the domain expert. This works even with "anatagonistic constraints" which were excluded from the Sisyphus challenge KB.

The structure of the rest of the paper is as follows: Section 2 describes the VT design task, the Sisyphus-II challenge, and gives an overview of constraint satisfaction techniques; Section 3 describes the form of the generated constraint knowledge suitable for a CLP solver; Section 4 describes how we investigated the solution space and how we refined the knowledge format to deal with serious performance problems; Section 5 gives the experimental results, while Section 6 discusses related work, future work, and our overall conclusions.

2 The VT problem and VT Sisyphus-II Challenge

2.1 VT Problem

The Vertical Transportation (VT) domain is a complex configuration task involving the interaction of the components required to design a lift/elevator system. Parameters such as physical dimensions, weight and choice of components are regulated by physical constraints. The VT domain [3] was initially used to solve real-world lift design by the Westinghouse Elevator Company.

The Sisyphus [10] version of the VT domain was created so that researchers would have a common KB for experimentation. It is the Protégé version of the VT system from Stanford University which has been used in this project [9].

2.2 An Overview of Constraint Satisfaction Techniques

Constraint Satisfaction techniques attempt to find solutions to constrained combinatorial problems and there are a number of efficient CSP toolkits in a variety of programming languages. The definition of a constraint satisfaction problem (CSP) is:

- a set of variables $X = \{X_1, \cdots, X_n\}$,

- for each variable X_i, a finite set D_i of possible values (its domain), and
- a set of constraints $C_j \subseteq D_{j1} \times D_{j2} \times \cdots \times D_{jt}$, restricting the values that subsets of the variables can take simultaneously.

A solution to a CSP is a set of assignments to each of the variables in such a way that all constraints are satisfied. The main CSP solution technique is consistency enforcement, in which infeasible values are removed from the problem by reasoning about the constraints using algorithms such as node consistency and arc consistency checking. Two important features introduced in CLP are goal suspension and constraint propagation, and these concepts are described in the following paragraphs.

Goal Suspension: In brief, suspension improves on Prolog by delaying the processing of arithmetic constraints until all their variables are full instantiated. For example the Prolog statement, $2 < Y + 1, Y = 3$ would result in an error since in the first occurrence of Y, it is not sufficiently instantiated. Using the ECLiPSe statement, $(2 < Y + 1)$, the query is suspended until Y is fully instantiated and the query is ready for evaluation. This allows statements to be written in an order which is natural to the user but is still executable.

Constraint Propagation: Constraint propagation results in the removal of all values that cannot participate in any solution to a CSP. In ECLiPSe constraint propagation is activated (triggered) as soon as a new constraint is encountered, and this mechanism attempts to reduce the domains of all related variables including variables that may have already been considered during the processing of other constraints. If while enforcing arc-consistency, the set of acceptable values for a node is reduced to zero, then the entire sub-tree of potential solutions can be pruned. This is the real power of CSP.

2.3 ECLiPSe - Constraint Logic Programming System

ECLiPSe [11] is a software system for the development and execution of constraint programming applications. It contains several constraint solver libraries, a high-level modelling and control language, interfaces to third-party solvers, an integrated development environment, and interfaces to allow embedding in host environments.

ECLiPSe Libraries (sd and ic): The ECLiPSe system is an extension of Prolog. The sd (symbolic domains) library is the ECLiPSe library used to process domains of symbols e.g. {x, motor, current_value, ...}, which makes constraints more easily readable. This extends the utility of the ic (interval constraints) library, which is the ECLiPSe library used to process simple numeric interval data e.g. [3, 4, 5, 6] or more complex ranges e.g. [2..5, 8, 9..14]. The sd and ic libraries implement node-consistency, arc-consistency, suspend and constraint propagation.

ECLiPSe (Bounded Reals): In addition to the basic numeric variable data types (integers, floats, and rationals), ECLiPSe also supports the numeric data type "bounded real". Each bounded real is represented by a pair of floating point numbers. For example, the statements X > 3.5 and X < 9.2, assign X the value {3.5 ... 9.2}. The true value of the number may not be known, but it is definitely known to lie between the two bounds. Fortunately, many of the techniques used for finite domain (lists of values) have been extended in ECLiPSe[1] to apply to bounded reals, even though these represent potentially infinite sets of reals. Without this extension, CLP techniques would be too weak to solve the VT design problem because many of the crucial variables are lengths or weights represented as reals. The *locate/2* predicate can also be used to direct search for real variables. *Locate* works by non-deterministically splitting the domains of the variables until they are narrower than a specified precision. For example, locate([Cable_length], 0.01), can be used to split the domain of Cable_length into a set of discrete values to find a value to satisfy the constraints.

3 An Overview of Structure

3.1 Initial Structure of ExtrAKTor Generated Code

The format for the generated constraints and declarations was deliberately structured so as to create a compact structure that was eminently readable by knowledge engineers yet at the same time solvable. This was made possible by the declarative nature of the code. The format uses widely known logical and arithmetical syntax with the usual semantics, and so is easy to use for a wide range of configuration problems encountered in engineering. There was a big gain over the thousands of lines in the original CLIPS version. In the new version, the code segments each contain around 50 lines of code which are summarised below.

Within each code segment, statements can come in any order yet still give the same results on execution. For convenience the code was sorted into the most readable form with variables ordered alphabetically. Each section is described here in detail since the structure had a major bearing on the next stage of the project.

Prolog Data Tables (Tuples)
This is a standard Prolog data table structure. Each predicate represents a different entity and each parameter represents a specific attribute, as in a record structure or relational database. The "_" (underscore) represents "anything" in terms of Prolog pattern matching.

```
hoistcable(0.5,   0.03,   14500.0).
```

There are 28 of these tables in the system, with an average of 10 rows per table.

Variable Declarations
The following example shows integer variable declarations with lower and upper bounds. Note the "#::" syntax used to declare integers and also the use of "1.0Inf" to declare no upper bound (Infinity).

```
%Integers with Constraints
```

```
[Car_buffer_blocking_height] #:: 0 .. 120,
[Platform_width] \#:: 60 .. 1.0Inf
```

Real declarations have a similar syntax to integers but without the use of "#". The following example shows real variable declarations with lower and upper bounds.

```
%Reals with Constraints
[Car_runby] :: 6.0 .. 24.0,
[Car_return_left] :: 1.0 .. 1.0Inf
```

Data Table Functions
The data predicates pattern match against the tuples declared in the "Prolog Data Tables". The Prolog predicate unifies with the rows in the tables, and the Prolog variables are instantiated to the column values.

```
hoistcable(Hoistcable_diameter,Hoistcable_unit_weight,
Hoistcable_ultimate_strength),
```

Assignments
These are simple assignments where the value of the right hand side of the equation is assigned to the left hand side of the equation. The "ic:" syntax tells ECLiPSe to use the ic solver when processing this line of code. Since ECLiPSe is a CLP system, any of the variables on the left and right side can be unknown at this point. For example, the assignment

```
ic:(2.5 =:= A + B)
```

is a perfectly acceptable construct, as is:

```
ic:(Car_buffer_striking_speed_maximum =:=
1.15 * Car_speed)
```

Constraints
Constraints are used to limit the values that variables can take. ECLiPSe uses this information when performing arc-consistency checks and rapidly eliminates impossible combinations of values. General arithmethic expressions (even non-linear) may be included, for example:

```
ic:(Car_buffer_load >= Car_buffer_loadmin)
```

3.2 ExtrAKTor Structure Summary

As stated earlier, the code structure made it very easy to visually scan for variable names during debugging. It is worth noting that variable names are identical to the slot names used in the original ontology.

4 Investigating the Sisyphus-VT Solution Space

4.1 Constraint Types for Relaxation

The constraints in VT can be classified as one of 3 types:

- Universal Constraints
- Site Specific Constraints
- Design Specific Constraints

Universal Constraints: These express physical limits on certain parameters that apply to every VT design. Examples of this class are angles which can only be between 0.0 and 360.0 (expressed in degrees), and positive real values which must be greater than 0.0. *Site Specific Constraints*: These are physical limits of certain values that apply only to a specific site. An example is "the building has 8 floors". *Design Specific Constraints*: These are physical limits of certain values that apply only to a specific design. An example is "the lift must be able to support a load of 10 passengers".

4.2 Early Performance Issue

Surprisingly, processing of the ExtrAKTor generated code for the tasks specified by the Sisyphus VT challenge is completed in seconds. Universal constraints apply to all real world problems and Site Specific constraints cannot physically be altered for a given site, so it was therefore decided to relax the "Design Specific Constraints" to investigate an enlarged solution space. Relaxing the constraints and expanding the search space had a massive detrimental effect on the processing time for the original problem. Execution times increased from 0.01 seconds to periods in excess of 1 hour (in fact the code never ran to completion). The performance degradation was traced to significant backtracking that was required for "component" selection.

The explanation seems to be as follows: Initially the unification process selects a set of components. Next, when constraints are specified, ECLiPSe determines that some of the initial choices of components violate the constraints. The system must then *backtrack* using standard Prolog techniques to select an alternative "component". This then forces the assignments to be recalculated. Consider the following simple code fragment that demonstrates the problem.

```
a(999), a(998), ... a(1).
...
a(X), ... ic:(Z =:= X * 1.34 ),
ic:(Y =:= (Z * Z) / 2.33 ),
...
ic:(Y>3),  %Constraint C2
ic:(X<2),  %Constraint C1
```

First, X is instantiated to 999, and constraint C1 fails. Then, X is instantiated to 998, and constraint C1 fail ... After 1000 instantiations, X is instantiated to 1, and constraint C1 is satisfied. With this style of code, hundreds of complex calculations may be performed on the instantiated values of X before C1 and C2 are tested and fail, forcing backtracking and recalculation of all intermediate values.

4.3 Performance Enhancement - "domain" & "infers most"

It was disappointing that ECLiPSe which had performed so well in most numeric constraint solving seemed to have such poor handling of lists of values and data tables. However, this prompted a more detailed review of the more esoteric capabilities of ECLiPSe which eventually led to the discovery of the "domain" and "infers most" constructs.

The "domain" and "infers most" constructs were not documented to any great extent in the ECLiPSe manuals, and are not mentioned in the ECLiPSe reference book [1]. Fortunately, one of the authors recalled its use in a previous project [13] and this showed how to use this construct to instantiate variables in "'Data Table Functions'" without backtracking. Initially, it took considerable trial and error to get the code to work, but the effort paid handsome dividends. Although the use of "domain" is independent of the "infers most" declaration it greatly extends its effectiveness. The following paragraphs document how we extended our format to keep it declarative while greatly enhancing the KBS's performance.

The "infers most" [2, 8] construct requires the ECLiPSe Propia library to be loaded. This library implements the Generalised Constraint Propogation technique developed by Le Provost and Wallace [2]. The construct was able to use the implied constraint information in Prolog Data Tables far more efficiently than by standard backtracking, as described in the following paragraphs.

4.3.1 Domain Declaration

The first part of this construct declares a domain by providing a (domain) name and (domain) values. Importantly, domain values must be unique within the ECLiPSe KB; ie declaration of two domains; domain1('A', 'B', 'C') and domain2('C', 'D', 'E'), where element 'C' appears in two domains, is not allowed. The string constants act as a kind of object identifier, whose associated values (e.g. Power of motor model) are taken from the tables.

```
%Domain Declaration
:-local domain(motor_model("motor_10HP","motor_15HP",
"motor_20HP","motor_25HP", "motor_30HP","motor_40HP").
```

4.3.2 Tuple Declaration

The second part of the construct is to declare the data tuples using standard Prolog syntax. Comments starting with "%" are generated as documentation.

```
%Tuples
%motor(model,power_min,power_max,weight,current_max)
motor("motor_10HP",  0, 10, 374, 150).
motor("motor_15HP", 10, 15, 473, 250).
motor("motor_20HP", 15, 20, 539, 260).
```

4.3.3 Domain Assignment

The third part of the construct is to assign the domain to a variable.

```
%Domain Assignment
Motor_model &:: motor_model,
```

This is absolutely necessary since without it "Motor_model" in the above example would be treated as a standard Prolog variable, and backtracking of the data structure, which was the main cause of performance degradation, would be the primary method of searching for plausible components.

4.3.4 Infers Most

The fourth and final part of the construct is the "infers most" annotation.

```
motor(Motor_model, Power_min, Power_max, Motor_weight,
Motor_max_current) infers most,
```

Any *Goal* in Prolog can be turned into a constraint by using the annotation *Goal infers most*. In fact we only use it for a "Goal" in the form of a term structure such as "motor(, ,)" where some of the variables have assigned domains (as in 4.3.3). Propia needs this information in order to explore alternative domain values efficiently within the solver, without defaulting to backtracking. The new constraint accepts and rejects the same symbolic values as when using standard backtracking techniques, however the processing is significantly different. Propia extracts as much information as possible from the constraint before processing the Prolog goal. Note that the variable Motor_model is assigned to domain motor_model declared previously.

4.3.5 Final Code Structure

The code described in sections "Domain Declaration", "Tuple Declaration", "Domain Assignment", and "Infers Most" was replicated for each of the symbolic values in each of the fifteen VT component selections. This again made the generated code very readable by comparison with the CLIPS original.

4.3.6 Summary

If you consider the ECLiPSe solver to have two levels of processing namely Prolog and the CSP, then the addition of the "infers most" has the effect of pushing the Prolog tuple definitions down into the CSP level enabling the power of the CSP to be invoked. Thus the CSP is able to choose combinations of alternative values from the local domains provided, instead of repeatedly having to suspend constraint solving and backtracking to get another value in a sequence over which it has no control. A further advantage is that just adding a simple Design Specific goal as a constraint followed by an output statement:

```
ic:(Power_min =< 12),
write("Motor_model is "), write(Motor_model), nl,
```

returns the solution as ranges of symbolic or numeric values.

```
Motor_model is Motor_model{[motor_10HP, motor_15HP]}
```

Thus where Prolog would only return the first instantiation of motor_model, ECLiPSe returns all feasible values.

4.4 ExtrAKTor Upgrade

The ExtrAKTor system was upgraded to generate an enhanced form of ECLiPSe code. This entailed adding the following three programming constructs for each of the lift components. Firstly, a local domain was created for each component,

```
:- local domain(motor_model("motor_10HP", ... )).
```

Secondly, a domain assignment was created for each component,

```
Motor_model &:: motor_model
```

Thirdly, "infers most" was added to the end of the Prolog database predicate for each component,

```
motor(Motor_model, Power_min, ... Motor_max_current)
infers most
```

4.4.1 Summary

By pushing the Prolog tuple definitions down into the CSP level, the performance of the loosely constrained KB returns to that of the highly constrained KB without affecting the readability of the code. By reducing Prolog backtracking, processing time was very significantly reduced from hours to seconds, and most importantly the performance of this structure is largely independent of clause ordering. This then made it possible to explore the solution space in detail which was not achieved by previous researchers.

5 Experimentation - Exploring The VT Solution Space

A key value in the Sisyphus-VT KB is the Car_weight, as this affects the two most important values in the solution space namely, Machine_groove_pressure(MGP) and Hoist_cable_traction_ratio(HCTR), as described in the original paper [3]. Car_weight is calculated as the simple sum of several variables described in the following equation:

```
Car_weight = Car_cab_weight + Platform_weight +
Sling_weight + Safetybeam_weight + Car_fixture_weight
+ Car_supplement_weight + Car_misc_weight
```

All of these variables have dependencies except Car_supplement_weight(CSW) which is defined in the VT Sisyphus documentation as taking only one of two discrete values either 0 or 500. We decided to remove this limitation and to iterate CSW over a range of values from 0 to 1000 in steps of 50 (manually running the KBS for each new value of CSW). The initial experiments did not show the expected relationship between CSW, MGP and HCTR and this led to the discovery of an error in the Protégé Sisyphus-VT ontology. In the ExtrAKTor version of the KB derived from the original Sisyphus-VT code from Stanford there was a statement for constraint C-48 as follows:

```
%ic:(Hoist_cable_traction_ratio > (Groove_multiplier
* Machine_angle_of_contact) + Groove_offset)
```

However, on further investigation we realised that the original full Sisyphus-VT Documentation states, "the HOIST CABLE TRACTION RATIO is constrained to be *at most* 0.007888 Q + 0.675 ...(where Q = machine_angle_of_contact)" This would suggest that the ">" should in fact be a "$<=$" and that the version of the Protégé Sisyphus-VT ontology used up to this point had a significant error. After correcting the error, we then decided to iterate over a range of values 0 to 1000 in steps of 1, this time automatically running the KBS for each new value of CSW. Figure 1 shows the outcome of this test. As had been suggested in the original VT paper, as CSW increases MGP increases and HCTR decreases. With steps of 50, both variables appeared to change in linear fashion, but steps of 1 showed that HCTR actually behaved in a sawtooth fashion.

In order to experiment over such a wide range of CSW constraints known as C-31 and C-42 were disabled. Without this, at CSW$>=$721 the MGP exceeds the Maximum Machine_Groove_Pressure (MaxMGP=119) and the solver correctly identifies that there are no solutions.

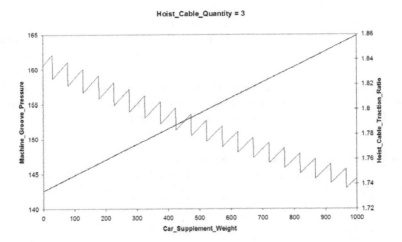

Hoist_Cable_Quantity = 3

Fig. 1 CSW 0 to 1000 Step 1: sawtooth shows HCTR; straight line shows MGP

Prior to this experiment, we knew that if a task is consistently and fully represented that it can be solved by a CSP system; but of course this might take a very
long time. What we were not sure about before this experiment was whether some
vital information was contained in the fixes which meant that the formulation would
be incomplete until the information inherent in the fix was added to the formulation
of the task. The experiment showed that this perspective / hypothesis was not correct
for the VT task with a particular contemporary CSP system. In retrospect, we now
view the role of fixes as changing the focus of the search and hence we believe they
would be useful in very large search spaces. Again empirically we have seen that
sizable tasks / search spaces are handled efficiently by CLP and so to date we have
not needed to use these heuristics (fixes) in conjunction with CLP searches for the
VT tasks.

6 Discussion of Related Work

6.1 Comparison with VITAL Results

Seven papers were presented at KAW94, each of which described a methodology
for modelling and solving VT Sisyphus II; these are: Soar / TAQL, Protégé II [6],
VITAL [5], CommonKADS, Domain-Independent Design System (DIDS), KARL
/ CRLM and DESIRE.

Of these seven papers, only one reported multiple runs of their implementation
and that was VITAL [5]. Further, Menzies [4] reviewing this work emphasises that
little testing was conducted on the various methods beyond this one example. Table

1 recreats the table presented in the VITAL paper. The most immediate observation is the apparent random nature of success and failure in finding a solution. For example, using the initial design constraints 3500lbs weight capacity and a 200ft/min lift speed, VITAL was successful in finding a solution. It is intuitively obvious that the same lift design would also be a valid solution for any lower weight i.e. the lift design which is valid ("success") for 3500lbs would be a valid solution for 3000lbs, 2500lbs, and 2000lbs; but as can be seen in Table 1, this was not the case; further, VITAL could not find a solution for 3000lbs and 2500lbs.

Table 1 Recreation of Experimentation Table for VITAL

	200 ft/min	250 ft/min	300 ft/min	350 ft/min	400 ft/min
2000lbs	success	success	fail	success	success
2500lbs	fail	fail	success	success	success
3000lbs	fail	fail	fail	fail	fail
3500lbs	success	fail	fail	fail	fail
4000lbs	fail	fail	fail	fail	fail

For comparison purposes, the same set of tasks were solved by the ECLiPSe VT Sisyphus KB; these results are shown in Table 2. Motta, Zdrahal et al [5] argued that the failure of VITAL to find a solution was due to the VT Sisyphus problem specification. As such, the other six implementations should have seen similar problems, and since this was not reported by any other research group, it suggests that the other systems had not been tested extensively [4].

Table 2 Recreation of Experimentation Table for VITAL

	200 ft/min	250 ft/min	300 ft/min	350 ft/min	400 ft/min
2000lbs	success	success	success	success	success
2500lbs	success	success	success	success	success
3000lbs	success	success	success	fail	fail
3500lbs	success	success	fail	fail	fail
4000lbs	fail	fail	fail	fail	fail

6.2 Future Work

Our previous paper [7] focussed on the extraction of KB components from the VT-Sisyphus domain so that they can be reformulated and re-used in conjunction with different problem solvers. This led to the automated extraction of an ontology, formulae, constraints, and fixes. In this paper the extracted information has been used to solve real problems with a powerful CLP problem solver which is capable of using real number domains. Further, as far as we have ascertained, no other research has used constraint solvers with the VT domain.

There are a number of areas for further investigation. These include:

1) extension of the KB to support a "Sketch and Refine" interactive design process. This would accept initial design ranges, solve the KB followed by output of new acceptable ranges, and then allow user input of refined ranges.

2) investigation of the performance of CLP with more complex problems than VT, perhaps involving non-linear constraints.

6.3 Conclusion

We have shown that a classic AI problem, VT configuration design, is very well suited to solution by advanced CLP techniques, as provided in the ECLiPSe library. Much more significantly, we were able to code generate the CLP description of the problem direct from the Protégé knowledge base used in the Sisyphus II challenge. This means that a person with almost no experience of CLP or of programming in Prolog can now use these powerful techniques with confidence to get solutions to this class of problem.

Formulating problems in such a way that a powerful solver (in this case ECLiPSe) can get solutions has always been an important AI goal. Here we have shown a systematic way to generate the CLP automatically from a KB in a widely used representation (Protégé) which is accessible to many engineers through its graphic front end. This in turn uses a widely taught object model (ontology) based on entities, attributes, relationships and constraints. Thus the knowledge engineer has a clear way to think about and represent the problem, and a good graphic tool to capture the information. Further, there is no need to worry about how to order the information to achieve a solution, as one does with a programming language. Details of this knowledge capture method are given in our EKAW06 paper [7].

Here we have described how we used the various features of ECLiPSe to get very fast performance on this class of problem – far quicker than any other published study on VT. Some of these features were not at all obvious, but now we have refined and tested them on VT they can be code generated for future users to use on various kinds of configuration problem. Without these features we could not have done the in-depth study of the VT solution space that is presented here.

The original Protégé KB for Sisyphus II contained information on entity types, attribute names (variables), initial values, constraints and fixes for use with the propose-and-revise algorithm. The CLP solver proved so powerful that we did not have to use any *fix* information. We thought we might have to use it to write a *labelling* predicate which is commonly used to guide the CLP solver about the order in which variables should be solved; and whether to increase or decrease values. It was not needed. This was so even though we re-introduced pairs of antagonistic constraints into the Sysyphus description, that had to be treated very specially in the

[3] paper in order to avoid thrashing. Instead these constraints were just entered like any others and were not specially labelled for ECLiPSe.

We have described in section 3 how the Protégé information, some of it in tables of alternative values, is represented in ECLiPSe. This is to convince the reader that it really is very straightforward to code generate for any configuration problem. Some problems might need more complex non-linear constraints, but these can also be generated. They do not affect the code generator, only the speed of finding solutions.

Acknowledgments

We acknowledge useful discussions of Research issues with Tomas Nordlander & David Corsar. Additionally, we acknowledge discussions with the Protégé team at Stanford University, including Mark Musen who also made available their version of the Sisyphus-VT code.

References

1. K. R. Apt and M. G. Wallace. *Constraint Logic Programming using ECLiPSe*. Cambridge University Press, 2007.
2. T. Le Provost and M. Wallace. Generalised Constraint Propagation Over the CLP Scheme. *JPL*, 16:319–359, 1991.
3. S. Marcus, J. Stout, and J. McDermott. VT: An Expert Designer That Uses Knowledge-Based Backtracking. *AI Magazine*, pages 95–111, 1988.
4. T. Menzies. Evaluation Issues for Problem Solving Methods. In *KAW98*, 1998.
5. E. Motta, K. O'Hara, N. Shadbolt, A. Stutt, and Z. Zdrahal. Solving VT in VITAL: a study in model construction and knowledge reuse. *IJHCS*, 44(3/4):333–371, 1996.
6. T. E. Rothenfluh, J. H. Gennari, H. Eriksson, A. R. Puerta, S. W. Tu, and M. A. Musen. Reusable ontologies, knowledge-acquisition tools, and performance systems: PROTÉGÉ-II solutions to Sisyphus-2. *IJHCS*, 44(3/4):303–332, 1996.
7. D. Sleeman, T. Runcie, and P. M. D. Gray. Reuse: Revisiting Sisyphus-VT. In *Lecture Notes in Computer Science*, pages 59–66, Podebrady, 2006. Springer.
8. P. Van Hentenryck. *Constraint Satisfaction in Logic Programming*. MIT Press, 1989.
9. Protégé VT Sisyphus Ontology. *ftp://ftp-smi.stanford.edu/pub/protege/S2-WFW.ZIP*, August 2004.
10. Sisyphus II. *http://ksi.cpsc.ucalgary.ca/KAW/Sisyphus*, December 2005.
11. ECLiPSe. *http://eclipse.crosscoreop.com/eclipse*, April 2006.
12. Online Guide to Constraint Programming. *http://ktiml.mff.cuni.cz/ bartak/constraints/*, March 2006.
13. Kit ying Hui and Peter M. D. Gray. Developing finite domain constraints - a data model approach. In *CL '00: Proceedings of the First International Conference on Computational Logic*, pages 448–462, London, UK, 2000. Springer-Verlag.

On a Control Parameter Free Optimization Algorithm

Lars Nolle[1]

Abstract This paper introduces SASS2, a novel control parameter free optimization algorithm, which combines a population based self-adaptive Hill-Climbing strategy with a stopping criterion and a heuristic for selecting the population size for the hill-climbing component. Experiments presented in this paper demonstrate that the algorithm is very effective and also very efficient whilst removing the need for tuning the algorithm to match an optimization problem at hand. This provides practitioners with a powerful tool, which can be used as a black-box optimizer by an end-user without the need to become an expert in optimization algorithms.

1 Introduction

Many scientific and engineering problems can be viewed as search or optimization problems, where an optimum input parameter vector for a given system has to be found in order to maximize or to minimize the system response to that input vector. Often, auxiliary information about the system, like its transfer function and derivatives, etc., is not known and the measures might be incomplete and distorted by noise. This makes such problems difficult to be solved by traditional mathematical methods. Here, heuristic optimization algorithms, like Genetic Algorithms (GA) [1] or Simulated Annealing (SA) [2], can offer a solution. But because of the lack of a standard methodology for matching a problem with a suitable algorithm, and for setting the control parameters for the algorithm, practitioners often seem not to consider heuristic optimization.

The main reason for this is that a practitioner, who wants to apply an algorithm to a specific problem, and who has no experience with heuristic search algorithms, would need to become an expert in optimization algorithms before being able to choose a suitable algorithm for the problem at hand. Also, finding suitable control parameter settings would require carrying out a large number of experiments. This

1 Nottingham Trent University, NG11 8NS, UK
lars.nolle@ntu.ac.uk

might not be an option for a scientist or engineer, who simply wants to use heuristic search as a tool.

For such practitioners, an optimization algorithm that would have no control parameters to choose, while still being effective and efficient for a wide variety of problems, would clearly be of benefit. Hence, the aim of this project was to develop a control parameter free search algorithm that is still effective for solving black-box optimization tasks. In previous work, Self-Adaptive Step size Search (SASS), a self adaptive hill-climbing strategy, was proposed [3] and applied to a number of optimization applications [4,5]. However, the SASS algorithm has still two control parameters, the number of iterations and the number of particles in the population. This led into the development of SASS2, which has no control parameters to tune.

2 SASS2

For heuristic search algorithms, like Hill-Climbing (HC), it was previously shown that the definition of the neighborhood, and in particular the chosen step size s, the length of the steps, is crucial to the success of the algorithm [6], not only for continuous parameter search, but also for discrete parameters, when the search space is too large to consider direct neighbors of a candidate solution for performance reasons. It was shown that selection schemes with random step sizes with an upper limit (maximum step size s_{max}) outperform neighborhood selection schemes with a constant step length s_{const}. The following section explains the effect of step size on simple Hill-Climbing strategies.

2.1 Effect of Step Size s on Hill-Climbing

Figure 1 shows examples of typical search runs of a simple Hill-Climbing algorithm, using the different selection schemes for function minimization. Each dot represents an accepted solution, i.e. the rejected solutions are not shown. The starting point for all experiments is on top of the local hill at about -200. Figure 1a and Figure 1b show the results for using a constant step size s_{const}, Figure 1c, Figure 1d and Figure 1e show the results for experiments using a maximum random step size s_{max}. As it can be seen from Figure 1a, if s_{const} is chosen to be too small, the algorithm gets trapped in an adjacent local optimum. If s_{const} is large enough, it is capable of jumping over local optima (Figure 1b), but because the steps are of constant length, the number of points, which can be reached from a certain position, is limited. For example, in Figure 1b, it is not possible to jump from the last point (near +400) to a point with lower associated costs, because all these points are within the constant step width.

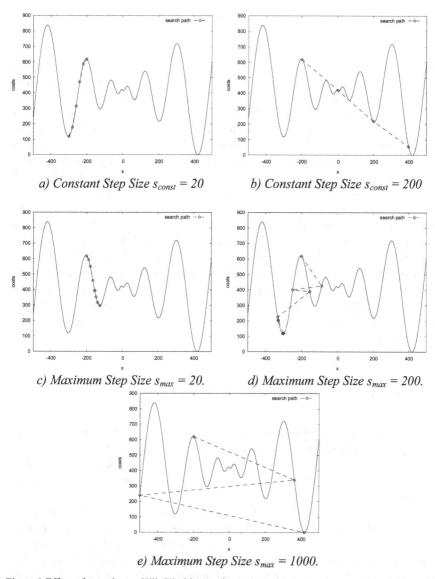

a) Constant Step Size $s_{const} = 20$ b) Constant Step Size $s_{const} = 200$

c) Maximum Step Size $s_{max} = 20$.   d) Maximum Step Size $s_{max} = 200$.

e) Maximum Step Size $s_{max} = 1000$.

Figure 1 Effect of step size on Hill-Climbing performance.

When using a random step with a maximum length s_{max}, the effect for choosing small values is similar to that for using a constant step width (Figure 1c), but with increasing s_{max}, the ability to reach points with a better cost value increases. In Figure 1d for example, the algorithm was able to jump out of the valley on the right hand side of the start point into the valley of the left hand side, and it was also able to decent into the valley on the left hand side. However, because the maximum step width was not large enough to jump into the right hand side of the search space, which contains the global minimum, the algorithm only exploited the local optimum. In Figure 1e, the maximum step length is large enough to jump into the right hand side of the search space, but this time, because of the large steps that are possible, it does not fully exploit this global optimum. The results given above show, that, if the step width is chosen to be too small, both selection schemes will eventually get trapped in the nearest local optimum, whereas using a larger step width increases the ability to overcome local optima. However, for a constant step width it is more difficult to reach the global optimum, because of the limited number of possible search points that can be reached from a certain position. This is overcome by using a maximum random step length, but this needs to be carefully selected: if it is chosen to be too large, the algorithm will lose its ability to exploit a potential region. But if the step width is chosen to be too small, it is not guaranteed that the algorithm can jump over local optima in order to reach the region that contains the global optimum. Therefore, the careful selection of appropriate values for s_{max} seems to be crucial for the success of the algorithm for a particular application. However, it would clearly be of benefit if the maximum step length would be more adaptive to the search progress itself. Therefore, in previous research, a novel population-based adaptation scheme with a self-adaptive step size, referred to as Self-Adaptive Step-size Search (SASS) has been developed. This algorithm, which is explained in the following section, forms the basis for the new SASS2 algorithm.

2.2 Basic SASS

Previously, a population-based adaptation scheme with a self-adaptive step size, referred to as Self-Adaptive Step-size Search (SASS) has been developed where the temporary neighborhood of a particle p_i is determined by the distance between itself and a randomly selected sample particle s_i of the population during each iteration [3].

At the beginning of a search, this distance is likely to be large, because the initial population is uniformly distributed over the search space and the chances are high that s_i is drawn from a different region within the input space. When the search is progressing, each particle is attracted by a local optimum and hence the population is clustered around a number of optima. If both, p_i and s_i are located in different clusters, p_i has the chance to escape its local optimum if it samples from a region with a higher fitness, i.e. lower costs. Towards the end of the search, most particles have reached the region of the global optimum and hence their mean distance is much smaller than in the initial population. As a result, the maximum step size s_{max} is sufficiently small to yield the global optimum. Figure 2 shows pseudo code of the algorithm.

```
Procedure selfAdaptiveStepSizeSearch
Begin
   initialise population of n particles
   While stopping criterion not met
   Begin
     For every particle p in population
     Begin
       select random particle s ≠ p
       For every component pᵢ in particle p
       Begin
           sₘₐₓ ← | pᵢ - sᵢ |
           generate random value r ∈ [-sₘₐₓ; +sₘₐₓ]
           p'ᵢ ← pᵢ + r
       End
       If f(p') better than f(p) then p ← p'
     End
   End
   Return best result
End
```

Figure 2 Pseudo code of the basic SASS algorithm.

SASS has two control parameters that have to be chosen in advance, the number of particles n in the population and the number of iterations of the algorithm. Although the algorithm is very simple, it has been shown that it is capable to find near optimal solutions.

In order to demonstrate the effectiveness and the efficiency of SASS, a set of experiments was conducted using two well-established standard test functions, the inverted Schwefel function and the inverted Griewank function [7]. The first test function, the n-dimensional inverted Schwefel function (1), was chosen because of its interesting characteristic that the second best optimum is located far away from the global optimum, which can cause an optimization algorithm to converge towards one of the local optima. The global optimum of zero is located at the coordinate x=(420.969, 420.969, ...).

$$f(x) = 418.98288n + \sum_{i=1}^{n} -x_i \sin(\sqrt{|x_i|}) \tag{1}$$

Where: $-500 \leq x_i \leq +500$

The second test function, the n-dimensional inverted Griewank function (2), was chosen because the product term introduces a correlation between the function variables and hence a high degree of epistasis [8]. This can disrupt optimization techniques that work on one function's variable at a time.

$$f(x) = 1 + \sum_{i=1}^{n} \frac{x_i^2}{4000} - \prod_{i=1}^{n} \cos(\frac{x_i}{\sqrt{i}}) \qquad (2)$$

Where: $-30 \le x_i \le +30$

The global optimum of zero is located at the point x=(0, 0, ...). There are many local optima in the landscape of this function. An increase in the number of variables decreases the number of local optima since it makes the function surface flat. The 2, 5, and 10 dimensional versions of both test functions have been used. The population sizes were varied from 3 to 30 particles and every experiment was repeated 100 times in order to prove reproducibility. The number of iterations was constant for all the experiments. Figure 3a shows the average costs of the 100 experiments per population size for the different versions of the Schwefel function, whereas Figure 3b shows the same for the different versions of the Griewank function.

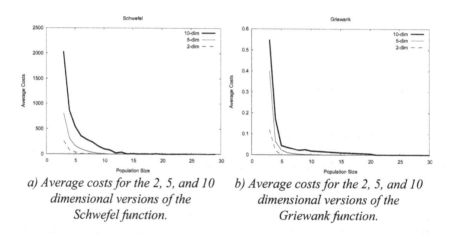

a) Average costs for the 2, 5, and 10 dimensional versions of the Schwefel function.

b) Average costs for the 2, 5, and 10 dimensional versions of the Griewank function.

Figure 3 Results of the experiments with the basic SASS algorithm.

As it can be seen, SASS was able to find the global optima with a very high reproducibility of about 99%, provided that the population sizes used exceeded a certain minimum. For example, for the 2 dimensional Schwefel function, the algorithm proved to be very robust if the population size was greater than 12, whereas for the 10 dimensional version, it was necessary to use population sizes greater than 20. Similar behavior was observed for the different versions of the Griewank function. The need for selecting the number of iterations and for guessing a suitable number of particles in the population makes SASS less usable as an 'out of the box' black-box optimization algorithm.

This disadvantage of pre-setting the number of iterations is overcome in the SASS2 algorithm. This will be explained in section 2.4. The next section explains the stopping criterion of SASS2, which can detect convergence of the algorithm.

2.3 Stopping Criterion

For an efficient algorithm, it is important to detect when the algorithm is converged in order to avoid unnecessary computational costs. In this section, a typical search run of SASS for the 2 dimensional Schwefel function is analyzed and a stopping criterion is derived from the analysis.

Figure 4a shows the development of the average costs of the population and the lowest costs found in a population over time, i.e. iterations. It can be seen that the population converged after approximately 800 iterations. Figure 4b shows the actual development of the average s_{max} in the population over time for the same search run. It can be seen that it starts off with relatively large values compared to the size of the input space and that it finally settles on very small numbers after approximately 800 iterations. This is in line with Figure 5a, which shows that the population has converged after approximately 800 iterations. Figure 5a shows a contour plot of the initial population for the same search run. Here, Parameter 1 and Parameter 2 are the input parameters of the 2 dimensional Schwefel function. It can be seen that the population is more or less uniformly distributed over the input space, although no particle starts near the global optimum at (420.969, 420.969).

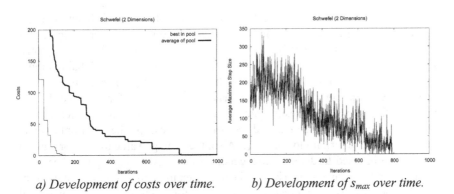

a) Development of costs over time.   b) Development of s_{max} over time.

Figure 4 *Typical run of SASS algorithm for the 2 dimensional Schwefel function.*

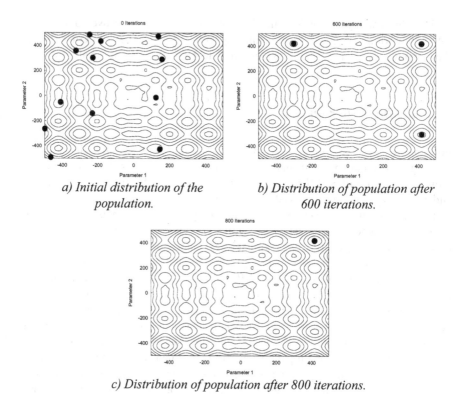

a) Initial distribution of the
population.

b) Distribution of population after
600 iterations.

c) Distribution of population after 800 iterations.

Figure 5 Contour plot of population over time.

After 600 iterations, all particles have settled into three different clusters (Figure 5b), which are located relatively far away from each other. Algorithms like GA, SA, and HC would be very unlikely to escape from the local optima, while SASS was able to achieve this and to converge towards the global optimum after about 800 iterations (Figure 5c). In other words, whereas these large distances between the clusters would make it impossible for SA and HC to converge, for SASS they result into large values for s_{max} for particles from different clusters, and hence enabled the particles to escape the local optima and hence enable the algorithm to converge. Also, the average value of s_{max} for a given iteration can be used to detect convergence: if the average s_{max} approaches zero, the algorithm has converged. This has been chosen to be the stopping criterion for SASS2. The next section presents a heuristic for determining the number of particles needed for a given optimization problem.

2.4 Population Size

The chosen population size is curial for the success of SASS: if the population is too small, the algorithm might converge towards a local optimum rather than towards the global one. If the population size is chosen to be too large, this leads to inefficiency of the search. Therefore, a method for automatically determining a population size that is as small as possible and as large as necessary for a given optimization problem is needed.

In order to develop a method for determining the population size needed for a particular problem, a set of experiment was carried out on a 10 dimensional version of the Schwefel function and a five dimensional version of the Griewank function. For the Schwefel function the population size was varied from 10 to 20 and for the Griewank function from five to 15. The average s_{max} stopping criterion was used for both functions. Each experiment was repeated 10 times and the results are given in Figure 6 below. Figure 6a shows the average costs achieved versus population size for both functions, Figure 6b shows the achieve standard deviation versus population size for both functions and Figure 6c presents the average number of iterations needed to converge versus population size for both functions.

It can be observed from Figure 6 that there is a strong correlation between the average costs and the standard deviation for both functions, whereas no correlation exists between these two factors and the average number of iterations. This means, in Figure 6, both the costs and the standard deviation approach zero if 15 particles are used for the Schwefel function and if nine particles are used for the Griewank function. The average costs achieved over a number of trials and the achieved standard deviation, can be used to determine the optimal population size. However, because in a typical application, there is no target value for the costs but an ideal standard deviation, i.e. zero, the standard deviation is used to determine the optimum population size: starting with a population size that is equal to the dimensionality of the problem, a number of trials is carried out an the standard deviation is calculated. If the standard deviation is greater than zero, the population size is increased by one and another set of trials is carried out. This will be repeated until the standard deviation approaches zero.

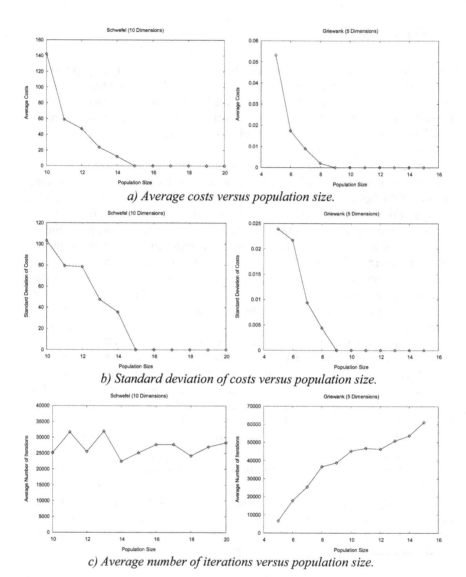

a) *Average costs versus population size.*

b) *Standard deviation of costs versus population size.*

c) *Average number of iterations versus population size.*

Figure 6 Experimental results for determining the population size.

2.5 SASS2 Algorithm

The SASS2 algorithm combines the SASS algorithm with the stopping criterion derived from section 2.3 and the heuristic for determining the population size, developed in section 2.4. Figure 7 gives the pseudo code of the new SASS2 algorithm.

```
Procedure selfAdaptiveStepSizeSearch2
Begin
  population n ← number of dimensions of search problem
  standard deviation std ← ∞
  While std > 0
  Begin
    For m iterations
    Begin
      initialise population of n particles
      While average s_max > 0
      Begin
        For every particle p in population
        Begin
          select random particle s ≠ p
          For every component p_i in particle p
          Begin
            s_max ← | p_i - s_i |
            generate random value r ∈ [-s_max; +s_max]
            p'_i ← p_i + r
          End
          If f(p') better than f(p) then p ← p'
        End
        calculate average s_max for iteration
      End
    End
    calculate std for m iterations
    n ← n + 1
  End
  Return best result
End
```

Figure 7 Pseudo code of the SASS2 algorithm.

3 Conclusion

This paper introduced SASS2, a novel population based Hill-Climbing algorithm with a self-adaptive step size, a well-defined stopping criterion and a heuristic for determining the population size needed for a particular application. The algorithm is control parameter free and hence can be used by inexperienced practitioners as a black-box optimizer, without the need for becoming an expert in computational optimization. Other optimization algorithms usually require a large number of experiments in order to find a suitable control parameter set, which can be seen as an optimization problem itself and hence requires a considerable amount of time and afford. This is a real obstacle for practitioners who simply want to use heuristic search as a problem-solving black-box tool. The advantage of the SASS2 algorithm is that it is fully self adaptive whilst still effective and efficient. There is a computational overhead caused by the fact that a number of trials are needed to determine the optimum number of particles in the populations, but this can easily be overcome by using parallel computing, which SASS2 is very well suited for.

References

1. Goldberg, D.E.: Genetic Algorithms in Search, Optimization and Machine Lerning, Addison-Wesley, 1989
2. Kirkpatrick, S., Gelatt Jr, C. D., Vecchi, M. P.: Optimization by Simulated Annealing, Science, 13 May 1983, Vol. 220, No. 4598, pp 671-680
3. Nolle, L.: On a Hill-Climbing Algorithm with Adaptive Step Size: Towards a Control Parameter-Less Black-Box Optimisation Algorithm, In Reusch, B. (ed) Computational Intelligence, Theory and Applications, Springer, 2006
4. Nolle, L.: SASS Applied to Optimum Work Roll Profile Selection in the Hot Rolling of Wide Steel, Knowledge-Based Systems, Vol. 20, Issue 2, March 2007, pp 203-208
5. Nolle, L.: SASS Applied to Automated Langmuir Probe Tuning, Proceedings of Asia Modelling Symposium 2007, Phuket, Thailand, 27-30 March, 2007, pp 421-425
6. Nolle, L.: On the Effect of Step Width Selection Schemes on the Performance of Stochastic Local Search Strategies, Proceedings of the 18th European Simulation Multiconference, Magdeburg, Germany, 13-14 June 2004, pp 149-153
7. Muehlenbein H.: Evolution in Time and Space - the Parallel Genetic Algorithm. In: Rawlins G.J.E. (ed) Foundations of Genetic Algorithms, Morgan Kaufmann, 1991
8. Davidor Y.: Epistasis Variance: Suitability of a Representation to Genetic Algorithms. Complex Systems, Vol. 4, 1990, pp 369-383

ARGUMENTATION AND NEGOTIATION

PISA - Pooling Information from Several Agents: Multiplayer Argumentation from Experience

Maya Wardeh, Trevor Bench-Capon and Frans Coenen[1]

Abstract In this paper a framework, PISA (*Pooling Information from Several Agents*), to facilitate multiplayer (three or more protagonists), "argumentation from experience" is described. Multiplayer argumentation is a form of dialogue game involving three or more players. The PISA framework is founded on a two player argumentation framework, PADUA (*Protocol for Argumentation Dialogue Using Association Rules*), also developed by the authors. One of the main advantages of both PISA and PADUA is that they avoid the resource intensive need to predefine a knowledge base, instead data mining techniques are used to facilitate the provision of "just in time" information. Many of the issues associated with multiplayer dialogue games do not present a significant challenge in the two player game. The main original contributions of this paper are the mechanisms whereby the PISA framework addresses these challenges.

1 Introduction

In many situations agents need to pool their information in order to solve a problem. For example in the field of classification one agent may have a rule that will give the classification, but that agent may be unaware of the facts which will enable the rule to be applied, whereas some other agent does know these facts. Individually neither can solve the problem, but together they can. One method to facilitate information sharing is to enable a dialogue between the two agents. Often this dialogue takes the form of a persuasion dialogue where two agents act as advocates for alternative points of view. A survey of such approaches is given in (Prakken 2006). The systems discussed by Prakken suppose that agent knowledge is represented in the form of belief bases, essentially a set of rules and facts. In consequence dialogue moves are strongly related to knowledge represented in this form. A typical set of moves for the systems in (Prakken 2006) are:

- *Claim P*: P is the head of some rule
- *Why P*: Seeks the body of rule for which P is head
- *Concede P*: agrees that P is true

---

[1] Department of Computer Science, The University of Liverpool, UK.

- *Retract P*: denies that *P* is true
- *P since S*: A rule with *P* head and *S* body.

In (Wardeh et al, 2007, 2008) we introduced an alternative basis for such persuasion dialogues to enable what we termed arguing from experience to solve classification problems. Here the agents do not have belief bases, but only a database of previous examples. When presented with a new case the agents use data mining techniques to discover associations between features of the case under consideration and the appropriate classification according to their previous experience. We argued that this has several advantages:

- Such arguments are often found in practice: many people do not develop a theory from their experience, but when confronted with a new problem recall past examples;
- It avoids the knowledge engineering bottleneck that occurs when belief bases must be constructed;
- There is no need to commit to a theory in advance of the discussion: the information can be deployed as best meets the need of the current situation;
- It allows agents to share experiences that may differ: one agent may have encountered types of case that another has not.

The moves made in arguments based directly on examples contrast with those found in persuasion dialogues based on belief bases, and have a strong resemblance to those used in case based reasoning systems, e.g. (Ashley 1990) and (Aleven 1997). The work in (Wardeh et al 2007, 2008) describes an implementation allowing argumentation from experience of this sort, called PADUA (Protocol for Argumentation Dialogue Using Association Rules). PADUA, however, is, like the systems of (Prakken 2006), restricted to just two agents. In this paper we extend the approach to allow a number of agents to participate in the discussion.

The rest of this paper is orgnaised as follows: *Section 2* will motivate the need for the extension to more than two players, and discuss some of the key issues involved in doing so. *Section 3* will briefly describe the distinctive argument moves made in PADUA and *Section 4* will recall the two player PADUA protocol. *Section 5* describes the changes made to the two player version to allow multiple participants. Finally *Section 6* offers some concluding remarks.

2 Need for Multiparty Dialogue

The focus of argumentation dialogues in work on agents has largely been limited to two party dialogues. Typically these dialogues have been adversarial. In practice, however, such dialogues can take place with more than two parties. The two party scenario is not always the ideal way to handle certain situations. For some classification problems there may be a set of possibilities, and it is desirable to allow each possibility to have its own advocate, so that each possibility can be given fair consideration. Examples are numerous. In debates within political institutions the representatives of different parties and factions may look at the same issue from several different angles, and each propose different solutions. In medicine, several diseases may share similar symptoms. Hence doctors may confuse one with the other and only by consulting and arguing with each other can the right diagnosis can emerge. At an everyday level, consider a group of friends, each with their own favourite restaurant, deciding where to eat. By allowing these parties to all take part in the dialogue they can pool their experience, increase their chances of winning over their opponents, and of the correct solution being reached.

The above real life examples not only illustrate the frequency and importance of multiparty argumentation dialogues, but also highlight several issues that must be taken into consideration when trying to model and implement multiparty dialogues in general and argumentation dialogue in particular. There are several different models for multi-party dialogue: formal meetings, informal meetings, bulletin boards, seminars, brainstorming sessions and so on. Some of the most important issues arising from this variety of models are discussed in (Dignum and Vreeswijk 2004). For each of these issues, choices must be made to yield a particular flavour of dialogue. The most important features for our purposes here are:

1. *System openness*: multiparty argumentation can either be closed, which means that the dialogue starts with n players and continues with n players until it is terminated, so that new participants are not allowed to join the dialogue once it has started, and players cannot leave the dialogue while it is in progress. Open systems are rather the opposite as players in such systems are free to join in or leave whenever they want.
2. *Players' roles*: in 2-party argumentation dialogues the roles of players are limited to one proponent and one opponent, while in multiparty argumentation dialogues the situation is more complicated. We may have several proponents and several opponents of the thesis. Alternatively we may have several participants each with their own distinct option. Also, some parties within the dialogue can take a neutral point of view, or stand as mediator between the opposing parties (other dialectical roles may also be taken into consideration). Also, linguistically speaking, in two player dialogues one (and only one) player can speak per turn (be the speaker) while the other listens (be the listener or hearer). In multiparty dialogues there can be more than one hearer per turn, and the roles of those hearers may also vary (e.g. addressee, auditor, over-hearer etc...). Besides, one can argue that there can be more than one speaker per turn, since in real life people may start talking at the same time, or interrupt each other, or even start yelling at each other --- the loudest winning the situation!
3. *Addressing*: this is also a solved issue in 2-party dialogues, which one can picture as two players facing each other so when one talks the other realizes this and starts to listen! In multiparty dialogue the issue of deciding to whom a player is addressing his speech is not as clear. Different strategies can be used

to solve this problem. These include: public broadcasting where all the players listen to what the speaker is saying; or targeted broadcasting of the *speech act* to some players (but not all of them); or just addressing the speech act to one particular player. In some situations the possibility of private communication can play an important strategic role.

4. *Turn taking*: In 2-party dialogues "turn switching" is straightforward, the listener becomes the speaker when the current speaker finishes. This is not the case in multiparty dialogue, as more than one player may wish to talk at the same time and they all may request to take the next turn. In argumentation the decision whether the turn can be given to some player, or to more than one player at the same time, or whether the turn passes from one player to another in a certain order can greatly influence the final result of the argumentation process. Additional turn taking can give rise to significant fairness issues.

5. *Termination*: The termination of 2-party argumentation dialogues happens once one of them has convinced the other (or once one of them has run out of things to say). In multiparty argumentation the dialogue may be terminated either when *all* the other players are convinced or once the *majority* of them are. Another issue regarding termination is that sometimes players may fail to convince each other and could end up playing for ever; therefore there should be a mechanism to end such dialogues. Finally in some scenarios the game may end without one single player winning the majority of other players' votes: in these cases there should also be a mechanism to determine the winner of the game or simply by allowing ties to take place.

In the following we shall first recapitulate the current framework of the PADUA protocol and then describe the developments we have made in order to be able to host multiplayer argumentation dialogue games.

3 Arguing from Experience

In this section we consider what speech acts will be used of dialogues attempting to argue from experience. One field in which arguing on the basis of precedent examples is of importance is common law. Important work has been carried out by, amongst others Ashley (Ashley 1990) and Aleven (Aleven 1997). What has emerged from this work is there are three key types of move:

- Citing a case
- Distinguishing a case
- Providing a Counter Example

We will discuss each of these in turn, anticipating the next section by indicating in brackets the corresponding speech acts in the PADUA protocol described in section 4. One difference with case based reasoning that should be noted is that in argumentation from experience the whole database is used rather than identifying a single case as a "*precedent*". Unlike legal decisions the authority comes from the frequency of occurrence in the set of examples rather than endorsement of a particular decision by an appropriate court.

In legal argument, citing a case involves identifying a previous case with a particular outcome which has features in common with the case under consideration. Given the things in common, the suggestion is that the outcome should be the same. Applied to argumentation from experience in the case of classification, the argument is something like: *in my experience, typically things with these features are Cs: the current example has those features, so it is a C* (propose rule[2]). The features in common are thus presented as reasons for classifying the example as C, justified by the experience of previous examples with these features. Distinguishing is one way of objecting to this, giving reasons why the example being considered does not conform to this pattern. It often involves pointing to features present in the case which make it atypical, so that the "typical" conclusions do not follow. For example the feature may indicate an exception: *although typically things with these features are Cs, this is not so when this additional feature is present* (distinguish). As an example, swans are typically white, but this is not so for Australian swans. Another form of distinction is to find a missing feature that suggests that the case is not typical: *while things with these features are typically Cs, Cs with these features normally have some additional feature, but this is not present in the current example* (unwanted consequences). A third kind of distinction would be to supply a more typical case: *while many things with these features are Cs, experience would support the classification more strongly if some additional feature were also present* (increase confidence).

Thus we have three types of distinction, with differing strengths: (i) that the current example is an exception to the rule proposed; (ii) that there are reasons to think the case untypical, and so that it may be an exception to the rule proposed; and (iii) that the confidence in the classification would be increased if some additional features were present. In all cases, the appropriate response is to try to refine the proposed set of reasons to meet the objections and thus accommodate the exception. Confidence in arguments is important: arguments from experience are usually associated with a degree of confidence: experience will suggest that things with certain features are often/usually/almost always/without exception Cs. This is also why dialogues to enable experience to be pooled are important: one participant's experience will be based on a different sample from that of another's. In extreme cases one person may have had no exposure to a certain class of exceptions: a person classifying swans with experience only of the Northern hemisphere needs

---

[2] Note that "rule" in this context is not an axiom of a theory. Rules are merely proposed as a way of deciding the current case. They function in the same way as the decision rules or tests proposed in oral argument in US Supreme Court hearings, designed to serve as the basis for further probing (Ashley et al 2007) to see whether the test can be used.

this to be supplemented with experience of Australian swans. In less extreme cases, it may only be the confidence in the classification that varies.

Counter examples differ from distinctions in that they do not attempt to cast doubt on the reasons, but suggest that there are better reasons for believing the contrary. The objection here is something like: *while these features do typically suggest that the thing is a C, these other features typically suggest that it is not* (counter rule). Here the response is either to argue about the relative confidence in the competing reasons, or to attempt to distinguish the counter example. Thus a dialogue supporting argument from experience will need to accommodate these moves: in the next section we will describe how they are realized in the PADUA protocol.

4 PADUA Protocol

PADUA (*Protocol for Argumentation Dialogue Using Association Rules*) is an argumentation protocol designed to enable participants to debate on the basis of their experience. PADUA has as participants agents with distinct datasets of records relating to a classification problem. These agents produce reasons for and against classifications by mining association rules from their datasets using data mining techniques (Agrawal 1993, Goulbourne et al 1999, Coenen et al. 2004). By "*association rule*" we mean that the antecedent is a set of reasons for believing the consequent. In what follows $P \rightarrow Q$ should be read as "P are reasons to believe Q". A full description of PADUA is given in (Wardeh et al 2008).

PADUA adopts six dialogue moves, related to the argument moves identified in the previous section:

1. *Propose Rule*: allows generalizations of experience to be cited, by which a new association with a confidence higher than a certain threshold is proposed.
2. *Attacking moves:* these pose the different types of distinction mentioned above:

    – *Distinguish*: When a player p plays a *distinguish* move, it adds some new premise(s) to a previously proposed rule, so that the confidence of the new rule is lower than the confidence of the original rule.
    – *Counter Rule*: is very similar to *propose rule* and is used to cite generalizations leading to a different classification
    – *Unwanted Consequences*: Here the player p suggests that certain consequences (conclusions) of the rule under discussion do not match the case under consideration.

3. *Refining moves:* these moves enable a rule to be refined to meet objections:

    – *Increase Confidence*: a player p adds one or more premise(s) to a rule it had previously played to increase the confidence of this rule.

- *Withdraw unwanted consequences*: a player *p* plays this move to exclude the unwanted consequences of the rule it previously proposed, while maintaining a certain level of confidence.

The PADUA protocol defines for each of those six moves a set of legal next moves (i.e. moves that can possibly follow this move). Table 1 summarizes PADUA protocol rules, and indicates whether a new rule is introduced.

Move	Label	Next Move	New Rule
1	Propose Rule	3, 2, 4	Yes
2	Distinguish	3, 5, 1	No
3	Unwanted Cons	6, 1	No
4	Counter Rule	3, 2, 1	Nested dialogue
5	Increase Conf	3, 2, 4	Yes
6	Withdraw Unwanted Cons	3, 2, 4	Yes

Table 1. The protocol legal moves

5 PISA

Extending the PADUA system based on two players to support many players is not a trivial task, as there are a number of problems that need to be resolved, in particular:

1. PADUA is a closed system with exactly two players;
2. Limited players' roles: Roles in the present PADUA systems are very restricted, in virtue of the simplicity inherent in two player games. Thus decisions have to be made about turn taking, and the addressing issues discussed above;
3. The lack of a powerful control structure: The existing PADUA implementation is not provided with any sophisticated control structure, as in two player games everything is simple, from turn taking which is obvious as no choice as to who will have the next turn is needed, to addressing which basically follows the model of face to face conversations, to game termination, which occurs when a player runs out of moves. This simplicity of two player games does not apply to multiplayer situations, which needs more careful surveillance and enforcement to guarantee that everything goes according to the design choices made with respect to the player roles and the conduct of the dialogue.

Therefore it is very important to resolve these issues before extending PADUA to support multiparty argumentation dialogues. The changes to be introduced to PADUA system should not affect the basic protocol structure (i.e. the moves and rule mining), but rather complement the existing PADUA protocol with a control structure that makes it possible to organize the players and their turns within the games, and to identify the termination conditions for those games. Therefore we must first decide on the type of dialogue we will aim to produce, in terms of the issues identified in section 2. We will refer to this multiplayer version as PISA (*Pooling Information from Several Agents*).

The dialogue we will model is one where there are a range of options for classification, and each of the indefinite number of participants is the advocate of one of these options. Additionally there will be one agent, the chairperson, who will not be the advocate of any position, but rather manage the dialogue and facilitate communication between the advocates. This style of dialogue thus determines the roles of the players: a chairperson, and, for every option, one player acting as its advocate. Alternative models, where we might have several supporters for a particular option are no less valid, but we need to fix on one style of dialogue. The dialogue will be open, in that a participant (other than the chair) may enter or leave when they wish. For turn taking, we adopt a structure with rounds, rather than a linear structure where a given agent is selected as the next speaker. In each round, any agent who can make a move can do so: the chair then updates a central argument structure, and another round occurs. This is not perhaps the most usual structure for human meetings, but it can be found in some board games such as *Diplomacy*. We believe that the structure is particularly appropriate in order to achieve fairness in our situation where every advocate is playing for themselves, and has to regard every other advocate as an opponent (even though they may temporarily focus their efforts on a particular opponent). For addressing, every move after the first attacks a move of some other agent: that agent can be regarded as the addressee of that move, and the others as auditors. The game will terminate when no agent makes a contribution for two rounds (to ensure that they have really finished and not withheld a move for tactical reasons) or after some limiting number of rounds have been played. The model is essentially that of a facilitated discussion, with the chairperson acting as facilitator. We will now discuss the realization of this model, and the choices summarized above, in more detail in the following sub-sections.

5.1 Control Structure

The suggested control structure (Figure 1) can be pictured as a meeting room in which players can be seated and equipped with a blackboard like structure on which players can place their arguments (moves). The meeting is guided by a chairperson responsible for: organizing the dialogue, monitoring the players, controlling the turn taking procedure and applying the protocol rules. There is no distinction between the players other than their points of view regarding the case under discussion. When a new game commences the chairperson randomly chooses one player to start the dialogue; in the meeting room scenario this player (P_1) is given the first seat on the meeting table; the rest of the players are seated randomly around the table and given according names $(P_2 \dots P_n)$. Then P_1 proposes a new rule and pastes it on a black board, this is called the first argumentation round (R_1). The game continues in the same manner, and in each of the following rounds all the players who can and wish to attack any of the arguments played in the previous turn(s) are allowed to place their arguments (moves) on the black board. The suggested facilitated discussion scenario enjoys the following advantages:

1. It increases the flexibility of the overall PISA system: by assigning the majority of protocol surveillance to the chairperson the system gains great flexibility. For example the system can be switched between closed and open by applying a few limited changes to the chairperson, while the rest of the players remain unaffected.
2. It is a very simple structure: there is no complicated turn taking procedure involving a choice of the next player, allowing the internal implementation of the players to be kept as simple as possible.
3. It provides a fair dialogue environment: the organizational configuration of the dialogue is neutralized by restricting the control tasks to the chairperson who is not allowed to take sides in the dialogue. This means that no one can be privileged to speak while the others must remain silent.

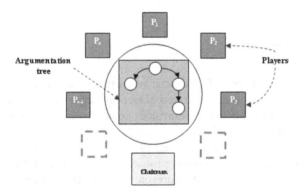

Fig. 1. The Suggested Structure

5.2 Turn Taking Policy

There is no strict turn taking procedure in PISA; any player who can make a legal move can participate in any round. There is no limitation on the number of players that can participate in a round, but each player is limited to one move per round:

the reason behind this restriction is mainly to simplify the dialogue, and contain the growth of the argument tree and repetition of moves within reasonable bounds.

This turn taking policy gives great freedom for players to apply their strategy in the way they think best to win the game; it also simplifies the game. Besides, if a strict turn taking procedure was applied it may affect the final result of the game, for example when the turn goes back to some player, the arguments against its proposition may be so numerous that deciding which one to defend against may be difficult. Also a player may not be able to defend itself against some attacks in its own turn, but might be able to do that after some other players have moved, In general the turn taking technique adopted here enjoys the following advantages:

1. It allows for turn skipping: Players who do not want to take part in a particular round can remain silent. (Although they can only remain silent for a limited number of rounds otherwise they will eventually lose).
2. Participants can play their attacks/counter attacks as soon as they want and they do not have to wait for an opportunity to contribute.
3. This way we solve the justice issue that rises from the fact that the turn taking process requires that some agent be favoured with the chance to speak. With turn taking a player can lose a game just because it is not given the opportunity to present its case at a favourable time. In other words all the players, under this policy, have an equal chance to win the game.

5.3 Game Termination

The chairperson terminates a PISA game when two rounds have passed and the argument state has not changed (i.e. no player has anything to say). The reason behind waiting two rounds is that sometimes some players (who are still capable of arguing) may choose to skip some rounds for strategic reasons. Therefore, if a round is passed without any move being played, the chairperson has to warn all the players that if they have anything to say the next round would be the last chance for them to say if they wish to prevent the game from ending.

Termination as described above is called "*legal termination*", but there are also cases in which the game should be exceptionally terminated (i.e. *exceptional termination*); the chairperson has the authority to terminate the game if any of the following events occur:

1. If only one player remains active after all the other players have withdrawn (in which case the surviving player wins the game).
2. If the game has taken more than n rounds (assuming that if the parties could not agree in n rounds were n is sufficiently large then they will not ever agree). In

this case no one wins the game. Of course, the value of n can differ from game to game, but it should allow for a large number of rounds.

5.4 Roles of the Players

Roles in PADUA are limited due to the inherent simplicity of two-player games, but in PISA more attention has to be paid to roles, and more importantly the way these roles change from round to round. The main distinction in players' roles is between attackers and defenders and between speakers and listeners as follows:

1. *Attacker(s) vs. defender(s):* while players are most certainly defenders of their point of views, they can take different positions regarding other players' proposals, therefore each player can decide whether to attack or defend other players' arguments. Enabling players to defend the arguments of other players (supposedly, and in the long term, their opponents) may be of strategic importance within the game. For example weak players may join forces to defeat stronger players, or a player may help another player to defeat a common opponent that it cannot defeat on its own. Once that opponent has been eliminated the remaining players can then attack one another.

2. *Speaker(s) vs. Listener(s) (addressee(s))***: in the first round of PISA there is only one speaker (P_1) while the rest of the players are addressees (the chairperson may be considered as an auditor). In all the subsequent rounds there are s speakers (where $s <= m$ number of players) where s is the number of the players participating in the given round. Once the speakers are done with their moves the addressees of the round are defined as the players whose arguments were attacked in this round and the rest of the players (i.e. those who did not participate and were not attacked in the given round) are assumed to be auditors.

5.5 Argumentation Tree

In PISA the notion of *Argumentation Tree* is used to describe the data structure used to represent the arguments played in each round, and the attack relations between those arguments. This tree acts as a mediating artifact for the dialogue as described in (Olivia et al 2008). Hence it is similar to other tree structures used in the literature, but this particular tree differs from other data structures because:

1. It consists of arguments played by more than one player
2. It implements three colours to mark the status of the arguments played so far.
3. It contains two types of links: explicit links (edges) and implicit links.

The *PISA Argumentation Tree* data structure consists of:

1. *Nodes*: represent the moves (i.e. arguments) played so far; each node has a number representing the player (the full structure of the node is described in the following subsection). The colour of the nodes changes from round to round as defined in the following Table 2:
2. *Links*: represent the explicit attack relationship between the nodes.
3. *Green Confidence*: is a global value (a real number) associated with the tree representing the highest confidence of the undefeated nodes (representing moves of types: 1, 4, 5 and 6 in Table 1). This value helps in defining the implicit attack relationships across multiple rounds (instead of physically representing those relationships as links in the tree).

Colour	Meaning	Shifting to
Green	The node is undefeated in the given round, and was added by one of the moves 1, 4, 5 and 6	(to red) If attacked by at least one undefeated node.
Red	The node is defeated in the given round.	(To green) if all attacks against a node are successfully defeated and the original node colour was green.
		(To blue) if all attacks against a node are successfully defeated and the original node colour was blue.
Blue	The node is undefeated in the given round, but nodes of this colour do not enforce new rules, their sole purpose is simply to undermine an argument played by another player using moves 2 and 3.	(To red) If attacked by at least one undefeated node.

Table 2. The Argumentation Tree Colours

When player P_i plays some move (m), this move must satisfy a number of conditions in order to be added as a node to the argumentation tree, otherwise the move will be rejected. The conditions of acceptance are as follows:

1. Move m is added to the tree if and only if it changes the colouring of the tree (consequently a player can not add an argument that enhances its position in the game if such a move does not change the tree colouring).
2. A player can put forward one move only per round (deciding which rule to play is strategy issue).
3. Moves (1, 4, 5, 6) implicitly attack all the other (1, 4, 5, 6) moves played by other players which have lower confidence.
4. Moves (2, 6) affect only the nodes they directly attack.
5. Moves (1, 4, 5, 6) explicitly attack the (2, 6) nodes they are associated with (if any).
6. Participants should not play moves that weaken their position (i.e. a player should not put forward moves that change the colouring of the argumentation

tree such that another player would take the lead). This condition holds when a player tries to attack blue nodes that were originally made to attack an argument proposed by other players.

5.6 *Winner Announcement*

Once a game has terminated, the chairperson consults the argumentation tree to determine the winner. The winner should satisfy one of the following rules:

1. If all the green nodes on the graph belong to the same player then this player wins the game.
2. If the green nodes on the graph belong to more than one player then the player which has played the green node with the highest confidence wins the game (as this node implicitly attacks the other nodes).
3. If there are no green nodes and all the blue nodes were played by the same player then this player wins the game.

Unfortunately not all the games end up with one clear winner, as there are cases where the decision as to who won the game may not be obvious. For example: If there is more than one green node with the same confidence on the argumentation tree at the end of the game belonging to different players and no green nodes with higher confidence. Also if the game ends without any green nodes on the argumentation tree and the blue ones belong to more than one player.

The first case is considered a *strong tie situation*, as the players have actually proposed classifications within the game. One possible solution may be starting a new game between the tying parties only and see how this game ends. But there is nothing to guarantee that this game will not also end up with a tie. In this case the chairperson may be forced to announce a tie (after the second game or after g number of mini games).

The second case is considered a *weak tie situation*, as the tied players did not actually have any proposed classifications at the end of the game. In such cases starting a new mini game may be of great benefit, but with the condition that the players should propose as many reasons for their classification as they can this time.

6 Conclusions

In this paper, PISA, a multiplayer argumentation from experience framework has been described and illustrated. The main original contribution of the paper is the mechanisms whereby the framework addresses the many challenges found in multiplayer dialogue games which are either not present in the two player game or are not of significance in the two player game. Of particular note is the control structure used in PISA, the turn taking policy, the approach to game termination and the definition of the roles of the players allowing them to adopt differing strategies. The supporting argumentation tree data structure is also significant. Current evaluation of the PISA implementation has provided the authors with encouraging results indicating that in its current form PISA is a genuinely useful tool to support agent based argumentation. The evaluation has also indicated areas for further investigation. These include the development of alternative game strategies, the potential for players to form dynamic groups and alliances and further variants on the current PISA model.

References

1. Agrawal R, Imielinski T, Swami A.N et al (1993). Association rules between sets of items in large databases. In: Proc. of ACM SIGMOD Int. Conf. on Management of Data, Washington, 207-216.
2. Aleven V (1997). Teaching Case Based Argumentation Through an Example and Models. PhD thesis, University of Pittsburgh, Pittsburgh, PA, USA.
3. Ashley K. D (1990). Modeling Legal Argument. MIT Press, Cambridge, MA, USA.
4. Coenen F. P, Leng P, Goulbourne G et al (2004). Tree Structures for Mining Association Rules. In: Journal of Data Mining and Knowledge Discovery, Vol 8, No 1, 25-51.
5. Dignum F and Vreeswijk G.A.W (2003). Towards a test bed for multi-party dialogues. In Advances in Agent Communication, F. Dignum, Ed. Springer Verlag. Berlin, 121-230.
6. Goulbourne G, Coenen F. P, Leng L et al (1999). Algorithms for Computing Association Rules Using a Partial Support Tree. In: Proc. of ES99, Springer, London, UK, 132-147.
7. Olivia, E, Viroli, M, Omicini and McBurney et al (2008). Argumentation and artifact for dialogue support. In Proc. ArgMAS 2008, the 5th Inter Workshop on Argumentation in Multi-Agent Systems, AAMAS 2008, Lisbon, Portugal.
8. Prakken H (2006). Formal systems for persuasion dialogue. In: The Knowledge Engineering Review 21, 163-188.
9. Wardeh, M, Bench-Capon, T, Coenen, F.P et al (2008). Arguments from Experience: The PADUA Protocol. To appear in Proc. COMMA'2008.
10. Wardeh, M, Bench-Capon, T, Coenen, F.P et al (2007). PADUA Protocol: Strategies and Tactics. In Proc. ECSQARU 2007, 9th European Conf. on Symbolic and Quantitative Approaches to Reasoning with Uncertainty, LNAI 4724: 465-476.

Agent-Based Negotiation in Uncertain Environments

John Debenham and Carles Sierra

Abstract An agent aims to secure his projected needs by attempting to build a set of (business) relationships with other agents. A relationship is built by exchanging private information, and is characterised by its intimacy — degree of closeness — and balance — degree of fairness. Each argumentative interaction between two agents then has two goals: to satisfy some immediate need, and to do so in a way that develops the relationship in a desired direction. An agent's desire to develop each relationship in a particular way then places constraints on the argumentative utterances. The form of negotiation described is argumentative interaction constrained by a desire to develop such relationships.

1 Introduction

This paper is in the area labelled: *information-based agency* [10]. An information-based agent has an identity, values, needs, plans and strategies all of which are expressed using a fixed ontology in probabilistic logic for internal representation and in an illocutionary language [9] for communication. All of the forgoing is represented in the agent's deliberative machinery. We assume that such an agent resides in a electronic institution [1] and is aware of the prevailing norms and interaction protocols.

[9] describes a rhetorical argumentation framework that supports argumentative negotiation. It does this by taking into account: the relative information gain of a new utterance, the relative semantic distance between an utterance and the dialogue history. Then [11] considered the affect that argumentative dialogue has on the ongoing *relationship* between a pair of negotiating agents. Neither of these contribu-

John Debenham

University of Technology, Sydney, Australia, e-mail: debenham@it.uts.edu.au and Carles Sierra
Institut d'Investigació en Intel·ligència Artificial - IIIA, Spanish Scientific Research Council, CSIC,08193 Bellaterra, Catalonia, Spain, e-mail: sierra@iiia.csic.es

tions addressed the relationship between argumentative utterances or strategies for argumentation.

This paper is based in rhetorical argumentation [8] — we attempt to edge our approach towards classical argumentation by modelling the criteria that the partner uses to gauge the effect of argumentation. For example, suppose I am shopping for a new car and have cited "suitability for a family" as a criterion. The salesman says "This LandMonster is great value.", and I reply "My grandmother could not climb into that." Classical argumentation may attempt to refute the matriarch's lack of gymnastic prowess or the car's inaccessibility. Taking a less confrontational and more constructively persuasive view we might note that this statement impacts negatively on the "suitability for a family" criterion, and attempt to counter that impact possibly with "Its been voted No 1 for children.". Although a smarter response may look for an argument that is semantically closer: "The car's height ensures a very comfortable ride over rough terrain that is popular with old people."

Our argumentation agent has to perform two key functions: to understand incoming utterances and to generate responses. In Section 2 we describe the communication model and an argumentation language that admits Prolog-like statements. The approach is founded on a model of contract acceptance that is described in Section 3. Section 4 details a scenario that provides the context for the discussion. Sections 5 and 6 consider the scenario from each side of the bargaining table. Reactive and proactive argumentation strategies are given in Section 7, and Section 8 concludes.

2 Communication Model

This paper is written from the point of view of an agent α that is engaged in argumentative interaction with agent β. The history of all argumentative exchanges is the agents' *relationship*. We assume that their utterances, u, can be organised into distinct dialogues, Ψ^t. For simplicity we assume that at most one dialogue exists at any time. We assume that α and β are negotiating with the mutual aim of signing a contract, where the contract will be an instantiation of the mutually-understood object $o(\Psi^t)$. We assume that this negotiation is taking place through the exchange of proposals accompanied by argumentative dialogue.

In order to define a language to structure agent dialogues we need an ontology that includes a (minimum) repertoire of elements: a set of *concepts* organised in a is-a hierarchy (e.g. platypus is a mammal, Australian-dollar is a currency), and a set of relations over these concepts (e.g. price(beer,AUD) [4]:

An ontology is a tuple $\mathcal{O} = (V, R, \leq, \sigma)$ where:

1. V is a finite set of concept symbols (including basic data types), i.e. a vocabulary;
2. R is a finite set of relation symbols;
3. $\leq$ is a reflexive, transitive and anti-symmetric relation on V (a partial order), and
4. $\sigma : R \to V^+$ is the function assigning to each relation symbol its arity

where $\leq$ is the traditional *is-a* hierarchy. To simplify computations in the computing of probability distributions we will assume that there is a number of disjoint *is-a* trees covering different ontological spaces (e.g. a tree for types of fabric, a tree for shapes of clothing, and so on). R contains relations between the concepts in the hierarchy, this is needed to define deals as tuples of issues. Semantic distance plays a fundamental role in strategies for information-based agency, see [10] for details.

The general argumentation language described here was first reported in [11]. The discussion is from the point of view of an information-based agent α in a multiagent system where α interacts with negotiating agents, β_i, and information providing agents, θ_j: $\{\alpha, \beta_1, \ldots, \beta_o, \theta_1, \ldots, \theta_t\}$.

The shape of the language that α uses to represent the information received and the content of its dialogues depends on two fundamental actions: (i) passing information, and (ii) exchanging proposals and contracts. A contract (a, b) between agents α and β is a pair where a and b represent the actions that agents α and β are responsible for respectively. *Contracts* signed by agents and *information* passed by agents, are similar to norms in the sense that they oblige agents to behave in a particular way, so as to satisfy the conditions of the contract, or to make the world consistent with the information passed. Contracts and Information can thus be thought of as normative statements that restrict an agent's behaviour.

α's communication language has two fundamental primitives: Commit(α, β, φ) to represent, in φ, the world that α aims at bringing about and that β has the right to verify, complain about or claim compensation for any deviations from, and Done(u) to represent the event that a certain action u^1 has taken place. In this way, norms, contracts, and information chunks will be represented as instances of Commit$(\cdot)$ where α and β are individual agents. Language $\mathscr{L}$ is the set of utterances u defined as:

$$u ::= illoc(\alpha, \beta, \varphi, t) \mid u; u \mid \textbf{Let } context \textbf{ In } u \textbf{ End}$$
$$\varphi ::= term \mid \text{Done}(u) \mid \text{Commit}(\alpha, \beta, \varphi) \mid \varphi \wedge \varphi \mid$$
$$\varphi \vee \varphi \mid \neg\varphi \mid \forall x.\varphi_x \mid \exists x.\varphi_x$$
$$context ::= \varphi \mid id = \varphi \mid prolog\_clause \mid context; context$$

where φ_x is a formula with free variable x, *illoc* is any appropriate set of illocutionary particles, ';' means sequencing, and *context* represents either previous agreements, previous illocutions, the ontological working context, that is a projection of the ontological trees that represent the focus of the conversation, or code that aligns the ontological differences between the speakers needed to interpret an (illocutionary) action u. Representing an ontology as a set predicates in Prolog is simple. The set *term* contains instances of the ontology concepts and relations.[2]

---

[1] Without loss of generality we will assume that all actions are dialogical.

[2] We assume the convention that $V(v)$ means that v is an instance of concept V and $r(v_1, \ldots, v_n)$ implicitly determines that v_i is an instance of the concept in the i-th position of the relation r.

3 Contract Acceptance

No matter what interaction strategy an agent uses, and no matter whether the communication language is that of simple bargaining or rich argumentation, a negotiation agent will have to decide whether or not to sign each contract on the table. We will argue in Section 5 that the buyer will be uncertain of his preferences in our Scenario described in Section 4. If an agent's preferences are uncertain then it may not make sense to link the agent's criterion for contract acceptance to a strategy that aims to optimise its utility. Instead, we pose the more general question: "how certain am I that $\delta = (\phi, \varphi)$ is a good contract to sign?" — under realistic conditions this may be easy to estimate. $\mathbb{P}^t(\text{sign}(\alpha, \beta, \chi, \delta))$ estimates the certainty, expressed as a probability, that α should sign[3] proposal δ in satisfaction of her need χ, where in (ϕ, φ) ϕ is α's commitment and φ is β's. α will accept δ if: $\mathbb{P}^t(\text{sign}(\alpha, \beta, \chi, \delta)) > c$, for some level of certainty c.

To estimate $\mathbb{P}^t(\text{sign}(\alpha, \beta, \chi, \delta))$, α will be concerned about what will occur if contract δ is signed. If agent α receives a commitment from β, α will be interested in any variation between β's commitment, φ, and what is actually observed, as the enactment, φ'. We denote the relationship between commitment and enactment:

$$\mathbb{P}^t(\text{Observe}(\alpha, \varphi') | \text{Commit}(\beta, \alpha, \varphi))$$

simply as $\mathbb{P}^t(\varphi' | \varphi) \in \mathcal{M}^t$, and now α has to estimate her belief in the acceptability of each possible outcome $\delta' = (\phi', \varphi')$. Let $\mathbb{P}^t(\text{acc}(\alpha, \chi, \delta'))$ denote α's estimate of her belief that the outcome δ' will be acceptable in satisfaction of her need χ, then we have:

$$\mathbb{P}^t(\text{sign}(\alpha, \beta, \chi, \delta)) = f(\mathbb{P}^t(\delta' | \delta), \mathbb{P}^t(\text{acc}(\alpha, \chi, \delta'))) \tag{1}$$

for some function f;[4] if f is the arithmetic product then this expression is mathematical expectation. f may be more sensitive; for example, it may be defined to ensure that no contract is signed if there is a significant probability for a catastrophic outcome.

There is no prescriptive way in which α should define $\mathbb{P}^t(\text{acc}(\alpha, \chi, \delta'))$, it is a matter for applied artificial intelligence to capture the essence of what matters in the application. In any real application the following three components at least will be required. $\mathbb{P}^t(\text{satisfy}(\alpha, \chi, \delta'))$ represents α's belief that enactment δ' will satisfy her need χ. $\mathbb{P}^t(\text{obj}(\delta'))$ represents α's belief that δ' is a fair deal against the open marketplace — it represents α's *objective* valuation. $\mathbb{P}^t(\text{sub}(\alpha, \chi, \delta'))$ represents α's belief that δ' is acceptable in her own terms taking account of her ability to meet her commitment ϕ [9] [10], and any way in which δ' has value to her personally[5] — it represents α's *subjective* valuation. That is:

---

[3] A richer formulation is $\mathbb{P}^t(\text{eval}(\alpha, \beta, \chi, \delta) = e_i)$ where eval$(\cdot)$ is a function whose range is some descriptive evaluation space containing terms such as "unattractive in the long term".

[4] β influences the equation in the sense that different βs yield different $\mathbb{P}^t(\delta' | \delta)$.

[5] For example, when buying a new digital camera, α may give a high subjective valuation to a camera that uses the same memory cards as her existing camera.

$$\mathbb{P}^t(\mathrm{acc}(\alpha,\chi,\delta')) = g(\mathbb{P}^t(\mathrm{satisfy}(\alpha,\chi,\delta')), \mathbb{P}^t(\mathrm{obj}(\delta')), \mathbb{P}^t(\mathrm{sub}(\alpha,\chi,\delta'))) \quad (2)$$

for some function g.

Suppose that an agent is able to estimate: $\mathbb{P}^t(\mathrm{satisfy}(\alpha,\chi,\delta'))$, $\mathbb{P}^t(\mathrm{obj}(\delta'))$ and $\mathbb{P}^t(\mathrm{sub}(\alpha,\chi,\delta'))$. The specification of the aggregating g function will then be a strictly subjective decision. A highly cautious agent may choose to define:

$$\mathbb{P}^t(\mathrm{acc}(\alpha,\chi,\delta')) = \begin{cases} 1 & \text{if: } \mathbb{P}^t(\mathrm{satisfy}(\alpha,\chi,\delta')) > \eta_1 \\ & \wedge\, \mathbb{P}^t(\mathrm{obj}(\delta')) > \eta_2 \wedge \mathbb{P}^t(\mathrm{sub}(\alpha,\chi,\delta')) > \eta_3 \\ 0 & \text{otherwise.} \end{cases}$$

for some threshold constants η_i. Whereas an agent that was prepared to permit some propagation of confidence from one factor to compensate another could define:

$$\mathbb{P}^t(\mathrm{acc}(\alpha,\chi,\delta')) = \mathbb{P}^t(\mathrm{satisfy}(\alpha,\chi,\delta'))^{\eta_1} \times \mathbb{P}^t(\mathrm{obj}(\delta'))^{\eta_2} \times \mathbb{P}^t(\mathrm{sub}(\alpha,\chi,\delta'))^{\eta_3}$$

where the η_i balance the influence of each factor.

The point of this is: if an agent aims to produce persuasive argumentative dialogue then in the absence of any specific information concerning the structure of g the agent should ignore g and concentrate on the three categories: $\mathbb{P}^t(\mathrm{satisfy}(\alpha,\chi,\delta'))$, $\mathbb{P}^t(\mathrm{obj}(\delta'))$ and $\mathbb{P}^t(\mathrm{sub}(\alpha,\chi,\delta'))$.

So how then will α specify: $\mathbb{P}^t(\mathrm{satisfy}(\alpha,\chi,\delta))$, $\mathbb{P}^t(\mathrm{sub}(\alpha,\chi,\delta))$ and $\mathbb{P}^t(\mathrm{obj}(\delta))$? Of these three factors only $\mathbb{P}^t(\mathrm{obj}(\delta))$ has a clear meaning, but it may only be estimated if there is sufficient market data available. In the case of selling sardines this may well be so, but in the case of Google launching a take-over bid for Microsoft it will not[6]. Concerning $\mathbb{P}^t(\mathrm{satisfy}(\alpha,\chi,\delta))$ and $\mathbb{P}^t(\mathrm{sub}(\alpha,\chi,\delta))$ we assume that an agent will somehow assess each of these as some combination of the confidence levels across a set of privately-known *criteria*. For example, if I am buying a camera then I may be prepared to define:

$$\mathbb{P}^t(\mathrm{satisfy}(\alpha,\chi,\delta)) = h(\mathbb{P}^t(\mathrm{easy\text{-}to\text{-}use}(\alpha,\delta)), \mathbb{P}^t(\mathrm{well\text{-}built}(\alpha,\delta))) \quad (3)$$

for some function h. Any attempt to model another agent's h function will be as difficult as modelling g above. *But*, it is perfectly reasonable to suggest that by observing my argumentative dialogue an agent could form a view as to which of these two criteria above was more important.

This paper considers how an agent may observe the argumentative dialogue with the aim of modelling, within each of the three basic factors, the partner's criteria and the relative importance of those criteria. In repeated dealings between two agents, this model may be strengthened when the objects of the successive negotiations are semantically close but not necessarily identical.

---

[6] In this example the subjective valuation will be highly complex.

4 The Scenario

Rhetorical argumentation is freed from the rigour of classical argumentation and descriptions of it can take the form of "this is how it works here" and "this is how it works there" without describing a formal basis. We attempt to improve on this level of vagary by using a general scenario and describing the behaviour of our agents within it.

In a general retail scenario there is a seller agent, α, and a buyer, β. The items for sale are abstracted from: digital cameras, mobile phones, PDAs, smart video recorders, computer software, sewing machines and kitchen mixers. The features of an item are those that are typically listed on the last few pages of an instruction booklet. For example, a camera's features could include the various shutter speeds that it is capable of, the various aperture settings, the number of years of warranty, and so on — together the *features* describe the capabilities of the item. For the purpose of comparison with other items, β will consider a particular item as a typed Boolean vector over the (possible) features of each item available, this vector shows which feature is present. The *state* of an item is then specified by identifying which of the item's features are 'on'. For example, the state of a camera could be: 'ready' with aperture set to 'f8' and shutter speed set to '1 500'th of a second'. In this scenario an *offer* is a pair (supply of a particular item, supply of some money) being α's and β's commitments respectively.

β may wish to know how well an item performs certain tasks. Software agents are not naturally endowed with the range of sensory and motor functions to enable such an evaluation. We imagine that the seller agent has an associated tame human who will demonstrate how the various items perform particular tasks on request, but performs no other function. We also imagine that the buyer agent has an associated tame human who can observe what is demonstrated, articulates an evaluation of it that is passed to its own agent, but performs no other function.

To simplify our set up we assume that the seller, α, is β's only source of information about what tasks each item can perform, and, as we describe below, what sequence of actions are necessary to make an item perform certain tasks[7]. That is, our multiagent system consists only of $\{\alpha, \beta\}$, and the buyer is denied access to product reviews, but *does* have access to market pricing data. This restriction simplifies the interactions and focusses the discussion on the argumentation.

For example, if the item is a camera the buyer may wish to observe how to set the camera's states so that it may be used for 'point-and-shoot' photography. If the item is a sewing machine she may wish to see how to make a button hole on a piece of cloth. If the item is graphics software she may wish to see how to draw a polygon with a two-pixel red line and to colour the polygon's interior blue. These tasks will be achieved by enacting a process that causes the item to pass though a sequence of states that will be explained to β by α. So far our model consists of: features, states, sequences and tasks.

---

[7] In other words, the sort of information that is normally available in the item's Instruction Booklet — we assume that α conveys this information accurately.

We assume that the object of the negotiation is clear where the object is an uninstantiated statement of what both agents jointly understand as the intended outcome — e.g. I wish to exchange a quantity of eggs of certain quality for cash. We assume that each agent is negotiating with the aim of satisfying some goal or need that is private knowledge. In determining whether a negotiation outcome is acceptable in satisfaction of a need we assume that an agent will blend the factors in our acceptance model described in Section 3. We assume that for each factor an agent will articulate a set of *criteria* that together determine whether the factor is acceptable. The criteria may include private information such as deadlines.

More formally, there is a set of feature names, $\mathscr{F}$, a set of item names, $\mathscr{I}$, a feature mapping: feature : $\mathscr{I} \rightarrow \times^n (\mathbb{B} : \mathscr{F})$ where there are n feature names, and $\mathbb{B}$ is a boolean variable that may be $\top$ or $\bot$. Each item name belongs to a unique concept — e.g.: "Nikon123 is-a camera". For any particular item name, v, feature(v) will be a typed Boolean vector indicating which features that item v possesses. Let $\mathscr{F}_v$ be the set of n_v features that item v possesses. At any particular time t, the state of an item is a mapping: state^t : $\mathscr{I} \rightarrow \times^{n_v} (\mathbb{B} : \mathscr{F}_v)$ where the value $\top$ denotes that the corresponding feature of that item is 'on'. A *sequence* is an ordered set of states, $(\mathbf{w}_i)$, where successive states differ in one feature only being on and off. A sequence is normally seen as performing a *task* that are linked by the mapping: to-do : $\mathscr{T} \rightarrow 2^{\mathscr{S}}$ where $\mathscr{T}$ is the set of tasks and $\mathscr{S}$ the set of all possible sequences — that is, there many be several sequences that perform a task. If a sequence is *performed* on an item then, with the assistance of a human, the agent rates how well it believes the sequence performs the associated task. The evaluation space, $\mathscr{E}$, could be {good, OK, bad}. A criterion is a predicate: criterion(v), meaning that the item v satisfies criterion 'criterion'. The set of criteria is $\mathscr{C}$.

5 The Buyer Assesses A Contract

In this Section we consider how the buyer might use the general framework in Section 3 to assess a contract[8]. In general an agent will be concerned about the enactment of any contract signed as described in Equation 1. In the scenario described in Section 4, enactment is not an issue, and so we focus on Equation 2. To simplify things we ignore the subjective valuation factor. Before addressing the remaining two factors we note that the buyer will not necessarily be preference aware.

First β must give meaning to $\mathbb{P}^t(\text{satisfy}(\beta, \chi, \delta))$ by defining suitable criteria and the way that the belief should be aggregated across those criteria. Suppose one of β's criteria is $\mathbb{P}^t(\text{ease-of-use}(\beta, \delta))$. The idea is that β will ask α to demonstrate how certain tasks are performed, will observe the sequences that α performs, and will use those observations to revise this probability distribution until some clear verdict appears.

---

[8] The seller will have little difficulty in deciding whether a contract is acceptable if he knows what the items cost.

Suppose the information acquisition process is managed by a plan π. Let random variable X represent $\mathbb{P}^t(\text{ease-of-use}(\beta, \delta) = e_i)$ where the e_i are values from an evaluation space that could be $\mathscr{E} = \{\text{fantastic, acceptable, just OK, shocking}\}$. Then given a sequence s that was supposed to achieve task τ, suppose that β's tame human rates s as evidence for ease-of-use as $e \in \mathscr{E}$ with probability z. Suppose that β attaches a weighting $\mathbb{R}^t(\pi, \tau, s)$ to s, $0 < \mathbb{R} < 1$, which is β's estimate of the *significance* of the observation of sequence s within plan π as an indicator of the true value of X. For example, the on the basis of the observation alone β might rate ease-of-use as $e = $ acceptable with probability $z = 0.8$, and separately give a weighting of $\mathbb{R}^t(\pi, \tau, s) = 0.9$ to the sequence s as an indicator of ease-of-use. For an information-based agent each plan π has associated *update functions*, $J_\pi(\cdot)$, such that $J_\pi^X(s)$ is a set of linear constraints on the posterior distribution for X. In this example, the posterior value of 'acceptable' would simply be constrained to 0.8.

Denote the prior distribution $\mathbb{P}^t(X)$ by $\mathbf{p}$, and let $\mathbf{p}_{(s)}$ be the distribution with minimum relative entropy[9] with respect to $\mathbf{p}$: $\mathbf{p}_{(s)} = \arg\min_{\mathbf{r}} \sum_j r_j \log \frac{r_j}{p_j}$ that satisfies the constraints $J_s^X(s)$. Then let $\mathbf{q}_{(s)}$ be the distribution:

$$\mathbf{q}_{(s)} = \mathbb{R}^t(\pi, \tau, s) \times \mathbf{p}_{(s)} + (1 - \mathbb{R}^t(\pi, \tau, s)) \times \mathbf{p} \qquad (4)$$

and then let:

$$\mathbb{P}^t(X_{(s)}) = \begin{cases} \mathbf{q}_{(s)} & \text{if } \mathbf{q}_{(s)} \text{ is more interesting than } \mathbf{p} \\ \mathbf{p} & \text{otherwise} \end{cases} \qquad (5)$$

A general measure of whether $\mathbf{q}_{(s)}$ is more interesting than $\mathbf{p}$ is: $\mathbb{K}(\mathbf{q}_{(s)} \| \mathbb{D}(X)) > \mathbb{K}(\mathbf{p} \| \mathbb{D}(X))$, where $\mathbb{K}(\mathbf{x} \| \mathbf{y}) = \sum_j x_j \log \frac{x_j}{y_j}$ is the Kullback-Leibler distance between two probability distributions $\mathbf{x}$ and $\mathbf{y}$, and $\mathbb{D}(X)$ is the expected distribution in the absence of any observations — $\mathbb{D}(X)$ could be the maximum entropy distribution. Finally, $\mathbb{P}^{t+1}(X) = \mathbb{P}^t(X_{(s)})$. This procedure deals with integrity decay, and with two probabilities: first, the probability z in the rating of the sequence s that was intended to achieve τ, and second β's weighting $\mathbb{R}^t(\pi, \tau, s)$ of the significance of τ as an indicator of the true value of X. Equation 5 is intended to prevent weak information from decreasing the certainty of $\mathbb{P}^{t+1}(X)$. For example if the current distribution is $(0.1, 0.7, 0.1, 0.1)$, indicating an "acceptable" rating, then weak evidence $\mathbb{P}(X = \text{acceptable}) = 0.25$ is discarded.

Equation 4 simply adds in new evidence $\mathbf{p}_{(s)}$ to $\mathbf{p}$ weighted with $\mathbb{R}^t(\pi, \tau, s)$. This is fairly crude, but the observations are unlikely to be independent and the idea is

---

[9] Given a probability distribution $\mathbf{q}$, the *minimum relative entropy distribution* $\mathbf{p} = (p_1, \ldots, p_I)$ subject to a set of J linear constraints $\mathbf{g} = \{g_j(\mathbf{p}) = \mathbf{a_j} \cdot \mathbf{p} - c_j = 0\}, j = 1, \ldots, J$ (that must include the constraint $\sum_i p_i - 1 = 0$) is: $\mathbf{p} = \arg\min_{\mathbf{r}} \sum_j r_j \log \frac{r_j}{q_j}$. This may be calculated by introducing Lagrange multipliers λ: $L(\mathbf{p}, \lambda) = \sum_j p_j \log \frac{p_j}{q_j} + \lambda \cdot \mathbf{g}$. Minimising L, $\{\frac{\partial L}{\partial \lambda_j} = g_j(\mathbf{p}) = 0\}, j = 1, \ldots, J$ is the set of given constraints $\mathbf{g}$, and a solution to $\frac{\partial L}{\partial p_i} = 0, i = 1, \ldots, I$ leads eventually to $\mathbf{p}$. Entropy-based inference is a form of Bayesian inference that is convenient when the data is sparse [2] and encapsulates common-sense reasoning [7].

that π will specify a "fairly comprehensive" set of tasks aimed to determine $\mathbb{P}^t(X)$ to a level of certainty sufficient for Equation 2.

$\mathbb{P}^t(\text{obj}(\delta))$ estimates the belief that δ is acceptable in the open-market that β may observe in the scenario. Information-based agents model what they don't know with certainty as probability distributions. Suppose that X is a discrete random variable whose true value is the open-market value of an item. First, β should be able to bound X to an interval $(x_{\min}, x_{\max})$ — if this is all the evidence that β can muster then X will be the flat distribution (with maximum entropy) in this interval, and $\mathbb{P}^t(\text{obj}((\text{item}, y))) = \sum_{x \geq y} \mathbb{P}(X = x)$. β may observe evidence, perhaps as observed sale prices for similar items, that enables him to revise particular values in the distribution for X. A method [9] similar to that described above is used to derive the posterior distribution — it is not detailed here. An interesting aspect of this approach is that it works equally well when the valuation space has more than one dimension.

6 The Seller Models the Buyer

In this Section we consider how the seller might model the buyer's contract acceptance logic in an argumentative context. As in Section 5 we focus on Equation 2 and for reasons of economy concentrate on the factor: $\mathbb{P}^t(\text{satisfy}(\alpha, \chi, \delta))$.

Suppose that β has found an item that he wants to buy, α will be interested in how much he is prepared to pay. In a similar way to Section 5, α can interpret β's proposals as willingness to accept the offers proposed, and counter-offers as reluctance to accept the agent's prior offer — all of these interpretations being qualified with an epistemic belief probability. Entropy-based inference is then used to derive a complete probability distribution over the space of offers for a random variable that represents the partner's limit offers. This distribution is "the least biased estimate possible on the given information; i.e. it is maximally noncommittal with regard to missing information" [3]. If there are n-issues then the space of limit offers will be an $(n-1)$-dimensional surface through offer space.

α's world model, $\mathcal{M}^t$, contains probability distributions that model the agent's belief in the world, including the state of β. In particular, for every criterion $c \in \mathscr{C}$ α associates a random variable C with probability mass function $\mathbb{P}^t(C = e_i)$.

The distributions that relate object to criteria may be learned from prior experience. If $\mathbb{P}^t(C = e | O = o)$ is the prior distribution for criteria C over an evaluation space given that the object is o, then given evidence from a completed negotiation with object o we use the standard update procedure described in Section 5. For example, given evidence that α believes with probability p that $C = e_i$ in a negotiation with object o then $\mathbb{P}^{t+1}(C = e | O = o)$ is the result of applying the constraint $\mathbb{P}(C = e_i | O = o) = p$ with minimum relative entropy inference as described previously, where the result of the process is protected by Equation 5 to ensure that weak evidence does not override prior estimates.

In the absence of evidence of the form described above, the distributions, $\mathbb{P}^t(C = e | O = o)$, should gradually tend to ignorance. If a decay-limit distribution [9] is known they should tend to it otherwise they should tend to the maximum entropy distribution.

In a multiagent system, this approach can be strengthened in repeated negotiations by including the agent's identity, $\mathbb{P}^t(C = e|(O = o, Agent = \beta))$ and exploiting a similarity measure across the ontology. So if β purchased a kitchen mixer apparently with the criterion "easy to carry" then that would increase the prior probability that β will use the criterion "easy to carry" in negotiating for a sewing machine. Two methods for propagating estimates across the world model by exploiting the $\text{Sim}(\cdot)$ measure are described in [9]. An extension of the $\text{Sim}(\cdot)$ measure to sets of concepts is straightforward, we will note it as $\text{Sim}*(\cdot)$.

Agent β's *disposition* is the underlying rationale that he has for a dialogue. α will be concerned with the confidence in α's beliefs of β's disposition as this will affect the certainty with which α believes she knows β's key criteria. Gauging disposition in human discourse is not easy, but is certainly not impossible. We form expectations about what will be said next; when those expectations are challenged we may well believe that there is a shift in the rationale.

The bargaining literature consistently advises (see for example [5]) that an agent should change its *stance* (one dimension of stance being the 'nice guy' / 'tough guy' axis) to prevent other agents from decrypting their private information, and so we should expect some sort of "smoke screen" surrounding any dialogue between competitive agents. It would be convenient to think of disposition as the mirror-image of stance, but what matters is the agent's confidence in its model of the partner. The problem is to differentiate between a partner that is skilfully preventing us from decrypting their private information, and a partner that has either had a fundamental change of heart or has changed his mind in a way that will significantly influence the set of contracts that he will agree to. The first of these is normal behaviour, and the second means that the models of the partner may well be inaccurate.

α's model of β's *disposition* is $D_C = \mathbb{P}^t(C = e|O = o)$ for *every* criterion in the ontology, where o is the object of the negotiation. α's confidence in β's disposition is the confidence he has in these distributions. Given a negotiation object o, confidence will be aggregated from $\mathbb{H}(C = e|O = o)$ for *every* criterion in the ontology. Then the idea is that if in the negotiation for a camera "for family use" α is asked to demonstrate how to photograph a drop of water falling from a tap then this would presumably cause a dramatic difference between $\mathbb{P}^t(C = e|(O = $ *"family use"*$))$ and $\mathbb{P}^t(C = e|(O = $ *"family use"*$, O' = $ *"photograph water drops"*$))$. This difference causes α to revise her belief in "family use", to revise the disposition towards distributions of higher entropy, and to approach the negotiation on a broader basis.

7 Strategies

In this section we describe the components of an argumentation strategy starting with tools for valuing information revelation that are used to model the fairness of a negotiation dialogue.

Everything that an agent communicates gives away information. The simple offer "you may purchase this wine for €3" may be intrepretd in a utilitarian sense (e.g. the profit that you could make by purchasing it), and as information (in terms of the reduction of your entropy or uncertainty in your beliefs about my limit price for the item). Information-based agents value information exchanged, and attempt to manage the associated costs and benefits.

Illocutionary categories and an *ontology* together form a framework in which the value of information exchanged can be categorised. The LOGIC framework for argumentative negotiation [11] is based on five illocutionary categories: Legitimacy of the arguments, Options i.e. deals that are acceptable, Goals i.e. motivation for the negotiation, Independence i.e: outside options, and Commitments that the agent has including its assets. In general, α has a set of illocutionary categories $\mathcal{Y}$ and a categorising function $\kappa : \mathcal{L} \to \mathcal{P}(\mathcal{Y})$. The power set, $\mathcal{P}(\mathcal{Y})$, is required as some utterances belong to multiple categories. For example, in the LOGIC framework the utterance "I will not pay more for a bottle of Beaujolais than the price that John charges" is categorised as both Option (what I will accept) and Independence (what I will do if this negotiation fails).

Then two central concepts describe relationships and dialogues between a pair of agents. These are *intimacy* — degree of closeness, and *balance* — degree of fairness. In this general model, the *intimacy* of α's relationship with β, A^t, measures the amount that α knows about β's private information and is represented as real numeric values over $\mathcal{G} = \mathcal{Y} \times V$.

Suppose α receives utterance u from β and that category $y \in \kappa(u)$. For any concept $x \in V$, define $\Delta(u,x) = \max_{x' \in concepts(u)} Sim(x',x)$. Denote the value of A^t_i in position (y,x) by $A^t_{(y,x)}$ then:

$$A^t_{(y,x)} = \rho \times A^{t-1}_{(y,x)} + (1-\rho) \times \mathbb{I}(u) \times \Delta(u,x)$$

for any x, where ρ is the discount rate, and $\mathbb{I}(u)$ is the *information*[10] in u. The *balance* of α's relationship with β_i, B^t, is the element by element numeric difference of A^t and α's estimate of β's intimacy on α.

We are particularly interested in the concept of intimacy in so far as it estimates what α knows about β's criteria, and about the certainty of α's estimates of the random variables $\{C_i\}$. We are interested in balance as a measure of the 'fairness' of the dialogue. If α shows β how to take a perfect photograph of a duck then it is reasonable to expect some information at least in return.

Moreover, α acts proactively to satisfy her needs — that are organised in a hierarchy[11] of *needs*, Ξ, and a function $\omega : \Xi \to \mathcal{P}(W)$ where W is the set of perceivable states, and $\omega(\chi)$ is the set of states that satisfy need $\chi \in \Xi$. Needs turn 'on' spontaneously, and in response to *triggers*. They turn 'off' because α believes they are

---

[10] Information is measured in the Shannon sense, if at time t, α receives an utterance u that may alter this world model then the (Shannon) *information* in u with respect to the distributions in $\mathcal{M}^t$ is: $\mathbb{I}(u) = \mathbb{H}(\mathcal{M}^t) - \mathbb{H}(\mathcal{M}^{t+1})$.

[11] In the sense of the well-known Maslow hierarchy [6], where the satisfaction of needs that are lower in the hierarchy take precedence over the satisfaction of needs that are higher.

satisfied. When a need fires, a plan is chosen to satisfy that need (we do not describe plans here). If α is to contemplate the future she will need some idea of her future needs — this is represented in her *needs model*: $\upsilon : T \to \times^{|\varXi|}[0,1]$ where T is time, and: $\upsilon(t) = (\chi_1^t, \ldots, \chi_{|\varXi|}^t)$ where $\chi_i^t = \mathbb{P}(\text{need } \chi_i \text{ fires at time } t)$.

Given the needs model, υ, α's *relationship model* (Relate$(\cdot)$) determines the target *intimacy*, A_i^{*t}, and target *balance*, B_i^{*t}, for each agent i in the known set of agents *Agents*. That is, $\{(A_i^{*t}, B_{*i}^t)\}_{i=1}^{|Agents|} = \text{Relate}(\upsilon, \mathbf{X}, \mathbf{Y}, \mathbf{Z})$ where, $\mathbf{X}_i$ is the trust model, $\mathbf{Y}_i$ is the honour model and $\mathbf{Z}_i$ is the reliability model as described in [9]. As noted before, the values for intimacy and balance are not simple numbers but are structured sets of values over $\mathscr{Y} \times V$.

When a need fires α first selects an agent β_i to negotiate with — the social model of trust, honour and reliability provide input to this decision, i.e. $\beta_i = $ Select$(\chi, \mathbf{X}, \mathbf{Y}, \mathbf{Z})$. We assume that in her social model, α has medium-term intentions for the state of the relationship that she desires with each of the available agents — these intentions are represented as the target intimacy, A_i^{*t}, and target balance, B_i^{*t}, for each agent β_i. These medium-term intentions are then distilled into short-term targets for the intimacy, A_i^{**t}, and balance, B_i^{**t}, to be achieved in the current dialogue Ψ^t, i.e. $(A_i^{**t}, B_i^{**t}) = \text{Set}(\chi, A_i^{*t}, B_i^{*t})$. In particular, if the balance target, B_i^{**t}, is grossly exceeded by β failing to co-operate then it becomes a trigger for α to terminate the negotiation.

For an information-based agent, an incoming utterance is only of interest if it reduces the uncertainty (entropy) of the world model in some way. In information-based argumentation we are particularly interested in the effect that an argumentative utterance has in the world model including β's disposition, and α's estimate of β's assessment of current proposals in terms of its criteria.

Information-based argumentation attempts to counter the effect of the partner's arguments, in the simple negotiation protocol used here, an argumentative utterance, u, will either contain a justification of the proposal it accompanies, a rating and justification of one of α demonstration sequences, or a counter-justification of one of α's prior proposals or arguments. If u requests α to perform a task then u may modify β's disposition i.e. the set of conditional estimates of the form: $\mathbb{P}^t(C = e | O = o)$). If β rates and comments on the demonstration of a sequence then this affects α's estimate of β's likelihood to accept a contract as described in Equation 1 (this is concerned with *how* β will apply his criteria).

Suppose that u rates and comments on the performance of a sequence then that sequence will have been demonstrated in response to a request to perform a task. Given a task, τ, and a object, s, α may have estimates for $P^t(C = e | (O = o, \mathscr{T} = \tau))$ — if so then this suggests a link between the task and a set of one or more criteria C_u. The effect that u has on β's criteria (what ever they are) will be conveyed as the rating. In the spirit of the scenario, we assume that for every criterion and object pair (C, o) α has a supply of positive argumentative statements $\mathscr{L}_{(C,o)}$. Suppose α wishes to counter the negatively rated u with a positively rated u'. Let Ψ_u be the set of all arguments exchanged between α and β prior to u in the dialogue. Let $M_u \subseteq \mathscr{L}_{(C,o)}$ for any $C \in C_\mu$. Let $N_u \subseteq M_u$ such that $\forall x \in N_u$ and $\forall u' \in \Psi_u$, Sim$*(concepts(x), concepts(u')) > \eta$ for some constant η. So N_u is a set of arguments all of which (a) have a positive effect on at least one criterion associated with the negative u, and (b) are at 'some distance' (determined by r) from arguments already exchanged. Then:

$$u' = \begin{cases} \arg\min_{u' \in N_u} \text{Sim}*(concepts(u), concepts(u')) & \text{if } N_u \neq \emptyset \\ \arg\min_{u' \in M_u} \text{Sim}*(concepts(u), concepts(u')) & \text{otherwise.} \end{cases}$$

So using only 'fresh' arguments, α prefers to choose a counter argument to u that is semantically close to u, and if that is not possible she chooses an argument that has some general positive effect on the criteria and may not have been used previously.

Suppose that u proposes a contract. α will either decide to accept it or to make a counter offer. We do not describe the bargaining process here, see [9].

8 Discussion

If β_i communicates u then α responds with:

$$u' = Argue(u, \mathcal{M}^t, \Psi^t, A^{**t}, B^{**t}, C_u, N_u, M_u, D_u))$$

where:

- the *negotiation* mechanisms as explained in Section 7 sets parameters A^{**t}, B^{**t}) (see e.g. [11] for further details);
- the *argumentation* process determines the parameters N_u, M_u needed to generate the accompanying arguments to the proposal, see Section 7;
- the *criteria* modeling process determines the set of criteria C_u used by our opponent to assess the proposals, see Section 6; and,
- the *disposition* modeling sets the distributions D_u used to interpret the stance of the opponent, see Section 6.

We have described an approach to argumentation that aims to:

- discover what the partner's key evaluative criteria are,
- model how the partner is evaluating his key criteria given some evidence,
- influence the partner's evaluation of his key criteria,
- influence the relative importance that the partner attaches to those criteria, and
- introduce new key criteria when it is strategic to do so.

The ideas described here are an attempt to develop an approach to argumentation that may be used in the interests of both parties. It aims to achieve this by unearthing the 'top layer' of the partner's reasoning apparatus and by attempting to work with it rather than against it. To this end, the utterances produced aim to influence the partner to believe what we believe to be in his best interests — although it may not be in fact. The utterances aim to convey what is so, and not to point out "where the partner is wrong". In the long term, this behaviour is intended to lead to the development of lasting relationships between agents that are underpinned both by the knowledge that their partners "treat them well" and that their partners act as they do "for the right reasons".

In previous work [11] we have advocated the gradual development of trust and intimacy[12] through successive argumentative exchanges as a way of building relationships between agents. In this paper we have gone one step further by including a modest degree of *understanding* in the sense that an agent attempts to understand what her partner likes. This augments the tools for building social relationships through argumentation by establishing:

- *trust* — my belief in the veracity of your *commitments*
- *intimacy* — my belief in the extent to which I know your private *information*
- *understanding* — my belief in the extent to which I know what you *like*

Acknowledgements This research has been supported by the Sabbatical Programme of the Catalan Government BE2007, the Australian Research Council Discovery Grant DP0557168, and by the Spanish Ministerio de Educación y Ciencia project "Agreement Technologies" (CONSOLIDER CSD2007-0022, INGENIO 2010).

References

1. Arcos, J.L., Esteva, M., Noriega, P., Rodríguez, J.A., Sierra, C.: Environment engineering for multiagent systems. Journal on Engineering Applications of Artificial Intelligence **18** (2005)
2. Cheeseman, P., Stutz, J.: Bayesian Inference and Maximum Entropy Methods in Science and Engineering, chap. On The Relationship between Bayesian and Maximum Entropy Inference, pp. 445 – 461. American Institute of Physics, Melville, NY, USA (2004)
3. Jaynes, E.: Information theory and statistical mechanics: Part I. Physical Review **106**, 620 – 630 (1957)
4. Kalfoglou, Y., Schorlemmer, M.: IF-Map: An ontology-mapping method based on information-flow theory. In: S. Spaccapietra, S. March, K. Aberer (eds.) Journal on Data Semantics I, *Lecture Notes in Computer Science*, vol. 2800, pp. 98–127. Springer-Verlag: Heidelberg, Germany (2003)
5. Lewicki, R.J., Saunders, D.M., Minton, J.W.: Essentials of Negotiation. McGraw Hill (2001)
6. Maslow, A.H.: A theory of human motivation. Psychological Review **50**, 370–396 (1943)
7. Paris, J.: Common sense and maximum entropy. Synthese **117**(1), 75 – 93 (1999)
8. Rahwan, I., Ramchurn, S., Jennings, N., McBurney, P., Parsons, S., Sonenberg, E.: Argumentation-based negotiation. Knowledge Engineering Review **18**(4), 343–375 (2003)
9. Sierra, C., Debenham, J.: Trust and honour in information-based agency. In: P. Stone, G. Weiss (eds.) Proceedings Fifth International Conference on Autonomous Agents and Multi Agent Systems AAMAS-2006, pp. 1225 – 1232. ACM Press, New York, Hakodate, Japan (2006)
10. Sierra, C., Debenham, J.: Information-based agency. In: Proceedings of Twentieth International Joint Conference on Artificial Intelligence IJCAI-07, pp. 1513–1518. Hyderabad, India (2007)
11. Sierra, C., Debenham, J.: The LOGIC Negotiation Model. In: Proceedings Sixth International Conference on Autonomous Agents and Multi Agent Systems AAMAS-2007, pp. 1026–1033. Honolulu, Hawai'i (2007)

---

[12] The revelation of private information.

Automated Bilateral
Negotiation and Bargaining Impasse

Fernando Lopes, A. Q. Novais and Helder Coelho

Abstract The design and implementation of autonomous negotiating agents involve the consideration of insights from multiple relevant research areas to integrate different perspectives on negotiation. As a starting point for an interdisciplinary research effort, this paper employs game-theoretic techniques to define equilibrium strategies for the bargaining game of alternating offers and formalizes a set of negotiation strategies studied in the social sciences. This paper also shifts the emphasis to negotiations that are "difficult" to resolve and can hit an impasse. Specifically, it analyses a situation where two agents bargain over the division of the surplus of several distinct issues to demonstrate how a procedure to avoid impasses can be utilized in a specific negotiation setting. The procedure is based on the addition of new issues to the agenda during the course of negotiation and the exploration of the differences in the valuation of these issues to capitalize on Pareto optimal agreements.

1 Introduction

Negotiation is a pervasive form of social interaction. Human negotiation has been extensively studied in the different branches of the social sciences (see, e.g., [12, 14]). Automated negotiation is an active area of research in artificial intelligence (AI). The demands for systems composed of computational agents that are owned by different individuals or organizations and are capable of reaching agreements through negotiation are becoming increasingly important (see, e.g., [3, 5]).

Fernando Lopes and A. Q. Novais
INETI, Dep. Modelação e Simulação, Est. Paço Lumiar, 1649-038 Lisboa, Portugal
e-mail: {fernando.lopes,augusto.novais}@ineti.pt

Helder Coelho
Universidade de Lisboa, Dep. de Informática, Campo Grande, 1749-016 Lisboa, Portugal
e-mail: hcoelho@di.fc.ul.pt

Automated negotiation promises a higher level of process efficiency and a higher quality of agreements [1]. In practice, the task of designing and implementing autonomous negotiating agents usually involves the consideration of insights from multiple relevant research areas to integrate different perspectives on negotiation. Yet, most existing models primarily use either game-theoretic techniques or methods from the social sciences as a basis to develop negotiating agents, and largely ignore the integration of the results from both areas. As a starting point for an interdisciplinary research effort, this paper employs game-theoretic techniques to define equilibrium strategies for the bargaining game of alternating offers and formalizes a set of negotiation strategies and tactics studied in the social sciences.

Negotiation may end in an agreement, wherein the parties mutually agree to a proposal, or in an impasse, wherein the parties do not reach a settlement. An impasse (a stalemate or a deadlock) is a condition or state of negotiation in which there is no apparent quick or easy resolution − the parties are unable to create mutually advantageous deals that satisfy their aspirations [6]. AI researchers have traditionally focused on understanding and formalizing "successful" negotiations − most researchers have assumed that negotiations result in agreement (see, e.g., [3, 4]). Few researchers have attempted to formalize "difficult" negotiations, *i.e.*, negotiations that can become contentious to the point of impasse (see, e.g., [2, 13]). Recently, we have proposed a model that accounts for systematic preparation and planning for negotiation and formalizes a procedure for assisting agents to avoid impasses [8]. The procedure involves the following main actions:

- re-definition of the agenda, *i.e.*, addition of new issues to the agenda during the course of negotiation;
- exploration of the differences in the valuation of the new issues to capitalize on Pareto optimal agreements.

This paper analyses a situation where two agents bargain over the division of the surplus of several distinct issues to demonstrate how the procedure can be utilized in a specific negotiation setting.

The work described here is complementary to the work described in [8, 9, 10]. In particular, it is complementary to the work described in [8, 9], because it uses both game-theoretic techniques and methods from the social sciences as a basis to develop autonomous negotiating agents, rather than game-theoretic techniques alone. It is also complementary to the work described in [10], because it concentrates both on "successful" and "difficult" negotiations, rather than on "successful" negotiations alone.

The remainder of the paper is structured as follows. Section 2 addresses the operational and strategic process of preparing and planning for negotiation (usually referred to as pre-negotiation). Section 3 describes the central process of moving toward agreement (usually referred to as actual negotiation or simply negotiation). Section 4 addresses negotiations that are "difficult" to resolve and can hit an impasse. Section 5 discusses related work and section 6 presents concluding remarks and indicates avenues for further research.

2 Pre-Negotiation

Pre-negotiation is the process of preparing and planning for negotiation and involves mainly the creation of a well-laid plan specifying the activities that negotiators should attend to before actually starting to negotiate [6]. That plan, and the confidence derived from it, is often a critical factor for achieving negotiation objectives. Accordingly, we describe below various activities that negotiators make efforts to perform in order to carefully prepare and plan for negotiation (see our earlier work for an in-depth discussion [8]).

Let $Ag = \{ag_1, ag_2\}$ be the set of autonomous negotiating agents. Let $I_i = \{is_{i1}, \ldots, is_{iz}\}$ be the set of independent issues of an agent $ag_i \in Ag$. The issues are quantitative variables, defined over continuous intervals. Negotiation usually involves a number of major or primary issues (e.g., price) and several minor or secondary issues (e.g., maintenance policies). Let $MI_i = \{is_{i1}, \ldots, is_{in}\}$ and $SI_i = \{is_{in+1}, \ldots, is_{iz}\}$ be the sets of major and minor issues of ag_i, respectively.

Effective pre-negotiation requires that negotiators prioritize the issues and establish the agenda. Priorities are set by rank-ordering the issues, *i.e.*, by defining the most important, the second most important, and so on. The priority pr_{il} of ag_i for each issue $is_{il} \in I_i$ is a number that represents its order of preference. The weight w_{il} of is_{il} is a number that represents its relative importance. The limit lim_{il} is the point where ag_i decides that it should stop to negotiate, because any settlement beyond this point is not minimally acceptable. The level of aspiration or target point trg_{il} is the point where ag_i realistically expects to achieve a settlement. The negotiating agenda is represented by *Agenda* and specifies the final set of issues to be deliberated. Its definition involves interaction with the opponent. Specifically, negotiators disclose and combine their individual sets of major issues. For the sake of simplicity, we consider that the sets MI_i and *Agenda* contain the same issues.

Additionally, effective pre-negotiation requires that negotiators agree on an appropriate protocol that defines the rules governing the interaction. The protocol can be simple, allowing agents to exchange only proposals. Alternatively, the protocol can be complex, allowing agents to provide arguments to support their negotiation stance. However, most sophisticated protocols make considerable demands on any implementation, mainly because they appeal to very rich representations of the agents and their environments (see, e.g., [4]). Therefore, we consider an alternating offers protocol [11]. Two agents or players bargain over the division of the surplus of $n \geq 2$ issues (goods or pies) by alternately proposing offers at times in $T = \{1, 2, \ldots\}$. The negotiation procedure, labelled the "joint-offer procedure", involves bargaining over the allocation of the entire endowment stream at once. An offer is a vector $(x_1, \ldots, x_n)$ specifying a division of the n goods. Once an agreement is reached, the agreed-upon allocations of the goods are implemented. This procedure permits agents to exploit the benefits of trading concessions on different issues.

The players' preferences are modelled by assuming that each player ag_i discounts future payoffs at some given rate δ_i^t, $0 < \delta_i^t < 1$, (δ_i^t is referred to as the discount factor). The cost of bargaining derives from the delay in consumption implied by a rejection of an offer. Practically speaking, the justification for this form of preferences takes into account the fact that money today can be used to make money tomorrow. Let U_i be the payoff function of ag_i. For simplicity and tractability, we assume that U_i is separable in all their arguments and that the per-period delay costs are the same for all issues:

$$U_i(x_1,\ldots,x_n,t) = \delta_i^{(t-1)} \sum_{l=1}^n w_{il} \, u_{il}(x_l)$$

where w_{il} is the weight of is_{il} and x_l denotes the share of ag_i for is_{il}. The component payoff function u_{il} for is_{il} is a continuous, strictly monotonic, and linear function. The distinguish feature of time preferences with a constant discount rate is the linearity of the function u_{il} [11]. The payoff of disagreement is normalized at 0 for both players.

Finally, effective pre-negotiation requires that negotiators be able to select an appropriate strategy. Traditionally, AI researchers have paid little attention to this pre-negotiation step. In the last several years, however, a number of researchers have developed models that include libraries of negotiation strategies (see, e.g., [3, 4, 5]). Some strategies are in equilibrium, meaning that no designer will benefit by building agents that use any other strategies when it is known that some agents are using equilibrium strategies (see, e.g., [11] for an in-depth description of the standard game-theoretic concept of equilibrium). Thus, for some situations of complete information, the agents can be designed to adopt equilibrium strategies (see subsection 3.1). However, for situations of incomplete information, the problem of strategic choice is rather complex. In these situations, many bargaining models have different equilibria sustained by different assumptions on what an individual in the game would believe if its opponent took an action that it was not supposed to take in equilibrium. Hence, our study differs from this line of work — we address the challenge of building agents that are able to negotiate under incomplete information by formalizing relevant strategies used by human negotiators and empirically evaluating the effectiveness of these strategies in different situations (see subsection 3.2 and the comments on future work in section 6).

3 Actual Negotiation

Actual negotiation is the process of moving toward agreement (usually by an iterative exchange of offers and counter-offers). The negotiation protocol defines the states (e.g., accepting a proposal), the valid actions of the agents in particular states (e.g., which messages can be sent by whom, to whom, at what stage), and the events that cause states to change (e.g., proposal accepted). It marks branching points at which negotiators have to make decisions according to their strategies. Hence, this section describes equilibrium strategies for the bargaining game of alternating offers and formalizes negotiation strategies studied in the social sciences (see our earlier work for an in-depth discussion [8, 10]).

3.1 Equilibrium Strategies

The negotiation process is modelled as an extensive game. For theoretical convenience, we consider the standard game-theoretic situation of two players completely informed about the various aspects of the game. The players are assumed to be rational, and each player knows that the other acts rationally. We also consider settings involving more than one issue. In particular, to reduce the complexity of the analysis, and without loss of generality, we consider a two-sided four-issue bargaining situation in which the players have different evaluations of the issues (other situations, involving a *different* number of issues, are handled similarly).

Two players are jointly endowed with a single unit of each of four goods, $\{X_1,\dots,X_4\}$, and alternate proposals until they find an agreement. Each good is modelled as an interval $[0,1]$ (or as a divisible pie of size 1). The players' preferences are as follows:

$$U_i = \delta_i^{(t-1)} (ax_1 + bx_2 + x_3 + x_4)$$
$$U_j = \delta_j^{(t-1)} [(1-x_1) + (1-x_2) + c(1-x_3) + d(1-x_4)]$$

where x_l and $(1-x_l)$, $l=1,\dots,4$, denote the shares of ag_i and ag_j for each pie, respectively. The parameters a, b, c, and d allow the marginal utilities of the players to differ across issues and players. We consider $a>b>1$ and $d>c>1$, i.e., ag_i places greater emphasis on goods X_1 and X_2 while ag_j values goods X_3 and X_4 more. Also, we consider that δ_i and δ_j are close to 1 and the parameters a, b, c, and d are close to one another. Let $p_{j\rightarrow i}^{t-1}$ and $p_{i\rightarrow j}^{t}$ denote the offers that ag_j proposes to ag_i in period $t-1$ and ag_i proposes to ag_j in period t, respectively. Consider the following strategies:

$$str_i^* = \begin{cases} \text{offer } (1,1,x_{i3}^*,0) & \text{if } ag_i\text{'s turn} \\ \text{if } U_i(p_{j\rightarrow i}^{t-1}) \geq U_i^* \text{ accept else reject} & \text{if } ag_j\text{'s turn} \end{cases}$$

$$str_j^* = \begin{cases} \text{offer } (1,x_{j2}^*,0,0) & \text{if } ag_j\text{'s turn} \\ \text{if } U_j(p_{i\rightarrow j}^{t}) \geq U_j^* \text{ accept else reject} & \text{if } ag_i\text{'s turn} \end{cases}$$

where $U_i^* = U_i(1,x_{j2}^*,0,0)$, $U_j^* = U_j(1,1,x_{i3}^*,0)$, and the shares are the following: $x_{i3}^* = \frac{\delta_i\delta_j(a+b)-\delta_j(a+b+bc+bd)+bc+bd}{bc-\delta_i\delta_j}$ and $x_{j2}^* = \frac{\delta_i(\delta_i\delta_j(a+b)-\delta_j(a+b+bc+bd)+bc+bd)+(bc-\delta_i\delta_j)(a\delta_i+b\delta_i-a)}{b(bc-\delta_i\delta_j)}$.

Remark 1. For the two-sided four-issue bargaining game of alternating offers with an infinite horizon, in which the players' preferences are as described above, the pair of strategies (str_i^*, str_j^*) form an equilibrium. The outcome is the following:

$$x_1^* = 1, \quad x_2^* = 1, \quad x_3^* = \frac{\delta_i\delta_j(a+b) - \delta_j(a+b+bc+bd) + bc+bd}{bc - \delta_i\delta_j}, \quad x_4^* = 0$$

Agreement is immediately reached with no delay. The outcome is Pareto optimal.

The formal proof is presented in [8]. In short, note that the familiar necessary conditions for equilibrium are that ag_i is indifferent between waiting one period to have its offer accepted and accepting ag_j's offer immediately, and that ag_j is indifferent between waiting one period to have its offer accepted and accepting ag_i's offer immediately. Let $\mathbf{x}_i^* = (x_{i1}^*, \ldots, x_{i4}^*)$ and $\mathbf{x}_j^* = (x_{j1}^*, \ldots, x_{j4}^*)$ be the equilibrium proposals of ag_i and ag_j, respectively. The problem for ag_i is stated as follows:

maximize:

$$U_i(x_1, \ldots, x_4, t) = \delta_i^{(t-1)} \left(ax_1 + bx_2 + x_3 + x_4 \right)$$

subject to:

$$(1 - x_{i1}^*) + (1 - x_{i2}^*) + c(1 - x_{i3}^*) + d(1 - x_{i4}^*) =$$
$$\delta_j[(1 - x_{j1}^*) + (1 - x_{j2}^*) + c(1 - x_{j3}^*) + d(1 - x_{j4}^*)]$$
$$0 \leq x_{il}^* \leq 1, \quad 0 \leq x_{jl}^* \leq 1, \quad \text{for} \quad l = 1, \ldots, 4$$

The problem for ag_j is stated in a similar way and is omitted. Solving both maximization problems yields the outcome specified in the statement of the Remark. In the limit, letting $\delta_i \to 1$ and $\delta_j \to 1$, the outcome of the equilibrium is $(1, 1, 0, 0)$. This outcome is on the Pareto frontier and corresponds to the utility pair $(a+b, c+d)$.

3.2 Concession and Problem Solving Strategies

Game theory can provide sound design principles for computer scientists. The last subsection has considered two fully informed agents and used game-theoretic techniques to define equilibrium strategies. The agents were creative and able to settle for the outcome that maximizes their benefit (resources were not wasted and money was not squandered). Yet, the assumption of complete information is of limited use to the designers of agents. In practice, agents have private information. Also, simple casual observation reveals the existence of concessions and long periods of disagreement in many actual negotiations. Furthermore, one agent, say ag_i, may wish to act rationally, but the other agent may not behave as a strategically sophisticated, utility maximizer − thus rendering conventional equilibrium analysis inapplicable.

Behavioural negotiation theory can provide rules-of-thumb to agent designers. The danger is that the designers may not be fully aware of the circumstances to which human practice is adapted, and hence use rules that can be badly exploited by new agents. Nevertheless, an increasing number of researchers consider that human practice is crucial to automated negotiation (see, e.g., [1]). There is a need to integrate the procedures and results from behavioural negotiation theory in bargaining models incorporating game-theoretic techniques. Accordingly, this subsection considers two incompletely informed agents about the various aspects of the bargaining game and formalizes relevant strategies studied in the social sciences.

Negotiation strategies can reflect a variety of behaviours and lead to strikingly different outcomes. However, the following two fundamental groups of strategies are commonly discussed in the behavioural negotiation literature [12, 14]:

1. *concession making* – negotiators who employ strategies in this group reduce their aspirations to accommodate the opponent;
2. *problem solving* – negotiators maintain their aspirations and try to find ways of reconciling them with the aspirations of the opponent.

Although it is important to distinguish among these two groups of strategies, we hasten to add several explanatory notes. First, most strategies are implemented through a variety of tactics. The line between strategies and tactics often seems indistinct, but one major difference is that of scope. Tactics are short-term moves designed to enact or pursue broad (high-level) strategies [6]. Second, concession making strategies are essentially unilateral strategies – the decision to concede is fundamentally a unilateral one. By contrast, problem solving strategies are essentially social strategies. Third, most negotiation situations call forth a combination of strategies from different groups. Finally, most strategies are only informally discussed in the behavioural literature. They are not formalized, as typically happens in the game-theoretic literature.

Concession making behaviour aims at partially or totally accommodating the other party. Consider two incompletely informed agents bargaining over n distinct issues $\{is_1,\ldots,is_n\}$. For convenience, each issue is_l is modelled as an interval $[min_l,max_l]$. The agents' preferences are as defined in subsection 2. The opening stance and the pattern of concessions are two central elements of negotiation. Three different opening positions (extreme, reasonable and modest) and three levels of concession magnitude (large, moderate and small) are commonly discussed in the behavioural literature [6]. They can lead to a number of concession strategies, notably:

1. *starting high and conceding slowly* – negotiators adopt an optimistic opening attitude and make successive small concessions;
2. *starting reasonable and conceding moderately* – negotiators adopt a realistic opening attitude and make successive moderate concessions.

Let $p_{j \to i}^{t-1}$ be the offer that ag_j has proposed to ag_i in period $t-1$. Likewise, let $p_{i \to j}^{t}$ be the offer that ag_i is ready to propose in the next time period t. The formal definition of a generic concession strategy follows.

Definition 1. Let $ag_i \in Ag$ be a negotiating agent. A concession strategy for ag_i is a function that specifies either the tactic to apply at the beginning of negotiation or the tactic that defines the concessions to be made during the course of negotiation:

$$conc \stackrel{def}{=} \begin{cases} \text{apply } tact_i^1 & \text{if } ag_i\text{'s turn and } t=1 \\ \text{apply } tact_i^t & \text{if } ag_i\text{'s turn and } t>1 \\ \text{if } U_i(p_{j \to i}^{t-1}) \geq U_i(p_{i \to j}^{t}) \text{ accept else reject} & \text{if } ag_j\text{'s turn} \end{cases}$$

where $tact_i^1$ is an opening negotiation tactic and $tact_i^t$ is a concession tactic.

The two aforementioned concession strategies are defined by considering different tactics. For instance, the "starting reasonable and conceding moderately" strategy is defined by: "$tact_i^1 = starting\_realistic$" and "$tact_i^t = moderate$" (but see below).

Problem solving behaviour aims at finding agreements that appeal to all sides, both individually and collectively. The host of problem solving strategies includes [12]:

1. *low-priority concession making* — negotiators hold firm on more important issues while conceding on less important issues;
2. *logrolling* — negotiators agree to trade-off among the issues under consideration so that each party concedes on issues that are of low priority to itself and high priority to the other party.

Low-priority concession making involves primarily the analysis of one's priorities and further concessions on less important issues. However, effective logrolling requires information about the two parties' priorities so that concessions can be matched up. This information is not always easy to get. The main reason for this is that negotiators often try to conceal their priorities for fear that they will be forced to concede on issues of lesser importance to themselves without receiving any repayment [12]. Despite this, research evidence indicates that it is often not detrimental for negotiators to disclose information that can reveal their priorities — a simple rank order of the issues does not put negotiators at a strategic disadvantage [14]. Hence, we consider that negotiators willingly disclose information that can help to identify their priorities (e.g., their interests).

Logrolling can be viewed as a variant of low-priority concession making in which the parties' priorities are in the opposite direction. The formal definition of a generic logrolling strategy follows (the definition of a low-priority concession making strategy is essentially identical, and is omitted).

Definition 2. Let $ag_i \in Ag$ be a negotiating agent and $ag_j \in Ag$ be its opponent. Let *Agenda* denote the negotiating agenda, $Agenda^{\oplus}$ the subset of the agenda containing the issues of high priority for ag_i (and low priority for ag_j), and $Agenda^{\ominus}$ the subset of the agenda containing the issues of low priority for ag_i (and high priority for ag_j). A logrolling strategy for ag_i is a function that specifies either the tactic to apply at the beginning of negotiation or the tactics to make trade-offs during the course of negotiation:

$$log \stackrel{def}{=} \begin{cases} \text{apply } tact_i^1 & \text{if } ag_i\text{'s turn and } t = 1 \\ \text{apply } tact_i^{t\oplus} \text{ and } tact_i^{t\ominus} & \text{if } ag_i\text{'s turn and } t > 1 \\ \text{if } U_i(p_{j\to i}^{t-1}) \geq U_i(p_{i\to j}^t) \text{ accept else reject} & \text{if } ag_j\text{'s turn} \end{cases}$$

where $tact_i^1$ is an opening negotiation tactic, $tact_i^{t\oplus}$ is a concession tactic (to apply to the issues on $Agenda^{\oplus}$), and $tact_i^{t\ominus}$ is another concession tactic (to apply to the issues on $Agenda^{\ominus}$). ∎

A number of logrolling strategies can be defined simply by considering different tactics. For instance, a strategy that specifies a realistic opening attitude, followed by null concessions on issues on $Agenda^{\oplus}$, and large concessions on issues on $Agenda^{\ominus}$, is defined by: "$tact_i^1 = starting\_realistic$", "$tact_i^{\oplus} = stalemate$", and "$tact_i^{\ominus} = soft$" (but see below).

Opening negotiation tactics are functions that specify the initial values for each issue is_l at stake. The following three tactics are commonly discussed in the behavioural literature [6]:

1. *starting optimistic* – specifies a value far from the target point;
2. *starting realistic* – specifies a value close to the target point;
3. *starting pessimistic* – specifies a value close to the limit.

The definition of the tactic "starting realistic" follows (the definition of the other two tactics is essentially identical, and is omitted).

Definition 3. Let $ag_i \in Ag$ be a negotiating agent and $is_l \in Agenda$ a negotiation issue. Let trg_{il} be the target point of ag_i for is_l. The tactic starting realistic for ag_i is a function that takes is_l and trg_{il} as input and returns the initial value $v[is_l]_i^1$ of is_l:

$$starting\_realistic(is_l, trg_{il}) = v[is_l]_i^1$$

where $v[is_l]_i^1 \in [trg_{il} - \varepsilon, trg_{il} + \varepsilon]$ and $\varepsilon > 0$ is small. ∎

Concession tactics are functions that compute new values for each issue is_l. The following five tactics are commonly discussed in the literature [6]:

1. *stalemate* – models a null concession on is_l;
2. *tough* – models a small concession on is_l;
3. *moderate* – models a moderate concession on is_l;
4. *soft* – models a large concession on is_l;
5. *accommodate* – models a complete concession on is_l.

The definition of a generic concession tactic follows (without loss of generality, we consider that ag_i wants to maximize is_l).

Definition 4. Let $ag_i \in Ag$ be a negotiating agent, $is_l \in Agenda$ a negotiation issue, and lim_{il} the limit of is_l. Let $v[is_l]_i^t$ be the value of is_l offered by ag_i at period t. A concession tactic for ag_i is a function that takes $v[is_l]_i^t$, lim_{il} and the concession factor $Cf \in [0, 1]$ as input and returns the new value $v[is_l]_i^{t+2}$ of is_l:

$$concession\_tactic(v[is_l]_i^t, lim_{il}, Cf) = v[is_l]_i^{t+2}$$

where $v[is_l]_i^{t+2} = v[is_l]_i^t - Cf(v[is_l]_i^t - lim_{il})$. ∎

The five tactics are defined by considering different values for Cf. In particular, the stalemate tactic by $Cf = 0$, the accommodate tactic by $Cf = 1$, and the other three tactics by different ranges of values for Cf (e.g., the tough tactic by $Cf \in]0.00, 0.05]$, the moderate tactic by $Cf \in]0.05, 0.10]$, and the soft tactic by $Cf \in]0.10, 0.15]$).

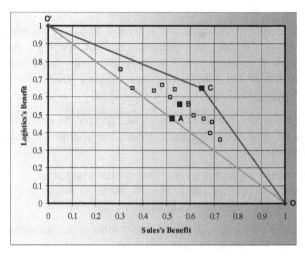

Fig. 1 Joint utility space for the Sales-Logistics example (line OCO' represents the Pareto frontier)

Example 1. Consider a sales agent and a logistics agent operating in a multi-agent supply chain system:

> David, the director of Sales, is trying to arrange for production of its two new orders, one for 10000 and the other for 5000 men's suits. Martin, the director of Logistics, is stating that the job will take four months. Together, they will gross over 25000 Euros. The problem is that David's customer wants a two-month turnaround.

There are four issues in the agenda, namely quantity_1 and date_1 (for the 10000 suit order), and quantity_2 and date_2 (for the 5000 suit order). The sales agent places greater emphasis on quantity_1 and date_1 (due to the inherent customer demands), and the logistics agent values quantity_2 and date_2 more. Additionally, there is one minor issue for the sales agent, namely the right to attend a number of Sales Division meetings that are of interest to the Logistics Division.

Generally speaking, negotiators who demand too much will often fail to reach agreement. Those who demand too little will usually reach agreement but achieve low benefits. The most successful negotiators are often those who are moderately firm [12]. However, if negotiators are moderately firm and do not try to devise new alternatives by means of problem solving, the result will probably be a compromise agreement with low benefits to both sides. For instance, David and Martin can agree on a five-week schedule for 10000 men's suits and a six-week schedule for 5000 men's suits. This compromise agreement is represented by point A in Figure 1 and provides a (normalized) benefit of 0.525 to David and 0.475 to Martin.

Alternatively, the two agents can pursue logrolling strategies and agree on a four-week schedule for 9750 suits and a six-week schedule for 4500 suits (see point B in Figure 1). Furthermore, they can pursue the strategies (str_i^*, str_j^*) and agree on a four-week schedule for 10000 suits and a six-week schedule for 4000 suits. This Pareto optimal agreement is represented by point C in Figure 1 and provides a (normalized) benefit of 0.65 to each party (letting $\delta_i \rightarrow 1$ and $\delta_j \rightarrow 1$).

4 Bargaining Impasse

Negotiators can adopt different orientations (and strategies) to accomplish their goals. Two bargaining orientations are commonly discussed in the literature [12]: individualistic or competitive and cooperative or problem solving. Individualistic negotiators show a strong interest in achieving only their own outcomes – getting this deal, winning this negotiation – and tend to pursue competitive strategies (see, e.g., [6, 14]). Cooperative negotiators are concerned with both their own and the other's outcomes – building, preserving, or enhancing a good relationship with the other party – and tend to pursue problem solving strategies (e.g., logrolling).

Subsection 3.1 has considered a typical bargaining situation of two cooperative agents and a "win-win" philosophy (formalized, at least in part, by the strategic choices of the players). The agents were able to settle for the outcome that maximizes their benefit (resources were not wasted and money was not squandered). This section addresses a different bargaining situation – it considers a cooperative agent, say ag_i, and a competitive agent, ag_j, who wants to "win" the negotiation. Now, ag_j pursues a strategy compatible with its negotiating style (e.g., starting with high demands and making a few small concessions [7]). In period 1, ag_i proposes the offer $\mathbf{x}_i^*$ specified in Remark 1, and ag_j either accepts this offer or rejects it. We restrict attention to the case in which ag_j rejects the offer $\mathbf{x}_i^*$. The play passes to period 2 and ag_j proposes an offer $\mathbf{y}_j$, which ag_i rejects (considering that $U_i(\mathbf{y}_j, 2) < U_i(\mathbf{x}_i^*, 3)$). The agents continue to negotiate in this manner and, therefore, negotiation can become "difficult" to the point of impasse.

In this situation, ag_i can try to draw ag_j into a more constructive process. Specifically, ag_i can manage the sets of major and minor issues constructively by performing the following actions [8]:

- analysis of the set SI_i of minor issues; selection of issues that are believed to cost less than they are worth to ag_j;
- addition of new issues to the set MI_i of major issues (and subsequent re-definition of the agenda);
- exploration of the differences in the valuation of the new issues.

The basic idea is to allow ag_i to prepare a new proposal that maximizes its benefit and simultaneously is more favourable to ag_j (than any previous proposal). Taken together, the suggested actions add an evolutionary dimension to the analysis. They can enable the enlargement of the space of feasible settlements, thus facilitating movement towards an optimal agreement.

Consider a new two-sided five-issue bargaining situation obtained from the two-sided four-issue situation introduced in subsection 3.1 by changing the agenda, *i.e.*, by adding a new good X_5 (again, to reduce the complexity of the analysis, and without loss of generality, we consider a particular bargaining situation – other situations, involving a *different* number of issues, are handled similarly). For the new bargaining game of alternating offers, time starts at period 1. However, the players' preferences take into account the costs of bargaining derived from the delays in consumption implied by the rejection of offers in the "initial" situation, *i.e.*,

$$U_i = \delta_i^{(t-1)+\tau}(ax_1 + bx_2 + x_3 + x_4) + \delta_i^{(t-1)}x_5$$

$$U_j = \delta_j^{(t-1)+\tau}[(1-x_1)+(1-x_2)+c(1-x_3)+d(1-x_4)] + \delta_j^{(t-1)}e(1-x_5)$$

where τ is a time period, $a > b > 1$ and $d > c > e > 1$. Consider the following strategies:

$$str_i^{**} = \begin{cases} \text{offer } (1, 1, 0, 0, x_{i5}^{**}) & \text{if } ag_i\text{'s turn} \\ \text{if } U_i(p_{j \to i}^{t-1}) \geq U_i^{**} \text{ accept else reject} & \text{if } ag_j\text{'s turn} \end{cases}$$

$$str_j^{**} = \begin{cases} \text{offer } (1, x_{j2}^{**}, 0, 0, 0) & \text{if } ag_j\text{'s turn} \\ \text{if } U_j(p_{i \to j}^{t}) \geq U_j^{**} \text{ accept else reject} & \text{if } ag_i\text{'s turn} \end{cases}$$

where
$$U_i^{**} = U_i(1, x_{j2}^{**}, 0, 0, 0), \qquad\qquad U_j^{**} = U_j(1, 1, 0, 0, x_{i5}^{**}),$$

$$x_{i5}^{**} = \frac{(a+b)\delta_i^{\tau}\delta_j^{\tau+1} - (a+b+bc+bd)\delta_i^{\tau-1}\delta_j^{\tau+1} + (bc+bd)\delta_i^{\tau-1}\delta_j^{\tau} - be\delta_i^{\tau-1}(\delta_j-1)}{be\delta_i^{\tau-1} - \delta_j^{\tau+1}}, \qquad \text{and}$$

$$x_{j2}^{**} = \frac{(abe+b^2e)\delta_i^{\tau} - abe\delta_i^{\tau-1} - (b+bc+bd)\delta_j^{\tau+1} + (bc+bd)\delta_j^{\tau} - be(\delta_j-1)}{b(be\delta_i^{\tau-1} - \delta_j^{\tau+1})}.$$

Remark 2. For the new bilateral five-issue bargaining game of alternating offers with an infinite horizon, in which the players' preferences are as described above, the strategies (str_i^{**}, str_j^{**}) form an equilibrium. The outcome is Pareto optimal:

$$x_1^{**} = 1, \qquad x_2^{**} = 1, \qquad x_3^{**} = 0, \qquad x_4^{**} = 0,$$

$$x_5^{**} = \frac{(a+b)\delta_i^{\tau}\delta_j^{\tau+1} - (a+b+bc+bd)\delta_i^{\tau-1}\delta_j^{\tau+1} + (bc+bd)\delta_i^{\tau-1}\delta_j^{\tau} - be\delta_i^{\tau-1}(\delta_j-1)}{be\delta_i^{\tau-1} - \delta_j^{\tau+1}}$$

Agreement is immediately reached with no delay.

The formal proof is presented in [8]. At this stage, it is worth noting that the offer specified in Remark 2 is more favourable to ag_j than the offer specified in Remark 1. Thus, this new offer can be accepted, *i.e.*, the negotiation process may end successfully and the Pareto optimal agreement may be implemented.

Example 2. David and Martin are still at it. David has proposed an optimal solution involving a four-week schedule for the production of 10000 suits and a six-week schedule for the production of 4000 suits (see point C in figure 2). However, Martin has rejected this solution and has stated that it will take two months to complete each task. Following the initial exchange of proposals, the agents have become entrenched in their positions and productive negotiation has almost stopped.

This is an example of a mismatched situation involving two intra-organisational agents – David tries to negotiate to an optimal solution and Martin wants to "win" the negotiation. Hence David can propose the addition of a new issue to the agenda – the right to attend future Sales Division meetings that are of interest to the Logistics Division. Consider that Martin feels reasonably about this new issue and agrees to add it to the agenda. Its inclusion unveils a new opportunity to exploit the

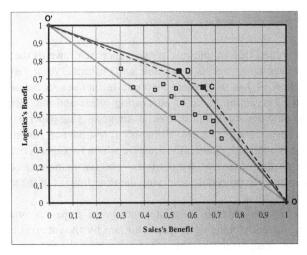

Fig. 2 New joint utility space for David and Martin (line ODO' represents the Pareto frontier)

differences in the valuation of the issues, thus changing the location of the Pareto frontier (see figure 2). Now, David can pursue the strategy str_i^{**} and propose a new optimal solution involving a four-week schedule for 10000 suits, a six-week schedule for 4000 suits, and the right to attend future Sales Division meetings. This solution is represented by the point D and provides a (normalized) benefit of 0.725 to Martin (letting $\delta_i \rightarrow 1$ and $\delta_j \rightarrow 1$). It is more favourable to Martin than the previous optimal solution. Thus, Martin may re-analyze the negotiation situation, adopt a different negotiating style, and respond favourably to this new solution.

5 Related Work

AI researchers have investigated the design of negotiating agents from both a formal perspective (see, e.g., [5]) and a computational perspective (see, e.g., [3, 4]). Most existing models use either game-theoretic techniques or methods from the social sciences, and largely ignore the integration of results from both areas. Yet, the task of designing negotiating agents involves the consideration of insights from multiple research areas to integrate different perspectives on negotiation. This paper has used game-theoretic techniques to define equilibrium strategies and has formalized a set of negotiation strategies studied in the social sciences.

Also, AI researchers have focused on modelling "successful" negotiations. Few researchers have attempted to model negotiations that are "difficult" to resolve and can hit an impasse (see, e.g., [2, 7, 13]). At present, despite these and other relevant pieces of work, the study of "difficult" negotiations and the formalization of effective approaches to impasse avoidance are still very much in its infancy. This paper has addressed these issues in a specific negotiation setting.

6 Conclusion

This paper has argued that an interdisciplinary approach towards the development of autonomous negotiating agents is possible and desirable. As a starting point for this research effort, it has used game-theoretic techniques to define equilibrium strategies for the bargaining game of alternating offers and has formalized a set of negotiation strategies studied in the social sciences. This paper has also shifted the emphasis to negotiations that are "difficult" to resolve and can hit an impasse. Specifically, it has analysed a particular situation where two agents bargain over the division of the surplus of several distinct issues and has demonstrated the benefits of an impasse avoidance procedure involving the re-definition of the agenda during the course of negotiation.

Autonomous agents able to negotiate and avoid impasses under complete information are currently being developed. Our aim for the future is to empirically evaluate the key components of the agents. We also intend to develop more sophisticated agents that are able to negotiate and avoid impasses under incomplete information.

References

1. Bichler, M., Kersten, G., Strecker, S.: Towards a Structured Design of Electronic Negotiations. Group Dec. and Neg. **12**, 311–335 (2003)
2. Faratin, P.: Automated Service Negotiation Between Autonomous Computational Agents. Ph.D. Thesis, Queen Mary & Westfield College, UK (2000)
3. Ito, T., Hattori, H., Zhang, M., Matsuo, T.: Rational, Robust, and Secure Negotiations in Multi-Agent Systems. Springer, Heidelberg (2008)
4. Jennings, N., Faratin, P., Lomuscio, A., Parsons, S., Wooldridge, M., Sierra, C.: Automated Negotiation: Prospects, Methods and Challenges. Group Dec. and Neg. **10**, 199–215 (2001)
5. Kraus,S.: Strategic Negotiation in Multi-Agent Environments. MIT Press, Cambridge (2001)
6. Lewicki,R., Barry, B., Saunders, D., Minton, J.: Negotiation. McGraw Hill, New York (2003)
7. Lopes, F., Mamede, N., Novais, A.Q., Coelho, H.: A Negotiation Model for Autonomous Computational Agents: Formal Description and Empirical Evaluation. Journal Intelligent & Fuzzy Systems **12**, 195–212 (2002)
8. Lopes, F., Fatima, S., Wooldridge, M.: Pre-Negotiation and Impasse in Automated Negotiation. Group Dec. and Neg. (submitted 2007)
9. Lopes, F., Novais, A., Coelho, H.: The Evolution of Negotiation and Impasse in Two-Party Multi-Issue Bargaining. In: Geffner, H. (ed.) Advances in AI (LNAI 5290), pp. 213-222. Springer, Heidelberg (2008)
10. Lopes, F., Novais, A., Coelho, H.: Towards an Interdisciplinary Framework for Automated Negotiation. In: Psaila, G., Wagner, R. (eds.) E-Commerce and Web Technologies (LNCS 5138), pp. 81-91. Springer, Heidelberg (2008)
11. Osborne, M., Rubinstein, A.: Bargaining and Markets. Academic Press, London (1990)
12. Pruitt, D., Kim, S.: Social Conflict: Escalation, Stalemate, and Settlement. McGraw Hill, New York (2004)
13. Sycara, K.: Problem Restructuring in Negotiation. Management Sci. **37**, 1248–1268 (1991)
14. Thompson, L.: The Mind and Heart of Negotiator. Prentice-Hall, Englewood Cliffs (2005)

INTELLIGENT SYSTEMS

Exploring Design Space For An Integrated Intelligent System

Nick Hawes and Jeremy Wyatt and Aaron Sloman

Abstract Understanding the trade-offs available in the design space of intelligent systems is a major unaddressed element in the study of Artificial Intelligence. In this paper we approach this problem in two ways. First, we discuss the development of our integrated robotic system in terms of its trajectory through design space. Second, we demonstrate the practical implications of architectural design decisions by using this system as an experimental platform for comparing behaviourally similar yet architecturally different systems. The results of this show that our system occupies a "sweet spot" in design space in terms of the cost of moving information between processing components.

1 Introduction

Intelligent systems (e.g. intelligent service robots) are a product of the many design decisions taken to ensure that the final system meets the requirements necessary to fit in its particular niche [1]. In nature, evolution creates behaviours and bodies that suit an animal's ecological niche. In the field of intelligent artifacts, choices about the design and implementation of hardware and software may be taken by a designer, or enforced by project or resource constraints. Few, if any, of these choices are truly independent; using a particular solution for one part of the system will constrain the space of solutions available for other parts of the system. For example, the number of degrees of freedom of an effector will restrict the design of the control software and behaviours required to use the effector, and the choice of middleware

Nick Hawes
School of Computer Science, University of Birmingham, UK e-mail: n.a.hawes@cs.bham.ac.uk

Jeremy Wyatt
School of Computer Science, University of Birmingham, UK e-mail: j.l.wyatt@cs.bham.ac.uk

Aaron Sloman
School of Computer Science, University of Birmingham, UK e-mail: a.sloman@cs.bham.ac.uk

for software components will restrict the communication patterns that components can use. Understanding the *trade-offs available in the design space of intelligent artifacts* is a major open issue in the understanding of integrated intelligent systems, and thus AI.

In this paper we focus on the design space of architectures for intelligent robots. We discuss the design of, and the trade-offs created by, an *architecture schema* for intelligent agents based on a model of shared working memories. Following this we present a novel exploration of the design space of information sharing models for architectures for integrated intelligent systems based on this schema. This exploration uses an intelligent robot as an experimental platform. The robot's architecture is varied in principled ways to generate quantitative information demonstrating the costs and benefits of the different designs.

2 Background

In the field of intelligent systems, the term "architecture" is still used to refer to many different, yet closely related, aspects of a system's design and implementation. Underlying all of these notions is the idea of a collection of units of functionality, information (whether implicitly or explicitly represented) and methods for bringing these together. At this level of description there is no real difference between the study of architectures in AI and software architectures in other branches of computer science. However, differences appear as we specialise this description to produce architectures that integrate various types of functionality to produce intelligent systems. Architectures for intelligent systems typically include elements such as fixed representations, reasoning mechanisms, and functionaly or behavioural component groupings. Once such elements are introduced, the trade-offs between different designs become important. Such trade-offs include the costs of dividing a system up to fit into a particular architecture design, and the costs of using a particular representation. Such trade-offs have been ignored by previous work on integrated systems, yet these factors are directly related to the efficacy of applying an architecture design to a particular problem. Our research studies architectures for integrated, intelligent systems in order to inform the designers of these systems of the trade-offs available to them.

An important distinction to make when studying the information-processing architectures used in intelligent systems is the distinction between architectures that are entirely-specified in advance (e.g. those used in [2, 3]), and architectures that are partially specified. This latter type can then be specialised to produce different *instantiations* of the architecture. We will refer to such partially specified architectures as architecture *schemas* as they provide outlines from which many different concrete instantiations can be designed. Examples of such schemas include cognitive modelling architectures such as ICARUS [4], ACT-R, [5], and Soar [6]; more general frameworks such as CogAff [1] and APOC [7]; and robotic architectures such as 3T [8]. It is worth noting that the freedom in specialisation available to the designer varies greatly across these schemas.

As architecture schemas can be instantiated in various ways, each one provides a framework for exploring a limited region of design space for possible architecture instantiations: the use of a particular schema restricts the available design space to be those designs that can be created within the schema. Although instantiations produced from a schema may vary considerably, they will all share certain characteristics as a consequence of occupying similar regions of design space. It is difficult to study these characteristics directly, particularly in implemented systems, because it is difficult to separate the effects of the schema (i.e. the aspects of the architecture that will exist in all instantiations of the schema) from the effects of the specialisation (i.e. any additional components and implementation work) in the finished system.

As we wish to study the effects of variations in architecture schema in implemented systems we need an experimental approach that overcomes the problem of separating schema effects from specialisation effects. Our approach involves taking a single task (i.e. a problem requiring a fixed set of known behaviours) and creating instantiations of a number of different architecture schemas to solve it. In this way the task-specific elements of the instantiations are invariant (e.g. the algorithms used to process input and generate output), whilst the schema-level elements change between instantiations (e.g. the nature of the connections between input and output modules). Assuming task-specific invariance exists, comparing instantiations of different schemas on a single task will then provide information about the trade-offs between the different design options offered by the schemas.

Such single-task comparisons could be performed using existing systems. For example, driving tasks have been tackled in ACT-R [9] and ICARUS [10], spatial reasoning tasks by SOAR [11] and ACT-R [12], and natural language understanding has been tackled with almost every architecture schema, e.g. in APOC [13]. The drawback of this approach is that the different instantiations performed by different researchers using different technology will almost certainly introduce variations in behaviour that may mask the underlying effects of the various architectures, making comparisons worthless. To make comparisons between implemented systems informative, the variation in instantiations must be controlled. This is an approach we explore in Section 4. An alternative approach is to perform these comparisons theoretically (cf. [14]), although this risks overlooking the critical aspects that only become apparent when building integrated systems.

3 From Requirements to Robots

To further explore the idea of design decisions constraining the design space available for a particular intelligent system, it is worth considering an example. Our current research project is studying the problem of building intelligent systems. We are approaching the problem from various perspectives including hardware control, subsystem design (including vision, planning etc.) and architectures. As the project has progressed we have made strong commitments to particular designs for elements of the overall system. These design commitments have constrained the space of solutions available for subsequent developments. Although the following description is anecdotal, it demonstrates one possible type of development trajectory[1] for an integrated intelligent system.

Prior to any design or development we analysed our target scenarios. From these scenarios we extracted a number of requirements for our integrated systems to satisfy, providing some initial constraints on design space. These requirements are too numerous to explore fully here, but the following proved important for subsequent developments:

- The system must feature concurrently active elements in order to respond to a dynamic world whilst processing.
- The system must represent and reason about hypothetical future states, thus requiring explicit representations.
- The system must support specialised reasoning in its subsystems, requiring support for multiple representations.

Although these requirements do not appear too restrictive, they rule out design approaches that require a single unified representation and that do not support concurrency. This prevents the use of many architectures for modelling human-level intelligence, and logic-based robotics approaches.

Our first design for a system to satisfy the scenario's requirements was constructed using the Open Agent Architecture (OAA) [15]. It featured concurrent components for language interpretation and generation, object category recognition using a modified variant of SIFT, generation of multiple forms of spatial representations, and cross-modal information fusion. The use of OAA constrained us to design the system as a network of exhaustively pair-wise connected components that exchanged information directly. Although the resulting system satisfied our requirements and demonstrated the desired behaviour, the architecture structure had a number of drawbacks. The main drawback was that the direct exchange of information made it difficult to share the same information between more than two components in a system, making it difficult to explore the consequences of component collaboration (e.g. using scene information to incrementally reduce the hypothesis space during parsing [13]). This is a clear of example of a design choice (the connection model enforced by the architecture) limiting the subsequently available design space (the design space of information sharing models). It is worth noting that in theory we could have implemented a different information sharing model on top of OAA, but this would not have been a natural fit with the underlying architecture. These kinds of specialisation costs (i.e. the cost of implementing one system given the constraints of another) are hard to measure, but typically very important in the design and implementation of intelligent systems.

---

[1] It is arguable that this development trajectory has much in common with a large number of intelligent and integrated system projects.

Because of the drawbacks of our OAA-based system, we decided to explore designs for architectures based on commonly accessible information stores. This led to the development of the CoSy Architecture Schema (CAS) [16, 17, 18], a schema that groups concurrently active processing components into separate *subarchitectures* via limited connections to *shared working memories*. In CAS all communication between components occurs via these working memories (rather than directly between components), enforcing the requirement of data sharing (see Figure 1(a)). However, the separation of components into groups around working memories brings its own set of design constraints, and these have become apparent in the systems we have built on top of CAS.

The systems we have built with CAS feature subarchitectures designed around particular representations, e.g. a visual subarchitecture containing 3D representations of objects, and a communication subarchitecture containing logical interpretations of utterances. Although these representations are shared, they are only intelligible by the components in the same subarchitecture. To obtain a complete view of all the information in the system, our instantiations have had to include a *binding* subarchitecture, which abstracts from other subarchitectures to provide a single amodal representation of the current state [19]. It is arguable that a system based on a single unified data store would not require such augmentation (although such a design would not meet our requirements). This again demonstrates how a design decision (separating information is into different memories) influences the subsequent design choices for a system. In this instance, choices were not completely ruled out, but additional mechanisms were required to support functionality that would have been more easily obtained in an alternative design.

4 Exploring Information Sharing Designs

The preceding discussion presents insights into system design in an entirely qualitative manner. To further the principled exploration of the design space of integrated intelligent systems, we want to generate quantitative data that describes possible trade-offs between designs. Given our experience with information sharing in different architectures, we chose to explore this area of design space using the comparative methodology described in Section 2.

There is a space of possible models for information sharing between components, ranging from point-to-point communication in which components share information only with directly connected components (i.e. the model used by the OAA-based system described in Section 3), to a broadcast model where components share information with every component in a system. Between these two extremes exist a range of possible systems in which components share information with a designer-defined subset of components. Which model is chosen can have a great impact on the behaviour of the final system, but little information is available to designers of intelligent systems about the trade-offs associated with this dimension of design space. In the remainder of this paper we make an initial attempt at filling this void.

4.1 Experimental System

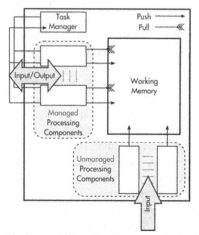

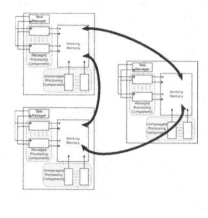

(a) The CAS subarchitecture design schema. All information passes via the working memory.

(b) A CAS architecture based on three subarchitectures. Cross-subarchitecture communication occurs via connections between working memories.

Fig. 1 Two views of the CoSy Architecture Schema.

The system which we have used to explore the effects of information sharing is derived from an intelligent robot cable of object manipulation and human-robot interaction [17]. It is based on the CAS architecture schema. This schema was briefly described in Section 3, and is pictured in Figure 1. This schema has a number of features relevant to developing integrated systems, but here we will focus on the approach it takes to passing information between components[2].

When information is operated on (added, overwritten or deleted) in a CAS working memory a *change event* is generated. This event structure contains information on the operation performed, the type (i.e. class name) of the information, the component which made the change, and the location of the information in the system. Components use this change event data to decide whether to perform some processing task with the changed information. To restrict the change events that are received, each component is able to *filter* the event stream based on change event contents. Components typically subscribe to relevant change information by registering callbacks on combinations of the fields in the change event. For example, a vision component may subscribe to additions of regions of interests. This filter would refer to the change event's operation type (addition) and data type (region of interest).

---

[2] For a more complete description of CAS, please see previous previous work, e.g. [16, 17, 18].

CAS groups components into subarchitectures around a working memory. These subarchitecture groupings influence the flow of change events, and thus the flow of information between components. Within a subarchitecture components a sent all the of change events generated by operations on that subarchitecture's working memory. They then use their filters to select the relevant events from this stream. Change events that describe operations on other working memories (i.e. those outside of the subarchitecture) are first checked against the union of all of the filters registered by components in a subarchitecture. If an event passes these filters then it is forwarded to all of the subarchitecture's components via the same mechanism used for local changes. This reuse of the existing filter mechanism adds redundancy to the change propagation mechanisms, but reduces the complexity of the system.

When a component reads information from, or writes information to, a working memory, or a change event is broadcast, a *communication event* occurs. A communication event abstracts away from the underlying communications infrastructure, hiding whether the information is being moved in memory, over a network or translated between programming languages. Within subarchitectures any operation requires a single communication event. When communication happens between two subarchitectures an additional communication event is required due to the separation (this is equivalent to the information passing over one of the dark lines in Figure 1(b)).

Change and communication events are implemented as part of our CoSy Architecture Schema Tookit (CAST) which realises the CAS schema in an open source, multi-language software framework [18]. In CAST the change event system is implemented as a callback mechanism modelled on event driven programming. The communication events are implemented as procedure calls or remote procedure calls depending on the languages and distribution methods used in the instantiation.

Using CAST we have built an integrated intelligent robot which featuring subarchitectures for vision, qualitative spatial reasoning (QSR), communication, continual planning, binding, manipulation and control [17]. To provide a simpler system useful for exploring the design space of information sharing mechanisms, reduced this system to a smaller number of subarchitectures: vision, binding, and QSR. This reduction was chosen because it provides a simpler system which still integrates two modalities with distinct representations (quantitative vision and qualitative spatial reasoning). For the experimental runs we replaced some of the components in the visual subarchitecture with simulated components. These not only simulated the results of visual processing, but also the interactions of the components via shared working memories (the important aspect of this study). This allowed us to fully automate interactions with the system in order to perform a large number of experimental runs. Aside from these alterations, the remaining components were taken directly from our original robotic system.

When presented with an object after a change to the visual scene, the system first determines its 3D position and then extracts some visual attributes. This information is abstracted into the binding subarchitecture where it become available in a simplified form to the rest of the system. The presence of object information in the binding subarchitecture triggers the QSR subarchitecture which computes spatial relations between the new object and any other known objects. This relational information is transmitted back to the binding subarchitecture where the relations are introduced between the existing object representations.

4.2 Methodology

We can use the shared memory-based design of CAS to explore the effects of varying information sharing patterns between components in our experimental system. We do this by altering the ratio of components to subarchitectures.

We start with an n-m design where n components are divided between m subarchitectures, where $n > m > 1$. This is our original system described above, in which components are assigned to subarchitectures based on functionality (vision, binding or QSR), although for this experimental work arbitrary n-m assignments are also possible (and would explore a wider area of design space). We then reconfigure this system to generate architectures at two extremes of the design space for information sharing models. At one extreme we have an n-1 design in which all n components from the original system are in the same subarchitecture. At the other extreme of design space we have an n-n design in which every component is in a subarchitecture of its own. Each of these designs can be considered a schema specialisation of the CAS schema from which a full instantiation can be made.

These various designs are intended to approximate, within the constraints of CAS, various possible designs used by existing systems. The n-1 design represents systems with a single shared data store to which all components have the same access. The n-m design represents systems in which a designer has imposed some modularity which limits how data is shared between components. The n-n design represents a system in which a no data is shared, but is instead transmitted directly between components. In the first two designs a component has do to extra work to determine what information it requires from the available shared information. In the latter two designs a component must do extra work to obtain information that is not immediately available to it (i.e. information that is not in it's subarchitecture's working memory).

In order to isolate the effects of the architectural alterations from the other runtime behaviours of the resulting systems, it is important that these architectural differences are the *only* differences that exist between the final CAS instantiations. It is critical that the systems are compared on the same task using the same components. CAST was designed to support this kind of experimentation: it allows the structure of instantiations to be changed considerably, with few, if any, changes to component code. This has allowed us to take the original implementation described above and create the n-1, n-m, and n-n instantiations without changing component code. This means that we can satisfy our original aim of comparing near-identical systems on the same tasks, with the only variations between them being architectural ones.

To measure the effects of the architecture variations, we require metrics that can be used to highlight these effects. We previously presented a list of possible metrics that could be recorded in an implemented CAS system to demonstrate the trade-offs in design space [20]. Ultimately we are interested in measuring how changes to the way information is shared impacts on the external behaviour of the systems, e.g. how often it successfully completes a task. However, given the limited functionality of our experimental system, these kind of behaviour metrics are relatively uninformative. Instead we have chosen to focus on lower-level properties of the system. We have compared the systems on:

1. variations in the number of **filtering operations** needed to obtain the change events necessary to get information to components as required by the task.
2. variations in the number of **communication events** required to move information around the system.

As discussed previously communication and change events underlie the behaviour of almost all of the processing performed by a system. Therefore changes in these metrics demonstrate how moving through the space of information sharing models supported by CAS influences the information processing profile of implemented systems.

We studied the three different designs in two configurations: one with vision and binding subarchitectures, and the second with these plus the addition of the QSR subarchitecture. This resulted in six final instantiations which we tested on three different simulated scenes: scenes containing one object, two objects and three objects. Each instantiation was run twenty times on each scene to account for variations unrelated to the system's design and implementation.

4.3 Results

The results for the filtering metric are based around the notion of a *relevant event*. A relevant event is a change event that a component is filtering for (i.e. an event that it has subscribed to). Figure 2 demonstrates the percentage of relevant events received per component in each instantiation. 100% means that a component only receives change events it is listening for. A lower percentage means that the connectivity of the system allows more than the relevant change events to get the component, which then has to filter out the relevant ones. This is perfectly natural in a shared memory system. The results demonstrate that a component in an n-1 instantiation receives the lowest percentage of relevant events. This is because within a subarchitecture, all changes are broadcast to all components, requiring each component to do a lot of filtering work. A component in an n-n instantiation receives the greatest percentage of relevant changes. This is because each component is shielded by a subarchitecture working memory that only allows change events that are relevant to the attached components to pass. In the n-n case because only a single component is in each subarchitecture this number is predictably high[3]. This figure demonstrates the benefits

---

[3] The events required by the manager component in each subarchitecture mean the relevant percentage for the n-n instantiations is not 100%.

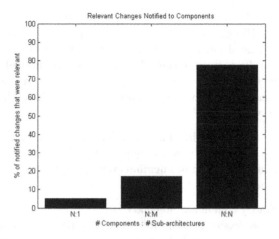

Fig. 2 Average number of relevant change events received per component.

of a directly connected instantiation: components only receive the information they need.

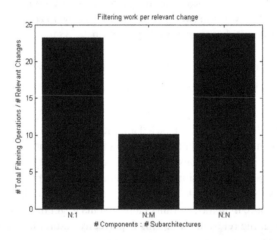

Fig. 3 Average filtering effort per relevant change event received.

However, this increase in the percentage of relevant changes received comes at a cost. If we factor in the filtering operations being performed at a subarchitecture level (which could be considered as "routing" operations), we can produce a figure demonstrating the total number of filtering operations (i.e. both those at a subarchitecture and a component level) per relevant change received. This is presented in Figure 3. This shows a striking similarity between the results for the n-1 and n-n instantiations, both of which require a larger number of filtering operations per rel-

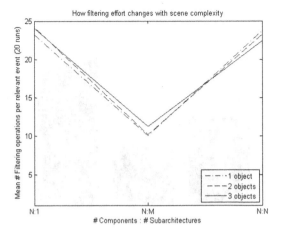

Fig. 4 Average filtering effort per relevant event compared to scene complexity.

evant change than the *n-m* instantiations. In the *n-m* systems, the arrangement of components into functionally themed subarchitectures results in both smaller numbers of change events being broadcast within subarchitectures (because there are fewer components in each one), and a smaller number of change events being broadcast outside of subarchitectures (because the functional grouping means that some changes are only required within particular subarchitectures). These facts mean that an individual component in an *n-m* instantiation receives fewer irrelevant change events that must be rejected by its filter. Conversely a component in the other instantiations must filter relevant changes from a stream of changes containing *all of the change events in the system*. In the *n-1* instantiations this is because all of these changes are broadcast within a subarchitecture. In the *n-n* instantiations this is because all of these changes are broadcast between subarchitectures. Figure 4 shows that these results are robust against changes in the number of objects in a scene. Also, the nature of the results did not change between the systems with vision and binding components, and those with the additional QSR components.

Figure 5 demonstrates the average number of communication events per system run across the various scenes and configurations for the three different connectivity instantiations. This shows that an *n-n* instantiation requires approximately 4000 more communication events on average to perform the same task as the *n-1* instantiation, which itself requires approximately 2000 more communication events than the *n-m* instantiation. Figure 6 demonstrates that this result is robust in the face of changes to the number of objects in a scene. The nature of the results also did not change between the systems with vision and binding components, and those with the additional QSR components.

This result is due to two properties of the systems. In the *n-n* system, every interaction between a component a working memory (whether it's an operation on information or the propagation of a change event) requires an additional commu-

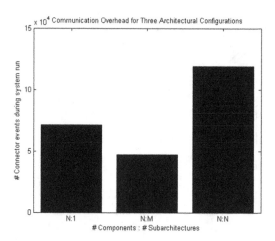

Fig. 5 Average total communication events per instantiation run.

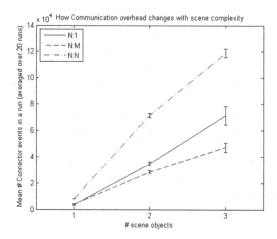

Fig. 6 Average total communication events per instantiation run compared to scene complexity.

nication event. This is because all components are separated by subarchitectures as well as working memories. In addition to this, the number of change events propagated through the systems greatly effect the amount of communication events that occur. In the *n-n* and *n-1* instantiations, the fact that they effectively broadcast all change events throughout the system contributes significantly to the communication overhead of the system.

5 Conclusions

From these results we can conclude that a functionally-decomposed n-m CAS instantiation occupies a "sweet spot" in architectural design space with reference to filtering and communication costs. This sweet spot occurs because having too much information shared between components in a system (the n-1 extreme) means that all components incur an overhead associated with filtering out relevant information from the irrelevant information. At the other extreme, when information is not shared by default (the n-n extreme) there are extra communication costs due to duplicated transmissions between pairs of components, and (in CAS-derived systems at least) the "routing" overhead of transmitting information to the correct components (i.e. the filtering performed by working memories rather than components).

In this simple example the existence of such a sweet spot, subject to well defined assumptions, could be established mathematically without doing any of these experiments. However, we have shown the possibility of running experiments to test such mathematical derivations, and also to deal with cases where no obvious mathematical analysis is available because of the particular features of an implementation.

It is clear that our results are not the end of the story. We have yet to explore n-m instantiations that are not designed along functional lines; it seems sensible to expect them not to perform as well as the n-m system presented here. It is also not clear that n-n instantiations in CAS accurately capture the benefits of a directly connected system, as CAS's design is tailored to information sharing as a default.

This observation leads us to consider an open question: what other appropriate metrics should be considered when evaluating trajectories through design space? In this paper we considered relatively low-level metrics because they could be captured and characterised relatively easily. Other relevant metrics include behavioural measures (e.g. how likely a system is to achieve a goal), expressiveness measures (e.g. how easy it is to encode a particular solution to a problem in an architecture), and meta-level measures (e.g. how easy it is for a designer, or the system itself, to reconfigure the architecture or alter its functionality). It is only when this whole space of possibilities is addressed can we truly start to judge the trade-offs of designing an architecture in a particular way (with reference to a particular task).

Even given these shortcomings, the novel experimental methodology presented in this paper points to a route forward for the principled study of integrated intelligent systems in AI. It is our hope that further work along these lines will provide system designers with a body of knowledge about the choices and trade-offs available in architectural design space, allowing them to build systems that satisfy their requirements in an informed and principled manner.

Acknowledgements This work was supported by the EU FP6 IST Cognitive Systems Integrated Project "CoSy" FP6-004250-IP, and the EU FP7 IST Cognitive Systems Integrated Project "CogX" ICT-215181-CogX.

References

1. Sloman, A.: The "semantics" of evolution: Trajectories and trade-offs in design space and niche space. In: IBERAMIA '98, pp. 27–38 (1998)
2. Mavridis, N., Roy, D.: Grounded situation models for robots: Where words and percepts meet. In: IROS '06 (2006)
3. Mcguire, P., Fritsch, J., Steil, J.J., Rothling, F., Fink, G.A., Wachsmuth, S., Sagerer, G., Ritter, H.: Multi-modal human-machine communication for instructing robot grasping tasks. In: IROS '02 (2002)
4. Langley, P., Choi, D.: A unified cognitive architecture for physical agents. In: AAAI '06 (2006)
5. Anderson, J.R., Bothell, D., Byrne, M.D., Douglass, S., Lebiere, C., Qin, Y.: An integrated theory of the mind. Psychological Review 111(4), 1036–1060 (2004)
6. Laird, J.E., Newell, A., Rosenbloom, P.S.: Soar: An architecture for general intelligence. AIJ 33(3), 1–64 (1987)
7. Andronache, V., Scheutz, M.: Integrating theory and practice: The agent architecture framework apoc and its development environment ade. In: AAMAS '04, pp. 1014–1021 (2004)
8. Gat, E.: On three-layer architectures. In: D. Kortenkamp, R.P. Bonnasso, R. Murphy (eds.) Artificial Intelligence and Mobile Robots (1997)
9. Salvucci, D.D.: Modeling driver behavior in a cognitive architecture. Human Factors (48), 362–380 (2006)
10. Choi, D., Morgan, M., Park, C., Langley, P.: A testbed for evaluation of architectures for physical agents. In: AAAI '07 WS: Evaluating Architectures for Intelligence (2007)
11. Wintermute, S., Laird, J.E.: Predicate projection in a bimodal spatial reasoning system. In: AAAI '07, pp. 1572 – 1577 (2007)
12. Kennedy, W.G., Bugajska, M.D., Marge, M., Adams, W., Fransen, B.R., Perzanowski, D., Schultz, A.C., Trafton, J.G.: Spatial representation and reasoning for human-robot collaboration. In: AAAI '07, pp. 1554–1559 (2007)
13. Brick, T., Scheutz, M.: Incremental natural language processing for hri. In: HRI '07, pp. 263–270 (2007)
14. Jones, R.M., Wray, R.E.: Comparative analysis of frameworks for knowledge-intensive intelligent agents. AI Mag. 27(2), 57–70 (2006)
15. Cheyer, A., Martin, D.: The open agent architecture. Autonomous Agents and Multi-Agent Systems 4(1), 143–148 (2001)
16. Hawes, N., Wyatt, J., Sloman, A.: An architecture schema for embodied cognitive systems. Tech. Rep. CSR-06-12, Uni. of Birmingham, School of Computer Science (2006)
17. Hawes, N., Sloman, A., Wyatt, J., Zillich, M., Jacobsson, H., Kruijff, G.J., Brenner, M., Berginc, G., Skočaj, D.: Towards an integrated robot with multiple cognitive functions. In: AAAI '07, pp. 1548 – 1553 (2007)
18. Hawes, N., Zillich, M., Wyatt, J.: BALT & CAST: Middleware for cognitive robotics. Tech. Rep. CSR-07-1, Uni. of Birmingham, School of Computer Science (2007). URL ftp://ftp.cs.bham.ac.uk/pub/tech-reports/2007/CSR-07-1.pdf
19. Jacobsson, H., Hawes, N., Kruijff, G.J., Wyatt, J.: Crossmodal content binding in information-processing architectures. In: Proceedings of the 3rd ACM/IEEE International Conference on Human-Robot Interaction (HRI). Amsterdam, The Netherlands (2008)
20. Hawes, N., Sloman, A., Wyatt, J.: Towards an empirical exploration of design space. In: Proc. of the 2007 AAAI Workshop on Evaluating Architectures for Intelligence. Vancouver, Canada (2007)

A User-Extensible and Adaptable Parser Architecture

John Tobin and Carl Vogel

Abstract Some parsers need to be very precise and strict when parsing, yet must allow users to easily adapt or extend the parser to parse new inputs, without requiring that the user have an in-depth knowledge and understanding of the parser's internal workings. This paper presents a novel parsing architecture, designed for parsing Postfix log files, that aims to make the process of parsing new inputs as simple as possible, enabling users to trivially add new rules (to parse variants of existing inputs) and relatively easily add new actions (to process a previously unknown category of input). The architecture scales linearly or better as the number of rules and size of input increases, making it suitable for parsing large corpora or months of accumulated data.

1 Introduction

The architecture described herein was developed as part of a larger project to improve anti-spam defences by analysing the performance of the set of filters currently in use, optimising the order and membership of the set based on that analysis, and developing supplemental filters where deficiencies are identified. Most anti-spam techniques are content-based (e.g. [3, 7, 11]) and require the mail to be accepted before determining if it is spam, but rejecting mail during the delivery attempt is preferable: senders of non-spam mail that is mistakenly rejected will receive an immediate non-delivery notice; resource usage is reduced on the accepting mail server (allowing more intensive content-based techniques to be used on the mail that is accepted); users have less spam mail to wade through. Improving the performance of anti-spam techniques that are applied when mail is being transferred via Simple Mail Transfer Protocol (SMTP)[1] is the goal of this project, by providing a platform

John Tobin e-mail: `tobinjt@cs.tcd.ie` · Carl Vogel e-mail: `vogel@cs.tcd.ie`
School of Computer Science and Statistics, Trinity College, Dublin 2, Ireland.
Supported by Science Foundation Ireland RFP 05/RF/CMS002.

for reasoning about anti-spam filters. The approach chosen to measure performance is to analyse the log files produced by the SMTP server in use, Postfix [13], rather than modifying it to generate statistics: this approach improves the chances of other sites testing and using the software. The need arose for a parser capable of dealing with the great number and variety of log lines produced by Postfix: the parser must be designed so that adding support for parsing new inputs is a simple task, because the log lines to be parsed will change over time. The variety in log lines occurs for several reasons:

- Log lines differ amongst versions of Postfix.
- The mail administrator can define custom rejection messages.
- External resources utilised by Postfix (e.g. DNS Black List (DNSBL) or policy servers [14]) can change their messages without warning.

It was hoped to reuse an existing parser rather than writing one from scratch, but the existing parsers considered were rejected for one or more of the following reasons: they parsed too small a fraction of the log files; their parsing was too inexact; they did not extract sufficient data. The effort required to adapt and improve an existing parser was judged to be greater than the effort to write a new one, because the techniques used by the existing parsers severely limited their potential: some ignored the majority of log lines, parsing specific log lines accurately, but without any provision for parsing new or similar log lines; others sloppily parsed the majority of log lines, but were incapable of distinguishing between log lines of the same category, e.g. rejecting a mail delivery attempt. The only prior published work on the subject of parsing Postfix log files that the authors are aware of is *Log Mail Analyser: Architecture and Practical Utilizations* [4], which aims to extract data from log files, correlate it, and present it in a form suitable for a systems administrator to search using the myriad of standard Unix text processing utilities already available. A full state of the art review is outside the scope of this paper but will be included in the thesis resulting from this work.

The solution developed is conceptually simple: provide a few generic functions (*actions*), each capable of dealing with an entire category of inputs (e.g. rejecting a mail delivery attempt), accompanied by a multitude of precise patterns (*rules*), each of which matches all inputs of a specific type and only that type (e.g. rejection by a specific DNSBL). It is an accepted standard to separate the parsing procedure from the declarative grammar it operates with; part of the novelty here is in the way that the grammar is itself partially procedural (each action is a separate procedure). This architecture is ideally suited to parsing inputs where the input is not fully understood or does not conform to a fixed grammar: the architecture warns about unparsed inputs and other errors, but continues parsing as best it can, allowing the developer of a new parser to decide which deficiencies are most important and require attention first, rather than being forced to fix the first error that arises.

---

[1] Simple Mail Transfer Protocol transfers mail across the Internet from the sender to one or more recipients. It is a simple, human readable, plain text protocol, making it quite easy to test and debug problems with it. The original protocol definition is RFC 821 [10], updated in RFC 2821 [9].

2 Architecture

The architecture is split into three sections: framework, actions and rules. Each will be discussed separately, but first an overview:

Framework   The framework is the structure that actions and rules plug into. It provides the parsing loop, shared data storage, loading and validation of rules, storage of results, and other support functions.
Actions   Each action performs the work required to deal with a single category of inputs, e.g. processing data from rejections.
Rules   The rules are responsible for classifying inputs, specifying the action to invoke and the regex that matches the inputs and extracts data.

For each input the framework tries each rule in turn until it finds a rule that matches the input, then invokes the action specified by that rule.

Decoupling the parsing rules from their associated actions allows new rules to be written and tested without requiring modifications to the parser source code, significantly lowering the barrier to entry for casual users who need to parse new inputs, e.g. part-time systems administrators attempting to combat and reduce spam; it also allows companies to develop user-extensible parsers without divulging their source code. Decoupling the actions from the framework simplifies both framework and actions: the framework provides services to the actions, but does not need to perform any tasks specific to the input being parsed; actions benefit from having services provided by the framework, freeing them to concentrate on the task of accurately and correctly processing the information provided by rules.

Decoupling also creates a clear separation of functionality: rules handle low level details of identifying inputs and extracting data; actions handle the higher level tasks of assembling the required data, dealing with the intricacies of the input being parsed, complications arising, etc.; the framework provides services to actions and manages the parsing process.

Some similarity exists between this architecture and William Wood's Augmented Transition Networks (ATN) [6, 16], used in Computational Linguistics for creating grammars to parse or generate sentences. The resemblance between the two (shown in table 1) is accidental, but it is obvious that the two approaches share a similar division of responsibilities, despite having different semantics.

Table 1 Similarities with ATN

ATN	Parser Architecture	Similarity
Networks	Framework	Determines the sequence of transitions or actions that constitutes a valid input.
Transitions	Actions	Assembles data and imposes conditions the input must meet to be accepted as valid.
Abbreviations	Rules	Responsible for classifying input.

2.1 Framework

The framework takes care of miscellaneous support functions and low level details of parsing, freeing the programmers writing actions to concentrate on writing productive code. It links actions and rules, allowing either to be improved independently of the other. It provides shared storage to pass data between actions, loads and validates rules, manages parsing, invokes actions, tracks how often each rule matches to optimise rule ordering (§3.2 [p. 9]), and stores results in the database. Most parsers will require the same basic functionality from the framework, plus some specialised support functions. The framework is the core of the architecture and is deliberately quite simple: the rules deal with the variation in inputs, and the actions deal with the intricacies and complications encountered when parsing.

The function that finds the rule matching the input and invokes the requested action can be expressed in pseudo-code as:

```
for each input:
    for each rule defined by the user:
        if this rule matches the input:
            perform the action specified by the rule
            skip the remaining rules
            process the next input
    warn the user that the input was not parsed
```

2.2 Actions

Each action is a separate procedure written to deal with a particular category of input, e.g. rejections. The actions are parser-specific: each parser author will need to write the required actions from scratch unless extending an existing parser. It is anticipated that parsers based on this architecture will have a high ratio of rules to actions, with the aim of having simpler rules and clearer distinctions between the inputs parsed by different rules. In the Postfix log parser developed for this project there are 18 actions and 169 rules, with an uneven distribution of rules to actions as shown in fig. 1 on the facing page. Unsurprisingly, the action with the most associated rules is DELIVERY_REJECTED, the action that handles Postfix rejecting a mail delivery attempt; it is followed by SAVE_DATA, the action responsible for handling informative log lines, supplementing the data gathered from other log lines. The third most common action is, perhaps surprisingly, UNINTERESTING: this action does nothing when executed, allowing uninteresting log lines to be parsed without causing any effects (it does not imply that the input is ungrammatical or unparsed). Generally rules specifying the UNINTERESTING action parse log lines that are not associated with a specific mail, e.g. notices about configuration files changing. The remaining actions have only one or two associated rules: some actions are required to address a deficiency in the log files, or a complication that

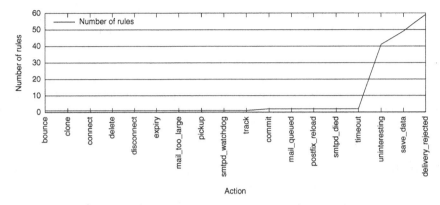

Fig. 1 Distribution of rules per action

arises during parsing; other actions will only ever have one log line variant, e.g. all log lines showing that a remote client has connected are matched by a single rule and handled by the CONNECT action.

Using the CONNECT action as an example: it creates a new data structure in memory for the new client connection, saving the data extracted by the rule into it; this data will be entered into the database when the mail delivery attempt is complete. If a data structure already exists for the new connection it is treated as a symptom of a bug, and the action issues a warning containing the full contents of the existing data structure, plus the log line that has just been parsed.

The ability to add special purpose actions to deal with difficulties and new requirements that are discovered during parser development is one of the strengths of this architecture. Instead of writing a single monolithic function that must be modified to support new behaviour, with all the attendant risks of adversely affecting the existing parser, when a new requirement arises an independent action can be written to satisfy it. Sometimes the new action will require the cooperation of other actions, e.g. to set or check a flag. There is a possibility of introducing failure when modifying existing actions in this way, but the modifications will be smaller and occur less frequently than with a monolithic architecture, thus failures will be less likely to occur and will be easier to test for and diagnose. The architecture can be implemented in an object oriented style, allowing sub-classes to extend or override actions in addition to adding new actions; because each action is an independent procedure, the sub-class need only modify the action it is overriding, rather than reproducing large chunks of functionality.

During development of the Postfix log parser it became apparent that in addition to the obvious variety in log lines there were many complications to be overcome. Some were the result of deficiencies in Postfix's logging (some of which were rectified by later versions of Postfix); others were due to the vagaries of process scheduling, client behaviour, and administrative actions. All were successfully accommodated in the Postfix log parser: adding new actions was enough to overcome several of the complications; others required modifications to a single existing action to work around the difficulties; the remainder were resolved by adapting existing actions to cooperate and exchange extra data, changing their behaviour as appropriate based on that extra data.

Actions may return a modified input line that will be parsed as if read from the input stream, allowing for a simplified version of cascaded parsing [1]. This powerful facility allows several rules and actions to parse a single input, potentially simplifying both rules and actions.

2.3 Rules

Rules categorise inputs, specifying both the regex to match against each input and the action to invoke when the match is successful. The Postfix log parser stores the rules it uses in the same SQL database the results are stored in, removing any doubt about which set of rules was used to produce a set of results; other implementations are free to store their rules in whatever fashion suits their needs. The framework warns about every unparsed input, to alert the user that they need to alter or extend their ruleset; the Postfix log parser successfully parses every log line in the 522 log files it is currently being tested with. The framework requires each rule to have `action` and `regex` attributes; each implementation is free to add any additional attributes it requires. The Postfix log parser adds attributes for several reasons: optimising rule ordering (§3.2 [p. 9]); restricting which log lines each rule can be matched against; and to describe each rule. Keywords in the rule's regex specify the data to be extracted from the input, but the Postfix log parser also provides a mechanism for rules to specify extra data to be saved.

Parsing new inputs is generally achieved by creating a new rule that pairs an existing action with a new regex. The Postfix log parser supplies a utility based on Simple Logfile Clustering Tool [12] to aid in producing regexes from unparsed log lines. Decoupling the rules from the actions and framework enables other rule management approaches to be used, e.g. instead of manually adding new rules, machine learning techniques could be used to automatically generate new rules. If this approach was taken the choice of machine learning technique would be constrained by the size of typical data sets (see §3 [p. 8]). Techniques requiring the full data set when training would be impractical; Instance Based Learning [2] techniques that automatically determine which inputs from the training set are valuable and which inputs can be discarded might reduce the data required to a manageable size. A parser might also dynamically create new rules in response to certain inputs, e.g. diagnostic messages indicating the source of the inputs has read a new configuration file. These avenues of research and development has not been pursued by the authors, but could easily be undertaken independently.

The architecture does not try to detect overlapping rules: that responsibility is left to the author of the rules. Unintentionally overlapping rules lead to inconsistent parsing and data extraction because the first matching rule wins, and the order in which rules are tried against each input might change between parser invocations.

Overlapping rules are frequently a requirement, allowing a more specific rule to match some inputs and a more general rule to match the remainder, e.g. separating SMTP delivery to specific sites from SMTP delivery to the rest of the world. Allowing overlapping rules simplifies both the general rule and the more specific rule; additionally rules from different sources can be combined with a minimum of prior cooperation or modification required. Overlapping rules should have a priority attribute to specify their relative ordering; negative priorities may be useful for catchall rules.

Decoupling the rules from the actions allows external tools to be written to detect overlapping rules. Traditional regexes are equivalent in computational power to Finite Automata (FA) and can be converted to FA, so regex overlap can be detected by finding a non-empty intersection of two FA. The standard equation for FA intersection (given for example in [17]) is: $FA1 \cap FA2 = \overline{(\overline{FA1} \cup \overline{FA2})}$, which has considerable computation complexity. Perl 5.10 regexes are more powerful than traditional regexes: it is possible to match correctly balanced brackets nested to an arbitrary depth, e.g. `/^[^<>]*(<(?:(?>[^<>]+)|(?1))*>)[^<>]*$/` matches `z<123<pq<>rs>j<r>ml>s`. Perl 5.10 regexes can maintain an arbitrary state stack and are thus equivalent in computational power to Pushdown Automata (PDA) or Context-Free Languages (CFL), so detecting overlap may require calculating the intersection of two PDA or CFL. The intersection of two CFL is not closed, i.e. the resulting language cannot always be parsed by a CFL, so intersection may be intractable in some cases e.g.: $a^*b^nc^n \cap a^nb^nc^* \rightarrow a^nb^nc^n$. Detecting overlap amongst n regexes requires calculating $n(n-1)/2$ intersections, resulting in $O(n^2x)$ complexity, where $O(x)$ is the complexity of calculating intersection. This is certainly not a task to be performed every time the parser is used: detecting overlap amongst the Postfix log parser's 169 rules would require calculating 14196 intersections.

It is possible to define pathological regexes which fall into two main categories: regexes that match every input, and regexes that consume excessive amounts of CPU time during matching. Defining a regex to match all inputs is trivial: `/^/` matches the start of every input. Usually excessive CPU time is consumed when a regex with a lot of alteration and variable quantifiers fails to match, but successful matching is generally quite fast (see [5] for in-depth discussion).

The example rule in table 2 matches the following sample log line logged by Postfix when a remote client connects to deliver mail:

```
connect from client.example.com[192.0.2.3]
```

Table 2 Example rule

Attribute	Value
regex	`^connect from (__CLIENT_HOSTNAME__)\[(__CLIENT_IP__)\]$`
action	CONNECT (described in §2.2 [p. 4])

2.4 Architecture Characteristics

Matching rules against inputs is simple: The first matching rule determines the action that will be invoked: there is no backtracking to try alternate rules, no attempt is made to pick a *best* rule.

Line oriented: The architecture is line oriented at present: there is no facility for rules to consume more input or push unused input back onto the input stream. This was not a deliberate design decision, rather a consequence of the line oriented nature of Postfix log files; more flexible approaches could be pursued.

Context-free rules: Rules can not take into account past or future inputs. In context-free grammar terms the parser rules could be described as:
$<$input$> \mapsto$ rule-1|rule-2|rule-3|...|rule-n.

Context-aware actions: Actions can consult the results (or lack of results) of previous actions during execution, providing some context sensitivity.

Cascaded parsing: Actions can return a modified input to be parsed as if read from the input stream, allowing for a simplified version of cascaded parsing [1].

Transduction: The architecture can be thought of as implementing transduction: it takes data in one form (log files) and transforms it to another form (a database); other formats may be more suitable for other implementations.

Closer to Natural Language Processing than using a fixed grammar: Unlike traditional parsers such as those used when compiling a programming language, this architecture does not require a fixed grammar specification that inputs must adhere to. The architecture is capable of dealing with interleaved inputs, out of order inputs, and ambiguous inputs where heuristics must be applied — all have arisen and been successfully accommodated in the Postfix log parser.

3 Results

Parsing efficiency is an obvious concern when the Postfix log parser routinely needs to parse large log files. The mail server which generated the log files used in testing the Postfix log parser accepts approximately 10,000 mails for 700 users per day; median log file size is 50 MB, containing 285,000 log lines — large scale mail servers would have much larger log files. When generating the timing data used in this section, 93 log files (totaling 10.08 GB, 60.72 million log lines) were each parsed 10 times and the parsing times averaged. Saving results to the database was disabled for the test runs, because the tests are aimed at measuring the speed of the Postfix log parser rather than the speed of the database. The computer used for test runs is a Dell Optiplex 745 described in table 3 on the next page, dedicated to the task of gathering statistics from test runs. Parsing all 93 log files in one run took 2 hours, 19 minutes and 17.293 seconds, mean throughput is 68.994 MB (435,942.882 log lines) parsed per minute; median throughput when parsing files separately was 80.854 MB (480,569.173 log lines) parsed per minute.

Table 3 Computer used to generate statistics

Component	Component in use
CPU	1 dual core 2.40GHz Intel® Core™2 CPU, with 32KB L1 and 4MB L2 cache.
RAM	2GB 667 MHz DDR RAM.
Hard disk	1 Seagate Barracuda 7200 RPM 250GB SATA hard disk.

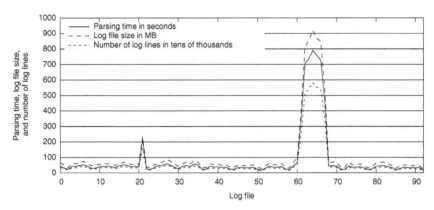

Fig. 2 Parsing time, log file size, and number of log lines

3.1 Architecture Scalability: Input Size

An important property of a parser is how parsing time scales relative to input size: linearly, polynomially, or exponentially? Figure 2 shows the parsing time in seconds, log file size in MB, and number of log lines in tens of thousands, for each of the 93 log files. The lines on the graph run roughly in parallel, giving the impression that the algorithm scales linearly with input size. This impression is borne out by fig. 3 on the next page: the ratios are tightly banded across the graph, showing that the algorithm scales linearly. The ratios increase (i.e. improve) for log files 22 and 62–68 despite their large size; that unusually large size is due to mail forwarding loops resulting in a greatly increased number of mails delivered and log lines generated.

3.2 Rule Ordering

Figure 4 on the following page shows the number of log lines in the 93 log files matched by each of the Postfix log parser's 169 rules. The top ten rules match 85.036% of the log lines, with the remainder tailing off similar to a Power Law distribution. Assuming that the distribution of log lines is reasonably consistent over time, parser efficiency should benefit from trying more frequently matching rules

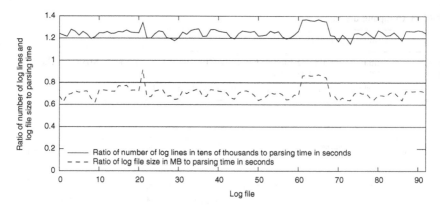

Fig. 3 Ratio of number of log lines and log file size to parsing time

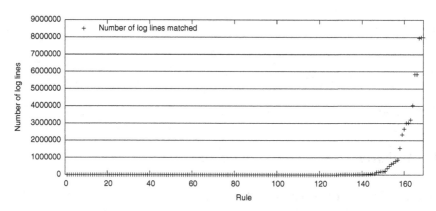

Fig. 4 Number of log lines matched by each rule

before those which match less frequently. To test this hypothesis three full test runs
were performed with different rule orderings:

optimal   Hypothetically the best order: rules which match most often will be tried
            first.

shuffled   Random ordering, intended to represent an unsorted rule set. Note that
            the ordering will change every time the parser is executed, so 10 different
            orderings will be generated for each log file in the test run.

reverse   Hypothetically the worst order: the most frequently matching rules will
            be tried last.

Figure 5 on the next page shows the parsing times of optimal and reverse orderings as a percentage of shuffled ordering parsing time. This optimisation provides a
mean reduction in parsing time of 14.785% with normal log files, 5.102% when a
mail loop occurs and the distribution of log lines is unusual. Optimal rule ordering
has other benefits, described in §3.3 on the facing page.

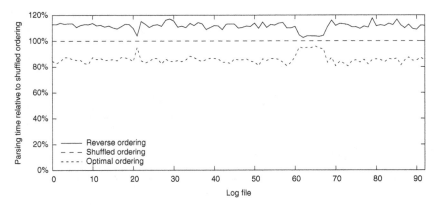

Fig. 5 Parsing time relative to shuffled ordering

3.3 Architecture Scalability: Number of Rules

How any architecture scales as the number of rules increases is important, but it is particularly important for this architecture because it is expected that typical parsers will have a large number of rules. There are 169 rules in the full Postfix log parser ruleset (parsing 522 log files), but the minimum number of rules required to parse the 93 log files is 115, 68.04% of the full ruleset. A second set of test runs was performed using the minimum ruleset, and the parsing times compared to those generated using the full ruleset: the percentage parsing time increase when using the full ruleset instead of the minimal ruleset for optimal, shuffled and reverse orderings is shown in fig. 6 on the next page. Clearly the increased number of rules has a noticeable performance impact with reverse ordering, and a lesser impact with shuffled ordering. The optimal ordering shows a mean increase of 0.63% in parsing time for a 46.95% increase in the number of rules. These results show that the architecture scales extremely well as the number of rules increases, and that optimally ordering the rules enables this.

3.4 Coverage

The Postfix log parser has two different types of coverage to be measured: log lines correctly parsed, and mail delivery attempts correctly understood (the former is a requirement for the latter to be achieved). Improving the former is less difficult, as usually it just requires new rules to be written; improving the latter is more difficult and intrusive as it requires adding or changing actions, and it can be much harder to notice that a deficiency exists.

Correct parsing of log lines must be measured first. Warnings are issued for any log lines that are not parsed; no such warnings are issued while parsing the 93 log

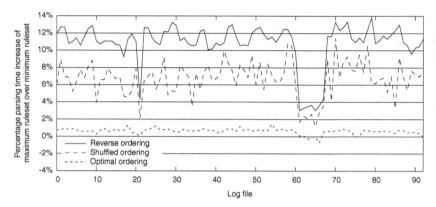

Fig. 6 Percentage parsing time increase of maximum ruleset over minimum ruleset

files, therefore there are zero false negatives. False positives are harder to quantify: manually verifying that the correct rule parsed each of the 60,721,709 log lines is infeasible. A random sample of 6,039 log lines (0.00994% of 60,721,709) was parsed and the results manually verified by inspection to ensure that the correct rule's regex matched each log line. The sample results contained zero false positives, and this check has been automated to ensure continued accuracy. The authors are confident that zero false positives occur when parsing the 93 log files.

The proportion of mail delivery attempts correctly understood is much more difficult to determine accurately than the proportion of log lines correctly parsed. The implementation can dump its state tables in a human readable form; examining these tables with reference to the log files and database is the best way to detect misunderstood mail delivery attempts. The Postfix log parser issues warnings when it detects any errors or discrepancies, alerting the user to the problem. There should be few or no warnings during parsing, and when parsing is finished the state table should only contain entries for mail delivery attempts starting before or ending after the log file. A second sample of 6000 log lines was parsed with all debugging options enabled, resulting in 167,448 lines of output. All 167,448 lines were examined in conjunction with the log segment and a dump of the resulting database, verifying that for each of the log lines the Postfix log parser performed correctly. The implementation produced 4 warnings about deficiencies in the log segment, 10 mails correctly remaining in the state tables, and 1625 correct entries in the database: it produced 0 false positives. No error or warning messages were produced, therefore there were no false negatives. Given the evidence detailed above, the authors are confident that zero false positives or negatives occur when parsing the 93 log files.

Experience implementing the Postfix log parser shows that full input coverage is relatively easy to achieve with this architecture, and that with enough time and effort full understanding of the input is possible. Postfix log files would require substantial time and effort to correctly parse regardless of the architecture used; this architecture enables an iterative approach to be used (similar to Stepwise Refinement [15]), as is practiced in many other software engineering disciplines.

4 Conclusion

This architecture's greatest strength is the ease with which it can be adapted to deal with new requirements and inputs. Parsing a variation of an existing input is a trivial task: simply modify an existing rule or add a new rule with an appropriate regex and the task is complete. Parsing a new category of input is achieved by writing a new action and appropriate rules; quite often the new action will not need to interact with existing actions, but when interaction is required the framework provides the necessary facilities. The decoupling of rules from actions allows different sets of rules to be used with the same actions, e.g. a parser might have actions to process versions one and two of a file format; by choosing the appropriate ruleset the parser will parse version one, or version two, or both versions. Decoupling also allows other approaches to rule management, as discussed in §2.3 [p. 6]. The architecture makes it possible to apply commonly used programming techniques (such as object orientation, inheritance, composition, delegation, roles, modularisation, or closures) when designing and implementing a parser, simplifying the process of working within a team or when developing and testing additional functionality. This architecture is ideally suited to parsing inputs where the input is not fully understood or does not follow a fixed grammar: the architecture warns about unparsed inputs and other errors, but continues parsing as best it can, allowing the developer of a new parser to decide which deficiencies are most important and require attention first, rather than being forced to fix the first error that arises.

The data gathered by the Postfix log parser provides the foundation for the future of this project: applying machine-learning algorithms to the data to analyse and optimise the set of anti-spam defences in use, followed by identifying patterns in the data that could be used to write new filters to recognise and reject spam rather than accepting it. The parser provides the data in a normalised form that is far easier to use as input to new or existing algorithm implementations than trying to adapt each algorithm to extract data directly from the log files. The current focus is on clustering and decision trees to optimise the order in which rules are applied; future efforts will involve using data gathered by the parser to train and test new filters. This task is similar to analysing a black box application based on its inputs and outputs, and this approach could be applied to analyse the behaviour of any system given sufficient log messages to parse. An alternate approach to black box optimisation that uses application profiling in conjunction with the application's error messages to improve the error messages shown to users is described in [8]; profiling data may be useful in supplementing systems that fail to provide adequate log messages.

The Postfix log file parser based on this architecture provides a basis for systems administrators to monitor the effectiveness of their anti-spam measures and adapt their defences to combat new techniques used by those sending spam. This parser is a fully usable application, built to address a genuine need, rather than a proof of concept whose sole purpose is to illustrate a new idea; it deals with the oddities and difficulties that occur in the real world, rather than a clean, idealised scenario developed to showcase the best features of a new approach.

References

1. Abney, S.: Partial parsing via finite-state cascades. Nat. Lang. Eng. **2**(4), 337–344 (1996). DOI http://dx.doi.org/10.1017/S1351324997001599. URL http://portal.acm.org/citation.cfm?coll=GUIDE&dl=GUIDE&id=974705. Last checked 2008/08/20
2. Aha, D.W., Kibler, D., Albert, M.K.: Instance-based learning algorithms. Mach. Learn. **6**(1), 37–66 (1991). DOI http://dx.doi.org/10.1023/A:1022689900470. URL http://portal.acm.org/citation.cfm?id=104717. Last checked 2008/07/29
3. Ahmed, S., Mithun, F.: Word stemming to enhance spam filtering. First Conference on Email and Anti-Spam CEAS 2004 (2004). URL http://www.ceas.cc/papers-2004/167.pdf. Last checked 2008/08/20
4. Aiello, M., Avanzini, D., Chiarella, D., Papaleo, G.: Log mail analyzer: Architecture and practical utilizations. Trans-European Research and Education Networking Association (2006). URL http://www.terena.nl/events/tnc2006/core/getfile.php?file_id=770. Last checked 2008/08/20
5. Friedl, J.E.F.: Crafting an efficient expression. Mastering regular expressions pp. 185–222 (2006). ISBN-10: 0596528124
6. Gazdar, G., Mellish, C.: Natural language processing in prolog. An Introduction to Computational Linguistics pp. 63–98 (1989). ISBN-10: 0201180537
7. Graham, P.: A plan for spam. Hackers & Painters pp. 121–129 (2004). ISBN-10: 0-596-00662-4
8. Ha, J., Rossbach, C.J., Davis, J.V., Roy, I., Ramadan, H.E., Porter, D.E., Chen, D.L., Witchel, E.: Improved error reporting for software that uses black-box components. SIGPLAN Not. **42**(6), 101–111 (2007). DOI http://doi.acm.org/10.1145/1273442.1250747. URL http://portal.acm.org/citation.cfm?id=1250747. Last checked 2008/08/20
9. Klensin, J.C.: Rfc 2821 — simple mail transfer protocol. The Internet Society Requests for Comment (2001). URL http://www.faqs.org/rfcs/rfc2821.html. Last checked 2008/08/20
10. Postel, J.B.: Rfc 821 — simple mail transfer protocol. The Internet Society Requests for Comment (1982). URL http://www.faqs.org/rfcs/rfc821.html. Last checked 2008/08/20
11. Sculley, D., Wachman, G.M.: Relaxed online svms in the trec spam filtering track. Text REtrieval Conference (TREC) (2007). URL http://trec.nist.gov/pubs/trec16/papers/tuftsu.spam.final.pdf. Last checked 2008/08/20
12. Vaarandi, R.: A data clustering algorithm for mining patterns from event logs. IP Operations and Management, 2003. (IPOM 2003). 3rd IEEE Workshop on pp. 119–126 (2003). URL http://ieeexplore.ieee.org/xpls/abs_all.jsp?arnumber=1251233. Last checked 2008/08/20
13. Venema, W.: Postfix home page. Postfix documentation (2008). URL http://www.postfix.org/. Last checked 2008/08/20
14. Venema, W.: Postfix smtp access policy delegation. Postfix documentation (2008). URL http://www.postfix.org/SMTPD_POLICY_README.html. Last checked 2008/08/20
15. Wirth, N.: Program development by stepwise refinement. Commun. ACM **14**(4), 221–227 (1971). DOI http://doi.acm.org/10.1145/362575.362577. URL http://portal.acm.org/citation.cfm?doid=362575.362577. Last checked 2008/08/20
16. Woods, W.A.: Transition network grammars for natural language analysis. Commun. ACM **13**(10), 591–606 (1970). URL http://portal.acm.org/citation.cfm?id=362773. Last checked 2008/08/20
17. Zafar, N.A., Sabir, N., Ali, A.: Construction of intersection of nondeterministic finite automata using z notation. Proceedings of World Academy of Science, Engineering and Technology **30**, 591–596 (2008)

The Reactive-Causal Architecture: Introducing an Emotion Model along with Theories of Needs

Ali Orhan Aydın, Mehmet Ali Orgun

Abstract In the entertainment application area, one of the major aims is to develop believable agents. To achieve this aim, agents should be highly autonomous, situated, flexible, and display affect. The Reactive-Causal Architecture (ReCau) is proposed to simulate these core attributes. In its current form, ReCau cannot explain the effects of emotions on intelligent behaviour. This study aims is to further improve the emotion model of ReCau to explain the effects of emotions on intelligent behaviour. This improvement allows ReCau to be emotional to support the development of believable agents.

1 Introduction

In the last two decades, the notion of agency became central to Artificial Intelligence. While simulating intelligence, agents have been developed by satisfying autonomy, situatedness and flexibility attributes [1]. The term autonomy refers to entities that can perform actions without assistance of other entities. The term situatedness implies entities that are capable of getting sensory data and performing actions to change their environment. Flexibility is the capability in performing flexible actions by being responsive, pro-active and social.

Believable agents employed in entertainment applications should have strong autonomy; since, they are interacting in real time with human actors. To have a stronger sense of autonomy Russell and Norvig [2] proposed that agents should be capable of learning. Luck and D'Inverno [3] proposed that to have a stronger autonomy, agents should also have motivations to generate goals. In addition to these, researches have indicated the importance of emotions [4]. They stressed that the core

Ali Orhan Aydın
Department of Computing, Macquarie University, Sydney e-mail: aaydin@ics.mq.edu.au

Mehmet Ali Orgun
Department of Computing, Macquarie University, Sydney e-mail: mehmet@ics.mq.edu.au

requirement for believable agents is being emotional. Therefore, believable agents should be capable of affect display by employing an emotional model.

In the literature, there are several agent architecture proposals for believable agents. However, these architectures lack in simulating strong autonomy and affect display together. To achieve this aim, such architectures should be capable of learning, having motivations to generate goals and displaying affect. By this study, our aim is to fill this gap by introducing an emotion model along with theories of needs. Theories of needs provide us the means for developing a framework for agents which have motivations. By extending the boundaries of theories of needs, we propose an emotion model for affect display. To support the development of believable agents, we adopt the proposed model in the Reactive-Causal Architecture (ReCau) [5].

This paper is organised as follows. In section two, architectures for believable agents are reviewed. In section three, the proposed framework which introduces an emotion model along with theories of needs is presented. Afterwards, the details of the Reactive-Causal Architecture are presented. Finally, the study ends with a conclusion.

2 Architectures for Believable Agents

To develop a believable agent the core requirement is stated as being emotional or displaying affect. Therefore, in this section of the study, we only review architectures that employ emotions and affect display. The pioneering believable agent architecture is called Tok [6]. Tok agents are capable of reactive, social and goal-directed behaviour, and employ emotions. Tok architecture also has natural language processing capabilities. Although several applications of Tok have been developed, it has no learning capabilities and it does not employ motives.

McCauley and Franklin [7] proposed an agent architecture called Conscious Mattie (CMattie). CMattie has the ability to display adaptive emotional states. CMattie is capable of learning more complicated emotions to interact in more complicated situations. CMattie tries to achieve its goals reinforced by the emotional worth of them. CMattie has learning capabilities. But it does not employ any motives.

Camurri and Coglio [8] proposed an architecture for affect display. By this architecture, they were not trying to model human like agents. Instead, they were trying to illustrate an architecture for affect display by providing practical behaviours. The proposed architecture leads to agents that are social, flexible and situated. But it is not highly autonomous; since, it does not employ any learning approach and motives.

In 1999, Sloman [9] proposed a generic schema which is called Cognition and Affect (CogAff). This schema includes three control layers: reactive, deliberative and meta-management. Each layer contains corresponding processes, and perception and action components. This cognitive architecture employs three different types of emotions each of which associated with one layer. Even though Sloman's architecture can be used to develop emotional and motivated agents, in its current form, it rather looks like a stand alone architecture without collaboration and cooperation capabilities.

In 2000, Gratch [10] proposed a model based on emotional reasoning and christened it as Èmile. Èmile is built on prior computational models of emotion, specifically En algorithm and Affective Reasoner. In its current form, Èmile can learn about the activites of other agents by observing their actions or communicating with them. Although Èmile does not employ motives to generate goals, it is one of the most significant architectures towards the development of believable agents.

In 2001, Sadio et. al. [11] proposed an emotion-based agent architecture which is an advanced version of DARE. This architecture employs two types of emotions: primary and secondary emotions. In this architecture, goals are generated from an agent's behaviours and needs. On the other hand, it does not support the development of social agents; since, it lacks in simulating cooperation and communication with other agents.

Baillie and Lukose [12] introduced an agent architecture in which affective decisions are made through emotion appraisal. The architecture is called Emotionally Motivated Artificial Intelligence (EMAI). EMAI enables agents to change their behaviours based on their emotional states in guide of the interactions with the environment. EMAI agents are capable of predicting future emotional states and deciding how to behave in case of change in their emotional state. EMAI includes a motivational drive generation component. However, EMAI only processes internal sensory data. Therefore, it does not employ motives to generate goals.

In 2005, Imbert and de Antonio [13] proposed an emotionally-oriented architecture called COGNITIVA. This architecture distinctively differs from conventional architectures which employ an emotion component. This architecture includes three layers which are reactive, deliberative and social. Components and processes of COGNITIVA are designed to deal with emotions. This architecture provides the means to build agents with emotionally influenced behaviour. COGNITIVA agents do not have strong autonomy; since, it does not employ any learning approach and motives.

The architectures for believable agents lack satisfying strong autonomy and affect display attributes together. Although Sloman's architecture provides higher sense of autonomy by employing motives, it does not support learning. Likewise, Gratch's architecture employs learning to achieve stronger autonomy, but it does not employ motives. The ReCau is proposed to provide stronger autonomy by employing learning and motives together. Therefore, it is a step towards the development of strongly autonomous agents with emotions.

3 Proposed Emotion Model

Our major aim in this study is to further improve the emotion model of ReCau. In this manner, we aim to explain the effects of emotions on intelligent behaviour. To achieve higher sense of autonomy, ReCau combines Alderfer's Existance, Related-ness, Growth theory (ERG) and Belief, Desire, Intention (BDI) approach [14, 15]. In this context, a ReCau agent acts intentionally driven by unsatisfied needs.

A ReCau agent continuously observes environment and internal state of itself. If the observed conditions are related with its needs then it generates a goal to satisfy the corresponding need. If the goal of an agent is to learn, it starts learning plans. To realise learning, ReCau adopts reinforcement learning in accordance with social learning theory [16, 17].

Based on the observed conditions, a ReCau agent develops plans. Each plan alter-native corresponds to a certain mean value of satisfaction degree (μ) and a variance value (σ^2). ReCau additionally employs pro-attitudes which have effect over the mean value of satisfaction degrees. In particular, pro-attitudes which are associated to certain plan alternatives can increase or decrease the mean value of satisfaction degrees of corresponding plan alternatives.

By using the mean value of satisfaction degree and variance value, the decision-making mechanism generates a satisfaction degree (ς) for each plan alternative. These satisfaction degrees are normally distributed random numbers that lie be-tween 0 and 1 coming from the corresponding mean and variance values. We adopt this approach, because satisfaction obtained under similar conditions by taking sim-ilar actions are more likely to be similar. Unlike the other approaches, our approach provides a higher degree of action flexibility. In particular, employing satisfaction degrees provides the means to simulate unpredictability of human behaviour. Be-sides, it supports routine activity when a lower variance value is assigned to the routine plan alternative.

The founder of the theories of needs, Maslow [18] considers emotions as post-cognitive by stating that the dissatisfaction of physiological needs results in negative emotions. Lazaruz [19] also considers affect to be post-cognitive. According to this point of view, experience of emotions is based on a prior cognitive process. In Re-Cau, we extend Maslow's approach by stating that satisfaction or dissatisfaction of not only physiological needs but also every need results in feeling different emo-tions.

To further improve the emotion model, we adopt Wukmir's approach. Wukmir [20] proposed that emotions are such a mechanism that they provide information about the degree of favourability of the percieved situation. If the situation seems to favourable to the survival of an intelligent being, then the being experiences a pos-itive emotion. The being experiences a negative emotion, when the situation seems to be unfavourable for survival.

When we consider theories of needs, we can claim that the survival of the beings depends on meeting their needs. From this point of view, we can combine Wuk-mir's approach and theories of needs. According to our proposal, every need in the hierarchy is associated with two different emotions. While one of these emotions is positive, the other one is negative. Whenever a particular need is adequately sat-isfied, it results in the generation of a positive emotion; since, it is favourable for survival. Likewise, if a particular need is not sufficiently satisfied, it results in a negative emotion. It is because of the fact that when a need is not satisfied, it is not favourable for survival.

In the proposed emotion model, emotions are classified in two levels: basic emotions and non-basic emotions. The basic emotions are the most primitive or universal emotions like pain, panic and anxiety. For our purposes, we consider the other emotions as non-basic emotions such as love and loneliness. Accordingly, the lowest level which includes existence needs corresponds to basic emotions. For example, if an agent meets its security need, this will result in the generation of comfort feeling. As long as the agent meets its security need, the agent is going to feel comfortable. In the ERG approach, higher level needs are existence needs and growth needs. These needs correspond to non-basic emotions. As an example, If an agent meets its affectionate relationship need, it is going to feel love.

In this context, it is proposed that the emotions emerge when needs of intelligent beings are satisfied or dissatisfied. Satisfaction of the needs results in positive emotions, while dissatisfaction of needs results in negative emotions. According to this viewpoint, while satisfaction of lower level needs triggers the primitive emotions; satisfaction of higher level needs results in non-basic emotions. Needs and associated emotions are shown in Table 1.

Table 1: Needs and Associated Emotions

Associated Negative Emotion	Needs	Associated Positive Emotion
Existence Needs and Basic Emotions		
Pain	Survival	Ease
Panic	Air	Relief
Anxiety	Water	Content
Anxiety	Food	Content
Irritation	Excretion	Calmness
Anger	Warmth	Delight
Anger	Sleep	Delight
Discontent	Sex	Pleasure
Discomfort	Security	Comfort
Despair	Health and Well-Being	Expectancy
Sadness	Stability	Elation
Fear	Religion	Assurance
Relatedness Needs and Social Emotions		
Lonelines	Affectionate Relationships	Love
Loneliness	Involvement with Family	Love
Envy	Involvement with Friends	Joy
Envy	Involvement with Others	Joy
Embarrassment	Being Needed	Respect
Embarrassment	Recognition	Respect
Shame	Dignity	Pride
		Continued on next page

Table 1 – continued from previous page

Associated Negative Emotion	Needs	Associated Positive Emotion
Shame	Dominance	Pride
Growth Needs and Non-Social Emotions		
Prejudice	Confidence	Detachment
Prejudice	Independence	Detachment
Mystery	Achievement	Familiarity
Mystery	Mastery	Familiarity
Confusion	Know and Understand	Discovery
Confusion	Fulfill Potentials	Discovery
Incompleteness	Transcendence	Completion
Incompleteness	Wholeness	Completion

To establish this table, we map the emotions with the needs. Ortony and Turner [21] studied basic emotions and established a list of basic emotions from the literature. Therefore, while mapping basic emotions, we adopt the emotions listed as fundamental emotions by them. However, in some cases we cannot find a corresponding negative or positive emotion in the list. In such conditions, we simply derived the corresponding positive or negative emotion from the present one.

Although lists of basic emotions vary from researcher to researher, we simply assumed that the emotions we mapped to the existence needs are the basic emotions. Accordingly, the other emotions are considered as non-basic emotions. Therefore, for the higher level needs we mapped non-basic emotions with needs. When considering ERG, we can easily observe that the relatedness needs are external needs, while the growth needs are internal. Pursuing relatedness needs involves other agents while pursuing growth needs do not involve interaction with other agents.

Likewise, social emotios emerge wholly from interpersonal concerns. In particular, social emotions occur only as a result of encounters with other agents. On the other hand, non-social emotions emerge from non-social events that do not involve interaction with other agents [22]. In this context, we map relatedness needs with social emotions while we map growth needs with non-social emotions.

While mapping social emotions with relatedness needs, we adopt the list of emotions established by Hareli and Parkinson [23]. In their study, Hareli and Parkinson lists several social emotions proposed in the literature. We adopt non-social emotions from an artificial language called Lojban. Lojban is a constructed language designed to remove the ambiguity from human communication [24]. Therefore, we derive non-social emotions from Lojban emotions.

In Table 1, we list the needs employed in our approach and associated emotions. To establish this table, we first gather the emotions proposed in the literature then we map several of them with the needs. As it can be seen in the table, several other emotions are not employed in our approach. But one can introduce additional needs and associate more emotions with these needs.

Wukmir [20] also states that emotions are expressed with a positive-negative scale and in variable magnitudes. For instance, one can say that "I feel quite calm", or "I feel calm". In this frame, Wukmir proposes that all emotions consist of two components:

1. Quantitative Component: Indicates the magnitude of the emotion.
2. Qualitative Component: Indicates the description of the emotion which determines the positiveness or negativeness of the emotional sign.

We can map these components in accordance with our proposal as it can be seen in Figure 1. In the figure, emotions are categorised as positive and negative. While satisfaction results in a positive emotion, dissatisfaction yiels a negative emotion. Additionally, we propose that the degree of satisfaction or dissatisfaction determines the strenght of emotions.

Emotion =	Needs	Quantitative Component	Needs	Qualitative Component
Positive	Satisfaction	Extraordinarily	Growth	Completion
		Quite	Relatedness	Love
		Very	Existence	Relief
		Little		Ease
Negative	Dissatisfaction	Little		Pain
		Very	Existence	Panic
		Quite	Relatedness	Loneliness
		Extraordinarily	Growth	Incompleteness

Fig. 1 Components of Emotions

According to this viewpoint, we categorise emotions as negative and positive. Then, we classify them further according to their magnitude. For this purpose, we propose two types of emotions as regular and strong emotions. To illustrate this approach, we propose four different emotion limits. If a satisfaction obtained is above or below these limits, it results in the generation of four different types of emotions as shown below:

1. Strong Positive Emotion Limit: If the satisfaction degree is above this limit, it results in a strong positive emotion.
2. Positive Emotion Limit: If the satisfaction degree is above this limit, it results in a regular positive emotion.
3. Negative Emotion Limit: If the satisfaction degree is below this limit, it results in a regular negative emotion.

4. Strong Negative Emotion Limit: If the satisfaction degree is below this limit, it
   results in a strong negative emotion.

We visually represent these emotions and emotion limits in Figure 2.

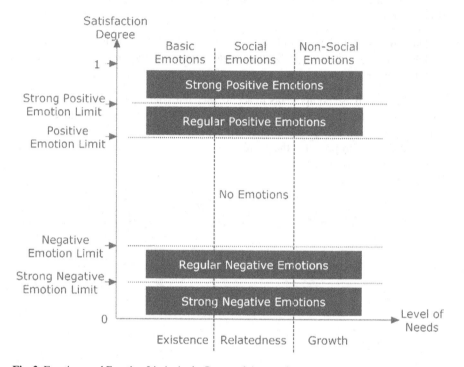

Fig. 2 Emotions and Emotion Limits in the Proposed Approach

The other issue is the effect of emotions on intelligent behaviour. We propose that
emotions have influence over the order of needs. Therefore, except for the existence
needs, the order of needs is not fixed. We propose that stronger emotion can change
the order of the associated need. If a particular need is strongly satisfied or dissatisfied, it results in a strong emotion. While strong positive emotion moves associated
need downwards in the hierarchy, strong negative emotion moves associated need
upwards.

If a need moves up in the hierarchy, it means that an agent is going to aviod
conditions associated with that need; since, the agent always pursue lower level
needs first. If a need moves down, it is more likely that an agent is going to pursue
that need more frequently.

As an example, we can consider an agent who meets its achievement need. If its
achievement need is strongly enough satisfied, the agent is going to feel familiarity
more strongly. The more familiarity the agent feel; the more the associated need
goes down. In this way, the agent is going to be more concerned about achievement.

The agent is going to focus more on his works which satisfies its achievement need. In some extreme conditions, we see people only think about their work and neglect their family and friends. It might be the result of this situation in which achievement need became a lower level need then other needs such as involvement with family and friends.

This proposal is also in accordance with approach of Wukmir [20]. He states that living organisms need to know if the conditions are useful and favourable for their survival. He adds that by the help of emotions, living beings try to find favourable situations to survive which produce positive emotions. Likewise, they refrain from unfavourable states for survival which produce negative emotions. Our proposal provides the means to recreate this mechanism.

Additionally, our approach provides the means to develop agents whose order of needs are different than those of the others. It can be observed that this approach provides personality to agents. Besides, Alderfer [14] also proposes that the order of needs of beings can be different.

4 The Reactive-Causal Architecture

We present Reactive-Causal Architecture (ReCau) which adopts the proposed emotion model. ReCau consists of three hierarchical layers: while the lowest layer is reactive, the highest layer is causal. The reactive layer controls perception and action to monitor internal and external conditions. The middle layer has deliberative capabilities such as action planning and task dispatching. The decision-making and emotion generation occurs in the causal layer. The overall structure and the components of the architecture are shown in Figure 3.

4.1 Reactive Layer

ReCau enables an agent to continuously observe internal and external conditions. This function is guided by the perception controller. This component receives and processes sensory data continuously. After receiving conditions, the perception controller sends data to a filtering mechanism.

The filtering mechanism is responsible for filtering out sensory data which is not related with the needs of the agent. Together with the motivation activator, the filtering mechanism puts condition-action rules into practical use. If the recieved conditions are not related with the needs of the agent, the filtering mechanism simply filters out those conditions. Otherwise, the motivation activator generates a goal to satisfy the corresponding need. Then the filtering mechanism further processes the goal by sending it to the deliberative layer. To realise these mechanisms, each condition is related with a need. To put ERG into the practice in ReCau, each need

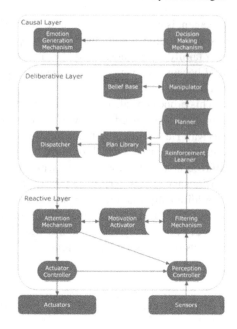

Fig. 3 Components of the
Reactive-Causal Architecture

in these levels is further orginised in a hierarchical order. The other function of the
filtering mechanism is to notify the motivation activator on completion of actions.

The motivation activator generates the goals of the agent. The goals are held in
a queue which includes goals in a hierarchical order. The hierarchical order of a
goal is determined in accordance with the level of the corresponding need. The goal
related with the lowest level need takes the first order.

Attention mechanism enables a ReCau agent to focus on meeting the active goal.
While executing certain actions to satisfy a particular need, it keeps the agent focused on that activity. To do so, it directs controlling mechanisms. While performing the actions, if the agent's active goal changes, the attention mechanism changes
the focus of the controllers.

The other important responsibility of the attention mechanism is to notify the
motivation activator to change the order of needs. As mentioned in the proposed
emotion model, strong emotions can change the order of the needs. To realise this
when a strong emotion is generated, the attention mechanism informs the motivation
activator to move the corresponding need up or down in the hierarchy. If the hierarchy of needs change, then the queue which holds the goals in hierarchical order is
updated as well.

The last component of the reactive layer is the actuator controller. This component provides the means to perform actions in the environment. The actuator controller performs tasks which are dispatched by the deliberative layer. The intentions
of the ReCau agent are also held in an ordered queue. The first intention in the queue
is executed first.

4.2 Deliberative Layer

The deliberative layer is the slowest layer of the ReCau. It employs a reinforcement learner, a planner with a plan library, a manipulator with a belief base and a dispatcher. When a goal and a condition are sent to the deliberative layer initially, this information reaches the reinforcement learner. The reinforcement learner first determines if learning is required or not. To achieve this aim, the reinforcement learner is linked to the plan library. It maps the conditions received with the conditions defined in the library. If the reinforcement learner cannot map conditions with the plans, the agent starts learning. Otherwise, the reinforcement learner sends the condition and goal directly to the planner. The reinforcement learning meant to realise the social learning theory. In other words, a ReCau agent learns plans from other agents.

The planner is responsible for developing plans. Whenever a condition is received from the lower layer, the ReCau agent develops plans by the help of the plan library. ReCau employs a discrete feasible planner. In ReCau, state space is defined discretely. The planning problem involves starting in an initial state and trying to arrive at a specified goal state. In our approach, a ReCau agent at a given pre-condition tries to reach a final state which meets the goal to satisfy a particular need.

In ReCau, each plan alternative corresponds to a certain mean value of satisfaction degree and a variance value. After developing plan alternatives with the mean and variance values and pre-condition are sent to the manipulator. The responsibilities of the manipulator are to update conditional pro-attitudes, judge alternatives and resolve conflicts between other agents by using the belief base. These pro-attitudes are explained in terms of beliefs; therefore, these are stored in the belief base.

When the manipulator receives a pre-condition, if it is required, conditional pro-attitudes are changed on the belief base. Some pre-conditions require taking some actions but at the same time they may result in changing the pro-attitudes of the agent due to changing conditions. Therefore, these pro-attitudes are updated by the manipulator whenever required. After making changes in the pro-attitudes, the manipulator simply checks post-conditions to see if there is an associated conditional pro-attitude. Whenever the manipulator finds a conditional belief associated to a plan alternative, it analyses the impact of the conditional belief on the plan alternative.

To realise this impact, each conditional pro-attitude has a certain impact factor (ψ). These impact factors can be positive or negative values. While a positive impact factor increases the satisfaction degree, a negative impact factor decreases the satisfaction degree. In the ReCau architecture, impact factors are real numbers that lie between -1 and 1. The influence factor 0 signifies no influence, while 1 signifies the strongest influence.

By using these impact factors, the manipulator simply recalculates the mean values of satisfaction degrees of each plan alternative. Recalculated mean values are called ameliorated mean values of satisfaction degrees ($\tilde{\mu}$) which are calculated as follows:

$$\tilde{\mu} = \begin{cases} 1 & \text{if } \mu + (\mu \times \psi) \geq 1 \\ \mu + (\mu \times \psi) & \text{if } 0 \leq \mu + (\mu \times \psi) < 1 \end{cases} \qquad (1)$$

After finding the ameliorated mean values of satisfaction degrees, the plan alternatives with these mean values are sent to the causal layer.

The last responsibility of the manipulator is to enable the agent to collaborate on pursuing common needs by resolving conflicts between other agents. When a ReCau agents have common needs, they will adjust unless they have contradicting pro-attitudes. The negotiation process is managed by the manipulator to collaborate on common needs. When an agent suggests a plan to a ReCau agent to collaborate on pursuing a common need, the ReCau agent tends to accept the plan alternative if it does not have contradicting pro-attitudes. If the ReCau agent has contradicting pro-attitudes, then it offers its plan alternative. If the other agent insists on its own plan alternative by providing additional conditional pro-attitudes, the ReCau agent considers this additional conditional pro-attitude.

The decision-making process is managed by the causal layer. Whenever the deliberative layer generates a plan alternative, it sends the selected plan alternatives to the causal layer. The decision is made and emotion is determined in the causal layer. Then they are sent to the deliberative layer specifically to the dispatcher.

The function of the dispatcher is to assign tasks to the components in the reactive layer. To assign tasks, according to the intention and emotional state the dispatcher gets the required data from the plan library. In the plan library, each action is described explicitly in such a way that each action corresponds to certain components.

Moreover, emotions are kinds of plans; therefore, they are held in the plan library. To realise emotions, the plan library also contains fully developed action sequences related with regular and strong emotions. Based on the emotion state and the intention, tasks are formed by the dispatcher. Finally, these tasks are sent to the attention mechanism to direct corresponding components for execution.

4.3 Causal Layer

Whenever the deliberative layer generates plan alternatives, it sends these alternatives to the causal layer. In particular, the agent sends desire alternatives with the ameliorated mean values of satisfaction degrees and mean values to the causal layer. Then according to these values, normally distributed random numbers, lying between 0 and 1 are generated for each plan alternative by the decision-making mechanism. These satisfaction degrees are generated by applying the polar technique. These random numbers are satisfaction degrees of the alternatives. According to these satisfaction degrees, the ReCau agent selects the most satisfactory alternative.

After determining the intention, the next process is to generate emotions. Each action taken does not guarantee the emotion generation. If the satisfaction degree is above or below a certain level, the emotion generation mechanism generates an emotion. In the ReCau architecture, if the satisfaction degree is above a positive emotion limit, it generates positive regular emotions. If the satisfaction degree is upper positive emotion limit, it generates positive strong emotions. Likewise, there are negative emotion limit and lower negative emotion limit. If the satisfaction degree is lower than these limits negative emotions are generated.

To realise emotion generation in ReCau, in the emotion generation mechanism each need is associated with a positive and a negative emotion. Whenever a need is sufficiently satisfied or dissatisfied, the corresponding emotional state is activated. After determining both emotional state and intention, they are sent to the deliberative layer.

5 Conclusion

Agent technologies enable us to develop human-like software programs by satisfying certain attributes. In the believable agent field, there are commonly accepted attributes for believable agents. These attributes are strong autonomy, situatedness, flexibility and affect display. To achieve strong autonomy and affection, architectures should be capable of learning from experience, having motivations to generate goals and displaying affect. By this study, we tried to satisfy these attributes by presenting a framework. This framework is established by combining needs theories and belief, desire, intention approach. Along with the needs theories, we introduced an emotion model for affect display.

In accordance with the proposed framework, we put forward an agent architecture called Reactive-Causal Architecture (ReCau) to support the development of believable agents. In the near future, we plan to perform a few social simulations to illustrate the working architecture. For this purpose, first we are going to undertake an organisational decision-making simulation which is called radar task. In the radar task simulation, a number of agents try to decide if an object observed in a radar is friend or foe.

References

1. Nicholas R. Jennings, Katia Sycara, and Michael Wooldridge. A roadmap of agent research and development. *Autonomous Agents and Multi-Agent Systems*, 1:738, 1998.
2. Stuart Russell and Peter Norvig. *Artificial Intelligence: A Modern Approach*. Prentice-Hall, second edition, 2002.
3. Michael Luck and Mark d'Inverno. A formal framework for agency and autonomy. In *the First International Conference on Multi-Agent Systems*, pages 254–260. AAAI Press / MIT Press, 1995.
4. Joseph Bates. The role of emotion in believable agents. *Communications of the ACM*, 37(7):122–125, 1994.
5. Ali Orhan Aydın, Mehmet Ali Orgun, and Abhaya Nayak. The reactive-causal architecture: Combining intentional notion and theories of needs. In *The 7th IEEE International Conference on Cognitive Informatics*, Stanford, 2008. Forthcoming.

6. Joseph Bates, A. Bryan Loyall, and W. Scott Reilly. An architecture for action, emotion, and social behavior. In *the Fourth European Workshop on Modeling Autonomous Agents in a Multi-Agent World*, pages 13–26, S.Martino, 1992.

7. T. Lee McCauley and Stan Franklin. An architecture for emotion. In *AAAI Fall Symposium Emotional and Intelligent: The Tangled Knot of Cognition*, pages 122–127, 1998.

8. Antonio Camurri and Alessandro Coglio. An architecture for emotional agents. *Multimedia*, 5(4):24–33, 1998.

9. Aaron Sloman. *Foundations of Rational Agency*, chapter What sort of Architecture is Required for a Human-Like Agent?, pages 35–52. Springer, 1999.

10. Jonathan Gratch. Èmile: Marshalling passions in training and education. In *Agents*, pages 325–332, 2000.

11. Rui Sadio, Gonalo Tavares, Rodrigo Ventura, and Luis Custodio. An emotion-based agent architecture application with real robots. In *the AAAI Fall Symposium on Emotional and Intelligent II*, pages 117–122, 2001.

12. Penny Baillie and Dickson Lukose. An affective decision making agent architecture using emotion appraisals. *Lecture Notes in Computer Science*, 2417:581–590, 2002.

13. Ricardo Imbert and Angèlica de Antonio. When emotion does not mean loss of control. *Lecture Notes in Computer Science*, 3661:152–165, 2005.

14. Clayton P. Alderfer. *Existence, Relatedness, and Growth: Human Needs in Organizational Settings*. Free Press, New York, 1972.

15. Anand S. Rao and Michael P. Georgeff. Modeling rational agents within a bdi-architecture. In *Knowledge Representation and Reasoning*, pages 473–484, San Mateo, California, 1991. Morgan Kaufmann Publishers.

16. Richard S. Sutton and Andrew G. Barto. *Reinforcement Learning: An Introduction*. MIT Press, Cambridge, Massachusetts, 1998.

17. Albert Bandura. *Social Foundations of Thought and Action*. Prentice-Hall, 1985.

18. Abraham Harold Maslow. *Motivation and Personality*. Harper and Row, 1987.

19. Richard S. Lazarus. Thoughts on the relations between emotions and cognition. *American Physiologist*, 37(10):1019–1024, 1982.

20. V. J. Wukmir. *Emocin y sufrimiento: Endoantropologa elemental*. Labor, Barcelona, 1967.

21. Andrew Ortony and Terence J. Turner. What is basic about basic emotions? *Psychological Review*, 97(3):315–331, 1990.

22. Larissa Z. Tiedens and Colin Wayne Leach. *The Social Life of Emotions*. Cambridge University Press, 2004.

23. Shlomo Hareli and Brian Parkinson. What's social about social emotions? *Journal for the Theory of Social Behaviour*, 38(2):131–156, 2008.

24. John Woldemar Cowan. *The Complete Lojban Language*. Logical Language Group Inc., 1997.

Automation of the Solution of Kakuro Puzzles

R. P. Davies, P. A. Roach, S. Perkins[1]

Abstract   Kakuro puzzles, also called cross sum puzzles, are grids containing clues to the completion of numerical 'words'. Being structured in a similar way to crossword puzzles, Kakuro grids contain overlapping continuous runs that are exclusively either horizontal or vertical. The 'clues' take the form of specified run totals, and a puzzle is solved by placing a value in each cell such that every run sums to its specified total, and no run contains duplicate values. While most puzzles have only a single solution, longer runs may be satisfied using many arrangements of values, leading to the puzzle having a deceptively large search space. The associated, popular Sudoku puzzle has been linked with important real-world applications including timetabling and conflict free wavelength routing, and more recently, coding theory due to its potential usefulness in the construction of erasure correction codes. It is possible that Kakuro puzzles will have similar applications, particularly in the construction of codes, where run totals may form a generalised type of parity check. A project has begun to investigate the properties of the class of Kakuro puzzles, and thereby establish its potential usefulness to real-world applications including coding theory. This paper reports some early findings from that project, specifically concerning puzzle complexity and the appropriateness of heuristic approaches for its automated solution. It highlights the use of heuristics to guide search by a backtracking solver, in preference to local search optimisation, and reports on the effectiveness of two heuristics and a pruning technique for reducing solution time. The authors believe this to be the first published work in the use of heuristics, in combination with pruning, for the automated solution of Kakuro puzzles.

1 Introduction

Kakuro puzzles are number puzzles that have strong similarities with the more familiar crossword puzzle, due to their use of 'clues' to specify correct numerical 'words' within a grid structure. Unlike crosswords, Kakuro puzzles more easily transcend language barriers due to their use of number sequences. Puzzles of this type typically consist of an $n \times m$ grid containing black and white cells. All white

---

1 Department of Computing and Mathematical Sciences, University of Glamorgan, Pontypridd, CF37 1DL, United Kingdom, rpdavies@glam.ac.uk

cells are initially empty and are organised into overlapping continuous runs that are exclusively either horizontal or vertical. A run-total, given in a black 'clue' cell, is associated with each and every run. The puzzle is solved by entering values (typically in the range $1,..., 9$ inclusive) into the white cells such that each run sums to the specified run-total and such that no value is repeated in any horizontal or vertical run.

Most published puzzles consist of an $n \times m$ grid and are *well-formed* [7], meaning that only one unique solution exists. Such puzzles are also called promise-problems (the promise being a unique solution) [1]. The puzzles are designed so that this unique solution may be determined through the employment of a range of types of logical deduction and reasoning; no guesswork should be needed. Many puzzles have reflective or rotational symmetry, although this is only to improve the visual appearance of the grid.

The name 'Kakuro' comes from the Japanese pronunciation of the English word 'cross' appended to the Japanese word for 'addition'. The name was part of a re-branding by Japan's Nikoli Puzzles Group of Dell Magazines' 'Cross Sum' puzzles, which can be traced back as early as 1966 [5]. Currently, the popularity of Kakuro in Japan is reported second only to Sudoku puzzles [5], but it is only during the last four years that the puzzle has gained wider global popularity, particularly in the West.

Related puzzles include: 'Cryptic Kakuro' [13], in which alphametric clues must be solved as a prerequisite to the Kakuro puzzle itself; 'Cross-sum Sudoku' [13], which combines the rules of standard Kakuro puzzles with the constraints of standard Sudoku puzzles; 'Cross Products', in which 'clue' cells suggest the product of digits in a run, rather than their sum; and 'Survo Puzzles' [9], in which the values $1,..., mn$ must be placed, once each, into an $n \times m$ grid that often contains givens, so as to satisfy row and column sums.

The associated, popular Sudoku puzzle has been linked with important real-world applications including timetabling [6] and conflict free wavelength routing [4], and more recently, coding theory due to its potential usefulness in the construction of erasure correction codes [12]. At present, very little has been published specifically on Kakuro and its related puzzles. The authors have previously reported on the use of binary integer programming and local search approaches to the solution of Kakuro [3], concluding on the need for heuristics to guide solution and for the need to reduce the size of the search space to be examined. The solution of Kakuro puzzles has been shown to be NP-Complete [11], through demonstrating the relationship between Kakuro and the Hamiltonian Path Problem, and 3SAT (the restriction of the Boolean satisfiability problem). It is possible that Kakuro-type puzzles will have similar applications to Sudoku, particularly in the construction of codes, where run totals may form a generalised type of parity check.

Tools for the automated solution of Kakuro puzzles are available online, either as a web-based applet or as a downloadable executable program file. In general, the methods employed are not revealed to the user. Most methods are implemented only for puzzles with a grid no larger than 12×12, and some report that memory-based issues will prevent the solution of larger puzzles that are deemed as "hard" [2]. It is likely, therefore, that an element of brute force may be employed by these solvers. Some solvers are also reported to use guesswork for larger puzzles [8]. The authors of the current paper wish to devise means of solving a Kakuro puzzle that may be scalable to larger puzzles, without recourse to guesswork. It is therefore unlikely that much useful information may be acquired from these existing tools.

A project has begun to investigate the properties of the class of Kakuro puzzles, and thereby establish its potential usefulness within a range of applications, including coding theory. This paper reports some early findings from that project, specifically concerning puzzle complexity and the appropriateness of heuristic approaches for its automated solution. It highlights the use of heuristics to guide search by a backtracking solver, in preference to local search optimisation. Evaluation is presented of the effectiveness of two heuristics for guiding search and a method for pruning the search space that need be considered by the solver. The authors believe this to be the first published work in the use of heuristics, in combination with pruning, for the automated solution of Kakuro puzzles.

2 Problem Analysis

Let a Kakuro grid be termed K, where K has dimension $n \times m$, and the cell at row i and column j is termed $k_{i,j}$. Each cell is either a white cell (to be assigned a numerical value in the range $1, ..., 9$) or a black 'clue' cell. Grid K contains a collection of runs of white cells. Each of these individual runs is exclusively either horizontal or vertical and is termed a tuple r_l ($l = 1, ..., p$) where $r_l \in r$, the set of all tuples, and p is the number of runs contained in the puzzle grid. We define the tuple r_l to be such that it contains no repeated elements.

Therefore r_l is described either as a tuple of connected horizontal white cells or of connected vertical white cells. A horizontal run is defined:

$$r_l = (k_{i,j_s}, ..., k_{i,j_e}) \qquad k_{i,j_x} \in r_l, \ s \leq x \leq e$$

where the run is in row i ($1 \leq i \leq n$), beginning in column j_s and ending in column j_e, ($1 \leq j_s < j_e \leq m$). A vertical run is defined:

$$r_l = (k_{i_s,j}, ..., k_{i_e,j}) \qquad k_{i_x,j} \in r_l, \ s \leq x \leq e$$

where the run is in column j $(1 \leq j \leq m)$, beginning in row i_s and ending in row i_e $(1 \leq i_s < i_e \leq n)$.

The values to be placed within each white cell, $k_{i,j}$, are governed by puzzle constraints, namely that:

- In each and every run, $r_l \in r$, the same value must appear in no more than one cell:

$$k_{i,j_u} \neq k_{i,j_v} \qquad k_{i,j_x} \in r_l, j_u \neq j_v$$

$$k_{i_u,j} \neq k_{i_v,j} \qquad k_{i_x,j} \in r_l, i_u \neq i_v.$$

- In each and every run, $r_l \in r$, the corresponding run-total, t_l, must be satisfied:

$$\sum_{k_{i,j} \in r_l} k_{i,j} = t_l$$

Kakuro grids can vary in the difficulty of their solution. Generally, the complexity of a given puzzle cannot be determined by the size of the grid alone, but should instead be determined from a combination of the number of empty (white) cells in its initial state, the grid size and the magnitudes of the run-totals.

In order to establish the potential size of the search space for a puzzle, we could consider the number of options for assigning values to a cell and thereby determine an upper bound for the number of different grid arrangements of values. (We note that, for a well-formed puzzle, all but one of these grids, the unique solution, would be invalid due to the puzzle constraints.)

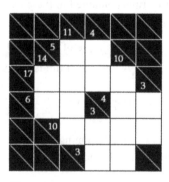

Fig. 1. A 5×5 initial puzzle grid

A crude upper bound for the number of grid arrangements for a puzzle grid with w white squares is 9^w, since each square can take any of nine numerical values, assuming the standard range of values $(1,...,9)$ is being used. The puzzle grid in Fig. 1, with sixteen white squares, would therefore have an upper bound of $9^{16} \approx 1.853 \times 10^{15}$ possible arrangements.

This upper bound is greatly reduced by considering which of the nine available values can legitimately be placed in each of the white cells, c_i, depending on the run(s), r_l (each with corresponding run-total t_l), in which the cell resides.

A set of values, P_l, that may be assigned to cells in a run r_l is constructed, such that:

$$P_l = \{1, \dots, 9\} \qquad \text{if } t_l > 9$$
$$P_l = \{1, \dots, a\text{-}1\} \qquad \text{if } t_l = a, \ a \le 9$$

The improved upper bound would then be:

$$\prod_{i=1}^{w} \min\{|P_l| \mid c_i \in r_l\}$$

For example, the white cell at the uppermost left of the grid in Fig. 1 is a member of a run totalling 11 and of another totalling 5. Concentrating on the lower of the two run-totals, only a value in the range $1,...,4$ can be placed in this cell. When all cells are considered in this way, a new upper bound equalling 1,133,740,800 arrangements can be calculated for this example.

The positioning of runs, and the selections of run totals of Kakuro puzzles can vary greatly. This makes the task of devising a general formula for the exact number of possible Kakuro grid arrangements of a given size difficult, if not impossible, to achieve. Instead we focus on determining the total number of arrangements of values within a single run which would satisfy the puzzle constraints – the run total constraint, and the requirement to have no duplicated values in the run. Different sets of distinct values might meet the run constraints, but each set can be permuted into different orderings – only one of which will match the puzzle solution. The total number of such arrangements of values can be derived from the coefficients obtained from a series expansion of the generating function:

$$F(x) = \prod_{i=1}^{9} (1 + x^i a)$$

The coefficient of $a^{|r_i|}x^{t_i}$ represents the number of unordered cell value partitions of length $|r_i|$ that have no repeated value and that sum to t_l. Multiplying this coefficient by $|r_i|!$ therefore gives the number of ordered cell value compositions.

This generating function has been used to develop a look-up table that is employed in a heuristic in Sect. 3.3.2. It is worth noting that the function is generalisable to Kakuro puzzles that use larger sets of assigned values (*i.e.* beyond the range $1, ..., 9$).

3 Automating the Solution

Automated approaches to the solution of a given Kakuro puzzle can be placed into two categories. One category of approaches would use similar methods to those used by a human solver, where the constraints of the puzzle (run-totals and non-duplication of values within runs) are considered in turn in some logical order until a valid solution is found. Alternatively, the secondary category would use search algorithms, possibly along with heuristics and objective functions for optimisation. These heuristics and objective functions would incorporate problem domain information.

3.1 Selecting a Suitable Approach

A given Kakuro puzzle could be solved exhaustively. That is, all possible values are tried in all cells, fully enumerating the search space in order to locate the solution. This approach is adequate for smaller grids or when a smaller range of numbers is to be used but very time consuming and inefficient for most puzzle grids where very large numbers of puzzle states would have to be checked.

The puzzle constraints, non-duplication of values within runs and the summation requirement of values to a specified run-total, make the puzzle seemingly appropriate for a constraint-based approach to a solution. Binary integer programming is one such approach, and such a formulation of the puzzle has previously been presented by the authors [3]. In that formulation, ten binary decision variables, $A_{i,j,k}$, are associated with every cell, where row i and column j specify the cell position, and k specifies an available value for assignment to the cell (with zero indicating a black square). Puzzle constraints and trivial constraints (such as there only being one value per cell and only values in the range $1, ..., 9$ can be added to white cells) are expressed explicitly. The solution is indicated by the collection of binary decision variables that are set to 1, showing which value k should be assigned to the cell at row *i* and column *j*. The results for this approach, using XPress MP (a suite of optimisation packages) showed that this approach works well for small puzzles [3]. However, the large number of binary decision variables for larger grids may make this an inefficient general approach.

The difficulty of search space size might be overcome by the use of heuristics in a local search optimisation approach [10]. This approach would employ some objective function to determine an efficient path through the search space, beginning from some *initial state*. This initial state might be a particular arrangement of values within cells such that run duplication constraints are met but not run-total constraints. An *operator* would then change the values within one or more of the cells so that *successor states*, different arrangements of values within cells, are produced following each iteration of the search (as illustrated in Fig. 2).

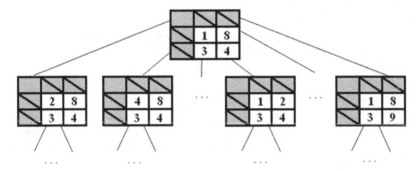

Fig. 2. A sample search space containing puzzle states

All states would then be evaluated and scored by the objective function, so that the state with highest 'score' would be explored next. However, such an approach is only feasible if a sensible and effective objective function can be constructed, such that it is possible to move reliably towards the goal state. Unfortunately, the amount of problem domain information that can usefully be incorporated into an effective objective function is limited. This puzzle information relates specifically to how closely the current horizontal and vertical run sums match the specified run-totals. There is a likelihood of many different states mapping to the same score and of the method becoming stuck in plateaus [10] in the search space. Similar difficulties have been reported in a local search optimisation approach to the solution to Sudoku puzzles [7]. Also, since each value in a particular cell can be replaced by up to eight alternative values, the search space can grow very rapidly. Solutions of larger puzzles would inevitably involve the storage of a very large number of states.

Meta-heuristic approaches might be employed to overcome the limitations of the objective function, however the authors wish to employ problem domain information more directly. For the above reasons, search optimisation approaches are not pursued here. Instead we employ a backtracking approach to solving Kakuro puzzles, as described below.

3.2 Backtracking Solver

An approach that takes more direct advantage of the problem complexity characteristics – notably the permutations of the values that may legitimately be assigned to runs – is desired. A backtracking algorithm, employing a depth-first approach to examining the search space, can be made appropriate for the solution of Kakuro puzzles if suitable heuristics to guide the backtracker, and effective pruning conditions can be determined to reduce search space size. In this section, a backtracking algorithm, implemented through the use of a stack, is described that incorporates conditions to prune parts of the search space in which valid solutions will definitely not be located.

BACKTRACKING ALGORITHM
Initialise puzzle information and stack.
Current_State becomes the initial-state. Add Current_State to stack.
Current_Cell is set to be the first available white cell.
Current_Value = 1.
WHILE [empty white cells exist]
    Place Current_Value into Current_Cell.
    Increment Iteration_Count.
    Determine runs in which Current_Cell resides, and corresponding run totals.
    IF [no duplicates in runs] and ([run-total(s) not exceeded] or [run(s) completed correctly])
        Push Current_State to stack.
        IF [empty white cells exist]
            Current_Cell becomes next available cell.
        END-IF
        Reset Current_Value to 1.
    ELSE-IF ([runs under target run-totals] or [duplicate in run(s)]) and [Current_Value<9]
        Current_Value = Current_Value +1.
    ELSE
        Pop state from stack to become Current_State.
        Current_Cell becomes previous cell.
        Current_Value becomes value within Current_Cell.
        WHILE [Current_Value = 9]
            Pop state from stack to become Current_State.
            Current_Cell becomes previous cell.
            Current_Value becomes value within Current_Cell.
        END-WHILE
        Current_Value = Current_Value +1.
    END-IF
END-WHILE
Output Current_State as solution.

This approach begins with an empty grid and attempts assignments of values to each white cell in turn, starting with the lowest numerical value, and beginning the placements from the top leftmost cell. It follows a depth-first [10] enumeration of the search space, favouring the assignment of low numerical values, but tests within the algorithm ensure that some fruitless paths through the search space are avoided. An apparently successful assignment of a value to a cell (one which does not violate puzzle constraints) results in the current grid being pushed onto the stack. Violations of the puzzle constraints – a duplicate value in a run, or an exceeded or under-target run total where all possible values have been considered for the final cell of a run – result in the algorithm backtracking, and popping the last successful grid state from the stack. The stack only stores incomplete states, that are apparently valid, along one branch of the search space, thus avoiding the memory based issues which can arise in search approaches in which all valid partial states encountered are stored (for example in the queue of a local search optimisation approach [10]). An iteration count is incremented each time an attempt is made to assign a value to a cell, and is used as a measure of algorithm performance in Sect. 4.

While this approach is ideal for smaller puzzles, the algorithm can be required to perform a great deal of backtracking in larger puzzles. This necessitates the addition of further components. The heuristics and pruning conditions that have been tested in this project are described in Sect. 3.3 below.

3.3 Modifications to the Backtracking Algorithm

In this section, three modifications to the Backtracking Algorithm of Sect. 3.2 are proposed. The results of using these approaches are presented and analysed in Sect. 4.

3.3.1 Cell Ordering

It is proposed here that the path taken through the search space be guided by consideration of how many valid arrangements of values there are for each run. The *cell ordering* heuristic employed is that by favouring the completion of cells in runs having fewest valid arrangements, a reduction can be achieved in the maximum amount of backtracking required due to incorrect assignments to cells considered near the start of the search process. Those cells in runs having most potential valid arrangements will be considered later, tending to push the consideration of cells requiring most backtracking to a deeper level in the search space.

As an example, a run-total of 6 over two cells can be filled using the tuples (1, 5), (5, 1), (2, 4) and (4, 2). (The tuple (3, 3) would be invalid due to the duplication constraint). Hence this run can be filled in four different ways.

A *look-up* table is constructed using the generating function of Sect. 2. This table explicitly states how many distinct compositions of values exist for each run-total t_l and all possible run lengths $|r_l|$.

As this approach uses calculations based on entire runs, rather than single cells, a cell inherits the lowest number of choices of any run in which it is situated. This represents an upper bound for the actual number of choices for that cell. (We note that a more accurate measure is to be found in the intersection of the arrangements in runs, which is more difficult to calculate, and remains as future work.)

3.3.2 Reverse Value Ordering

This heuristic favours the assignment of values in the range $1,...,9$ in reverse order, essentially being based on the 'assumption' that puzzles will be solved more quickly in this manner. Clearly, all values are equally likely to be the content of a cell of a puzzle solution, in a general sense; the actual likelihood of, for example, a 1 or 9 appearing more frequently in a solution will be puzzle-specific. This is a poor heuristic, but no worse in general that the reverse assumption. Hence it provides a useful test of the performance of the algorithm, when measuring the results of many puzzles. A puzzle having several high values in cells considered at the start of solution will probably solve more quickly when using this heuristic.

3.3.3 Projected Run Pruning

The Backtracking Algorithm of Sect. 3.2 checks for invalid assignments to a run on the completion of that run. This will still allow poor choices of values to be placed at the beginning of a run, such that the run total can not be met with legitimate value assignments in the remaining cells. As an example, consider a run of 5 cells having the run total 35. A placement of 1 in the initial cell will seem legitimate, but even the assignment of the largest values to the remaining cells – 9, 8, 7 and 6 – will only lead to a total of 31. In such a case, considerable processing time would be wasted attempting to fill the remaining cells, until the Backtracking Algorithm eventually places a value larger than 4 in the initial cell. By considering whether a run can possibly be completed to meet its total, each time an assignment is made, fruitless branches of the search space can be pruned.

An additional validity check is added to the Backtracking Algorithm of Sect. 3.2. On assigning a value to a cell in a run that still possesses unassigned cells, a calculation is performed of the sum of the largest possible values that may still legitimately be added to the remaining cells of that run. If this sum would yield a run total at least matching the specified run total for that cell, the backtracker continues, otherwise this branch of the search space is pruned. This approach will reduce the number of puzzle states that need to be considered and hence should, in general, decrease the time taken to obtain a solution to a given puzzle.

4 Results and Timings

There is no published work with which to compare the findings of this project, and so the results obtained using the heuristics and the projected run pruning from Sect. 3 will be compared to results obtained using the backtracking solver alone, for specific puzzles of varying sizes. Tests were performed on a Viglen Intel Core 2 Duo processor 2.66GHz, with 2GB RAM. Programs were developed in Java (using Oracle Jdeveloper 10.1.3.3.0) and executed in the J2SE runtime environment.

Initial experimentation focused on establishing the relative and general effectiveness of the methods proposed in Sect. 3, and results are shown in Table 1. Few puzzles of small size were available for testing, but those tested were deemed sufficient to examine the methods and to demonstrate the puzzle-specific nature of their effectiveness. The numbers of iterations (explained in Sect. 3.2) are shown for a range of puzzle sizes.

Table 1. Iteration counts for specific puzzles, in each method

		Heuristic Used				
		Backtracking Alone	Cell Ordering	Value Ordering	Projected Run Pruning	Projected Run Pruning & Cell Ordering
Puzzle Grid Size	2×2	96	96	16	42	42
	3×3	68	22	60	60	22
	4×4	444	311	40	86	131
	5×5(a)	142	213	309	142	213
	5×5(b)	2,917	209	2,562	2,383	100
	5×5(c)	983	423	424	149	111
	5×5(d)	2,735	237	1,353	429	195
	6×6	210	650	675	210	650
	7×7	20,393,677	1,052,747	2,495,945	12,455,461	24,636
	8×8	14,347	71,168	3,140	7,032	27,440

As would be expected, the reverse value ordering worked best on certain puzzles – these being ones in which the first few cells that considered had high values. Cell ordering was often effective, but seemed less so for larger puzzles – for certain puzzles it performed worse than backtracking alone. In contrast, the projected run pruning performed more consistently, never requiring more iterations than the backtracker alone (as would be expected), and often requiring far fewer iterations. A method that encourages rapid and early pruning is desired. The combination of cell ordering and projected run pruning occasionally reduced the number iterations below the count achieved by either approach individually, suggesting that the methods might combine well in guiding the search method to earlier pruning of the search space. However, this behaviour was not consistent.

Puzzles of small size generally solve quite rapidly, but the processing overhead of the methods is of interest here. Table 2 shows the average time taken per iteration, measured in milliseconds, for the puzzle set of Table 1, this time banded according to puzzle size. As would be expected, the average time per iteration is generally higher for smaller puzzles, as the search spaces are small, hence the benefits of pruning are less significant. It seems reasonably clear that the processing overheads of cell ordering (arising from a pre-processing step and indexing of an array) and pruning are small.

Table 2. Average time (milliseconds) taken per iteration

<table>
<tr><td colspan="2" rowspan="2"></td><td colspan="5">Heuristic Used</td></tr>
<tr><td>Backtracking Alone</td><td>Cell Ordering</td><td>Value Ordering</td><td>Project Run Pruning</td><td>Projected Run Pruning & Cell Ordering</td></tr>
<tr><td rowspan="3">Puzzle Grid Size</td><td>< 5x5</td><td>3.5107</td><td>3.8425</td><td>3.2736</td><td>3.6641</td><td>3.6108</td></tr>
<tr><td>5x5 & 6x6</td><td>3.3865</td><td>3.7496</td><td>3.4823</td><td>3.5374</td><td>3.6190</td></tr>
<tr><td>> 6x6</td><td>3.4648</td><td>3.5826</td><td>3.4903</td><td>3.5685</td><td>3.5518</td></tr>
</table>

While few puzzles of small sizes are available, a larger number of published puzzles exist for a more 'standard' challenge. For a test set of puzzles of size 9×9, we pursue the most promising methods of projected run pruning and its combination with cell ordering. Table 3 shows results for thirteen puzzles of grid size 9×9.

Table 3. Iteration statistics for thirteen puzzles with grid size 9x9.

	Minimum Iterations	Maximum Iterations	Median Iterations	Average Iterations	% of cases where method performed best
Projected Run Pruning	5,829	1,554,208	65,760	256,455	76.92%
Projected Run Pruning & Cell Ordering	2,543	28,039,107	284,512	5,795,832	23.08%

In a small number of cases, the combination of the cell-ordering heuristic and pruning improved results (shown by the minimum number of iterations and the percentage of cases where improvement occurred), but the median and maximum number of iterations show both that the combination is an unreliable approach and that on certain puzzles, performance is greatly worsened. Hence the projected run pruning method is considered here to be the most reliable approach.

An extended test set of 20 puzzles of size 9×9 were solved using just projected run pruning. The fastest solution time (in milliseconds) was 21,096, the longest 36,075,603, the median 323,694 and the average 4,675,317. The average time per iteration was 3.6738 ms to 4 decimal places. This approach is relatively promising, but further pruning methods to force an earlier and more rapid reduction in search space size, and heuristics to guide search, are sought to enable more rapid solution.

5 Conclusion

This paper has analysed the size of a Kakuro search space. This includes establishing an improved upper bound for the number of possible arrangements of values in a Kakuro grid. More significantly, a generating function has been presented to determine the exact number of valid arrangements of values in any given run; this function can be used for different grid sizes and different numbers of values to be assigned. The suitability of a range of search approaches for the solution of Kakuro has been considered, and a backtracking approach has been presented as the preferred approach. A cell ordering heuristic, based on the number of valid arrangements of values in a given run, has been proposed and evaluated. Lastly, a pruning method has been proposed to reduce the part of the search space that need be examined, by checking whether a run total can possibly be met each time an assignment is made to a cell in that run.

The pruning method proved to be most effective in reducing solution time for a range of puzzle grids. The cell ordering heuristic performed unreliably, making reasonable improvements in the solution time in some cases, but greatly increased solution time in other cases. This heuristic might be improved by establishing the intersection of the arrangements in runs, rather than allowing a cell to inherit the lowest number of possible arrangements of valid solutions of the two runs in which it is situated, thus giving a better measure of possibilities for a single cell. The completion of a started run, in preference to continually jumping to the next single cell with fewest apparent choices, might also allow the earlier detection of fruitless branches.

The usefulness of Kakuro for applications, including Coding Theory, will depend in part on the development of methods to reliably enumerate the search spaces of specific puzzles more rapidly. A more detailed understanding of the size of the search spaces of puzzles will also be required. For this, it is proposed that the results of this paper be extended through further improvements to the upper bound for the number of possible arrangements of values in solution grids, through consideration of the intersection of runs.

Acknowledgments   The authors wish to thank Sian K. Jones for many helpful discussions relating to this work.

References

1. Cadoli, M., Schaerf, M.: Partial solutions with unique completion. Lect. Notes Comput. Sci. **4155**, 101-10, (2006)
2. Chandrasekaran, K R: Kakuro Puzzle Solver, Internal Report (2008) http://www.geocities.com/krcgee/kakuro/index.html
3. Davies, R.P., Roach P.A., Perkins, S.: Properties of, and Solutions to, Kakuro and related puzzles. In: Roach, P., Plassman, P. (eds.) Proceedings of the 3rd Research Student Workshop, University of Glamorgan, pp. 54-58 (2008)
4. Dotu, I., del Val, A., Cebrian, M.: Redundant modeling for the quasigroup completion problem. In: Rossi, F. (ed.), Principles and Practice of Constraint Programming, CP 2003 (Lect. Notes Comput. Sci. **2833**), Springer-Verlag, Berlin, pp 288-302 (2003)
5. Galanti, G.: The History of Kakuro,. Conceptis Puzzles (2005). http://www.conceptispuzzles.com/articles/kakuro/history.htm. Cited 22 Feb 2008
6. Gomes, C., Shmoys, D.: The promise of LP to boost CP techniques for combinatorial problems. In: Jussien, N., Laburthe, F. (eds.) Proceedings of the Fourth International Workshop on Integration of AI and OR techniques in Constraint Programming for Combinatorial Optimisation Problems, CPAIOR, France, pp 291–305 (2002)
7. Jones, S.K., Roach P.A., Perkins S.: Construction of heuristics for a search-based approach to solving Sudoku. In: Bramer M., Coenen F., Petridis M. (eds) Research and Development in Intelligent Systems XXIV: Proceedings of AI-2007, the Twenty-seventh SGAI International Conference on Artificial Intelligence, pp. 37-49 (2007)
8. KakuroPlay: Kakuro Solver. Internal Report (2006) http://kakuro-solver.blogspot.com/
9. Mustonen, M.: On certain Cross Sum puzzles. Internal Report (2006) http://www.survo.fi/papers/puzzles.pdf. Cited 22 Feb 2008
10 Rich, E., Knight, K.: Artificial Intelligence, 2nd Edition. McGraw-Hill, Singapore (1991)
11. Seta, T.: The complexities of puzzles, cross sum and their another solution problems (ASP),. Senior thesis. Dept. Information Science, University of Tokyo (2002)
12. Soedarmadji, E., McEliece, R.: Iterative decoding for Sudoku and Latin Square codes. In: Forty-Fifth Annual Allerton Conference, Allerton-07, University of Illinois (2007)
13. Yang, X.: Cryptic Kakuro and Cross Sums Sudoku. Exposure Publishing (2006)

FROM MACHINE LEARNING TO E-LEARNING

The Bayesian Learning Automaton — Empirical Evaluation with Two-Armed Bernoulli Bandit Problems

Ole-Christoffer Granmo

Abstract The two-armed Bernoulli bandit (TABB) problem is a classical optimization problem where an agent sequentially pulls one of two arms attached to a gambling machine, with each pull resulting either in a *reward* or a *penalty*. The reward probabilities of each arm are unknown, and thus one must balance between exploiting existing knowledge about the arms, and obtaining new information.

In the last decades, several computationally efficient algorithms for tackling this problem have emerged, with *Learning Automata* (LA) being known for their ε-optimality, and *confidence interval based* for logarithmically growing regret. Applications include treatment selection in clinical trials, route selection in adaptive routing, and plan exploration in games like Go. The TABB has also been extensively studied from a Bayesian perspective, however, in general, such analysis leads to computationally inefficient solution policies.

This paper introduces the Bayesian Learning Automaton (BLA). The BLA is inherently Bayesian in nature, yet relies simply on counting rewards/penalties and on random sampling from a pair of twin beta distributions. Extensive experiments demonstrate that, in contrast to most LA, BLA does not rely on external learning speed/accuracy control. It also outperforms recently proposed confidence interval based algorithms. We thus believe that BLA opens up for improved performance in an extensive number of applications, and that it forms the basis for a new avenue of research.

1 Introduction

The conflict between exploration and exploitation is a well-known problem in reinforcement learning, and other areas of artificial intelligence. The two-armed bandit problem captures the essence of this conflict, and has thus occupied researchers for

Dr. Ole-Christoffer Granmo, Associate Professor
Department of ICT, University of Agder, Grimstad, Norway e-mail: ole.granmo@uia.no

over forty years [20]. This paper introduces a new family of techniques for solving the classical two-armed Bernoulli bandit problem, and reports empirical results that demonstrate its advantages over recent solution approaches such as UCB-Tuned [1], but also established schemes like the L_{R-I} and Pursuit Learning Automata [13].

1.1 The Two-Armed Bernoulli Bandit Problem

The two-armed Bernoulli bandit (TABB) problem is a classical optimization problem that explores the trade off between exploitation and exploration in reinforcement learning. The problem consists of an agent that sequentially pulls one of two arms attached to a gambling machine, with each pull resulting either in a *reward* or a *penalty*[1]. The sequence of rewards/penalties obtained from each arm $i \in \{1,2\}$ forms a Bernoulli process with *unknown* reward probability r_i and penalty probability $1 - r_i$. This leaves the agent with the following dilemma: Should the arm that so far seems to provide the highest chance of reward be pulled once more, or should the inferior arm be pulled in order to learn more about *its* reward probability? Sticking prematurely with the arm that is presently considered to be the best one, may lead to not discovering which arm is truly optimal. On the other hand, lingering with the inferior arm unnecessarily, postpones the harvest that can be obtained from the optimal arm.

With the above in mind, we intend to evaluate an agent's arm selection strategy in terms of so-called regret — *the difference between the sum of rewards expected after N successive arm pulls, and what would have been obtained by only pulling the optimal arm*. To exemplify, assume that a reward amounts to the value (utility) 1 and that a penalty possesses the value 0. We then have that the expected value of pulling arm i becomes r_i. Thus, if the optimal arm is arm 1, the regret after N plays would become:

$$r_1 N - \sum_{n=1}^{N} \hat{r}_n, \tag{1}$$

with $\hat{r}_n$ being the expected reward at arm pull n, given the agent's arm selection strategy. In other words, as will be clear in the following, we consider the case where rewards are *undiscounted*, as discussed in [1].

1.2 Applications

Solution schemes for bandit problems have formed the basis for tackling a number of applications. For instance, UCB-Tuned [1] is used for move exploration in MoGo, a top-level Computer-Go program on 9×9 Go boards [5]. Furthermore, UCB1 has

---

[1] A penalty may also be seen as the absence of a reward. However, we choose to use the term *penalty* as is customary in the LA literature.

formed the basis for guiding Monte-Carlo planning, improving planning efficiency significantly in several domains [9].

The applications of LA are many – the following more recent. LA have been used to allocate polling resources optimally in web monitoring, and for allocating limited sampling resources in binomial estimation problems [7]. LA have also been applied for solving NP-complete SAT problems [6]. Furthermore, in [2], LA optimize throughput in MPLS traffic engineering [2]. Note that regret minimizing algorithms also have found applications in network routing [4].

1.3 Contributions and Paper Organization

The contributions of this paper can be summarized as follows. In Sect. 2 we briefly review a selection of main TABB solution approaches, including LA and confidence interval based schemes. Then, in Sect. 3 we present the Bayesian Learning Automaton (BLA). In contrast to the above discussed schemes, the BLA is inherently Bayesian in nature, yet relies simply on counting and random sampling. Thus, to the best of our knowledge, BLA is the first TABB algorithm that takes advantage of the Bayesian perspective in a computationally efficient manner. In Sect. 4 we provide extensive experimental results that demonstrate that, in contrast to the L_{R-I} and Pursuit schemes, BLA does not rely on external learning speed/accuracy control. The BLA also clearly outperforms UCB-Tuned in all but one tested environments. Accordingly, in the above perspective, it is our belief that the BLA represent a new avenue of research, and in Sect. 5 we list open BLA related research problems, in addition to providing concluding remarks.

2 Related Work

The TABB problem has been studied in a disparate range of research fields. From a machine learning point of view, Sutton et. al put an emphasis on computationally efficient solution techniques that are suitable for reinforcement learning. A selection of main approaches that also have had a significant impact when it comes to applications are *briefly* reviewed here.

2.1 Learning Automata (LA) — The L_{R-I} and Pursuit Schemes

LA have been used to model biological systems [10, 12–15, 17, 18] and have attracted considerable interest in the last decade because they can learn the optimal action when operating in (or interacting with) unknown stochastic environments.

Furthermore, they combine rapid and accurate convergence with low computational complexity.

More notable approaches include the family of linear updating schemes, with the Linear Reward-Inaction (L_{R-I}) automaton being designed for stationary environments [13]. In short, L_{R-I} maintains an arm probability selection vector $\bar{p} = [p_1, p_2]$, with $p_2 = 1 - p_1$. Which arm to be pulled is decided randomly by sampling from $\bar{p}$. Initially, $\bar{p}$ is uniform and each arm is selected with equal probability. The following linear updating rules summarize how rewards and penalties affect $\bar{p}$ with p_1' and $1 - p_1'$ being the resulting updated arm selection probabilities:

$$p_1' = p_1 + (1 - a) \times (1 - p_1) \text{ if pulling arm 1 results in a reward} \qquad (2)$$

$$p_1' = a \times p_1 \text{ if pulling arm 2 results in a reward} \qquad (3)$$

$$p_1' = p_1 \text{ if pulling arm 1 or arm 2 results in a penalty.} \qquad (4)$$

Above the parameter a ($0 \ll a < 1$) governs learning speed. As seen, after an arm i has been pulled, the associated probability p_i is increased using the linear updating rule upon receiving a reward, with p_{1-i} being decreased correspondingly. Note that $\bar{p}$ is left unchanged upon a penalty.

A distinguishing feature of L_{R-I}, and indeed the field of LA as a whole, is its ε-optimality [13]: *By a suitable choice of some parameter of the LA, the expected reward probability obtained from each arm pull can be made arbitrarily close to the optimal reward probability, as the number of arm pulls tends to infinity.*

The *pursuit scheme* (P-scheme) makes the updating of $\bar{p}$ more goal-directed in the sense that it maintains maximum likelihood (ML) estimates $(\hat{r}_1, \hat{r}_2)$ of the reward probabilities (r_1, r_2) associated with each arm. Instead of using the rewards/penalties received to update $\bar{p}$ directly, the rewards/penalties are instead used to update the ML estimates. The ML estimates, in turn, are used to decide which arm selection probability p_i to increase. In brief, the Pursuit scheme increases the arm selection probability p_i associated with the currently largest ML estimate $\hat{r}_i$, instead of the arm actually producing the reward. Thus, unlike L_{R-I}, when the inferior arm produces rewards in the Pursuit scheme, these rewards will not influence learning progress (assuming that the ranking of the ML estimates are correct). Accordingly, the pursuit scheme usually outperforms L_{R-I} when it comes to rate of convergence.

Variants of the Pursuit scheme has been proposed [10, 12–15, 17, 18], with slightly improved performance, however, the pursuit scheme can be seen as representative for these additional approaches.

2.2 The ε-Greedy and ε_n-Greedy Policies

The ε-greedy rule is a well-known strategy for the bandit problem [16]. In short, the arm with the presently highest average reward is pulled with probability $1 - \varepsilon$, while a randomly chosen arm is pulled with probability ε. In other words, the balancing of exploration and exploitation is controlled by the ε-parameter. Note that the ε-greedy strategy persistently explores the available arms with constant effort, which clearly is sub-optimal for the TABB problem (unless the reward probabilities are changing with time).

As a remedy for the above problem, ε can be slowly decreased, leading to the ε_n-greedy strategy described in [1]. The purpose is to gradually shift focus from exploration to exploitation. The latter work focuses on algorithms that minimizes regret, i.e., the expected loss caused by the fact that a strategy does not always select the optimal arm. It turns out that the ε_n-greedy strategy provides a *logarithmically* increasing regret asymptotically. Indeed, it has been proved that logarithmically increasing regret is the best possible [1].

2.3 Confidence Interval Based Algorithms

A promising line of thought is the interval estimation methods, where a confidence interval for the reward probability of each arm is estimated, and an "optimistic reward probability estimate" is identified for each arm. The arm with the most optimistic reward probability estimate is then greedily selected [8, 19].

In [1], several confidence interval based algorithms are analysed. These algorithms also provide logarithmically increasing regret, with *UCB-Tuned* – a variant of the well-known UCB1 algorithm — outperforming both *UCB1*, *UCB2*, as well as the ε_n-greedy strategy. In brief, in UCB-Tuned, the following optimistic estimates are used for each arm i:

$$\mu_i + \sqrt{\frac{\ln n}{n_i} \min\{1/4, \sigma_i^2 + \sqrt{\frac{2\ln n}{n_i}}\}} \tag{5}$$

with μ_i and σ_i^2 being the sample mean and variance of the rewards that have been obtained from arm i, n is the number of arms pulled in total, and n_i is the number of times arm i has been pulled. Thus, the quantity added to the sample average of a specific arm i is steadily reduced as the arm is pulled, and uncertainty about the reward probability is reduced. As a result, by always selecting the arm with the highest optimistic reward estimate, UCB-Tuned gradually shifts from exploration to exploitation.

2.4 Bayesian Approaches

The TABB has also been extensively analysed from a Bayesian perspective. Assume that one always limits oneself to only considering the rewards/penalties that will be obtained from a limited number of succeeding arm pulls, thus, introducing a finite horizon of play artificially. Also assume that the rewards/penalties and probabilities of each possible sequence of events can be obtained. Then, obviously, one can calculate the Bayes optimal way of balancing exploration and exploitation simply by considering all of the possible sequences of arm selections and rewards/penalties that may occur. Such brute force enumeration is, of course, computationally intractable for the general case [16]. However, note that in [3] the TABB is modelled as a partially observable Markov decision processes, and it is shown that the difference in rewards between stopping learning and acquiring full information goes to zero as the number of arm pulls grows large.

Another related example is the probability matching algorithms proposed in [20]. Bayesian analysis is used to obtain a closed form expression for the probability that each arm is optimal given the rewards/penalties observed so far. The policy consists of always pulling the arm which has the greatest probability of being optimal. Unfortunately, computation time is unbounded, rising with the number of arm pulls [20]. Accordingly, the approach is of theoretical interest, but has limited applicability in practice.

3 The Bayesian Learning Automaton (BLA)

Bayesian reasoning is a probabilistic approach to inference which is of significant importance in machine learning because it allows quantitative weighting of evidence supporting alternative hypotheses, with the purpose of allowing optimal decisions to be made. Furthermore, it provides a framework for analyzing learning algorithms [11].

We here present a scheme for solving the TABB problem that inherently builds upon the Bayesian reasoning framework. We coin the scheme *Bayesian Learning Automaton* (BLA) since it can be modelled as a state machine with each state associated with unique arm selection probabilities, in an LA manner.

A unique feature of the BLA is its computational simplicity, achieved by relying *implicitly* on Bayesian reasoning principles. In essence, at the heart of BLA we find the *beta distribution*. Its shape is determined by two positive parameters, usually denoted by α and β, producing the following probability density function:

$$f(x; \alpha, \beta) = \frac{x^{\alpha-1}(1-x)^{\beta-1}}{\int_0^1 u^{\alpha-1}(1-u)^{\beta-1}du}, \quad x \in [0,1] \tag{6}$$

and the corresponding cumulative distribution function:

$$F(x; \alpha, \beta) = \frac{\int_0^x t^{a-1}(1-t)^{b-1}dt}{\int_0^1 u^{\alpha-1}(1-u)^{\beta-1}du}, \quad x \in [0,1]. \tag{7}$$

Essentially, BLA uses the beta distribution for two purposes. First of all, the beta distribution is used to provide a *Bayesian estimate* of the reward probabilities associated with each of the available bandit arms. Secondly, a novel feature of BLA is that it uses the beta distribution as the basis for a *randomized arm selection mechanism*. The following algorithm contains the essence of the BLA approach.

Bayesian Learning Automaton Algorithm.

- **Initialization:** $\alpha_1 := \beta_1 := \alpha_2 := \beta_2 := 1$.
- **Loop:**

    1. Draw a value x_1 randomly from beta distribution $f(x_1, \alpha_1, \beta_1)$ with parameters α_1, β_1.
    2. Draw a value x_2 randomly from beta distribution $f(x_2, \alpha_2, \beta_2)$ with parameters α_2, β_2.
    3. **If** $x_1 > x_2$ **then** pull *Arm* 1 **else** pull *Arm* 2. Denote pulled arm: *Arm i*.
    4. Receive either *Reward* or *Penalty* as a result of pulling *Arm i*.
    5. Increase α_i with 1 upon *Reward* ($\alpha_i := \alpha_i + 1$), and increase β_i with 1 upon *Penalty* ($\beta_i := \beta_i + 1$).
    6. **Goto** 1.

As seen from the above BLA algorithm, the parameters $(\alpha_1, \beta_1, \alpha_2, \beta_2)$ form a infinite discrete four dimensional state space Φ, within which the BLA navigates by iteratively increasing either α_1, β_1, α_2, or β_2 with 1.

Also note that for any parameter configuration $(\alpha_1, \beta_1, \alpha_2, \beta_2) \in \Phi$ we have that the probability of selecting *Arm* 1, $P(Arm\ 1)$, is equal to $P^\Phi(X_1 > X_2)$ — the probability that a randomly drawn value $x_1 \in X_i$ is greater than a randomly drawn value $x_2 \in X_2$, when the associated stochastic variables X_1 and X_2 are beta distributed, with parameters α_1, β_1 and α_2, β_2, respectively.

The probability $P^\Phi(X_1 > X_2)$ can also be interpreted as the probability that *Arm* 1 is the optimal one, given the observations α_1, β_1 and α_2, β_2. This means that BLA will gradually shift its arm selection focus towards the arm which most likely is the optimal one, as observations are received.

Finally, observe that BLA does not rely on any external parameters that must be configured to optimize performance for specific problem instances. This is in contrast to the traditional Learning Automata family of algorithms, where a "learning speed/accuracy" parameter is inherent in ε-optimal schemes.

4 Empirical Results

In this section we evaluate the BLA by comparing it with UCB-Tuned, the best performing algorithm from [1], as well as the L_{R-I} and Pursuit schemes from the LA field.

For the sake of fairness, we base our comparison on the experimental setup for the TABB found in [1]. Although several experiments were conducted using various reward distributions, we report, for the sake of brevity, only results for the following five reward/penalty distributions. The first distribution, **Distribution 1** ($r_1 = 0.9$, $r_2 = 0.6$), forms the most simple environment, with low variance and a large difference between the two arms. By gradually reducing the arm difference, we increase the difficulty of the TABB problem, and it is of interest to observe how the different schemes react as the challenge increases. **Distribution 2** ($r_1 = 0.9$, $r_2 = 0.8$) fulfills this purpose in [1], however, in order to stress the schemes further, we also apply **Distribution 3** ($r_1 = 0.9$, $r_2 = 0.85$) and **Distribution 4** ($r_1 = 0.9$, $r_2 = 0.89$). The challenge of **Distribution 5** ($r_1 = 0.55$, $r_2 = 0.45$) is its high variance combined with the small difference between the two arms.

For these distributions, an ensemble of 1000 independent replications with different random number streams was performed to minimize the variance of the reported results. In each replication, BLA, UCB-Tuned, L_{R-I}, and the Pursuit scheme conducted 100 000 arm pulls.

Fig. 1 and 2 contains the comparison on distribution 1. The former plot shows the probability of choosing the optimal arm as each scheme explores the two arms, with n being the number of arm pulls performed. The latter plot shows the accumulation of regret with number of arm pulls.

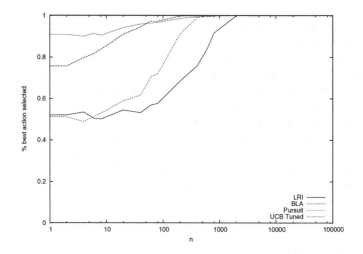

Fig. 1 Probability of selecting best arm for distribution 1 ($r_1 = 0.9$; $r_2 = 0.6$).

Because of the logarithmically scaled x-axis, it is clear from the plots that both BLA and UCB-Tuned attain a logarithmically growing regret. Moreover, the performance of BLA is significantly better than that of UCB-Tuned. Surprisingly, both of the LA schemes converge to constant regret. This can be explained by their ε-optimality and the relatively low learning speed parameter used ($a = 0.01$). In brief, the LA converged to only selecting the optimal arm in all of the 1000 replications.

Fig. 3 and 4 contains the comparison on distribution 2. As shown, the LA still achieve constant regret, and again, the BLA outperforms UCB-Tuned.

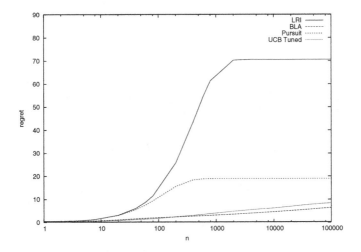

Fig. 2 Regret for distribution 1 ($r_1 = 0.9$; $r_2 = 0.6$).

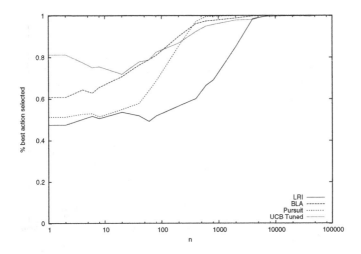

Fig. 3 Probability of selecting best arm for distribution 2 ($r_1 = 0.9$; $r_2 = 0.8$).

For Distribution 3, however, it turns out that the set learning accuracy of the LA is too low to always converge to only selecting the optimal arm. In some of the replications, the LA also converges to selecting the inferior arm only, and as seen in Fig. 5 and 6, this leads to linearly growing regret. As also seen, the BLA continues to provide significantly better performance than UCB-Tuned.

The latter property of LA becomes even more apparent with even more similar arms, as seen in the Fig. 7 and 8. Yet, we observe that the performance of both BLA

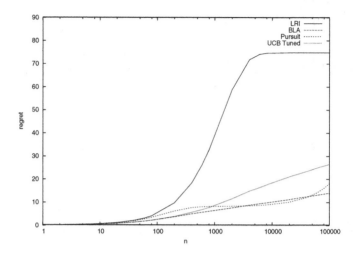

Fig. 4 Regret for distribution 2 ($r_1 = 0.9$; $r_2 = 0.8$).

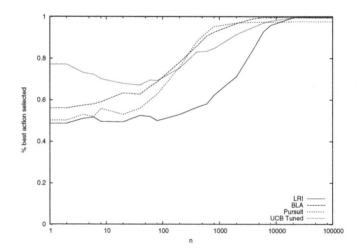

Fig. 5 Probability of selecting best arm for distribution 3 ($r_1 = 0.9$; $r_2 = 0.85$).

and UCB-Tuned are surprisingly unaffected by the increased difficulty. Indeed, the performance advantage of BLA becomes even more apparent in terms of regret.

Finally, for Distribution 5 we observe that the performance gap between BLA and UCB-Tuned is reduced, as seen in Fig. 9 and 10, leaving UCB-Tuned with slightly lower regret compared to BLA.

A distinguishing feature of Distribution 5 is its high variance. It is thus reasonable to conclude that UCB-Tuned has a *slight* performance advantage in that particular class of environments. In all of the other classes of environments we tested, how-

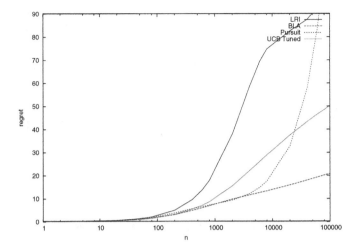

Fig. 6 Regret for distribution 3 ($r_1 = 0.9$; $r_2 = 0.85$).

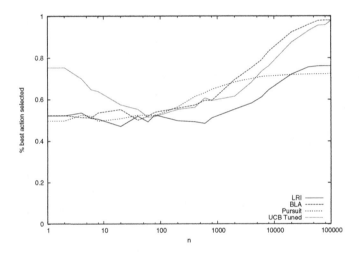

Fig. 7 Probability of selecting best arm for distribution 4 ($r_1 = 0.9$; $r_2 = 0.89$).

ever, BLA is clearly superior, with a significantly larger performance gap. Thus, overall, in the perspective of the experimental results, BLA can be seen as the most advantageous choice when the environment is unknown.

Note that the LA can achieve constant regret in all of the latter experiments too, by increasing learning accuracy. However, this significantly reduces learning speed, which for the present distributions already is worse than that of BLA and UCB-Tuned. Thus, adjusting the learning speed of the LA would not change the overall ranking of the algorithms when it comes to regret. In contrast, BLA and UCB-Tuned

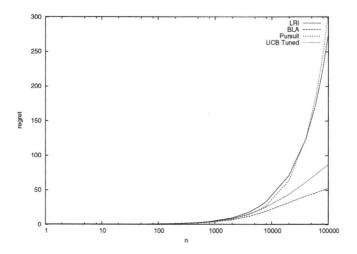

Fig. 8 Regret for distribution 4 ($r_1 = 0.9$; $r_2 = 0.89$).

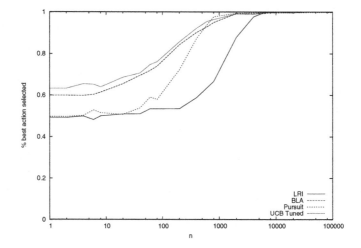

Fig. 9 Probability of selecting best arm for distribution 5 ($r_1 = 0.55$; $r_2 = 0.45$).

are not relying on externally set parameters to control their performance — in this sense, they can be applied in a plug-and-play manner not supported by the LA.

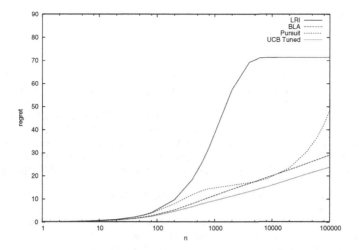

Fig. 10 Regret for distribution 5 ($r_1 = 0.55$; $r_2 = 0.45$).

5 Conclusion and Further Work

In this paper we presented the Bayesian Learning Automaton (BLA) for tackling the classical two-armed Bernoulli bandit (TABB). In contrast to previous LA and regret minimizing approaches, BLA is inherently Bayesian in nature. Still, it relies simply on counting of rewards/penalties and random sampling from a pair of twin beta distributions. Thus, to the best of our knowledge, BLA is the first TABB algorithm that takes advantage of Bayesian estimation in a computationally efficient manner.

Extensive experimental results demonstrated that, unlike L_{R-I} and Pursuit schemes, BLA does not rely on external learning speed/accuracy control. The BLA also clearly outperformed UCB-Tuned under all but one tested reward distribution, achieving logarithmically growing regret.

Accordingly, in the above perspective, it is our belief that the BLA represents a new avenue of research, opening up for an array of research problems. First of all, the BLA can quite straightforwardly be extended to handle the multi-armed bandit problem. Indeed, preliminary experimental results indicate that the observed qualities carry over from the TABB problem case. Secondly, a rigorous formal analysis of BLA is further work. We also intend to study systems of BLA from a game theory point of view, where multiple BLAs interact forming the basis for multi-agent systems.

References

1. Auer, P., Cesa-Bianchi, N., Fischer, P.: Finite-time Analysis of the Multiarmed Bandit Problem. Machine Learning **47**, 235–256 (2002)
2. B. J. Oommen, S.M., Granmo, O.C.: Routing Bandwidth Guaranteed Paths in MPLS Traffic Engineering: A Multiple Race Track Learning Approach. IEEE Transactions on Computers **56**(7), 959–976 (2007)
3. Bhulai, S., Koole, G.: On the Value of Learning for Bernoulli Bandits with Unknown Parameters. IEEE Transactions on Automatic Control **45**(11), 2135–2140 (2000)
4. Blum, A., Even-Dar, E., Ligett, K.: Routing Without Regret: On Convergence to Nash Equilibria of Regret-Minimizing Algorithms in Routing Games. In: Proceedings of the Twenty-Fifth Annual ACM SIGACT-SIGOPS Symposium on Principles of Distributed Computing (PODC 2006), pp. 45–52. ACM (2006)
5. Gelly, S., Wang, Y.: Exploration exploitation in Go: UCT for Monte-Carlo Go. In: Proceedings of NIPS-2006. NIPS (2006)
6. Granmo, O.C., Bouhmala, N.: Solving the Satisfiability Problem Using Finite Learning Automata. International Journal of Computer Science and Applications, **4**(3), 15–29 (2007)
7. Granmo, O.C., Oommen, B.J., Myrer, S.A., Olsen, M.G.: Learning Automata-based Solutions to the Nonlinear Fractional Knapsack Problem with Applications to Optimal Resource Allocation. IEEE Transactions on Systems, Man, and Cybernetics, Part B **37**(1), 166–175 (2007)
8. Kaelbling, L.P.: Learning in embedded systems. Ph.D. thesis, Stanford University (1993)
9. Kocsis, L., Szepesvari, C.: Bandit Based Monte-Carlo Planning. In: Proceedings of the 17th European Conference on Machine Learning (ECML 2006), pp. 282–293. Springer (2006)
10. Lakshmivarahan, S.: Learning Algorithms Theory and Applications. Springer-Verlag (1981)
11. Mitchell, T.M.: Machine Learning. McGraw-Hill (1997)
12. Najim, K., Poznyak, A.S.: Learning Automata: Theory and Applications. Pergamon Press, Oxford (1994)
13. Narendra, K.S., Thathachar, M.A.L.: Learning Automata: An Introduction. Prentice Hall (1989)
14. Obaidat, M.S., Papadimitriou, G.I., Pomportsis, A.S.: Learning automata: Theory, paradigms and applications. IEEE Transactions on Systems Man and Cybernetics **SMC-32**, 706–709 (2002)
15. Poznyak, A.S., Najim, K.: Learning Automata and Stochastic Optimization. Springer-Verlag, Berlin (1997)
16. Sutton, R.S., Barto, A.G.: Reinforcement Learning: An Introduction. MIT Press (1998)
17. Thathachar, M.A.L., Sastry, P.S.: Networks of Learning Automata: Techniques for Online Stochastic Optimization. Kluwer Academic Publishers (2004)
18. Tsetlin, M.L.: Automaton Theory and Modeling of Biological Systems. Academic Press (1973)
19. Vermorel, J., Mohri, M.: Multi-armed bandit algorithms and empirical evaluation. In: Proceedings of the 16th European Conference on Machine Learning (ECML 2005), pp. 437–448. Springer (2005)
20. Wyatt, J.: Exploration and inference in learning from reinforcement. Ph.D. thesis, University of Edinburgh (1997)

Acknowledgements I want to thank Chancellor's Professor B. John Oommen from Carleton University, Canada, for introducing me to the field of Learning Automata and for his valuable feedback and insight, both as a friend and as a colleague.

Discovering Implicit Intention-Level Knowledge from Natural-Language Texts[*]

John Atkinson and Anita Ferreira and Elvis Aravena

Abstract In this paper we propose a new approach to automatic discovery of implicit rhetorical information from texts based on evolutionary computation methods. In order to guide the search for rhetorical connections from natural-language texts, the model uses previously obtained training information which involves semantic and structural criteria. The main features of the model and new designed operators and evaluation functions are discussed, and the different experiments assessing the robustness and accuracy of the approach are described. Experimental results show the promise of evolutionary methods for rhetorical role discovery.

1 Introduction

For many advanced text mining tasks, applying natural-language processing technology is a key issue in order to extract relevant underlying information.

One problem with natural-language texts is that their unstructured representation makes it hard to recognize and interpret source data hence many on-line applications assume simple keyword-based representations. However, several information

John Atkinson
Department of Computer Sciences, Universidad de Concepcion, Concepcion, Chile, e-mail: atkinson@inf.udec.cl

Anita Ferreira
Department of Spanish Linguistics, Universidad de Concepcion, Concepcion, Chile, e-mail: aferreir@inf.udec.cl

Elvis Aravena
Department of Computer Sciences, Universidad de Concepcion, Concepcion, Chile, e-mail: elvarn@udec.cl

[*] This research is partially sponsored by the National Council for Scientific and Technological Research (FONDECYT, Chile) under grant number 1070714 *"An Interactive Natural-Language Dialogue Model for Intelligent Filtering based on Patterns Discovered from Text Documents"*

processing tasks require to analyze more meaningful information from texts such as semantic relationships, entities, etc., for which several Natural-Language Processing (NLP) techniques [10] are widely available. This usually becomes the previous step for complex language-based systems such as text mining.

Any state-of-the art NLP method can make use of linguistic knowledge obtained from text documents this to identify entities, simple relationships between concepts (i.e., X cause Y) and so on.

However, an important portion of this potentially useful knowledge is often implicit in the document. In order to interpret it, underlying relations between the different units of a text need to be detected so to uncover the intentions of the abstract's author. (i.e., what the abstract's author consciously expresses about what he/she wants to transmit). For example, if one wants to extract information concerning the goals of the work, the obtained results, etc from the above abstract, in order to, let say, fill in structured data bases, the sentences of the text should first be understood individually. We should then identify connections between these sentences by using some explicit "markers" when available (i.e., in the example above: "the results indicate .. ","in addition to .. "). Unfortunately, most of these relationships are implicit (i.e., *background*, *conclusions*, *methods*, etc) and require specific-purpose techniques for their treatment. The knowledge acquired at this level is usually called rhetoric knowledge or *discourse* knowledge [20, 12].

In this context, identifying implicit knowledge at the discourse level (aka. rhetorical knowledge) can be seen as the task of supervised learning in which a model learns to detect implicit relationships connecting the units (i.e., paragraphs, sentences, etc) of a text. All of these as a whole represent the overall intention that a document's author wants to transmit.

This work proposes a new approach to classification of rhetorical information based on evolutionary computation (EC) methods. Our working hypothesis is that evolutionary methods can be effective for discovery of rhetorical information from natural language texts. EC methods, particularly Genetic Algorithms (GA) exhibit interesting properties for finding solutions in complex search state spaces: they explore solutions in parallel, they cope well with attribute interaction, they are capable of producing better hypotheses by combining material of other hypotheses, they can deal with domain knowledge to assess the quality of the solutions being generated, etc.

2 Related Work

Although there is no direct approaches to identify rhetorical information for data-intensive analysis, there is a plenty of related techniques to identify and extract key information from texts for summarization or text categorization purposes [2]. Automatic summarization has interesting features as this carries out information extraction and classification tasks to identify the most relevant sentences of the full text which will be part of the generated summary. Summarization usually involves phrase extraction techniques and models for recognizing the discourse's structure [2]. The summarization problem can be seen as that which identifies the most relevant units (i.e., sentences, paragraphs) from the texts so to be included in the resulting summary.

One of the main advantages of phrase extraction based approaches is that they are simple, they do not generate deep semantic representations from text documents and no additional domain resources are usually required [9]. The problem of summarization involves ordering different phrases extracted from a full document according to their relevance in such a way that the connection between units is semantically coherent. The phrase relevance is measured by computing a relative weight of its compression rate (i.e., the length of the summary divided by the length of the source document), and the relevance of its contents [1]. Early efforts to automatic summarization are due to [11] who proposed an adaptive model for summarization using machine learning techniques. For training the model, pairs of documents and their corresponding summaries are used. Units to be extracted (i.e., phrases) are then analyzed in terms of relevant linguistic features. Thus a feature vector is computed for each phrase of the source text which is tagged according to its similarity to the text's summary. Vectors are used to build a classifier which will determine which phrases are likely to be part of the summary. Furthermore, a tagging task compares the document's phrases with its summary to decide which ones contain information existing in the summary [3]. Other powerful model for dealing with discourse relations is called *Rhetorical Structure Theory* (RST) [13] which suggests the use of rhetorical analysis techniques and nucleus detection methods to extract efficiently (and organize) the most relevant units of a text as compared with human discourse comprehension [13, 15]. The model defines relations as *Background*, *Elaboration*, *Preparation*, *Contrast*, etc., which occur between spans of text, one of which, more central to the authors purposes, is called a nucleus, and the other span, which is not so essential, is a satellite. For example, the *Evidence* relation occurs between *Claim* (nucleus) and *Evidence* (satellite), i.e., information intended to increase the reader's belief in the claim; Summary is a relation between Text (nucleus) and a short summary of the text (satellite). The main drawback of RST is that the authors don't give any logical or linguistic distinctions of relations and spans of text, and the criteria for distinguishing between them are not clear enough.

An alternative approach uses RST to extract rhetorical structures. Here, the discourse's structure can be seen as a composition of relations between sentences of a text. This can usually be represented into two layers: an intra-paragraph structure (i.e., an organization in which a sentence is the main unit of representation) and an inter-paragraph structure (i.e., an organization in which a paragraph is the main unit of representation).

Despite being an effective model to generate summaries from extracted rhetoric-based sentences, defining hierarchical relations poses several problems for developers such as the manual way new relationships should be incorporated. To cope with this, [20] propose a statistical-based approach for identifying and annotating non-hierarchical rhetorical information using Bayesian learning techniques [20]. Sentences are extracted according to their argumentative role into different levels which represent the intentional *movements* usually found in scientific documents. As a benefit, the model does not only extract relevant sentences but also has them classified into rhetorical roles. To this end, frequent rhetorical patterns (aka. moves) are defined [20] and further used to classify sentences and build the summary according to rhetorical roles such as *Background*, *Theme*, *Related work*, *Aim/Problem*, *Solution/Method*, *Results*, *Conclusion/Discussion*, etc. Nevertheless, due to the statistical nature of the method, its robustness is highly dependent on the amount of training samples being used and the ability to define the rhetorical patterns. Instead of defining and applying patterns to identify rhetorical roles, other approaches use discourse markers.

3 Discovering Rhetorical Relationships

The proposed evolutionary model receives a natural-language text, divides it into units and searches for the best sequence of rhetorical roles by taking into account semantic and structural criteria. As new hypotheses are generated, evaluation of individuals' quality is carried out through a multi-objective optimization strategy.

The model can be divided into three phases: pre-processing and training, classification (or tagging) and hypotheses evaluation.

From a set of natural-language scientific texts (training texts), the pre-processing task removes non-relevant information from the documents that may affect the quality of the further classification. Training texts are manually annotated by human experts with the correct rhetorical roles using a XML-like format. The method then computes and extracts two kinds of underlying information from the annotated texts:

1. *Semantic information:* this is used to generate multi-dimensional semantic vectors of co-occurrence based on Latent Semantic Analysis [12].
2. *Sequencing data:* based on a statistical language model, sequences of n-grams are obtained using Hidden Markov Models [10, 14].

Resulting training information is further used to guide the GA that classifies rhetorical roles for the sentences of a document. The initial population for the GA is generated by randomly combining candidate tags for the roles of the sentences contained in each document (the GA is ran for each document separately). Each individual is thus represented as a random sequence of (rhetorical) roles assigned to each sentence.

Thus, the problem can be seen as finding a decision variables vector that satisfies optimizing criteria of the text based on semantic and structural criteria. Optimization usually searches for a set of non-dominated solutions which contain acceptable values for all the vector's objective functions [4]. Each solution within this set is said to be a *Pareto Optimum* which is represented in a search space of objective functions.

All the decision vectors that are not dominated by other vectors in a given set of solutions is referred to as a *non-dominated* solution which are part of the Pareto

Optima set. Once the objective functions are determined, the fitness of the hypotheses are obtained by using a multi-objective optimization strategy [4]. This stores the solutions computed for each generation in a temporary population using an elitist selection strategy. The ordering of the obtained individuals is based on their strengths which are computed for each member of this temporary population as the proportion of individuals this dominates on the population. The strategy then uses a clustering method on the space of non-dominated individuals to preserve the diversity of the population and to avoid the evolution toward a unique solution.

3.1 Preprocessing and Training

To carry out the roles classification, a set of natural-language texts as informative abstracts was used as training data. Informative abstracts are those in which specific rhetorical roles can be found for the sentences such as those describing the used *methodology*, the *results*, etc. By using this corpus of documents, six different roles (moves) [20] were identified and tagged as seen in table 1.

Rhetoric Role	Tag	Explanation
Background	role_back	Introduces background information.
Purpose	role_purp	Briefly describes the research.
Objective	role_obje	Describes the goal(s) of the research.
Methodology	role_meth	Describes the procedures being used to deal with the underlying problem.
Results	role_resu	Presents and explains the results of the research.
Conclusions	role_conc	Presents the conclusions of the work.

Table 1 Defined Rhetorical Roles Based on a Training Corpus

Two human experts were asked to manually annotate these training documents with the rhetorical role tags previously identified in table 1. Non-relevant information such as stopwords was then removed and a lemmatization task was performed to extract stems from source words within the texts. For capturing training data, statistical language models were applied to extract knowledge which will guide the GA. In particular, n-gram language models [16] and Latent Semantic Analysis (LSA) for extracting co-occurring semantic vectors were used [12].

The n-gram model predicts the occurrence of a symbol in a sequence based on the $n-1$ previous contexts, in words, this makes explicit the structure of the symbols. For our approach, a 2-gram (aka. bi-gram) language model was applied to the training corpus with the symbols being the role tags. The benefit of bi-gram modeling is based on the assumption that there is a relevant connection between contiguous rhetorical information.

The bi-gram model computes the probability of a sequence of roles r based on the previous context according to $P(r) = P(r_1) \prod_{i=2}^{n} P(r_i \mid r_{i-1})$. Therefore, the probability of assigning a role r_i (of a sentence) given a previous role r_{i-1} is calculated as $P(r_i \mid r_{i-1}) = \frac{N(r_{i-1}, r_i)}{N(r_{i-1})}$, where $N(r_{i-1}, r_i)$ is the number of occurrences of a sequence of roles (r_{i-1}, r_i) within the training corpus, and $N(r_{i-1})$ is the number of occurrences of role r_{i-1}. Final role sequences were computed from 500 documents which were annotated with 1246 role tags.

This bi-gram model captures probabilities based on structural relations between roles only. However, it does not state anything about the semantic knowledge involved in the sentences. Accordingly, a corpus-based strategy was applied to extract underlying semantic relationships from the texts using Latent Semantic Analysis (LSA). In our model, LSA is used to generate semantic vectors representing implicit co-occurrence relationships between concepts within a corpus of texts. This knowledge is then used by the GA to determine the semantic closeness between sentences and their assigned roles. The example below shows a sentence and its role tag obtained from the training corpus:

```
role_meth For the statistical analysis, the
          proportion of eclossioned eggs was
          calculated and   ...
```

In the training phase, LSA generates multi-dimensional semantic vectors for each of the words of a sentence[2] as follows:

```
For role tag (role_meth):[0.455,0.626,0.227,0.2515,..]
For sentence  above     :[0.137,0.243,0.789,0.4674,..]
```

The semantic vector for each sentence is computed as the sum of the vectors of each relevant word of this sentence. We then take both semantic vectors and compute the closeness (semantic similarity) between these vectors by using a cosine function which gets a closeness value of 0.0567. This provides a flavor of how likely is the role to be associated with the sentence: the closer the value to 1, the higher the similarity between the sentence and the role tag.

3.2 Evolutionary Classification

In our evolutionary approach, roles discovery can be seen as an optimization problem in which the best rhetorical roles must be assigned to the sentences of an abstract. For this, the GA requires new representation codings, genetic operators and evaluation metrics for the hypotheses.

---

[2] Role tags are also considered as being words.

The model assumes each text (i.e., abstract) to be represented as a sequence of candidate rhetorical roles (the chromosome). For this, role tags can be seen as genes so that a chromosome is represented as a sequence of roles. Role tags are randomly assigned by the GA for each sentence of a text. For the initial population, chromosomes are generated from random sequences of roles for one abstract.

We used a tournament selection strategy [5] to select individuals to be reproduced. Here, the population is mixed and chromosomes compete in fixed-size groups. Winners are those having the highest fitness values. For binary tournament (i.e., competition by pairs), the population is mixed twice which guarantees multiple copies of the best individual from the parents of the next generation. Thus, for binary tournament, the best individual will be selected twice.

3.2.1 Reproduction Operators

In order to generate new combinations of rhetorical roles for a text, new crossover and mutation operators were designed.

The crossover operator allows for the GA to exchange rhetorical roles from different hypotheses given certain crossover probability P_c. The operation is performed at a single randomly selected position. All the genes after the crossing point are exchanged so two new sequences of roles are added to the population (see example of figure 1).

For the mutation operator, a random modification (with probability P_m) of each role is performed for a sequence from a set of available role tags. An example of mutation is presented in figure 2 in which the position 5 of the chromosome is randomly mutated with a new role `role_resu`. Note that both mutation and crossover are carried out on the chromosome's role tags, that is, the sentences of the chromosome remain unchanged during the evolution.

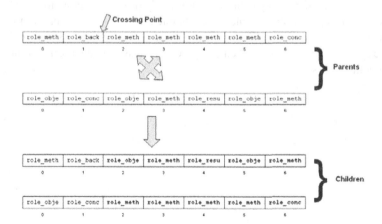

Fig. 1 The Crossover Operation

3.2.2 Fitness Evaluation

The quality of the hypotheses generated by the model is assessed according to two objective functions that must be maximized: the quality of the structure of roles and the semantic coherence, which is the semantic closeness between the assigned rhetorical role and the corresponding sentence. The GA searches for maximum values for these metrics using a multi-objective optimization strategy. The metrics are defined as follows:

1. **Quality of the Sequence of Roles:** this objective assesses the connectivity of chromosome's sequence of roles by using previously computed training information which provides the probability of a sequence of roles for the actual chromosome. The evaluation proceeds as follows: using bi-gram probabilities, the method determines how likely the sequence is (`role_purp` - `role_meth` - `role_resu` - `role_resu`) for the sentence *sent*000 by computing the probability of a sequence giving $P(< sequence \ of \ roles \ for \ sent000 >) = 0.52 * 0.62 * 0.27 * 0.72 = 0.062674$ (the probability of the first role of the sentence, `role_purp` is obtained. Based on the training data, these probability data suggest that it is very unlikely for the document's author to describe the *method* (`role_meth`) before the *results* (`role_resu`) used in his/her research, so this chromosome should have a lower fitness in the evaluation step of the GA.
2. **Coherence between role and sentence:** this metrics assesses the semantic similarity between a sentence and the assigned role based on the training information provided by LSA. In order to see how this works, have a look at the following gene (sentence) of a chromosome representing sentence *sent*000:

```
role_meth    For the statistical analysis, the
             proportion of eclossioned eggs was...
```

The method obtains the semantic vector for role `role_meth` and the sentence *sent*000 from the training data. Since LSA only provides vectors for words/tags, the vector representing a sentence is obtained by adding the vectors of each of the words of a sentence. The similarity (*sim*) between the role's vector (U) and the sentence's vector (V) is then computed by measuring the cosine of the angle of both vectors:

Fig. 2 The Mutation Operation

$$sim(U,V) = cos(\theta) = \frac{U*V}{\|U\|*\|V\|}$$

The total similarity measure for a chromosome is finally computed as the semantic similarity for all the p sentence-role pairs of a chromosome:

$$sim(Sentence, Role) = \frac{\sum_{i=1}^{p} sim(U_i, V_i)}{p}$$

The final fitness of an individual which considers the objective functions above is computed by a multi-objective optimization (MOO) strategy. Several MOO methods were assessed being the *SPEA* algorithm [4] the one that got the best results in terms of Pareto dominance. SPEA determines the non-dominated solutions (the Pareto front) for each generation and keeps them apart (elitism) in an external set. The ordering of the obtained individuals is made by computing a *strength* for each vector of the external set (P') which is a value proportional to the number of individuals that a solution in P' dominates. Specifically, the algorithm assigns a fitness value or *strength* for each individual of the set of non-dominated solutions (P') from an initial population (P). The *strength* of an individual is directly related to the number of the solutions of the population for which its objective values are equal or better, that is, the higher the number of covered solutions, the higher the *strength* of the current individual. Since the algorithm can potentially generate too many non-dominated objective vectors in the Pareto front, a clustering method is then applied to reduce the number of solutions and preserve the diversity of the search space.

At the beginning, the GA creates a population P of size N, and an external set P' of non-dominated solutions. As the GA goes on, non-dominated solutions of the population P are copied into P' from which solutions covered by any other member are removed. This optimization step aims at maximizing the objective functions values so that the *strength* of the external set gets improved.

Note that since there are two different groups of solutions (the population and the external set), the goodness value for the individuals must be computed differently. Firstly, the *strength* is computed for the non-dominated individuals whereas fitness values are obtained for dominated solutions. On the other hand, the fitness value of a dominated individual is computed as the inverse of its *strength* value. *Strength* values for the individuals $P[j] \in P$ are then computed from the *strengths* of all the external non-dominated solutions $P'[i] \in P'$.

Furthermore, the fitness value for individual $P[j]$ is obtained by computing the inverse of its *strength*'s value.

As a consequence, individuals in P' covering a lower number of individuals in P get a higher fitness value than other members of the population. Once the goodness values have been computed, the selection of chromosomes is performed using a binary tournament strategy which uses individuals from both populations. Mutation and crossover operations are then carried out on the selected chromosomes. In order to generate the next population, a *Steady-state* replacement strategy is used. This updates the individuals with lower fitness with those having higher strengths.

4 Analysis and Results

In order to evaluate the performance of our evolutionary model for role extraction, two sets of experiments were carried out. A first set aimed to tune different parameters of the GA so as to provide a robust search and classification. The second set provides insights regarding the effectiveness of the model based on its accuracy and precision when comparing to other classification methods.

For experimentation purposes, a corpus of 1300 medium-size scientific documents (i.e., abstracts) of university MSc/B.Sc theses on the topics of *Agriculture*, *Agronomy* and *Veterinary Medicine* was used. Each plain abstract contained 13 long sentences in average and none of these included explicit discourse markers. Note that a manual annotation by experts is mandatory, and that is actually costly hence larger amounts of tagged data are difficult to obtain. From this corpus, two set of datasets were obtained:

1. A random set of 500 abstracts was extracted for training purposes. Four human experts were used to annotate the training documents with role tags.
2. A set of 800 abstracts different from above was extracted for testing the evolutionary model.

A prototype was implemented and preliminary tuning experiments were carried out to determine the best parameter settings for the GA. Common criteria included the convergence toward the best solutions, fitness evolution, robustness of the GA along different runs and the final classification accuracy (i.e., the proportion of correctly assigned roles).

For these tuning purposes, 500 random abstracts were selected with four basic parameters being the number of generations (*NumGen*), population size (*PopSize*), probability of crossover (P_c) and probability of mutation (P_m). The different analyses considered the average behavior of the evolutionary model for all the selected documents on six GA runs. Finally, best experimental values were obtained for the GA-based model and included $NumGen = 120$, $PopSize = 200$, $Pc = 0.85$, $P_m = 0.05$.

In order to analyse the performance of our model for classifying rhetorical roles, the finally tuned evolutionary model was applied to the testing dataset. The evaluation included the predictive accuracy of the model for classifying different role types, and the standard *precision* and *recall* metrics.

A group of four human experts annotated the training dataset using rhetorical role tags as defined in the previously described set of tags. LSA-based semantic information and bi-grams statistics were then obtained using the methods described in section 3. The evolutionary model used the best previously obtained parameters $NumGen = 120, PopSize = 200, P_c = 0.85, P_m = 0.05$. Once the GA reached the final solutions, the human annotators were asked to compare the resulting assigned tags with the correct ones. Correlation between the model and human judgement was then computed and producing a (Pearson) value of $r = 0.84$ ($t - test = 3.11, p < 0.004$). This shows the promise of the GA in terms of predictive ability when compared with humans.

The real overall effectiveness of the model using different metrics can be seen in table 2. This used a testing corpus of 800 documents which contained 1500 roles tags. Metrics included the classification accuracy for each type of rhetorical role tag (i.e., proportion of correctly tagged roles), the standard measures of *Precision* and *Recall*.

Table 2 shows the number of role tags for each role type (#*Roles*), the number of correctly classified roles of a kind (*Correct Roles*), the number of incorrectly classified roles which is composed of positive falses (*YES*−) and negative falses (*NO*−), the classification accuracy for a role type (*Acc*), the precision (*P*), and the recall (*R*). Results show that the GA model for rhetorical labeling does well for most of the role tags having relatively high values of accuracy and precision/recall ($p < 0.001, t - test = 3.060$). One exception is the classification of role *role_obje* which got an accuracy of 63%. This may partially be due to the low number of *objective* roles found in the whole corpus (72) which affect the significance. In addition, role labeling was observed to be very ambiguous in the corpus and, in particular for *role_obje*, even human experts had troubles to identify the correct tags. Even so, the experiments show the promise of evolutionary methods for role tagging using a reasonable number of documents and role tags.

Role Tag	#Roles	Correct Roles	Incorrect Roles YES-	NO-	Acc	P	R
role_back	111	77	10	24	69%	0,89	0,76
role_purp	170	135	0	35	80%	1	0,8
role_obje	72	45	3	24	63%	0,94	0,65
role_meth	450	381	29	40	85%	0,93	0,9
role_resu	580	502	43	35	86%	0,92	0,93
role_conc	117	78	23	16	66%	0,77	0,83

Table 2 Effectiveness of the GA Model (total= 1500 roles)

In order to determine whether the method generalized well when comparing to other state-of-the-art learning methods, a series of experiments were performed. All machine learning performance tests were conducted using 10 fold cross-validation, using random splits in the data. The used methods included *Support Vector Machines (SVM)* [18, 21, 6] and *Naive Bayes Classification* [17, 8]. The performance tests for the SVM and Naives Bayes can be seen at tables 3 and 4 respectively. Results show that the results for SVM are very competitive with those obtained for our GA method. However, performance does not increase significantly for the Naive Bayes classifier. Results show that the GA model outperforms the other classifiers. Note also that the nature and ambiguity of the corpus affected the three methods in classifying the role *role_obje*, all the methods got the lowest performance.

In nearly all experiments, the increased number of role tags improves the GA and SVM performance. The addition of more roles for the types *role_meth* and

Role Tag	#Roles	Correct Roles	Incorrect Roles		Acc	P	R	F1
			YES-	NO-				
role_back	111	61	17	33	55%	0,78	0,65	0,71
role_purp	170	101	21	48	60%	0,83	0,68	0,75
role_obje	72	37	13	22	52%	0,74	0,63	0,68
role_meth	450	292	33	125	65%	0,9	0,7	0,79
role_resu	580	414	41	125	71%	0,91	0,77	0,83
role_conc	117	63	20	34	54%	0,76	0,65	0,7

Table 3 Effectiveness of the SVM classifier (total= 1500 roles)

role_resu improved classification for the methods and results but is of little help for the *objectives* and *conclusions* types.

Role Tag	#Roles	Correct Roles	Incorrect Roles		Acc	P	R	F1
			YES-	NO-				
role_back	111	50	20	41	45%	0,71	0,55	0,62
role_purp	170	100	24	46	59%	0,81	0,69	0,75
role_obje	72	26	10	36	36%	0,72	0,42	0,53
role_meth	450	220	31	199	49%	0,88	0,53	0,66
role_resu	580	410	45	125	71%	0,9	0,77	0,83
role_conc	117	59	21	37	50%	0,74	0,61	0,67

Table 4 Effectiveness of the Naive Bayes classifier (total= 1500 roles)

The lower performance of the Bayesian method can partially be explained because this relies on some significant training data to generate candidate most probable hypotheses for a multi-class problem. However, its non-adaptive nature prevents it from generating multiple hypotheses for a class and creating new hypotheses. Instead, the role of training data for our GA is twofold: this allows to guide the search for new solutions and assess the quality of newly created hypotheses as the GA goes on.

On the other hand, the accuracy of the SVM strongly relies on the samples and the text representation (vector of keywords). This text representation for the SVM may not be complete enough as the method is not always capable of capturing interrelationships between components of the vector. Other drawback of the tests with SVM is that domain knowledge could not explicitly be incorporated into the model and so this must rely on the implicit patterns being generated and generalized at the training step. Instead, proposed multi-objective fitness function for our model is capable of explicitly incorporating domain knowledge to assess the quality of the solutions. This also may explain the higher performance of the GA above SVM.

5 Conclusions

In this work, a new approach to discover implicit rhetorical knowledge from texts using evolutionary methods was proposed. The model uses previously computed training information to guide the search for solutions. Solutions involve optimum sequences of rhetorical role tags assigned to sentences of natural-language texts. Furthermore, evaluation of candidate solutions was carried out by using a multi-objective optimization strategy which considers statistical structure criteria (bi-gram language models) and semantic coherence criteria (corpus-based semantic analysis).

Different setting experiments were carried out to obtain the best configuration for the evolutionary model and annotate the target documents to compute training data. Real evaluations were then performed by assessing the predictive ability and precision of the model.

A distinctive feature of the experiments with our GA-based model is that, unlike other rhetorical data intensive tasks such as summarization, these do not require defining explicit (discourse) markers to identify a role's location within a text. Instead, the corpus-based approach allows the GA to learn associations between roles and semantic features learned from previously annotated pairs of roles and sentences (training set). This also let the model adapt to new structures of rhetorical roles as long as suitable annotated examples have been provided to the GA.

The corpus-based nature of the evolutionary method makes it possible to extract implicit relationships between units of a text without using any defined discourse markers. One additional advantage is that the model can be applied to analyze texts in different human languages with no major changes.

As a future work, new evaluation metrics to assess the quality of solutions can be incorporated such as techniques for recognizing sentences' connectors similar to those found in discourse markers based methods. In addition, further experiments may be required to determine the extent to which large training data affects the quality of the solutions generated by the model.

References

1. R. Barzilay and M. Elhadad. Lexical chains for text summarization. *Proceedings Meeting of the Association for Computational Linguistics of the ACL97/EACL97 Workshop on Intelligent Scalable Text Summarization*, pages 10–17, 1997.
2. R. Bekkerman, R. El-Yaniv, and M. Tishby. On feature distributional clustering for text categorization. *Proceedings of SIGIR-01, 24th ACM International Conference on Research and Development in Information Retrieval*, pages 146–153, 2001.
3. C. Bishop. *Pattern Recognition and Machine Learning*. Springer, 2006.
4. K. Deb. *Multi-Objective Optimization using Evolutionary Algorithms*. John Wiley and Sons, 2001.
5. K. DeJong. *Evolutionary Computation*. MIT Press, 2006.
6. R. Duda, P. Hart, and D. Stork. *Pattern Classification, Second Edition*. Wiley, 2000.
7. D. Hand, H. Mannila, and P. Smyth. *Principles of Data Mining*. MIT Press, 2001.
8. T. Hastie, R. Tibshirani, and J. Friedman. *The Elements of Statistical Learning*. Springer, 2003.

9. G. Jones, A. Robertson, and C. Santimetvirul. Non-hierarchical document clustering using a genetic algorithm. *Information Research*, 1, April 1995.
10. D. Jurafsky and J. Martin. *Speech and Language Processing: An Introduction to Natural Language Processing, Computational Linguistics and Speech Recognition*. Prentice Hall, 2000.
11. J. Kupiec, J. Pedersen, and F. Chen. A trainable document summarizer. *Proceedings of the 18th ACM-SIGIR Conference*, pages 68–73, 1995.
12. T. Landauer, D. McNamara, S. Dennis, and W. Kintsch. *Handbook of Latent Semantic Analysis (University of Colorado Institute of Cognitive Science Series)*. Lawrence Erlbaum Associates, 2007.
13. W. Mann and S. Thompson. Rhetorical structure theory: Toward a functional theory of text organization. *Text*, 8(3):243–281, 1998.
14. C. Manning and H. Schütze. *Foundations of Statistical Natural Language Processing*. The MIT Press, 1999.
15. D. Marcu. *The rhetorical parsing, summarization, and generation of natural language texts*. PhD thesis, Department of Computer Science, University of Toronto, 1997.
16. E. Miller, D. Shen, J. Liu, and C. Nicholas. Performance and scalability of a large-scale n-gram based information retrieval system. *Journal of Digital Information*, 1(5):1–25, 2000.
17. R. Neapolitan. *Learning Bayesian Networks*. Prentice Hall, 2003.
18. J. Shawe and N. Cristianini. *Support Vector Machines and other kernel-based learning methods*. Cambridge University Press, 2000.
19. E. Siegel. Learning methods for combining linguistic indicators to classify verbs. In Claire Cardie and Ralph Weischedel, editors, *Proceedings of the Second Conference on Empirical Methods in Natural Language Processing*, pages 156–163. Association for Computational Linguistics, Somerset, New Jersey, 1997.
20. S. Teufel and M. Moens. Argumentative classification of extracted sentences as a first step towards flexible abstracting. In I. Mani and M. Maybory, editors, *Advances in Automatic Text Summarization*. The MIT Press, 1999.
21. L. Wang. *Support Vector Machines: Theory and Applications*. Springer, 2005.

EMADS: An Extendible Multi-Agent Data Miner

Kamal Ali Albashiri, Frans Coenen, and Paul Leng

Abstract In this paper we describe EMADS, an Extendible Multi-Agent Data mining System. The EMADS vision is that of a community of data mining agents, contributed by many individuals, interacting under decentralised control to address data mining requests. EMADS is seen both as an end user application and a research tool. This paper details the EMADS vision, the associated conceptual framework and the current implementation. Although EMADS may be applied to many data mining tasks; the study described here, for the sake of brevity, concentrates on agent based data classification. A full description of EMADS is presented.

1 Introduction

Multi-Agent Systems (MAS) offer a number of general advantages with respect to Computer Supported Cooperative Working, distributed computation and resource sharing. Well documented advantages [1] include:

1. Decentralised control.
2. Robustness.
3. Simple extendability.
4. Sharing of expertise.
5. Sharing of resources.

Decentralised control is, arguably, the most significant feature of MAS that serves to distinguish such systems from distributed or parallel approaches to computation. Decentralised control implies that individual agents, within a MAS, operate in an

Kamal Ali Albashiri, Frans Coenen, and Paul Leng
Department of Computer Science, The University of Liverpool,
Ashton Building, Ashton Street, Liverpool L69 3BX, United Kingdom
e-mail: {ali,frans,phl}@csc.liv.ac.uk

autonomous manner and are (in some sense) self deterministic. Robustness, in turn is a feature of the decentralised control, where the overall system continues to operate even though a number of individual agents have "crashed". Decentralised control also supports extendability in that additional functionality can be added simply by including further agents. The advantages of sharing expertise and resources are self evident. The advantages offered by MAS are particularly applicable to Knowledge Discovery in Data (KDD) where a considerable collection of tools and techniques are current. MAS also has some particular advantages to offer with respect to KDD, and particularly data mining, in the context of sharing resources and expertise. KDD is concerned with the extraction of hidden knowledge from data. Very often data relevant to one search is not located at a single site, it maybe widely-distributed and in many different forms. There is a clear advantage to be gained from an organisation that can locate, evaluate and consolidate data from these diverse sources. KDD has evolved to become a well established technology that has many commercial applications. It encompasses sub-fields such as classification, clustering, and rule mining. Research work in these fields continues to develop ideas, generate new algorithms and modify/extend existing algorithms. A diverse body of work therefore exists. KDD research groups and commercial enterprises, are prepared (at least to some extent) to share their expertise. In addition, many KDD research groups have made software freely available for download[1]. This all serves to promote and enhance the current "state of the art" in KDD. However, although the free availability of data mining software is of a considerable benefit to the KDD community, it still require users to have some programming knowledge — this means that for many potential end users the use of such free software is not a viable option. One of the additional advantages offered by a MAS approach is that it would support greater end user access to data mining techniques.

A second advantages offered by MAS, in the context of data mining, is that of privacy and (to an extent) security. By its nature data mining is often applied to sensitive data. MAS allows data to be mined remotely. Similarly, with respect to data mining algorithms, MAS can make use of algorithms without necessitating their transfer to users, thus contributing to the preservation of intellectual property rights.

In this paper the authors propose the Extendible Multi-Agent Data mining System (EMADS). The EMADS vision is that of an anarchic collection of persistent, autonomous (but cooperating) KDD agents operating across the Internet. Individual agents have different functionality; the system currently comprises data agents, user agents, task agents, mining agents and a number of "house-keeping" agents. Users of EMADS may be data providers, data mining algorithm contributors or miners of data. The provision of data and mining software is facilitated by a system of *wrappers*. Users wishing to obtain (say) classifiers or collections of patterns, need have no knowledge of how any particular piece of data mining software works or the location of the data to be used. The operation of EMADS is illustrated in this paper

---

[1] See for example the Weka Tool Kit $http://www.cs.waikato.ac.nz/ml/weka/$, and the LUCS-KDD Software Library $http://www.csc.liv.ac.uk/\tilde{f}rans/KDD/Software/$

through the application of a collection of classifier data mining agents to a number of standard "benchmark" data sets held by data agents.

The paper is organised as follows. A brief review of some related work on Multi-Agent Data Mining (MADM) is presented in Section 2. The conceptual framework for EMADS is presented in Section 3. The current implementation of EMADS, together with an overview of the wrapper principle is given in 4. The operation of EMADS is illustrated in Section 5 with a classification scenario. Some conclusions are presented in Section 6.

2 Previous Work

There are a number of reports in the literature of the application of Agent techniques to data mining. Some example systems are briefly presented here. One of the earliest references to MADM is Kargupta et al. [2] who describe a parallel data mining system (PADMA) that uses software agents for local data accessing and analysis, and a Web based interface for interactive data visualisation. PADMA has been used in medical applications. Gorodetsky et al. [3] correctly consider that the core problem in MADM is not the data mining algorithms themselves (in many case these are well understood), but the most appropriate mechanisms to allow agents to collaborate. Gorodetsky et al. present a MADM system to achieve distributed data mining and, specifically, classification. They describe a distributed data mining architecture and a set of protocols for a multi-agent software tool. Peng et al. [4] present an interesting comparison between single-agent and multi-agent text classification in terms of a number of criteria including response time, quality of classification, and economic/privacy considerations. Their results indicate, not unexpectedly, in favour of a multi-agent approach.

Agent technology has also been employed in *meta-data mining*, the combination of results of individual mining agents. One example is meta classification, also sometimes referred to as meta-learning, this is a technique for generating a *global* classifier from N distributed data sources by first computing N *base* classifiers which are then collated to build a single *meta* classifier (see for example [14]). The meta-learning strategy offers a way to mine classifiers from homogeneously distributed data.

Perhaps the most mature agent-based meta-learning systems are: JAM [5], BODHI [6], and Papyrus [7]. In contrast to JAM and BODHI, Papyrus can not only move models from site to site, but can also move data when that strategy is desired. Papyrus is a specialised system which is designed for clustering while JAM and BODHI are designed for data classification. Basically, these systems try to combine local knowledge to optimise a global objective. The major criticism of such systems is that it is not always possible to obtain an exact final result, i.e. the global knowledge model obtained may be different from the one that might have been obtained by applying the one model approach to the same data.

It should be noted that the domains of distributed and multi-agent data mining tend to overlap, with much discussion amongst authors as to what a MADM system is. In this paper the authors concur with Wooldridge's [1] definition of what an agent is as itemised in Section 1.

3 The EMADS Conceptual Framework

Conceptually EMADS is a hybrid peer to peer agent based system comprising a collection of collaborating agents that exist in a set of *containers*. Agents may be created and contributed to EMADS by any EMADS user/contributor. One of these containers, the *main container*, holds a number of house keeping agents that have no direct connection with MADM, but provide various facilities to maintain the operation of EMADS. In particular the main container holds an Agent Management System (AMS) agent and a Directory Facilitator (DF) agent. The terminology used is taken from the JADE (Java Agent Development) [9] framework in which EMADS is implemented (JADE implementation details are discussed further in Section 4). Briefly the AMS agent is used to control the life cycles of other agents in the platform, and the DF agent provides an agent *lookup service*. Both the main container and the remaining containers can hold various MADM agents. Note that the EMADS main container is located on the EMADS host organisation site (currently The University of Liverpool in the UK), while the other containers may be held at any other sites world wide.

Other than the house keeping agents held in the main container EMADS currently supports four categories of MADM agents:

1. **User Agents**: User agents are the interface agents that connect users to EMADS. User agents allow users to pose requests and receive responses to such requests. Individual users create and launch their own EMADS user agents, which reside in the users' EMADS containers and are hosted at the users' site [2]. User agents interact with task agents (see below) in order to process data mining requests.
2. **Task Agents**: Task agents are specific temporary agents that are automatically created by user agents to address specific data mining requests. Task agents are located at the user's site and persist till the response to the associated requests is complete. A user can cause any number of task agents to be created. The nature of individual task agents depends on the nature of the requests, for example a classification task agent will be launched to respond to a classification request while (say) a meta Association Rule Mining task agent will be launched to respond to a meta-ARM request. Individual task agents posses meta-knowledge about data mining processes, which in turn define the methodology/approach best suited to respond to a particular data mining request; this includes input format requirements for specific data mining agents (see below). This meta-knowledge is used

---

[2] The EMADS user software is available from the EMADS mediator site at $http : //www.jade.csc.liv.ac.uk/$, although currently EMADS is only available to local users

in initiate and execute a required data mining process. Task agents are also responsible for communication to/from data mining agents, and (if appropriate) the activation and synchronisation of data mining agents. To execute a data mining process a task agent typically seeks the services of a group of data mining and data agents (see below) to obtain the desired result and return it to the user agent.

3. **Mining Agents**: Mining agents are an implementation of a specific data mining technique or algorithm. Mining agents contain the methods for initiating and carrying out a data mining activity and communicating results back to the appropriate task agent. Note that to release the full potential of EMADS mining agents, in either the same or different containers, typically collaborate to resolve some data mining task; although they are not obliged to so. Data mining agents are contributed by any EMADS *developer*, and reside in their owner's EMADS container hosted at the owner's site.

4. **Data Agents**: An agent, located at a local site, that holds meta-data about specified data sources held at the same site. The data may be a single data set, part of a data set or a number of data sets. Data agents are provided by EMADS *data contributors*. One of the advantages offered by data agents is that of privacy preservation.

A high level view of the EMADS conceptualisation showing the various categories of agents and their interaction is given in Figure 1. The figure shows a mediator host (main container) and three local hosts (local containers). The mediator host holds a AMS and a DF agent. One of the local hosts has a user and a task agent, while the other two hosts hold data and mining agents.

It should be noted that EMADS containers may contained both mining and data agents simultaneously as well as user agents. It should also be noted that data mining and data agents are *persistent*, i.e. they continue to exist indefinitely and are not created for a specific data mining exercise. Communication between agents is facilitated by the EMADS network.

3.1 EMADS End User Categories

EMADS has several different modes of operation according to the nature of the *participant*. Each mode of operation (participant) has a corresponding category of user agent. Broadly, the supported categories are as follows:

- **EMADS Users**: These are participants, with restricted access to EMADS, who may pose data mining requests.
- **EMADS Data Contributors**: These are participants, again with restricted access, who are prepared to make data available to be used by EMADS mining agents.
- **EMADS Developers**: Developers are EMADS participants, who have full access and may contribute data mining algorithms.

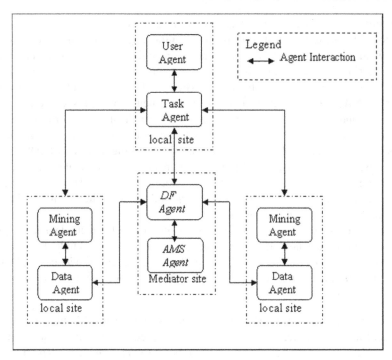

Fig. 1 High level view of EMADS conceptual framework.

Note that in each case, before interaction with EMADS can commence, appropriate software needs to be downloaded and launched by the participant. Note also that any individual participant may be a user as well as a contributor and/or developer.

Conceptually the nature of EMADS data mining requests, that may be posted by EMADS users, is extensive. In the current implementation, the following types of generic request are supported:

- Find the "best" classifier (to be used by the requester at some later date in off line mode) for a data set provided by the user.
- Find the "best" classifier for the indicated data set (i.e. provided by some other EMADS participant).
- Find a set of Association Rules (ARs) contained within the data set(s) provided by the user.
- Find a set of Association Rules (ARs) contained within the indicated type of data set(s) (i.e. provided by other EMADS participants).

A "best" classifier is defined as a classifier that will produce the highest accuracy on a given test set (identified by the mining agent) according to the detail of the request. To obtain the "best" classifier EMADS will attempt to access and communicate with as many classifier generator data mining agents as possible and select the best result. The classification style of user request will be discussed further in Section 5 to illustrate the operation of EMADS in more detail.

The Association Rule Mining (ARM) style of request is not discussed further in this paper. However, the idea here was that an agent framework could be used to implement a form of Meta-ARM where the results of the parallel application of ARM to a collection of data sets, with not necessarily the same schema but conforming to a global schema, are combined. Details of this process can be found in Albashiri et al. [8].

4 The EMADS Implementation

EMADS is implemented using the JADE framework. JADE is FIPA (Foundation for Intelligent Physical Agents) [10] compliant middleware that enables development of peer to peer applications based on the agent paradigm. JADE defines an agent platform that comprises a set of containers, which may be distributed across a network as in the case of EMADS. A JADE platform includes a main container in which is held a number of mandatory agent services. These include the AMS and DF agents whose functionality has already been described in Section 3. Recall that the AMS agent is used to control the lifecycles of other agents in the platform, while the DF agent provides a lookup service by means of which agents can find other agents. When a data mining or data agent is created, upon entry into the system, it announces itself to the DF agent after which it can be recognised and found by other agents.

Within JADE agents are identified by name and communicate using the FIPA Agent Communication Language (ACL). More specifically, agents communicate by formulating and sending individual messages to each other and can have "conversations" using interaction protocols that range from query request protocols to negotiation protocols. ACL message communication between agents within the same container uses event dispatching. Message communication between agents in the same JADE platform, but in different containers, is founded on RMI. Message communication between agents in different platforms uses the IIOP (Internet Inter-ORB Protocol). The latter is facilitated by a special Agent Communication Channel (ACC) agent also located in the JADE platform main containers.

Figure 2 gives an overview of the implementation of EMADS using JADE. The figure is divided into three parts: at the top are listed N user sites. In the middle is the JADE platform holding the main container and N other containers. At the bottom a sample collection of agents is included. The solid arrows indicates a "belongs to" (or "is held by") relationship while the dotted arrows indicate a "communicates with" relationship. So the data agent at the bottom left belongs to *container* 1 which in turn belongs to *User Site* 1; and communicates with the *AMS agent* and (in this example) a single *mining agent*.

The principal advantage of this JADE architecture is that it does not overload a single host machine, but distributes the processing load among multiple machines. The results obtained can be correlated with one another in order to achieve computationally efficient analysis at a distributed global level.

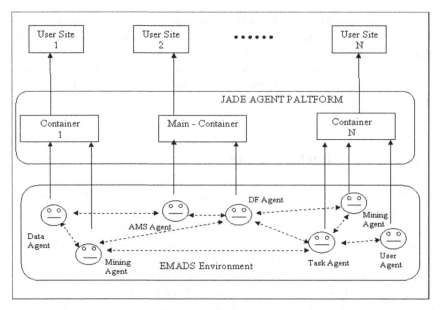

Fig. 2 EMADS Architecture as Implemented in Jade

4.1 EMADS Wrappers

One of the principal objectives of EMADS is to provide an easily extendible framework that could easily accept new data sources and new data mining techniques. In
general, extendibility can be defined as the ease with which software can be modified to adapt to new requirements or changes in existing requirements. Adding a new
data source or data mining techniques should be as easy as adding new agents to the
system. The desired extendability is achieved by a system of wrappers. EMADS
wrappers are used to "wrap" up data mining artifacts so that they become EMADS
agents and can communicate with other EMADS agents. As such EMADS wrappers
can be viewed as agents in their own right that are subsumed once that have been
integrated with data or tools to become data mining agents. The wrappers essentially provide an application interface to EMADS that has to be implemented by the
end user, although this has been designed to be a fairly trivial operation. Two broad
categories of wrapper have been defined: (i) data wrappers and (ii) tool wrappers.
Each is described in further detail in the following two sections.

4.1.1 Data Wrappers

Data wrappers are used to "wrap" a data source and consequently create a data
agent. Broadly a data wrapper holds the location (file path) of a data source, so that
it can be accessed by other agents; and meta information about the data. To assist

end users in the application of data wrappers a data wrapper GUI is available. Once created, the data agent announces itself to the DF agent as consequence of which it becomes available to all EMADS users.

4.1.2 Tool Wrappers

Tool wrappers are used to "wrap" up data mining software systems and thus create a mining agent. Generally the software systems will be data mining tools of various kinds (classifiers, clusters, association rule miners, etc.) although they could also be (say) data normalisation/discretisation or visualisation tools. It is intended that EMADS will incorporate a substantial number of different tool wrappers each defined by the nature of the desired I/O which in turn will be informed by the nature of the generic data mining tasks that it us desirable for EMADS to be able to perform. Currently the research team have implemented two tool wrappers:

1. The binary valued data, single label, classifier generator.
2. The meta AR generator.

Many more categories of tool wrapper can be envisaged. Mining tool wrappers are more complex than data wrappers because of the different kinds of information that needs to be exchanged. For example in the case of a "binary valued, single label, classifier generator" wrapper the input is a binary valued data set together with meta information about the number of classes and a number slots to allow for the (optional) inclusion of threshold values. The output is then a classifier expressed as a set of Classification Rules (CRs). As with data agents, once created, the data mining agent announce themselves to the DF agent after which they will becomes available for use to EMADS users.

5 EMADS Operation: Classifier Generation

In this section the operation of EMADS is illustrated in the context of a classifier generation task; however much of the discussion is equally applicable to other generic data mining tasks such as clustering and ARM. The scenario is that of an end user who wishes to obtain a "best" classifier founded on a given, pre-labelled, data set; which can then be applied to further unlabelled data. The assumption is that the given data set is binary valued and that the user requires a single-label, as opposed to a multi-labelled, classifier. The request is made using the individual's user agent which in turn will spawn an appropriate task agent.

For this scenario the task agent identifies mining agents that hold single labelled classifier generators that take binary valued data as input. Each of these mining agents is then accessed and a classifier, together with an accuracy estimate, requested. The task agent then selects the classifier with the best accuracy and returns this to the user agent.

The data mining agent wrapper in this case provides the interface that allows input for: (i) the data; and (ii) the number of class attributes (a value that the mining agent cannot currently deduce for itself) while the user agent interface allows input for threshold values (such as support and confidence values). The output is a classifier together with an accuracy measure. To obtain the accuracy measures the classifier generator (data mining agent) builds the classifier using the first half of the input data as the "training" set and the second half of the data as the "test" set. An alternative approach might have been to use Ten Cross Validation (TCV) to identify the best accuracy.

From the literature there are many reported techniques available for generating classifiers. For the scenario the authors used implementations of eight different algorithms [3]:

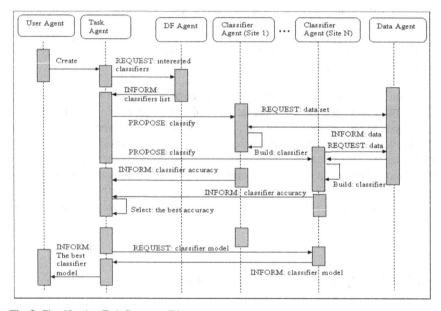

Fig. 3 Classification Task Sequence Diagram.

1. FOIL (First Order Inductive Learner) [11] the well established inductive learning algorithm for generating Classification Association Rules (CARs).
2. TFPC (Total From Partial Classification) CAR generator [12] founded on the P- and T-tree set enumeration tree data structures.
3. PRM (Predictive Rule Mining) [15] an extension of FOIL.
4. CPAR (Classification based on Predictive Association Rules) [15] a further development from FOIL and PRM.

---

[3] taken from the LUCS-KDD repository at $http://www.csc.liv.ac.uk/\tilde{f}rans/KDD/Software/$

5. IGDT (Information Gain Decision Tree) classifier, an implementation of the well established decision tree based classifier using most information gain as the "splitting criteria".
6. RDT (Random Decision Tree) classifier, a decision tree based classifier that uses most frequent current attribute as the "splitting criteria" (so not really random).
7. CMAR (Classification based on Multiple Association Rules) is a Classification Association Rule Mining (CARM) algorithm [16].
8. CBA (Classification Based on Associations) is a CARM algorithm [17].

These were placed within an appropriately defined tool wrapper to produce eight (single label binary data classifier generator) data mining agents. This was a trivial operation indicating the versatility of the wrapper concept.

Thus each mining agent's basic function is to generate a classification model using its own classifier and provide this to the task agent. The task agent then evaluates all the classifier models and chooses the most accurate model to be returned to the user agent. The negotiation process amongst the agents is represented by the sequence diagram given in Figure 3 (the figure assumes that an appropriate data agent has ready been created). In the figure includes N classification agents. The sequence of events commences with a user agent which spawns a (classification) task agent, which in turn announces itself to the DF agent. The DF agent returns a list of classifier data mining agents that can potentially be used to generate the desired classifier. The task agent then contacts these data mining agents who each generate a classifier and return statistical information regarding the accuracy of their classifier. The task agent selects the data mining agent that has produced the best accuracy and requests the associated classifier, this is then passed back to the user agent.

Table 1 Classification Results

Data Set	Classifier	Accuracy	Generation Time (sec)
connect4.D129.N67557.C3	RDT	79.76	502.65
adult.D97.N48842.C2	IGDT	86.05	86.17
letRecog.D106.N20000.C26	RDT	91.79	31.52
anneal.D73.N898.C6	FOIL	98.44	5.82
breast.D20.N699.C2	IGDT	93.98	1.28
congres.D34.N435.C2	RDT	100	3.69
cylBands.D124.N540.C2	RDT	97.78	41.9
dematology.D49.N366.C6	RDT	96.17	11.28
heart.D52.N303.C5	RDT	96.02	3.04
auto.D137.N205.C7	IGDT	76.47	12.17
penDigits.D89.N10992.C10	RDT	99.18	13.77
soybean-large.D118.N683.C19	RDT	98.83	13.22
waveform.D101.N5000.C3	RDT	96.81	11.97

Note that the users make the data that they desire to be mined (classified) available by launching their own data agents (which in turn publish their name and description using the DF agent as described above). The data sets used for the illustration were taken from the UCI machine learning data repository [18]. To simplify the scenario these data sets were preprocessed so that they were discretized/normalized into a binary form [4]. It should be noted here that the research team is currently implementing a normalisation/discretisation agent.

The results from a sequence of user requests, using different data sets, are presented in Table 1. Each row in the table represents a particular request and gives the name of the data set, the selected best algorithm, the best accuracy and the total EMADS execution time from creation of the initial task agent to the final classifier being returned to the user agent. The naming convention used in the Table is that: D equals the number of attributes (after discretisation/normalisation), N the number of records and C the number of classes (although EMADS has no requirement for the adoption of this convention).

The results demonstrate firstly that EMADS works (at least in the context of the current scenario). Secondly that operation of EMADS is not significantly hindered by agent communication overheads, although this has some effect. The results also reinforce the often observed phenomena that there is no single best classifier generator suited to all kinds of data set.

6 Conclusions and Future Work

This paper describes EMADS, a multi-agent framework for data mining. The principal advantages offered are that of experience and resource sharing, flexibility and extendibility, and (to an extent) protection of privacy and intellectual property rights. The paper presents the EMADS vision, the associated conceptualisation and the JADE implementation. Of note are the way that wrappers are used incorporate existing software into EMADS. Experience indicates that, given an appropriate wrapper, existing data mining software can be very easily packaged to become an EMADS data mining agent. The EMADS operation is illustrated using a classification scenario.

A good foundation has been established for both data mining research and genuine application based data mining. The current functionality of EMADS is limited to classification and Meta-ARM. The research team is at present working towards increasing the diversity of mining tasks that EMADS can address. There are many directions in which the work can (and is being) taken forward. One interesting direction is to build on the wealth of distributed data mining research that is currently available and progress this in an MAS context. The research team are also enhancing the system's robustness so as to make it publicly available. It is hoped that once the system is live other interested data mining practitioners will be prepared to contribute algorithms and data.

---

[4] The discretized data sets are available at $http://www.csc.liv.ac.uk/\tilde{f}rans/KDD/Software/LUCS-KDD-DN/DataSets/dataSets.html$

References

1. Wooldridge, M. (2003). *An Introduction to Multi-Agent Systems.* John Wiley and Sons (Chichester, England).
2. Kargupta, H., Hamzaoglu, I. and Stafford B. (1997). *Scalable, Distributed Data Mining Using an Agent Based Architecture.* Proceedings of Knowledge Discovery and Data Mining, AAAI Press, 211-214.
3. Gorodetsky, V., Karsaeyv, O., Samoilov, V. (2003). *Multi-agent technology for distributed data mining and classification.* Proc. Int. Conf. on Intelligent Agent Technology (IAT 2003), IEEE/WIC, pp438-441.
4. Peng, S., Mukhopadhyay, S., Raje, R., Palakal, M. and Mostafa, J. (2001). *A Comparison Between Single-agent and Multi-agent Classification of Documents.* Proc. 15th International Parallel and Distributed Processing Symposium, pp935-944.
5. Stolfo, S., Prodromidis, A. L., Tselepis, S. and Lee, W. (1997). *JAM: Java Agents for Meta-Learning over Distributed Databases.* Proceedings of the International Conference on Knowledge Discovery and Data Mining, pp. 74-81.
6. Kargupta, H., Byung-Hoon, et al. (1999). *Collective Data Mining: A New Perspective Toward Distributed Data Mining.* Advances in Distributed and Parallel Knowledge Discovery, MIT/AAAI Press.
7. Bailey, S., Grossman, R., Sivakumar, H. and Turinsky, A. (1999). *Papyrus: a system for data mining over local and wide area clusters and super-clusters.* In Proc. Conference on Supercomputing, page 63. ACM Press.
8. Albashiri, K.A., Coenen, F.P., Sanderson, R. and Leng. P. (2007). *Frequent Set Meta Mining: Towards Multi-Agent Data Mining.* In Bramer, M., Coenen, F.P. and Petridis, M. (Eds.), Research and Development in Intelligent Systems XXIII., Springer, London, (proc. AI'2007), pp139-151.
9. Bellifemine, F. Poggi, A. and Rimassi, G. (1999).*JADE: A FIPA-Compliant agent framework.* Proc. Practical Applications of Intelligent Agents and Multi-Agents, pg 97-108 (See http://sharon.cselt.it/projects/jade for latest information).
10. Foundation for Intelligent Physical Agents, FIPA 2002 Specification. Geneva, Switzerland.(See http://www.fipa.org/specifications/index.html).
11. Quinlan, J. R. and Cameron-Jones, R. M. (1993). *FOIL: A Midterm Report.* Proc. ECML, Vienna, Austria, pp3-20.
12. Coenen, F., Leng, P. and Zhang, L. (2005). *Threshold Tuning for Improved Classification Association Rule Mining.* Proceeding PAKDD 2005, LNAI3158, Springer, pp216-225.
13. Schollmeier, R. (2001). *A Definition of Peer-to-Peer Networking for the Classification of Peer-to-Peer Architectures and Applications.* First International Conference on Peer-to-Peer Computing (P2P01) IEEE.
14. Prodromides, A., Chan, P. and Stolfo, S. (2000). *Meta-Learning in Distributed Data Mining Systems: Issues and Approaches.* In Kargupta, H. and Chan, P. (Eds), Advances in Distributed and Parallel Knowledge Discovery. AAAI Press/The MIT Press, pp81-114.
15. Yin, X. and Han, J. (2003). CPAR: Classification based on Predictive Association Rules. Proc. SIAM Int. Conf. on Data Mining (SDM'03), San Fransisco, CA, pp. 331-335.
16. Li W., Han, J. and Pei, J. (2001). CMAR: Accurate and Efficient Classification Based on Multiple Class-Association Rules. Proc ICDM 2001, pp369-376.
17. Liu, B. Hsu, W. and Ma, Y (1998). Integrating Classification and Assocoiation Rule Mining. Proceedings KDD-98, New York, 27-31 August. AAAI. pp80-86.
18. Blake, C.L. and Merz, C.J. (1998). *UCI Repository of machine learning databases http : //www.ics.uci.edu/m̃learn/MLRepository.html,* Irvine, CA: University of California, Department of Information and Computer Science.

Designing a Feedback Component of an Intelligent Tutoring System for Foreign Language[*]

Anita Ferreira and John Atkinson

Abstract In this paper, we provide a model of corrective feedback generation for an intelligent tutoring system for Spanish as a Foreign Language. We have studied two kind of strategies: (1) Giving-Answer Strategies (GAS), where the teacher directly gives the desired target form or indicates the location of the error, and (2) Prompting-Answer Strategies (PAS), where the teacher pushes the student less directly to notice and repair their own error. Based on different experimental settings and comparisons with face-to-face tutoring mode, we propose the design of a component of effective teaching strategies into ITS for Spanish as a foreign language.

1 Motivation

The design of Intelligent Tutorial Systems (ITS) is founded on two fundamental assumptions about learning. First, individualized instruction by a competent tutor is far superior to the classroom style because both the content and the style of the instruction can be continuously adapted to best meet the needs of the situation. Secondly, students learn better in situations which more closely approximate the situations in which they will use their knowledge, i.e. they learn by doing, by making mistakes, and by constructing knowledge in a very individualized way. Empirical evidence has shown that tutorial mode is superior to normal learning experiences

Anita Ferreira
Department of Spanish Linguistics, Universidad de Concepcion, Concepcion, Chile, e-mail: aferreir@udec.cl

John Atkinson
Department of Computer Sciences, Universidad de Concepcion, Concepcion, Chile, e-mail: atkinson@inf.udec.cl

 * This research is sponsored by the National Council for Scientific and Technological Research (FONDECYT, Chile) under grant number 1080165 "*A Blended Learning Task-based Model and Cooperative Approaches for Teaching Spanish as Foreign Language* "

in traditional classroom settings, and it is mainly due to conversational dialogue patterns [8] which facilitate the treatment of errors and correction in tutorial mode. Chi and colleagues [3] have suggested that students have greater opportunities to be constructive in tutorial mode than in a traditional classroom.

Feedback and guidance moves (such as prompting, hinting, scaffolding, and pumping) have been investigated at some length by researchers working on Intelligent Tutoring Systems (ITS) for teaching procedural skills in domains such as algebra, geometry, physics and computer programming [2, 15, 10, 3]. However, little attention has been paid to feedback in the domain of ITS for foreign languages. As suggested by [7], this situation seems to have arisen for at least the following reasons :

- *The specific and complex nature of errors and corrective feedback in ITS for Foreign Language:* The main finding of studies of error treatment is that it is an enormously complex process. This can be seen in the different models of feedback and the different taxonomies of feedback strategies that have been proposed. Some of these strategies are markedly different from those typically found in ITSs for procedural domains.
- *The relative merits of different types of feedback are still not fully understood in the area of Second Language Acquisition (SLA)*: The results of empirical investigations indicate that the relative merits of different types of feedback are not fully understood. Furthermore, the relative effectiveness of feedback strategies depends on multiple variables, including the particular aspects of the language being corrected, conditions relating to the provision of teacher correction, and characteristics of the students (e.g., sophisticated grammatical explanations are not appropriate for beginning students).
- *The lack of empirical research on the effectiveness of ICALL for foreign language, in general, and feedback strategies in particular*: ITS and ICALL systems have not yet incorporated the strategies that are typically used by second and foreign language teachers and studied by SLA researchers.
- *The lack of awareness of results from SLA research by researchers in the ICALL and ITS communities*: Most ITS and ICALL systems appear to be created without reference to the many research studies concerning language learners' abilities, that is, how they may best learn languages, and how teachers deal with students' errors. We believe that to improve the effectiveness of ICALL systems for teaching foreign language, designers should pay more attention to the results emerging from SLA research.

ITS systems for foreign language (FL) learning have incorporated Natural-Language Processing (NLP) techniques to analyze learners' language production or model their knowledge of a FL, in order to provide learners with flexible feedback and guidance in their learning process. These systems use parsing techniques to analyze the student's response and identify errors or missing items. This allows systems to produce sophisticated types of feedback, such as meta-linguistic feedback and error reports, to correct particular student errors [4, 9].

In this paper, we have designed a model of corrective feedback based on the main tendencies suggested by results obtained from previous empirical studies [7]. Our main contribution is to experimentally identify the main factors that indicate which learning strategy to use for corrective feedback in a given tutoring situation. This aims at informing the design of intelligent CALL systems for foreign language learning.

2 Feedback in ITS for FL

ITS for FL have incorporated NLP techniques e.g., analyzing language learners' language production or modeling their knowledge of a second language to provide the learners with more flexible feedback and guidance in their learning process [4, 11]. An outstanding example is the E-Tutor, an online Intelligent Language Tutoring System developed by [9] for German. It provides error-specific and individualized feedback by performing a linguistic analysis of student input and adjusting feedback messages suited to learner expertise. The E-Tutor also provides individualized, context-sensitive help on the errors students are making. The web-based E-tutor system ranks student errors by using a flexible Error Priority Queue: the grammar constraints can be reordered to reflect the desired emphasis of a particular exercise. In addition, a language instructor might choose not to report some errors. The experience with E-tutor supports the need for a CALL system that addresses multiple errors by considering language teaching pedagogy.

Other successful ITS system called *BANZAI* [16] for Japanese employs NLP technology to enable learners to freely produce Japanese sentences and to provide detailed feedback concerning the specific nature of the learner's errors. The tutor incorporates twenty-four lessons covering the grammatical constructions encountered in a standard undergraduate curriculum. It accepts inputs in kana and kanji, and presents relevant photographic and graphical images of Japan and of everyday situations. In addition, BANZAI allows the learner to produce any sentence because it can identify parts of speech and syntactic patterns in the learner's sentence, on the basis of the general principles of Japanese grammar. Based on these grammatical principles, BANZAI determines whether the sentence is grammatical or not and generates intelligent feedback targeted to specific deficiencies in the learner's performance.

The BANZAI NLP analyzer consists of a lexicon, a morphological generator, a word segmentor, a morphological parser, a syntactic parser, an error detector, and a feedback generator. Japanese writing does not leave a space between words, so the BANZAI word segmentor divides the learner's input sentence (a typed character string) into lexical items, referring to the BANZAI lexicon. Several different segmentations and lexical assignments are often possible for one character string. For example, nihon can be identified as nihon 'Japan,' ni 'two' and hon (counter for long objects), or ni (particle) and hon 'book,' etc. The word segmentor finds all possible segmentations and lexical assignments. The BANZAI morphological parser combines segmented words into noun compounds or final verb forms (if any) in the input sentence. On the other hand, the BANZAI syntactic parser determines whether the input string is a grammatical (well formed) or ungrammatical (ill formed) sentence. The parser uses context free phrase structure rules to build words into phrases and phrases into sentences by means of a bottom-up parsing technique. If it cannot build all of the words in the given string into a sentence, the string is ungrammatical. The BANZAI syntactic parser includes 14 context free phrase structure rules, and each rule is consecutively applied to process the input.

3 Empirical Studies in Spanish Feedback Corrective

Errors and corrective feedback constitute a natural part of the teaching-learning process in a FL. Errors can be defined as deviations from the norms of the target language. They reveal the patterns of learners' development of inter-language systems, showing where they have over-generalized a FL rule or where they have inappropriately transferred a first language rule to the FL [12]. Corrective feedback is an indication to a learner that his or her use of the target language is incorrect, and includes a variety of responses that a language learner receives. Corrective feedback can be explicit (e.g., "No you should say goes, not go.") or implicit (e.g., "Yes, he goes to school every day."), and may or may not include meta-linguistic information (e.g., "Don't forget to make the verb agree with the subject.") [12]. In our studies, we classified corrective feedback strategies identified in SLA [13] into two groups:

1. **Giving-Answer Strategies (GAS):** Types of feedback moves in which the teacher directly gives the target form corresponding to the error in a student's answer, or shows the location of the student's error. These include:

    a. **Repetition** of the error or the portion of the learner's phrase containing the error, using stress or rising intonation to focus the student's attention on the problematic part of the utterance. E.g., S: "Future" (Incorrect tense); T: "¿Future?"

    b. **Recast:** reformulation of all or part of the student's answer, providing the target form. E.g,. S: "En el segundo piso, hay cuatro dormitorio y dos baño." (*On the second floor, there are four bedroom and two bathroom.*) T: "Qué grande es tu casa! Tiene cuatro dormitorios y dos baños." (*What a big house you have. It has four bedrooms and two bathrooms.*)

    c. **Explicit correction:** The teacher provides the correct target form. E.g., S: "Cuando ella andó." (*When she went*); T: "andaba." This differs from recast because the teacher directly corrects the error without rephrasing or reformulating the student's answer.

    d. **Give answer:** Used in cases when the student does not know or is unsure of the answer. E.g., S: "Ella compró mucha fruta y..." (Student can not finish his answer because he does not know how to say vegetables). T: "Fruta y verduras." (Teacher completes the answer with the word verduras.)

Our definitions of the repetition and recast strategies are based on those used in Doughty and Varela's [5] study.

2. **Prompting-Answer Strategies (PAS)**. Types of feedback moves in which the teacher pushes students to notice a language error in their response and to repair the error for themselves. We have called this group prompting answer strategies because of the similarity these strategies bear to the notion of "prompting" described in [3]. This group includes three types of strategies:

a. **Meta-linguistic cues:** The teacher provides information or asks questions regarding the correctness of the student's utterance, without explicitly providing the target form. E.g., S: "Compra" (to buy); T: "Tienes que poner un condicional." *(You have to use a conditional.)*

b. **Clarification requests:** Questions intended to indicate to the student that his/her answer has been misunderstood due to a student error, or that the utterance is ill-formed in some way and that a repetition or a reformulation is required. Clarification requests often include phrases such as "Pardon me.", "What?", "What do you mean?". E.g., S: "Me gustaría un jugo de cilantro." *(I would like a coriander juice)*; T: "¿Qué cosa?" *(What do you mean?)*.

c. **Elicitation:** The teacher encourages the student to give the correct form by pausing to allow the student to complete the teacher's utterance, by asking the student to reformulate the utterance, or by asking questions to elicit the correct answer, such as "How do we say that in Spanish?" E.g., T:"¿Qué debe hacer Roberto?" (What does Roberto need to do?) S: Brush his teeth. T: "How do we say that in Spanish?"

We have carried out three types of empirical research [6, 7] with the purpose of establishing the most frequent and effective feedback strategies in different teaching modes, with a view towards informing the design of feedback strategies for an ITS for Spanish as a second language. Our studies included:

- *An observational study of face-to-face classroom interactions:* an analysis of naturalistic data from traditional classrooms. The aim was to investigate, at a fine level of structure, how human teachers deal with particular issues, such as the treatment of errors, and learning.

  Specifically, this study involved two types of positive feedback: Repetition (i.e teacher repeats the student's correct answer) and rephrasing (i.e., the teacher displays a new structure which rephrases the correct answer given by the student). For corrective feedback, two groups of strategies were investigated: Giving-answer Strategies (GAS) and Prompting-answer Strategies (PAS).

- *A case study of one-on-one tutorial interactions:* a case study in which we compared the feedback between traditional and tutorial mode. We studied feedback strategies in tutorial interaction by comparing tutoring sessions with classroom interactions. Our approach considered the use of empirical data on student-teacher interactions to guide the design of feedback strategies in the context of ITS for learning Spanish as FL.

- *An experimental study:* involved a longitudinal experiment aimed at looking for further evidence about the effectiveness of the two classes of feedback strategies (GAS and PAS).

  In order to determine whether the tendencies found in the first two studies can be experimentally reproduced, we carried out a longitudinal experiment on grammar aspects. We controlled feedback strategies so as to observe the results in learning gain after a treatment process. We used a Web tutoring interface to gather empirical data on students' interactions.

The results of these three studies [6, 7] suggest as shown in table 1 that although GAS are the most frequently used strategies for all error types in both teaching modes, PAS are more effective for dealing with grammatical and vocabulary errors, whereas GAS are more effective for dealing with pronunciation errors. For grammar and vocabulary errors, an ITS should implement ways to prompt students' answers using meta-linguistic cues, elicitation and clarification-requests. There is a tendency for Prompting Answer Strategies feedback (PAS) to be more effective than Giving Answer Strategies (GAS) for dealing with grammar errors. The prompting strategies seem to promote more constructive student learning in a tutorial context [3] because they encourage the student to respond more constructively than when the teacher gives a simple repetition of the answer or a correction of the error.

Classroom Error Type	GAS	Repair	PAS	Repair
Grammar	74	36/74 (48%)	49	39/49 (80%)
Vocabulary	23	9/23 (39%)	19	18/19 (95%)
Pronunciation	80	67/80 (83%)	0	0
Total	177	112/177 (63%)	68	57/68 (84%)

Tutorial Error Type	GAS	Repair	PAS	Repair
Grammar	24	13/24 (54%)	21	16/21 (76%)
Vocabulary	13	3/13 (23%)	5	4/5 (80%)
Pronunciation	64	56/64 (87%)	1	0/1 (0%)
Total	101	72/101 (72%)	27	20/27 (74%)

Table 1 Rate of GAS and PAS Repair in Classroom and Tutorial Mode

The top part of Table 1 shows the rate of GAS and PAS repair in classroom mode. Overall, the proportion of repairs after PAS was higher than that after GAS. A statistical analysis considering the number of repaired and non-repaired errors following GAS and PAS for each type of error showed that for grammar ($\chi^2 = 11.86$, $p < 0.0005$) and vocabulary errors ($\chi^2 = 14.01$, $p < 0.0001$), PAS are more effective than GAS. For pronunciation errors, GAS are the only strategies used and they elicit a high rate of repair.

The lower part of Table 1 shows that there is a similar pattern in tutorial mode. When we look at effectiveness broken down by error type, we see that a higher percentage of grammar errors are repaired after PAS than after GAS, but the results are not significant. For vocabulary errors, PAS are more effective than GAS ($\chi^2 = 4.92$, $p < 0.05$). Finally, virtually all pronunciation errors invite GAS feedback, and there is a high rate of repair. Note that the chi-square analysis on vocabulary feedback in tutorial mode is right at the margin of valid application due to the limited amount of data.

In summary, these results indicate that PAS are more effective than GAS in eliciting repair for the errors they were used to treat. Despite this, teachers use GAS more frequently for all error types in both classroom and tutorial mode. With regard to repair, there seems to be agreement in the pedagogical literature that self-repair (i.e., students correcting their own linguistic errors) is more effective for learning than teacher-repair for several reasons. First, self-repair leads to knowledge construction as students actively confront errors and extend or revise their hypotheses about the target language. Second, self-repair allows students to automatize retrieval of the target language knowledge they already have. And finally, self-repair may be more conducive to acquisition than other-repair because it is less likely to result in a negative affective response. Therefore, when considering the effectiveness of feedback strategies, it is important to distinguish other-initiated self-repair (teacher notices student's error and prompts repair but the student generates the correct form him/herself) from other-initiated other-repair (teacher notices the student's error and the teacher corrects the error).

For the purposes of informing the design of ICALL systems for FL, it is important to identify the factors that indicate which strategy to use for corrective feedback in a given situation. We have already seen that the type of error is one factor that influences this decision. We then analyzed our data broken down by learner level as well as the type of error. As we can see from Table 2 for the different learning levels (Beginner, Intermediate and Advanced). Overall, the results show that PAS are more effective than GAS for learners at all levels. However, the following are the main trends that we observed.

First for the treatment of grammar errors, among GAS, recast was the most frequent strategy at beginner and intermediate levels, whereas explicit correction was the most frequent strategy at the advanced level. However, recast led to repair just 36% of the time overall. Give answer evoked a high rate of repair among learners at beginner and intermediate levels, but was not used to correct grammar errors of advanced learners. Explicit correction was used at all levels, and evoked a high rate of repair from intermediate students, but was less successful with beginner and advanced learners. Finally, there are too few cases of repetition to draw any conclusions.

Among the PAS strategies for grammar errors, elicitation is the most frequently used strategy, however, whereas [14] found this to be the most effective strategy, we observed it leading to repair less often than metalinguistic cues or clarification requests. Metalinguistic cues are extremely effective for beginning and advanced students, but less so for learners at the intermediate level. A more detailed look at

Level	Beg.	Interm.	Adv.	Total
GAS	82/110 (75%)	15/36 (42%)	15/31 (48%)	112
PAS	25/27 (93%)	22/32 (69%)	9/9 (100%)	56
All	107/137 (78%)	37/68 (54%)	24/40 (60%)	168

Table 2 Proportion of Repair of GAS and PAS by Learner Level

the instances of meta-linguistic prompts showed that they were especially effective for improving aspects of grammar (i.e., the subjunctive mood) in high-intermediate and advanced levels (experimental study). Our corpus did not include any instances of clarification requests for beginners, but this strategy always led to repair in the few cases where it was used for intermediate and advanced learners.

For vocabulary errors, the situation is less clear due to the small number of occurrences of this type of error in our corpora. Overall, although recast was the most frequently used strategy of the GAS group, it yielded only 27% repaired errors. Explicit correction was the most effective strategy with 71% of the errors repaired. The results for the PAS group indicate that all strategies are used with similar frequency, and that all strategies evoke high rates of repair. This is consistent with the high rates of uptake for PAS strategies found by [14].

For pronunciation errors, we focus on the strategies in the GAS group because the overwhelming majority of these errors were corrected by GAS. Overall, explicit correction is the most frequently used strategy and leads to repair 85% of the time. Give answer and recast were used with similar frequency, but give answer was much more effective at eliciting repairs (92% vs. 58%). At the beginner and advanced levels, give answer and explicit correction were the most effective GAS strategies for treating pronunciation errors. There were too few repairs at the intermediate level to draw any conclusions. The results of this provide useful guidance for the design of feedback in ICALL systems, which we discuss further in Section 4.

4 A Model for Generating Effective Strategies in Spanish as a FL

The implementation of strategies in our PAS group requires that the ITS for FL be able to carry on an appropriate interaction with the student. Although unconstrained conversation of the type that human teachers employ is beyond reach, recent advances in tutorial dialogue systems research make the interactive techniques we propose more feasible than they were at the time many ITS for FL were designed. This research shows that sophisticated interactions can be carried on in domains for which rich underlying models have been developed [17], or for which possible correct and incorrect responses have been enumerated and feedback moves for each case have been authored [8, 18]. In addition, recent work has shown that an ITS in which students produced self explanations by making selections from a menu led to learning outcomes that were equivalent to a version of the system in which students explained their problem-solving steps in their own words [1].

We defined a model for the design of a feedback component for ITS for Spanish as a FL, which takes into account the type of error the learner has made (grammar, vocabulary or pronunciation error), and the learner's level of proficiency (beginner, intermediate, advanced). In our model, we assume that error analysis is performed by an interpreter/analyzer.

In our model, the feedback sequence starts when a student's answer contains at least one error. If the answer contains more than one error, the system must determine which error should be treated first, and in our model this decision is based on the learner level. For beginners, grammar and pronunciation errors are the most frequent, and thus we suggest that priority should be given to the treatment of these types of errors. For intermediate and advanced learners, grammar and vocabulary errors should be addressed first. Once an error is identified, a feedback strategy must be chosen.

Using the data obtained from the above-mentioned empirical studies, we built a decision tree (see figure 4) aiming to drive the generation of feedback strategies for the treatment of errors according to the different learning levels. The selection of a GAS or a PAS type of feedback after the first error is then performed by following the branches of the obtained decision tree.

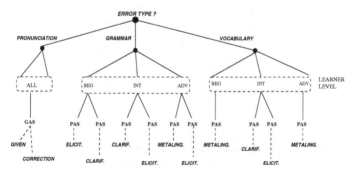

Fig. 1 Decision Tree for Feedback Generation after the first error.

After the feedback has been generated, the student may produce several types of responses (uptake):

1. An immediate uptake in which the student modifies his/her answer correctly, either by self-repair (if PAS was generated) or by other-repair (if GAS was generated). This indicates that the student has noticed the error and the given assistance, and the correct answer may indicate a first step towards improvement.
2. An uptake which still contains the error. This may occur because the student did not notice the target form provided by the teacher's feedback or the student does not know how to correct the error. In cases such as this, our human teachers

either try an alternative feedback strategy or continue the discussion with the next question, an accept turn, or a domain turn.

3. An uptake in which the student repairs the original error, but his/her answer contains another error. In this case, a feedback strategy is selected according to the algorithm for presenting the first corrective feedback move over an error given above.

4.1 Example of Feedback Generation

In order to produce feedback based on the students' errors in an ITS context, we propose a simple semi-deterministic mechanism which uses the resulting data concerning effectiveness from our studies. The input to our procedure is basically summarized by two tables whose values are extracted from our results in observational and experimental studies:

1. Table of effectiveness of strategy versus learning level (*ES*) per error type (table 3), where $ES_{(e,l,s)}$ represents the effectiveness value (between 0 and 100%) for the error type (e), for the level (*l*), and using a given strategy (*s*).

Error Type e	Strategy	
Level	PAS	GAS
beginner	$ES_{(e,b,pas)}$	$ES_{(e,b,gas)}$
intermediate	$ES_{(e,i,pas)}$	$ES_{(e,i,gas)}$
advanced	$ES_{(e,a,pas)}$	$ES_{(e,a,gas)}$

Table 3 Effectiveness Table for Strategy per Learning Level (ES)

2. Table of effectiveness of individual strategies versus learning level (*ET*) per error type (table 4), where $ET_{(e,l,t)}$ represents the effectiveness value for the error type (*e*), for the level (*l*), and using an individual strategy (*t*).

Error type e	Individual Strategy (i.e., PAS)		
Level	PAS_1	PAS_2	..
beginner	$ET_{(e,b,pas_1)}$	$ET_{(e,b,pas_2)}$	..
intermediate	$ET_{(e,i,pas_1)}$	$ET_{(e,i,pas_2)}$	..
advanced	$ET_{(e,a,pas_1)}$	$ET_{(e,a,pas_2)}$	..

Table 4 Effectiveness Table for Type of Strategy per Learning Level (ET)

From this input data, assume that the procedure is embedded in an ITS as a tutorial interface which contains the following steps:

```
Let L be the student's learning level
Let Sq be the set of questions

FOR  each question Q in Sq DO
  Generate Question Q
  Get Answer Ans
  IF Ans is correct THEN
    DISPLAY repaired
  ELSE
    Eq = Detect type of error
    Produce_feedback(Ans,Eq,L)
  END-IF
END-FOR
```

Here, Produce_feedback(Ans,Eq,L) is the process that produces the feedback given the current answer *Ans* and handles any subsequent error for this question, the detected error *Eq* and the student's level *L*. This first determines whether a PAS strategy must be given (GAS otherwise) and then produces the corresponding type of strategy:

```
PROCEDURE  Produce_feedback(Ans,Eq,L)

OUTPUT: Type of Strategy (T)

  Let AllowedErrors be the fixed number of
        allowed errors (2)
  Current_Error = 0
  WHILE (Current_Error < AllowedErrors)
    AND  (Ans is not repaired) DO
   IF    give_PAS(L,Eq)     THEN
      T = select_feedback_type(PAS,Eq,L)
   ELSE
      T = select_feedback_type(GAS,Eq,L)
   END-IF
   DISPLAY feedback depending on type T
   Determine Effect (uptake):
        Get new Answer Ans
   IF (Ans is repaired) THEN
     student's effect is self_repair
            if strategy is PAS
     or other_repair if strategy is  GAS.
   END-IF
   ELSE student's effect is "unrepaired"
    Current_Error = Current_Error + 1
  END-while
END-Procedure
```

When the first error is detected, the feedback is given based on the strategy with the highest effectiveness value in input table ES. Next, the type of feedback is generated in decreasing order of effectiveness of table ET providing that the generated type is not repeated for the same question.

When an error is made for the second time, the strategy with the highest effectiveness value is produced if the current error is the same as the previous one. If there is a new type of error, a probabilistic selection of a strategy is performed by choosing the strategy whose effectiveness value exceeds a randomly generated value between 0 and 1. The probability of choosing PAS or GAS is given by a real value which is proportional to each strategy's effectiveness. For example, the probability of selecting PAS as the next produced strategy will be given by:

$$Prob(\text{``}pas\text{''}) = \frac{<Effectiveness\_of\_PAS>}{<Total\_effectiveness(PAS+GAS)>}$$

For example, the probability for choosing a PAS feedback considering grammar errors at beginner level in table 2 is calculated as:

$$Prob(\text{``}pas\text{''}) = \frac{91}{91+53} = \frac{91}{144} = 0.63$$

Accordingly, the procedure to determine whether a PAS strategy should be produced or GAS otherwise, proceeds as follows:

```
FUNCTION  give_PAS(L,Eq)

OUTPUT: TRUE if PAS is given
        FALSE otherwise
  IF (<first error>
      OR (Eq = <previous error>) THEN
    IF ES(Eq,L,pas)>ES(Eq,L,gas) THEN
        return TRUE
    ELSE return FALSE
  ELSE  ** Probabilistic Step **
    Let TES be the
        total effectiveness for L:
    TES = ES(Eq,L,pas)+ES(Eq,L,gas)
    Let P_pas  be the probability of
          choosing a PAS strategy
    P_pas    = ES(Eq,L,pas) / TES
    P_random =
      <random value between 0 and 1>
    ** Determine whether PAS is chosen **
    IF (P_random < P_pas)  THEN
        return TRUE
    ELSE return FALSE
  END-IF
END
```

Once the strategy (S) is selected, the specific type of feedback is generated according to S, the error type (Eq) and the level (L) by using the following procedure:

```
ALGORITHM     select_feedback_type(S,Eq,L)

INPUT: Strategy (S), Error type (Eq),
       Learner Level (L)
OUTPUT: type of strategy T

Let St be the values of effectiveness
 of possible individual strategies for
 S from {ET(Eq,L,t)}
Select the type of strategy with
 effectiveness value T from St
 such that:
 1) T is the highest effectiveness
     value in St
 2) The type of strategy with
     effectiveness T has not been
     used before in the same question
END
```

A remaining issue that must be addressed in any implementation of our model is how the feedback strategies should be realized in natural language and presented to the student. This will depend on aspects of the overall ICALL system, such as whether the student interacts with the system using speech or typing (or a combination), whether the ICALL system is taking a Focus on Forms or Focus on Meaning approach, and so on.

5 Conclusions

In this paper, we provided guidelines for researchers developing feedback strategies for ITS systems. To this end, we focused on identifying the factors that should be taken into account in order to determine the feedback strategy that is most likely to be effective in any given situation. From these results, we were able to provide an initial approach for a feedback component for an ITS system for Spanish as FL. However, this model is necessarily simplified, and leaves several issues for future research.

Preliminary results using the model for generating feedback strategies (i.e., GAS, PAS) show the promise of the approach in dealing with different types of error correction in tutorial dialogues. This is strongly due to the decision making process to select the most effective feedback strategy. Unlike other approaches, this also considers different learning levels and error types from real tutoring and classroom experiences.

The necessity of implementing feedback strategies in ITS for FL can expand our understanding of this key issue and enable us to envisage the kind of contribution that can be useful for ITS for FL systems, as well as teaching training in the context of FL instruction.

References

1. V. Aleven, Popescu, and O. Ogan. A formative classroom evaluation of a tutorial dialogue system that supports self-explanation. In V. Aleven, editor, *Procs. of the 11th Int. Conf. on Artificial Intelligence in Education*, pages 345–355, 2003.
2. J. Anderson, A. Corbett, K. Koedinger, and R. Pelletier. Cognitive Tutors: Lessons Learned. *Journal of the Learning Sciences*, 4(2):167–207, 1995.
3. Michelene T. H. Chi, Stefanie Siler, H. Jeong, T. Yamauchi, and Robert G. Hausmann. Learning from human tutoring. *Cognitive Science*, 25(4):471–533, 2001.
4. M. Dodigovic. Artificial Intelligence in second Language Learning: Raising Error Awareness. *Multilingual Matters*, 2005.
5. C. Doughty and E. Varela. Communicative focus on form. In C. Doughty and J. Williams, editors, *Focus on Form in classroom second language acquisition*, pages 114–138. Cambridge University Press, 1998.
6. A. Ferreira. Estrategias efectivas de feedback correctivo para el aprendizaje de lenguas asistido por computadores. *Revista Signos*, 40(65):521–544, 2007.
7. A. Ferreira, J. Moore, and C. Mellish. A Study of Feedback Strategies in Foreign Language Classrooms and Tutorials with Implications for Intelligent Computer Assisted Language Learning Systems. *International Journal of Artificial Intelligence in Education*, 17(4):389–422, 2007.
8. A.C. Graesser, S. Lu, G.T. Jackson, H. Mitchell, M. Ventura, A. Olney, and M.M. Louwerse. Autotutor: A tutor with dialogue in natural language. *Behavioral Research Methods, Instruments, and Computers*, 36:180–193, 2004.
9. T. Heift and M. Schulze. *Errors and Intelligence in Computer-Assisted Language Learning: Parsers and Pedagogues*. Routledge, 2007.
10. G. Hume, J. Michael, A. Rovick, and M. Evens. Hinting as tactic in one-on-one tutoring. *Journal of Learning Sciences*, 5(1):23–47, 1996.
11. M. Levy and G. Stockwell. *CALL Dimensions: Options and issues in computer assisted Language Learning*. Lawrence Erlbaum Associates, London, 2006.
12. P. Lightbown and N. Spada. *How Languages are Learned*. Oxford University Press, 1999.
13. R. Lyster. Differential effects of prompts and recasts in form-focused instruction. *Studies in Second Language Acquisition*, 26(4):399–432, 2004.
14. R. Lyster and L. Ranta. Corrective Feedback and Learner Uptake: Negotiation of form in Communicative Classrooms. *Studies in Second Language Acquisition*, 19(1):37–66, 1997.
15. D. Merrill, B. Reiser, M. Ranney, and J. Trafton. Effective Tutoring Techniques: Comparison of Human tutors and Intelligent Tutoring Systems. *Journal of the Learning Sciences*, 2(3):277–305, 1992.
16. N. Nagata. Banzai: Computer assisted sentence production practice with intelligent feedback. *Proceedings of the Third International Conference On Computer Assisted Systems for Teaching and Learning/Japanese (CASTEL/J)*, 2002.
17. E. Owen and K. Schultz. Empirical foundations for intelligent coaching systems. In *Procs. of the Interservice/Industry Training, Simulation and Education Conference*, Orlando, Florida, 2005.
18. C. P. Rosé, P. Jordan, and M. Ringenberg. Interactive conceptual tutoring in atlas-andes. In J. D. Moore, editor, *AI in Education: AI-ED in the wired and wireless future*, pages 256–266. IOS Press, 2001.

DECISION MAKING

An Algorithm for Anticipating Future Decision Trees from Concept-Drifting Data

Mirko Böttcher and Martin Spott and Rudolf Kruse

Abstract Concept-Drift is an important topic in practical data mining, since it is reality in most business applications. Whenever a mining model is used in an application it is already outdated since the world has changed since the model induction. The solution is to predict the drift of a model and derive a future model based on such a prediction. One way would be to simulate future data and derive a model from it, but this is typically not feasible. Instead we suggest to predict the values of the measures that drive model induction. In particular, we propose to predict the future values of attribute selection measures and class label distribution for the induction of decision trees. We give an example of how concept drift is reflected in the trend of these measures and that the resulting decision trees perform considerably better than the ones produced by existing approaches.

1 Introduction

The induction of decision trees is a relatively mature and well-researched topic. Aiming at an increased classification accuracy many algorithms which emphasise on different aspects of decision tree learning have been proposed and proven to be successful in many industrial and business applications. Many of these algorithms have been developed assuming that the samples used for learning are randomly drawn

Mirko Böttcher
University of Magdeburg, Faculty of Computer Science, 39106 Magdeburg, Germany, e-mail: miboettc@iws.cs.uni-magdeburg.de

Martin Spott
Intelligent Systems Research Centre, BT Group plc, Adastral Park, Ipswich IP5 3RE, United Kingdom, e-mail: martin.spott@bt.com

Rudolf Kruse
University of Magdeburg, Faculty of Computer Science, 39106 Magdeburg, Germany, e-mail: kruse@iws.cs.uni-magdeburg.de

from a stationary distribution. This assumption does not hold when dealing with real world data, because they are almost always collected over long periods of time and the data generating processes are almost always very complex. Many real world data sets are exposed to changes in their data generating process and hence also show changes in their underlying hidden structure. This phenomenon is referred to as concept drift in the literature.

In the first place decision trees are used in many applications to learn a classification model for a certain target attribute and, secondly, to get a deeper understanding of a domain by interpreting the tree as a set of rules. However, the presence of concept drift imposes two problems on these tasks. With regard to the first task, historic data used for learning is usually drawn from a different distribution than the future samples to be classified. Consequently, the relations of the decriptive attributes to the target attribute described by the learned decision tree are different from the ones which are present in current and future data. As a result the classification accuracy will never be optimal. With regard to the second task, the gained knowledge about a domain is only valid for the past but it yields no knowledge about the present or future when concept drift is present. Although obtaining such prospective knowledge is crucial for many businesses, the problem has received significant less attention in publications.

Several methods have been published to learn decision trees in the presence of concept drift [19, 8, 10]. They all use some form of incremental learning which aims to efficiently learn or maintain models such that they are always based on the most recent samples. However, those methods only account for the first of the aforementioned problems. Moreover, their major drawback is that the learned models will only yield good results if concept drift happens very slowly. The faster the distribution changes, maybe only in some subspaces, the less accurate the decision trees get.

Our aim is to solve the two problems outlined above. In this paper we will introduce the *PreDeT* algorithm which anticipates future decision trees from concept drifting data. *PreDeT* does not track or model distribution shift as such. Instead, it models how distribution shift affects those measures which control the process of decision tree induction and predicts their future values. For this reason it is able to cope even with fast changing domains. The decision trees learned by *PreDeT* can be seen as a domain's projection into the future. Therefore they help a user to obtain insight into the data's likely hidden structure in the near future.

The paper is organized as follows. In Section 2 we present related work from the fields of concept drift. Some background on decision tree induction will be given in Section 3. The *PreDeT* algorithm will be explained in Section 4 and some preliminary experimental results shown in Section 5.

2 Related Work

As already pointed out in the previous section, several methods have been published for learning models in the presence of concept drift [19, 8, 10]. In the following we will give some more details about the methods itself and outline their drawbacks.

The two basic techniques employed are *moving temporal windows* [19, 8] and *age dependent weighting* [10]. The method of moving temporal windows learns the decision tree from samples that were gathered within a certain, recent time window. For instance, in [19] a framework is described which heuristically and dynamically adapts the window size during the learn process. A moving temporal window approach to learn decision trees – the CVFDT algorithm – which scales up to very-large databases was proposed in [8]. It maintains class counts in each tree node and when new data arrives decides whether or not a subtree needs to be re-learned.

For window-based approaches the choice of an appropriate window size is a crucial and difficult problem. In general, a compromise has to be found between small windows, which are required for a fast adaptation to concept drift, and large windows, which are required for a good generalization. In [12, 6] upper bounds on the speed of concept drift are determined which are acceptable to learn a concept with a fixed minimum accuracy. Hence a window with a certain minimal fixed size allows to learn concepts for which the speed of drift does not exceed a certain limit. Taking all of the aforesaid into account this means that window based approaches – independent from whether they use a fixed or adaptive window size – perform well in domains with slow concept drift but may result in models with a low accuracy in very dynamic domains.

Age dependent weighting simulates a kind of a data-ageing process by crediting more recent samples higher than old ones in the learning process. In [10] methods for age dependent weighting are shown and compared with temporal window approaches. The weights are chosen such that learning emphasises for slowly changing domains on a suitable large set of samples and fast changing domains on only the most recent samples. This, however, leads to the same problem as for window-based approaches. The speed of concept drift may change considerably amongst subspaces for which a global sample weighting scheme obviously does not account for.

3 Decision Trees

In the following discussion we will use some notations that will be introduced in this section. As already stated above, we assume that a dataset S of sample cases is described by a set of nominal input attributes $\{A^{(1)}, \ldots, A^{(m)}\}$ and a class attribute C. We assume that the domain of attribute A has n_A values, i.e. $\mathrm{dom}(A) = \{a_1, \ldots, a_{n_A}\}$, and that the domain of attribute C has n_C values, i.e. $\mathrm{dom}(C) = \{c_1, \ldots, c_{n_C}\}$.

A decision tree is a well-known type of classifier. As the name already indicates a decision tree is an acyclic graph having a tree-structure. Each inner node of the tree is labeled with an attribute A which is also called split attribute. For each attribute value $a \in \text{dom}(A)$ an edge to a child node exists and is labeled with a. Each leaf node has a class $c \in \text{dom}(C)$ assigned to it.

Given a new sample case for which the value of the class should be predicted, the tree is interpreted from the root. In each inner node the sample case is tested for the attribute stored within the node. According to the result of the test the corresponding edge is followed to a child node. When a leaf node is reached the class label assigned to it is taken as the class for the sample case.

A variety of algorithms to learn decision trees automatically from data have been published, for example the CART system [3] and C4.5 [13]. All algorithms for decision tree induction grow the three top-down using a greedy-strategy. Starting at the root node an attribute A is selected that yields the highest score regarding an attribute evaluation measure. The dataset is then split into n_A subsets each corresponding to one attribute value of A and a child node for each of them is created. If all its cases have the same class label, a subset is not split further and hence no children are created. The current node then becomes a leaf and is assigned the class label of its associated subset. Apart from minor variations all decision tree algorithms that we are aware of follow the schema above. In fact, one of the major differences between algorithms is the attribute evaluation measure used.

An attribute evaluation measure $I(C,A)$ rates the value of an attribute A for predicting the class attribute C. The most well-known measures are probably the Gini index [3], information gain [14] and information gain ratio [13]. Since we use the latter two in the experimental evaluation of our algorithm we will introduce them very briefly in the following. The information gain $I_{gain}(C,A)$ measures the information gained, on average, about the class attribute C when the value of the attribute A becomes known. A disadvantage of the information gain is its bias towards attributes with many values. To overcome this problem the information gain ratio $I_{gr}(C,A)$ was proposed which penalises many-valued attributes by dividing the information gain $I_{gain}(C,A)$ by the entropy of the attribute itself [14, 13].

4 Predicting Decision Trees

4.1 Basic Idea

Formally, concept drift can be described as the shift over time of the samples' probability distribution. We assume that such shift is usually not arbitrary but follows a certain pattern. It should be stressed that we do not make any assumptions about the speed of those distribution shift.

As already mentioned in the Introduction, the *PreDeT* algorithm does not track or model distribution shift as such. Instead it models the development of the attribute evaluation measure and the class label distribution over time. These models are then

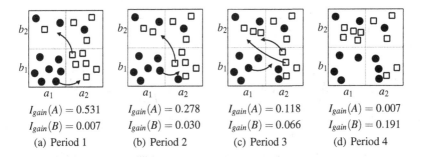

$I_{gain}(A) = 0.531$ $I_{gain}(A) = 0.278$ $I_{gain}(A) = 0.118$ $I_{gain}(A) = 0.007$

$I_{gain}(B) = 0.007$ $I_{gain}(B) = 0.030$ $I_{gain}(B) = 0.066$ $I_{gain}(B) = 0.191$

(a) Period 1   (b) Period 2   (c) Period 3   (d) Period 4

Fig. 1 Illustration of how concept drift can lead to trends in information gain

used to predict future values of the respective measure. The predictions, in turn, are used to control the decision tree induction.

Figure 1 illustrates the concept drift and the resulting change in information gain. It shows the distribution of samples over the attribute space at four consecutive time periods. Each sample belongs to one of two classes, squares and bullets, each described by two attributes A and B with domains $\{a_1, a_2\}$ and $\{b_1, b_2\}$, respectively. Lets assume that we learn a decision tree at the end of each period which predicts the samples in the next period. This is equivalent to a temporal window approach. In period 1, shown in Figure 1(a), the information gain of A is much higher than those of B and it therefore would have be chosen as the split attribute. However, the distribution of samples shifts over time which is indicated by arrows in Figure 1(a) to Figure 1(c). In period 3 the information gain of A is still higher than those of B and therefore A would be the split attribute. This would lead to an classification error of 8 using the samples from period 4 for testing. However, in period 4 attribute B would have been the superior split attribute. The choice solely based on the samples from period 3 was suboptimal. If we look at how the information gain developed between periods 1 and 3 we can see that it has a downward trend for A and an upward trend for B. Using an appropriate model for both time series it would have been possible to anticipate the change in the split attribute and to choose B. This choice leads to a much smaller classification error of 5.

Figure 2(a) shows an example obtained from the same real world dataset which we also use for our experimental evaluation in Section 5. The information gain history of the attribute $A^{(1)}$ is apart from noise stable whereas the information gain history of $A^{(2)}$ shows an upward trend. Furthermore, it can be seen that for the vast majority of time periods $T = 1, \ldots, 15$ attribute $A^{(1)}$ has more predictive power and would therefore been chosen as the split attribute. However, due to the observed upward trend in the information gain of $A^{(2)}$ both histories will intersect and $A^{(2)}$ will become the split attribute in the near future.

Figure 2(b) shows the two histories from Figure 2(a) each modeled by a quadratic regression polynomial. In period 16 are the – at the time of modeling unknown – information gain values of both attributes marked. As it can be seen, the predictions

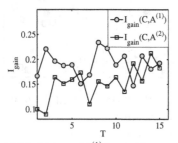 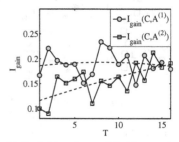

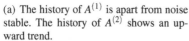

(a) The history of $A^{(1)}$ is apart from noise stable. The history of $A^{(2)}$ shows an upward trend.

(b) Both histories modeled by quadratic polynomials shown as dotted lines. In period 16 the values to be predicted are shown.

Fig. 2 Histories of information gain values for two different attributes

made by the regression models anticipate the change in the ranking of candidate split attributes which happens between period 15 and 16.

Summarising, the basic idea of *PreDeT* is to learn models which describe evaluation measure histories and class label distribution histories in each step of the decision tree induction. The models are then used to predict the value of the respective quantity for the next, future time period. Subsequently, the predictions are used to decide whether to grow a subtree and which class label to assign to a leaf node. As we already pointed out in Section 3 these two decisions are the main building blocks of the vast majority of decision tree learners. Because our algorithm leverages predictions for both it is finally capable to predict how a decision tree may look like in the future. In the context of concept drift this means that we are able to provide classifiers with a higher accuracy than those which are solely reflecting the characteristics of historic data.

4.2 Notation

Let S be a time-stamped data set and $[t_0,\ t_r]$ the minimum time span that covers all its samples. The interval $[t_0,\ t_r]$ is divided into $r > 1$ non-overlapping periods $[t_{i-1},t_i[$, such that the corresponding subsets $S^i \subset S$ each have a size $|S^i| \gg 1$. Let, without loss of generality, $\hat{T} := \{1,\ldots,r,(r+1),\ldots\}$ be the set of all past ($i \leq r$) and future ($i > r$) period indexes.

Assume that we have a family of time-dependent data sets $(S^1,\ldots,S^r)$ each described by the same attributes $A^{(i)}, i = 1,\ldots,m$ having the same domains in each time period. Quantities crucial for decision tree induction like attribute selection measure and the distribution of class labels are now related to a specific data set S^i and thus to a certain time period T_i. Therefore they form sequences of values which we will denote by $\mathbf{I} := (I(S^1, A), \ldots, I(S^r, A))$ for attribute evaluation measures and $\mathbf{P} := (P^1, \ldots, P^r)$ for the sequence of class label distributions. Thereby $P^k := (p^k_{1\cdot}, \ldots, p^k_{nC\cdot})$ is the distribution of class labels and $p^k_{i\cdot}$ is the relative frequency of class attribute value i in time period k. We will refer to these sequences as an attributes evaluation measure history and class label distribution history, respectively.

4.3 Predicting Attribute Evaluation Measures

A model φ for attribute evaluation measures is a function $\varphi : \hat{T} \longrightarrow \mathbb{R}$. In general, it will be determined based on a history $\mathbf{I} := (I(S^1, A), \ldots, I(S^r, A))$ of attribute evaluation measures which will be denoted by $\varphi[\mathbf{I}]$. A model φ is then used in each inner node to obtain a prediction $\varphi[\mathbf{I}](r + 1)$ for attribute evaluation measure's value in the next time period T_{r+1}.

As the set of potential candidate models we chose the set of polynomials $\varphi(T) = \sum_{i=0}^{q} a_i T^i$ fitted to $\mathbf{I}$ using least squared regression. Linear regression in contrast to other possible model classes, like neural networks [7] or support vector regression [16], offers the advantage that no large sample sizes (long histories) are required and that the underlying algorithms are fast. The latter aspect is in particular important because models for a vast number of histories need to be learned. The advantage of polynomial linear regression is, specifically, that it offers a simple way to obtain a set of candidate models by varying the degree q of the polynomial.

Having a set of fitted regression polynomials the best polynomial needs to be selected. In this case 'best' means that polynomial which provides the best trade-off between goodness of fit and complexity and is, for this reason, less prone to overfit the data. This can be measured using the Akaike information criterion (AIC) [1]. Let r be the number of observations, i.e. the length of the history, $q + 1$ the number of parameters of the polynomial and RSS the residual sum of squares of the fitted regression polynomial. Then AIC is defined as:

$$AIC = 2(q + 1) + r \ln \frac{RSS}{r} \qquad (1)$$

Commonly, the number of time periods for which data is available can be rather small. For example, the data we use for our experiments in Section 5 consists of 25 data sets obtained weekly. The original Akaike information criterion, however, should only be applied to data sets with large sample sizes [4], i.e. if $r/(q+1) > 40$. To overcome this limitation a number of corrections of the Akaike criterion for small sample sizes have been developed. In our *PreDeT* algorithm we use the following known as AIC_C [9]:

$$AIC_C = AIC + \frac{2(q + 1)(q + 2)}{r - q - 2} \qquad (2)$$

For large sample sizes $r\,AIC_C$ converges to AIC, therefore it is suggested that it is always used regardless of sample size [4].

4.4 Predicting the Majority Class in Leafs

A model ψ for histories of class label distributions is a function $\psi : \hat{T} \longrightarrow [0,1]^{n_C}$ It is learned from the history of class label distributions $\mathbf{P} := (P^1, \ldots, P^r)$. The dependency of ψ from $\mathbf{P}$ will be denoted by $\psi[\mathbf{P}]$. Within our *PreDeT* algorithm a model ψ is used in each leaf node to predict the class label distribution at time point T_{r+1}.

The prediction model ψ is a vector of functions $\phi_i : \hat{T} \longrightarrow [0,1]$ each of which models a dependency between the time period and the relative frequency (estimated probability) of a class label. Because the relative frequencies must sum to one $\sum_{i=1}^{n_C} \phi_i(T) = 1$ must hold, i.e.

$$\psi(\hat{T}) = \begin{pmatrix} \phi_1(T) \\ \phi_2(T) \\ \vdots \\ \phi_{n_C}(T) \end{pmatrix} = \begin{pmatrix} \phi_1(T) \\ \phi_2(T) \\ \vdots \\ 1 - \sum_{i=1}^{n_C-1} \phi_i(T) \end{pmatrix} \tag{3}$$

To model each ϕ we also use polyonomials of degree q, i.e. $\phi = \sum_{i=0}^{q} a_i T^i$. The degree of the polynomials is, similar to Section 4.3, determined using the Akaike information criterion.

Because values $\phi_i(T)$ are relative frequencies additional constraints have to be imposed on the choice of the function ϕ_i. In particular, $\forall T \in \{0, \ldots, r+1\} : 0 \leq \phi_i(T) \leq 1$ should always hold. In our experience, however, this constraint can be too strict. For example, in the case $p_i^k = p_i^{k+1} = 1$ and $p_i^j \neq 1$ for $j \neq k$ and $j \neq k+1$ it is rather difficult to find a continuous model class for ϕ. For this reason and because we only aim to predict values for the period $r+1$ we use the weaker constraint $0 \leq \phi_i(r+1) \leq 1$. Applying this constraint the model ϕ_i cannot be derived using standard regression analysis anymore. Instead, we obtain the coefficients $\mathbf{a} := (a_0, \ldots, a_q)^T$ of the polynomial $\phi_i = \sum_{i=0}^{q} a_i T^i$ by solving the constrained linear least-squares problem

$$\mathbf{a} = \underset{\mathbf{a}}{\operatorname{argmin}} \frac{1}{2} \|C\mathbf{a} - \mathbf{p}\|_2^2 \quad \text{with } C := \begin{pmatrix} 1^0 & \cdots & 1^q \\ \vdots & \ddots & \vdots \\ r^0 & \cdots & r^q \end{pmatrix} \text{ and } \mathbf{p} := \begin{pmatrix} p_i^1 \\ \vdots \\ p_i^r \end{pmatrix}$$

There exist several methods from the field of optimisation for solving constrained linear least-squares problems. They will not be discussed here in greater detail. For further reading see [5].

4.5 Putting the Parts Together

Having explained the main building blocks of our method in the previous two sections we will now go ahead and explain how they can be used in combination with a decision tree learner to predict future decision trees. This will lead us to the *PreDeT* algorithm.

Figure 3 shows the *PreDeT* algorithm. Similar to the vast majority of decision tree learners, like C4.5 and CART, it consists of two consecutive stages. In the first stage (lines 1–8) the split attribute for the current node is searched. In the second stage (lines 9–18) it is decided whether the current node is a leaf (line 9) or inner node (line 15). Respectively, either a class label is assigned to the leaf node based on the majority class in this node, or the data sets are split according to the split attribute and the *PreDeT* algorithm continues recursively (line 17). It should be clear that the basic ideas laid out in Section 4.3 and Section 4.4 can be used in connection with any decision tree learner that uses attribute evaluation measures to determine splits.

$\text{PREDE}T((S^1, \ldots, S^r))$
1    $I_{best} \leftarrow WORTHLESS$
2   **for** all untested attributes A
3   **do** $\mathbf{I} \leftarrow (I(S^1, A), \ldots, I(S^r, A))$
4   learn prediction model $\varphi[\mathbf{I}]$
5        $\tilde{I} \leftarrow \varphi[\mathbf{I}](r+1)$
6   **if** $\tilde{I} > I_{best}$
7   **then** $I_{best} \leftarrow \tilde{I}$
8                $A_{best} \leftarrow A$
9   **if** $I_{best} = WORTHLESS$
10   **then** create leaf node v
11            $P^k \leftarrow (p^k_{1\cdot}, \ldots, p^k_{n_C\cdot}), k = 1, \ldots, r$
12   learn prediction model $\psi[(P^1, \ldots, P^r)]$
13            $(\tilde{p}^{r+1}_{1\cdot}, \ldots, \tilde{p}^{r+1}_{n_c\cdot}) \leftarrow \psi[(P^1, \ldots, P^r)](r+1)$
14   assign $c = \text{argmax}_{c_i}(\tilde{p}^{r+1}_{1\cdot}, \ldots, \tilde{p}^{r+1}_{n_c\cdot})$ to v
15   **else** assign test on A_{best} to v
16   **for** all $a \in dom(A_{best})$
17   **do** $v.child[a] \leftarrow$
18                $\text{PREDE}T((S^1|_{A_{best}=a}, \ldots, S^r|_{A_{best}=a}))$
19   **return** v

Fig. 3 Outline of the *PreDeT* algorithm for predicting decision trees

In contrast to other decision tree learners *PreDeT* takes as input a sequence of data sets $(S^1, \ldots, S^r)$ representing time periods $1, \ldots, r$. It uses these data sets to estimate the value of the attribute evaluation measure in the next time period $r+1$ using a learned model φ (lines 4–5). The class label distribution within each data set is used to predict the likely class label distribution in time period $r+1$ using a learned model ψ (lines 11–13). Note that every decision about the structure of the tree – the choice of the split attribute in inner and of the class label in leaf nodes – is solely based on estimated future values of the used metrics but not directly on the historic or present data sets $(S^1, \ldots, S^r)$. For this reason the tree learned by *PreDeT* can be seen as a prediction of the decision tree in period $r + 1$.

5 Experimental Evaluation

The *PreDeT* algorithm does depend on a number of factors: first of all, the length r of the sequence of data sets $(S^1, \ldots, S^r)$, secondly, the attribute evaluation measure I, and thirdly, the size of the individual data set S^i. In our experiments we evaluated how these factors influence the accuracy of the anticipated decision trees and how this accuracy compares to the one of decision trees obtained by a temporal moving window approach which is typically used for learning decision trees from concept-drifting data.

For our experiments we chose a representative real-life dataset from the domain of Customer Relationship Management (CRM). The dataset contains answers of customers to a survey conducted by a telecommunications company over a period of 25 weeks. Each sample is described by 13 nominal attributes with a domain size between 2 and 9. Goal of the classification task is to predict whether a customer will be satisfied or dissatisfied with a certain service using the remaining 12 attributes, i.e. the data set has two classes to predict.

First of all we analysed the influence of the length r of the sequence of data sets and the choice of the attribute evaluation measure I on the classification accuracy. We split the original data set into 25 subsets S^i, each corresponding to a time period of one week. The subsets contain between 243 and 399 samples. For each experiment we chose a sequence of r consecutive data sets $(S^i, \ldots, S^{i+r-1})$ within the available 25 ones. For each i, $i = 0, \ldots, 25 - r$ we then learned a decision tree using the *PreDeT* algorithm and obtained classifications for the samples in the data set S^{i+r} that chronologically follows the sequence. For instance, for $r = 5$ we have 20 sequences, learn 20 decision trees and thus obtain the classification accuracy for 20 data sets.

To learn a decision tree with which the performance of PreDeT can be compared it has to be considered that *PreDeT* implicitly learns a sequence of r decision trees each corresponding to a data set S^i and then anticipates the tree in the future period $r + 1$ using a prediction model. As with any prediction model, the obtained result cannot have a better quality than its inputs used for learning. Since the quality of a decision tree is (amongst other factors) determined by the size of the data set used for training, it is clear that the tree anticipated by PreDeT does have a similar quality to a tree that would have been learned directly on a data set S^{r+1} with a size similar to those of each $S^i, i = 1, \ldots, r$. Since we assume S^{r+1} to be unknown at the time of learning we took the most recent data set S^r to learn a decision tree[1] for comparism because the characteristics of S^r are very likely best reflecting those of S^{r+1}.

Another advantage of comparing the accuracies obtained by PreDeT with those of a decision tree learned from only the most recent data is that the latter is basically a temporal moving window approach and thus common practise for learning decision trees in the presense of concept drift. Moreover, such a temporal moving window approach performs similar to age dependent weighting approaches – the alternative method to learn decision trees in the presence of concept drift – in case of smooth, non-abrupt concept drift [11, 10]. Such a type of concept drift is present in our data as we know from previous studies on change mining carried out on the same data set [2].

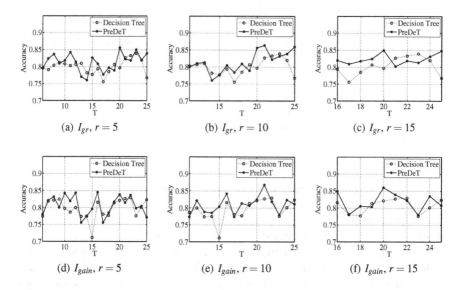

Fig. 4 Classification accuracy for two different attribute evaluation measures in several consecutive time periods T. Different sequences of a length of r time periods were used to learn the least squares models used by *PreDeT*. For comparison, the performance of a traditional decision tree approach using only the most recent data of each sequence for inducing the decision tree is shown.

Using the above experimental setup we carried out experiments using the information gain ratio I_{gr} and information gain I_{gain} and varied in each case the length of the sequence by using $r = 5, 10, 15$. Figure 4 shows the results of our experiments. As we can see, the classification accuracy of *PreDeT* is on average superior to the one of the traditional decision tree approach and also independent of the choice of the attribute evaluation measure and the parameter r. By comparing Figure 4(a) with

---

[1] We used the decision tree implementation by Christian Borgelt that can be obtained from http://www.borgelt.net/dtree

Figure 4(c) (Figure 4(d) with Figure 4(f), respectively) it can be seen that the gain in classification accuracy increases when longer sequences are used. This again leaves space for further optimisations of the *PreDeT* algorithm with respect to the optimal choice of the parameter r.

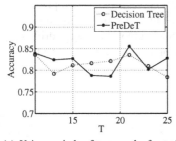
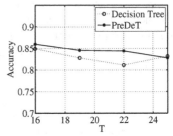

(a) Using periods of two weeks for training. The accuracy median for the decision tree is 0.8138 and for *PreDeT* 0.8256.

(b) Using periods of three weeks for training. The accuracy median for the decision tree is 0.83 and for *PreDeT* 0.8449.

Fig. 5 Classification accuracy for information gain I_{gain} and $r = 5$ using data sets covering periods of two and, respectively, three weeks for training and of one week for testing. For comparison, the performance of an approach using only the most recent data set of each sequence for inducing the decision tree is shown.

We now evaluate the influence of the size of the individual data sets S^i on the performance of *PreDeT*. This aspect is in particular interesting because it is known that the performance of a moving temporal window approach, which we use in our experiments for comparison, does strongly depend on it [6]. We use a similar experimental setup as in our first experiments but instead of using a size of one week for each data set S^i we increase the size to two and three weeks, respectively. In particular, we split our initial data set into 12 non-overlapping subsets each covering a period of two weeks. Likewise, we obtained another split of 8 subsets each covering a period of three weeks. Similar to our first experiment we used sequences of $r = 5$ to learn decision trees using *PreDeT* and classified the samples of the week that immediately follows the respective sequence. Again, we compared the classification accuracy of *PreDeT* with the one of decision trees learned by a temporal moving window approach.

The results of this experiment are shown in Figure 5(a) for a period length of two weeks and in Figure 5(b) for a period length of three weeks, respectively. As we can see, in both cases the classification accuracy of *PreDeT* is on average higher than the one of the temporal moving window approach, i.e. a decision tree learned only on the most recent data of each sequence. We can also see by comparing Figure 5(a) with Figure 5(b) that the performance gain offered by *PreDeT* seems to increase with the size of individual data sets.

6 Conclusion and Future Work

We presented a novel approach to learn decision trees in the presence of concept drift. Our *PreDeT* algorithm aims to anticipate decision trees for future time periods by modelling how attribute evaluation measure and class label distribution evolve over time. Our experimental results show that our approach is able to learn decision trees with a higher classification accuracy than trees learned by a temporal window approach.

Currently we are working on several enhancements of our algorithm. In the first place, we investigate the advantages of using more sophisticated and more robust regression methods, e.g. support vector regression [16], instead of regression polynomials. Secondly, at the moment a new decision tree has to be predicted every time a new batch of data arrives. For this reason it would be advantageous w.r.t. computational costs to enhance *PreDeT* in order to support incremental learning. One starting point could be to leverage existing incremental algorithms for linear regression [15] and support vector regression [17, 18].

References

1. Akaike, H.: A new look at the statistical model identification. IEEE Transactions on Automatic Control **19**(6), 716–723 (1974)
2. Boettcher, M., Nauck, D., Ruta, D., Spott, M.: Towards a framework for change detection in datasets. In: M. Bramer (ed.) Research and Development in Intelligent Systems, *Proceedings of AI-2006, the 26th SGAI International Conference on Innovative Techniques and Applications of Artificial Intelligence*, vol. 23, pp. 115–128. BCS SGAI, Springer (2006)
3. Breiman, L., Friedman, J., Olshen, R., Stone, C.: Classification and Regression Trees. Wadsworth, Belmont (1984)
4. Burnham, K.P., Anderson, D.R.: Multimodel inference: understanding AIC and BIC in model selection. Sociological Methods & Research **33**, 261–304 (2004)
5. Gill, P.E., Murray, W., Wright, M.H.: Practical Optimization. Academic Press, London (1989)
6. Helmbold, D.P., Long, P.M.: Tracking drifting concepts by minimizing disagreements. Machine Learning **14**(1), 27–45 (1994)
7. Hornik, K., Stinchcombe, M., White, H.: Multilayer feedforward networks are universal approximators. Neural Networks **2**(5), 359–366 (1989).
8. Hulten, G., Spencer, L., Domingos, P.: Mining time-changing data streams. In: Proceedings of the 7th ACM SIGKDD International Conference on Knowledge Discovery and Data Mining, pp. 97–106. ACM Press, New York, NY, USA (2001).
9. Hurvich, C.M., Tsai, C.L.: Regression and time series model selection in small samples. Biometrika **76**, 297–307 (1989)
10. Klinkenberg, R.: Learning drifting concepts: Example selection vs. example weighting. Intelligent Data Analysis **8**(3), 281–300 (2004)
11. Klinkenberg, R., Rueping, S.: Concept drift and the importance of examples. In: J. Franke, G. Nakhaeizadeh, I. Renz (eds.) Text Mining – Theoretical Aspects and Applications, pp. 55–77. Physica-Verlag, Berlin, Germany (2003)
12. Kuh, A., Petsche, T., Rivest, R.L.: Learning time-varying concepts. In: Advances in Neural Information Processing Systems, pp. 183–189. Morgan Kaufmann Publishers Inc., San Francisco, CA, USA (1990)
13. Quinlan, J.: C4.5: Programs for Machine Learning. Morgan Kaufmann (1992)

14. Quinlan, J.R.: Induction of decision trees. Machine Learning **1**(1), 81–106 (1996)
15. Scharf, L.: Statistical Signal Processing. Addison-Wesley (1991)
16. Smola, A.J., Schölkopf, B.: A tutorial on support vector regression. Statistics and Computing **14**(3), 199–222 (2004)
17. Syed, N.A., Liu, H., Sung, K.K.: Handling concept drifts in incremental learning with support vector machines. In: Proceedings of the 5th ACM SIGKDD International Conference on Knowledge Discovery and Data Mining, pp. 317–321. ACM Press, New York, NY, USA (1999).
18. Wang, W.: An incremental learning strategy for support vector regression. Neural Processing Letters **21**(3), 175–188 (2005).
19. Widmer, G., Kubat, M.: Learning in the presence of concept drift and hidden contexts. Machine Learning **23**(1), 69–101 (1996).

Polarity Assignment to Causal Information Extracted from Financial Articles Concerning Business Performance of Companies

Hiroyuki Sakai and Shigeru Masuyama

Abstract We propose a method of assigning polarity to causal information extracted from Japanese financial articles concerning business performance of companies. Our method assigns polarity (positive or negative) according to business performance to causal information, e.g. "*zidousya no uriage ga koutyou*: (Sales of cars are good)" (The polarity positive is assigned in this example.). First, our method classifies articles concerning business performance into positive articles and negative articles. Using this classified sets of articles, our method assigns polarity (positive or negative) to causal information extracted from the set of articles concerning business performance. We evaluated our method and it attained 75.3% precision and 47.9% recall of assigning polarity positive, and 77.0% precision and 58.5% recall of assigning polarity negative, respectively.

1 Introduction

Japanese Government recommends "From savings to investment" as a strategy for promoting the growth of Japanese economy[1]. Collecting information concerning business performance of companies is a very important task for investment. If the business performance of a company is good, the stock price of the company will rise in general. Moreover, causal information of the business performance is also important, because, even if the business performance of a company is good, its stock price will not rise when the main cause is the recording of an extraordinary profit not

Hiroyuki Sakai
Toyohashi University of Technology, 1-1 Hibarigaoka, Tempaku-cho, Toyohashi-shi 441-8580, Japan, e-mail: sakai@smlab.tutkie.tut.ac.jp

Shigeru Masuyama
Toyohashi University of Technology, 1-1 Hibarigaoka, Tempaku-cho, Toyohashi-shi 441-8580, Japan, e-mail: masuyama@tutkie.tut.ac.jp

[1] http://www.jasme.go.jp/jpn/summary/message041010.html

related to its core business (e.g. profit from sales of stocks). This is also the case for the bad business performance. Hence, causal information of the business performance is useful for investors in selecting companies to invest. However, since there are a number of companies that announce business performance, acquiring all of their causal information manually is a considerably hard and expensive task[2]. Hence, we proposed a method of identifying articles concerning business performance of companies and extracting causal information (e.g. "*zidousya no uriage ga koutyou*: Sales of cars are good") from them automatically[3][5]. We defined a phrase implying causal information as a "causal expression".

We expect that causal expressions may be used as data for computer trading and business trend forecast. However, in order to use causal expressions as more effective information, it is desirable to assign them polarity (positive or negative) according to business performance. For example, polarity of causal expression "car sales are good" is positive and polarity of causal expression "car sales are down" is negative[4].

If the number of causal expressions assigned polarity positive increases, business condition is expected to recover(e.g., see Figure 4.). Moreover, we may analyze content of articles concerning business performance circumstantially by using causal expressions assigned polarity by our method. Hence, we propose a method of assigning polarity (either positive or negative) to causal expressions automatically in this paper.

In our previous method, we defined causal expressions to be extracted as expressions that contain some "frequent expressions" and a "clue expression". Here, we defined a frequent expression as a phrase frequently appearing in a set of causal expressions and a clue expression as a phrase frequently modified by causal expressions. For example, in a causal expression "*zidousya no uriage ga koutyou*: (Sales of cars are good)", a frequent expression is "*uriage*: (sales)" and a clue expression is "*ga koutyou*: (are good)". Our previous method acquired such frequent expressions and clue expressions automatically and extracted causal expressions by using these frequent expressions and clue expressions.

Our method assigns polarity to the causal expressions by using statistical information of the combination of frequent expressions and clue expressions. In general, polarity of causal expressions containing a clue expression "*ga koutyou*: (are good)" is positive. However, the polarity is not able to be determined only by clue expressions. For example, although the polarity of a causal expression "*zidousya no uriage ga zouka*: (car sales are increasing)" containing a clue expression "*ga zouka*: (are increasing)" is positive, the polarity of a causal expression "*risutora hiyou ga zouka*: (restructuring cost is increasing)" containing the same clue expression is negative. Hence, it is necessary for assigning polarity to employ the combination of frequent expressions and clue expressions. However, since the number of combinations of frequent expressions and a clue expression is enormous, it is impossible to assign

---

[2] The number of listed companies is about 2401.

[3] We briefly introduce this method in Sec.3.

[4] Note that polarity "neutral" is not assigned to causal expressions since the causal expressions appear in articles concerning business performance when the business performance changes.

polarity to causal expressions manually. Moreover, machine learning methods can assign polarity to only causal expressions that contain the combinations of frequent expressions and a clue expression that appear in training data.

In contrast, our method classifies articles concerning business performance into two categories, positive articles and negative articles, according to business performance. That is, our method classifies an article that suggests business performance improves into the set of positive articles and classifies an article that suggests business performance declines into the set of negative articles. After that, our method assigns polarity to a causal expression by using probability that combinations of frequent expressions and a clue expression appear in a set of positive articles or that of negative ones. For example, the combination of a frequent expression "*risutora hiyou*: (restructuring cost)" and a clue expression "*ga zouka*: (is increasing)" is frequently contained in a set of negative articles. Hence, our method successfully assigns polarity "negative" to causal expressions containing the combination of a frequent expression "*risutora hiyou*: (restructuring cost)" and a clue expression "*ga zouka*: (is increasing)".

2 Related work

As related work, Takamura et al. proposed models for semantic orientations of phrases that consist of multiple words as well as classification methods based on the models by using a machine learning method [7]. They focused on "noun+adjective" and introduced latent variables into the model in order to capture the property of such phrases. However, the method is not able to classify phrases that consist of words not appearing in training dataset. In contrast, our method classifies articles concerning business performance into positive and negative ones. After that, our method assigns polarity to a causal expression by using probability that combinations of frequent expressions and a clue expression appear in a set of positive articles or that of negative ones. Although our method needs training dataset for classifying articles concerning business performance into positive and negative ones, our method does not need training dataset for assigning polarity to causal expressions. Hence, even if a causal expression not appearing in training dataset for classifying articles concerning business performance into positive and negative ones exists, our method is able to assign polarity to it by using statistical information of this classified sets of articles.

Turney proposed a method for classifying reviews as *recommended* (thumbs up) or *not recommended* (thumbs down) by calculating the mutual information between phrases in the review and a positive reference word "excellent", and a negative reference word "poor", respectively[8]. Wilson et al. proposed a method for recognizing contextual polarity in phrase-level sentiment analysis by using polarity of words that compose the phrase[9]. (Here, the polarity of words is assigned by hand.) Baron et al. proposed a method for classifying collocations extracted by Xtract[6] into "positive" and " negative" [1]. The method classifies them by using the orientations of the words in the neighboring sentences. However, since the number of frequent expressions and clue expressions necessary to extract causal expressions is enormous, assigning polarities to frequent expressions and clue expressions manually is a considerably hard task. Moreover, the polarity is not able to be determined only by clue expressions, e.g., "*ga zouka*: (are increasing)". Hence, a method that uses the polarity of words that compose a causal expression, e.g., [8][9][1], is not applicable in our task.

Kaji et al. proposed a method for acquiring polar phrases (adjectives and "noun + post-positional particles + adjective") by using frequency in polar sentence corpus[2]. Here, the polar sentences are extracted by using lexicon-syntactic patterns and manually created cue words list. In this method, the same polar phrases need to appear at least three times in both set of positive polar sentences and that of negative ones. However, since a causal expression consists of many words, the same causal expression does not appear in the set of articles concerning business performance. Hence, Kaji et al's method is not applicable to our task. In contrast, our method solves the problem that the same causal expression does not appear by replacing a causal expression that consists of many words with some "frequent expressions" and a "clue expression".

Koppel et al. proposed a method for classifying news stories about a company according to its apparent impact on the performance of the company's stock[3]. Lavrenko et al. proposed a method for identifying news stories that influence the behavior of financial markets[4]. In contrast, since our method assigns polarity to causal expressions extracted from newspaper articles concerning business performance, the task is different. In general, articles concerning business performance contain some content that influences the stock price. However, even if the business performance of a company is good, the stock price of the company will not rise if the main cause is not related to its core business. Hence, we consider that it is necessary not only to classify articles whether they influence the stock prise but also to analyze content of articles. We expect to be able to analyze content of the articles concerning business performance circumstantially by using causal expressions assigned polarity by our method.

3 Extraction of causal expressions

We proposed a method of extracting causal expressions from financial articles concerning business performance automatically[5]. In this section, we briefly introduce our previous method to help the understanding of our method of assigning polarity. We defined causal expressions to be extracted as expressions that contain some "frequent expressions" and one "clue expression" and our previous method extracts causal expressions by acquiring the frequent expressions and the clue expressions automatically. The method for acquiring frequent expressions and clue expressions is as follows.

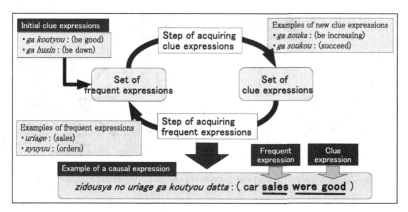

Fig. 1 Outline of our previous method

Step 1: Input a few initial clue expressions and acquire phrases that modify them. Here, we used two clue expressions, "*ga koutyou*: (be good)" and "*ga husin*: (be down)", as initial clue expressions.

Step 2: Extract phrases frequently appearing in a set of the phrases acquired in Step 1 as frequent expressions. Here, the phrases acquired in Step 1 are defined as frequent expression candidates and appropriate frequent expressions are selected from them.

Step 3: Acquire new clue expressions modified by the frequent expressions.

Step 4: Extract new frequent expressions from a set of phrases that modify the new clue expressions acquired in Step 3. (This step is the same as Step 2.)

Step 5: Repeat Steps 3 and 4 until they are executed predetermined times or neither new clue expressions nor new frequent expressions are extracted. □

An outline of our previous method is shown in Figure 1.

3.1 Selection of frequent expressions

Our previous method[5] selects appropriate frequent expressions from a set of frequent expression candidates. Here, our previous method calculates entropy $H(e)$ based on the probability $P(e,s)$ that frequent expression e modifies clue expression s and selects a frequent expression that is assigned entropy $H(e)$ larger than a threshold value calculated by Formula 2. Entropy $H(e)$ is used for reflecting "variety of clue expressions modified by frequent expression e". If entropy $H(e)$ is large, frequent expression e modifies various kinds of clue expressions and such a frequent expression is appropriate. (See Figure 2.) Entropy $H(e)$ is calculated by the following Formula 1:

$$H(e) = -\sum_{s \in S(e)} P(e,s) \log_2 P(e,s). \tag{1}$$

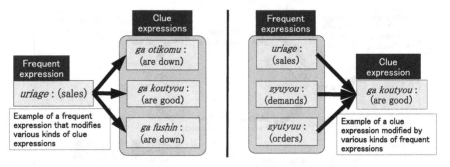

Fig. 2 Example of an appropriate frequent expression and an appropriate clue expression

Here, $S(e)$ is the set of clue expressions modified by frequent expression e in the set of articles concerning business performance. The threshold value is calculated by the following Formula 2:

$$T_e = \alpha \log_2 |N_s|. \tag{2}$$

Here, N_s is the set of clue expressions and α is a constant $(0 < \alpha < 1)$.

3.2 Acquisition of new clue expressions

Our previous method[5] acquires new clue expressions by using frequent expressions. First, our previous method extracts a *bunsetu*[5] modified by frequent expression e and acquires new clue expression s by adding a case particle contained in the frequent expression e to the *bunsetu*. Next, our previous method calculates entropy $H(s)$ based on the probability $P(s,e)$ that clue expression s is modified by frequent expression e and selects clue expression s that is assigned entropy $H(s)$ larger than a threshold value calculated by Formula 4 to be introduced hereafter:

$$H(s) = - \sum_{e \in E(s)} P(s,e) \log_2 P(s,e). \tag{3}$$

Here, $E(s)$ is the set of frequent expressions that modify clue expression s. The threshold value is calculated by the following Formula 4:

$$T_s = \alpha \log_2 |N_e|. \tag{4}$$

Here, N_e is the set of frequent expressions and α is the same constant value that in Formula 2.

---

[5] a *bunsetsu* is a basic block in Japanese composed of several words.

3.3 Extraction of causal expressions by using frequent expressions and clue expressions

Finally, our previous method extracts causal expressions by using frequent expressions and clue expressions. A causal expression consists of a clue expression and a phrase that modifies the clue expression. Moreover, the phrase that modifies the clue expression contains some frequent expressions. For example, "*tyuugoku muke no ekisyou kanren no denshi buhin ga kaihuku suru*: (Electronic parts related to liquid-crystal for China recover)" is extracted as a causal expression since phrase "*tyuugoku muke no ekisyou kanren no denshi buhin*: (Electronic parts related to liquid-crystal for China)" modifies clue expression "*ga kaihuku suru*: (recover)" and the phrase contains two frequent expressions "*denshi buhin*: (electronic parts)" and "*ekisyou kanren*: (related to liquid-crystal)".

4 Polarity assignment to causal expressions

Our method assigns polarity to causal expressions by using statistical information of combinations of "frequent expressions" and a "clue expression". For example, the combinations of a frequent expression "*uriage*: (sales)" and a clue expression "*ga zouka*: (are increasing)" is frequently contained in a set of articles that suggest business performance improves. In contrast, the combinations of a frequent expression "*risutora hiyou*: (restructuring cost)" and a clue expression "*ga zouka*: (are increasing)" is frequently contained in a set of articles that suggest business performance deteriorates. Hence, our method classifies articles concerning business performance into two categories, positive articles and negative articles, according to business performance. That is, our method classifies an article that suggests business performance improves into positive articles and classifies an article that suggests business performance declines into negative articles. After that, our method assigns polarity to a causal expression by using probability that combinations of frequent expressions and a clue expression appear in a set of positive articles or that of negative ones. An outline of our method is shown in Figure 3:

4.1 Classification of articles concerning business performance

We explain about the method of classifying articles concerning business performance in this subsection. Our method classifies articles into positive and negative ones by using Support Vector Machine(SVM). First, we extract articles concerning business performance from a set of financial articles and classify them into positive and negative ones manually. They are used as a training data of SVM. Note that the training data is used to classify the articles into positive and negative ones, and is

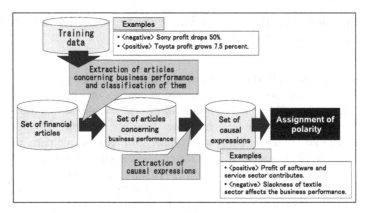

Fig. 3 Outline of our method

not used to assign polarity to causal expressions. Next, our method extracts content words effective for classifying articles as features from the training data. Actually, our method calculates score $W(t_i, S_p)$ of content word t_i contained in positive articles set S_p and score $W(t_i, S_n)$ of content word t_i contained in negative articles set S_n by the following Formula 5:

$$W(t_i, S_p) = P(t_i, S_p)H(t_i, S_p). \tag{5}$$

Here, $P(t_i, S_p)$ is the probability that word t_i appears in S_p and is calculated by the following Formula 6:

$$P(t_i, S_p) = \frac{Tf(t_i, S_p)}{\sum_{t \in Ts(S_p)} Tf(t, S_p)}. \tag{6}$$

Here, $Tf(t_i, S_p)$ is the frequency of word t_i in S_p and $Ts(S_p)$ is the set of words contained in S_p.

The entropy $H(t_i, S_p)$ is based on probability $P(t_i, d)$ that word t_i appears in document $d \in S_p$, and is calculated by the following Formula 7:

$$H(t_i, S_p) = - \sum_{d \in S_p} P(t_i, d) \log_2 P(t_i, d), \tag{7}$$

$$P(t_i, d) = \frac{tf(t_i, d)}{\sum_{d' \in S_p} tf(t_i, d')}. \tag{8}$$

Here, $tf(t_i, d)$ is the frequency of word t_i in document d. Entropy $H(t_i, S_p)$ is introduced for assigning a large score to a word that appears uniformly in each document contained in positive example set S_p.

Next, our method compares $W(t_i, S_p)$ with $W(t_i, S_n)$. If either score $W(t_i, S_p)$ is larger than $2W(t_i, S_n)$ or score $W(t_i, S_n)$ is larger than $2W(t_i, S_p)$, word t_i is selected as a feature for SVM. Some examples of words selected as features are shown in

Table 1 Examples of words selected as features

zyouhou syuusei: (upward adjustment)	*kahou syusei*: (downward adjustment)
tokubetu sonshitu: (extraordinary charge)	*zousyuu zoueki*: (profit increase)

Table 1. Here, each element of feature vectors used for learning by SVM is the appearance probability of words selected as features contained in each article in training data. We use a linear kernel as the kernel of SVM.

4.2 Polarity assignment to causal expressions

We explain about our method of assigning polarity to causal expressions. Here, we define a frequent expression as fp_i, a clue expression as cp, and a causal expression as x. Note that a causal expression contains a clue expression and at least one frequent expression.

$$x = (\langle fp_1, cp \rangle, \langle fp_2, cp \rangle, ..., \langle fp_n, cp \rangle). \tag{9}$$

Here, we define polarity of a causal expression as $c \in \{positive, negative\}$. Our method assigns polarity c to causal expression x by calculating probability $P(c|x)$ by the following Formula 10:

$$\hat{c} = \arg\max_c P(c|x) = \arg\max_c P(c)P(x|c) \tag{10}$$

The probability $P(x|c)$ is estimated by the following Formula 11:

$$P(x|c) \approx \prod_{i=1}^{n} P(\langle fp_i, cp \rangle | c_d), \tag{11}$$

where,

$c_d \in \{positive, negative\}$: the polarity of an article concerning business performance classified by our method.

$P(\langle fp_i, cp \rangle | c_d)$: the conditional probability that $\langle fp_i, cp \rangle$ contained in causal expressions appears in a set of articles concerning business performance classified to c_d.

Moreover, the probability $P(c)$ in Formula 10 is estimated by $P(c_d)$. Here, $P(c_d)$ is the probability that causal expressions appear in a set of articles concerning business performance classified to c_d.

Here, $P(c|x)$ at $c = positive$ is defined as P_p and $P(c|x)$ at $c = negative$ is defined as P_n, respectively. Our method assigns polarity "positive" in the case of $P_p > 2P_n$ and assigns polarity "negative" in the case of $P_n > 2P_p$. Otherwise, the polarity is not assigned.

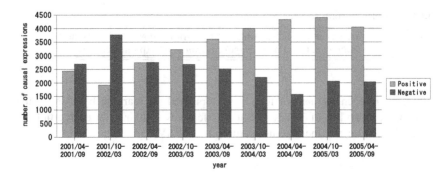

Fig. 4 The number of causal expressions assigned polarity by our method

5 Evaluation

5.1 Implementation

We implemented our method and evaluated it. We employ ChaSen[6] as a Japanese morphological analyzer, and CaboCha[7] as a Japanese parser and SVM^{light}[8] as an implementation of SVM. As training data, we manually extracted 2,920 articles concerning business performance from Nikkei newspapers published in 2000 and manually classified them into positive and negative ones. Causal expressions are extracted from Nikkei newspapers published from 1990 to 2005 (except 2000) by our previous method[5] and our method assigned polarity, "positive" or "negative", to them[9]. Some examples of causal expressions assigned polarity by our method are shown in Table 2 and the number of causal expressions assigned polarity positive and the number of causal expressions assigned polarity negative are shown in Figure 4. Note that business condition of Japan was marked bottom in 2001 and has gradually recovered since 2002.

5.2 Evaluation results

As a correct data set for evaluation, we manually extracted 623 causal expressions from 138 articles concerning business performance and assigned polarity to them. After that, our method extracted causal expressions and assigned polarity to them by our method from the same 138 articles as test data and we calculated precision and

---

[6] http://chasen.aist-nara.ac.jp/hiki/ChaSen/

[7] http://chasen.org/˜taku/software/cabocha/

[8] http://svmlight.joachims.org

[9] Although inappropriate causal expressions may be contained, they are not eliminated by hand.

Table 2 Examples of causal expressions assigned polarity by our method

causal expression	*tyuugoku muke no ekisyou kanren no denshi buhin ga kaihuku suru*:
	(Electronic parts related to liquid-crystal for China recover.)
frequent expression	*denshi buhin*: (electronic parts),
	ekisyou kanren: (related to liquid-crystal)
clue expression	*ga kaihuku suru*: (recover)
polarity	positive
causal expression	*keitai zyouhou tanmatu ya denshi debaisu ga husin datta*:
	(Portable terminal and electronic device were slack)
frequent expression	*denshi debaisu*: (electronic device)
clue expression	*ga husin datta*: (were slack)
polarity	negative

Table 3 Evaluation results

α	Num. of ce	$P_{pos}(\%)$	$R_{pos}(\%)$	F_{pos}	$P_{neg}(\%)$	$R_{neg}(\%)$	F_{neg}	$P_{ce}(\%)$	$R_{ce}(\%)$
0.3	139666	75.3	47.9	58.6	77.0	58.5	66.5	81.8	67.9
0.25	150719	71.4	51.4	59.8	74.9	60.3	66.8	78.3	70.3
0.2	171675	64.9	51.4	57.4	67.4	61.2	64.2	70.8	71.3

recall. Table 3 shows the results. For the purpose of reference, we also shows precision P_{ce} and recall R_{ce} of causal expressions extracted by our previous method[5] in Table 3. Here, *Num. of ce* is the number of causal expressions extracted by our previous method. Values $P_{pos}(P_{neg})$ and $R_{pos}(R_{neg})$ are precision and recall of causal expressions to which our method assigns polarity positive(negative), respectively. Value $F_{pos}(F_{neg})$ is F value of $P_{pos}(P_{neg})$ and $R_{pos}(R_{neg})$. Parameter α is used for determining the threshold value in Formula 2. Precision P_{pos} and recall R_{pos} is calculated by the following Formula 12:

$$P_{pos} = \frac{|A_{pos} \cap C_{pos}|}{|A_{pos}|}, \quad R_{pos} = \frac{|A_{pos} \cap C_{pos}|}{|C_{pos}|} \tag{12}$$

Here, A_{pos} is the set of causal expressions to which our method assigns polarity positive and C_{pos} is the set of causal expressions assigned polarity positive in a correct data set.

We compare our method with Semantic Orientation (*SO*) that is a criterion proposed by Turney[8]. The Semantic Orientation (*SO*) is calculated by the following formula13.

$$SO(ce) = \log_2 \frac{hits(ce\ NEAR\ ``koutyou(good)")hits(``husin(down)")}{hits(ce\ NEAR\ ``husin(down)")hits(``koutyou(good)")} \tag{13}$$

Note that although Turney calculated *SO* by using "excellent" and "poor", we calculated it by using "*koutyou*(good)" and "*husin*(down)" for applying *SO* to our task. Moreover, we set $hits(``koutyou(good)")$ as a number of articles containing "*koutyou*(good)" and $hits(ce\ NEAR\ ``koutyou(good)")$ as a number of articles containing both causal expression *ce* and "*koutyou*(good)". In our task, since

Table 4 Evaluation results (Semantic Orientation)

α	$P_{pos}(\%)$	$R_{pos}(\%)$	F_{pos}	$P_{neg}(\%)$	$R_{neg}(\%)$	F_{neg}
0.3	57.8	21.5	31.3	54.9	59.1	56.9
0.25	54.5	22.2	31.6	52.7	60.9	56.5
0.2	47.0	22.2	30.2	48.0	62.1	54.1

Table 5 Evaluation results (baseline method)

α	$P_{pos}(\%)$	$R_{pos}(\%)$	F_{pos}	$P_{neg}(\%)$	$R_{neg}(\%)$	F_{neg}
0.3	63.9	43.8	51.9	62.1	53.7	57.6
0.25	61.2	45.5	52.2	58.9	54.6	56.7
0.2	55.8	45.5	50.1	53.4	56.1	54.7

the same causal expression does not appear in the set of articles concerning business performance, the threshold value of $hits(ce\ NEAR\ "koutyou(good)")$ and $hits(ce\ NEAR\ "husin(down)")$ was not set. Table 4 shows the results. As a baseline method, we evaluate the method that assigns polarity corresponding to polarity of an article containing a causal expression to the causal expression. (For example, if an article containing a causal expression "*zidousya no uriage ga koutyou*: (Sales of cars are good)" is classified into negative one, polarity of the causal expression is also negative.) Table 5 shows the results.

6 Discussion

Table 3 shows that our method attained 75.3% precision of assigning polarity positive and 77.0% precision of assigning polarity negative to causal expressions extracted by our previous method. Note that if our method assigns polarity to inappropriate causal expressions extracted by our previous method (the precision of extracting causal expressions was 81.8%.), they are recognized as incorrect[10]. If our method assigns polarity to appropriate causal expressions selected manually in order to evaluate only our method, it attained 88.4% precision of assigning polarity positive and 92.5% precision of assigning polarity negative. Hence, we consider that our method achieved good performance.

For example, our method was able to assign polarity positive to a causal expression that contains a frequent expression "*uriage*: (sales)" and a clue expression "*ga zouka sita*: (are increasing)". In contrast, our method was able to assign polarity negative to a causal expression that contains a frequent expression "*shoukyaku hutan*: (extinguishment responsibility)" and a clue expression "*ga zouka sita*: (are increasing)". In general, the polarity of a causal expression containing a clue expression "*ga koutyou*: (are good)" is positive and the polarity of a causal expression containing a clue expression "*ga husin*: (are down)" is negative. However, the polarity is

---

[10] In this evaluation, we do not exclude inappropriate causal expressions manually.

not able to be determined only by clue expressions e.g., "*ga zouka*: (are increasing)". Our method classifies articles concerning business performance into positive and negative ones, and assigns polarity to a causal expression by using probability that combinations of frequent expressions and a clue expression appear in a set of positive articles or in that of negative articles. Hence, our method was able to assign appropriate polarity even if the polarity to be assigned changes by the combination of frequent expressions and clue expressions. In our method, the precision of classifying articles concerning business performance influences the polarity of assigning polarity to causal expressions. We evaluated the method of classifying articles concerning business performance and it attained 89.8% precision[11]. We consider that the method of classifying articles concerning business performance achieved good performance since our method is able to extract features efficient for classifying articles concerning business performance, e.g., "*zyouhou syuusei*: (upward adjustment)", "*tokubetu sonshitu*: (extraordinary charge)".

Table 4 shows that our method outperformed Semantic Orientation (*SO*) proposed by Turney. In our task, the *SO* is calculated by using frequency of cooccurrence of causal expressions and "*koutyou*(good)", and "*husin*(down)", respectively. However, since a causal expression consists of many words, the same causal expression does not appear in the set of articles concerning business performance. Since the frequency of co-occurrence of causal expressions and "*koutyou*(good)" and that of causal expressions and "*husin*(down)" are very low, the *SO* was not able to be calculated appropriately. In contrast, our method solves the problem that the same causal expression does not appear by replacing a causal expression that consists of many words with some "frequent expressions" and a "clue expression". Hence, we consider that our method outperformed Semantic Orientation (*SO*). Moreover, Table 5 shows that the precision of assigning polarity positive and the precision of assigning polarity negative of the baseline method were 63.9% and 62.1%, respectively. The reason why precision of the baseline method is low is that causal expressions that should assign polarity negative are frequently contained in articles classified into positive.

However, the recall value of assigning polarity positive and that of assigning polarity negative were 47.9% and 58.5%, respectively. The reason why the recall value is low is that the recall value of extracting causal expressions extracted by our previous method is 67.9%. Moreover, our method assigns polarity positive in the case of $P_p > 2P_n$ and assigns polarity negative in the case of $P_n > 2P_p$, otherwise, the polarity was not assigned. If our method does not execute this processing, the precision value and the recall value of assigning polarity positive were 68.7% and 51.0%, and the precision value and the recall value of assigning polarity negative were 73.6% and 63.0%, respectively. Hence, although the precision was improved, the recall was decreased by this processing.

---

[11] As a correct data set for calculating the precision of classifying articles, we manually classified 550 acrticles concerning business performance into positve and negative ones.

7 Conclusion

In this paper, we proposed a method of assigning polarity (positive or negative) to causal expressions extracted from articles concerning business performance of companies. Our method assigned polarity to them by using statistical information. First, our method classified articles concerning business performance into positive and negative ones. Next, our method assigned polarity to a causal expression by using probability that combinations of frequent expressions and clue expressions appear in a set of positive articles or that of negative ones. We evaluated our method and it attained 75.3% precision and 47.9% recall of assigning polarity positive, and 77.0% precision and 58.5% recall of assigning polarity negative.

Acknowledgment

This work was supported in part by Grant-in-Aid for Scientific Research(B)(20300058) from Japan Society for the Promotion of Science(JSPS).

References

1. Baron, F. and Hirst, G.: Collocations as Cues to Semantic Orientation, *AAAI Spring Symposium on Exploring Attitude and Affect in Text: Theories and Applications (AAAI-EAAT 2004)* (2004).
2. Kaji, N. and Kitsuregawa, M.: Building Lexicon for Sentiment Analysis from Massive Collection of HTML Documents, *Proceedings of the 2007 Joint Conference on Empirical Methods in Natural Language Processing and Computational Natural Language Learning (EMNLP-CoNLL)*, pp. 1075–1083 (2007).
3. Koppel, M. and Shtrimberg, I.: Good News or Bad News? Let the Market Decide, *Proceedings of the AAAI Spring Symposium on Exploring Attitude and Affect in Text*, pp. 86–88 (2004).
4. Lavrenko, V., Schmill, M., Lawrie, D. and Ogilvie, P.: Mining of Concurrent Text and Time Series, *Proceedings of the KDD 2000 Conference Text Mining Workshop* (2001).
5. Sakai, H. and Masuyama, S.: Cause Information Extraction from Financial Articles Concerning Business Performance, *IEICE Trans. Information and Systems*, Vol. E91-D, No. 4, pp. 959–968 (2008).
6. Smadja, F.: Retrieving collocations from text: Xtract, *Computational Linguistics*, Vol. 19, No. 1, pp. 143–177 (1993).
7. Takamura, H., Inui, T. and Okumura, M.: Latent Variable Models for Semantic Orientation of Phrases, *Proceedings of the 11th Conference of the European Chapter of the Association for Computational Linguistics (EACL2006)*, pp. 201–208 (2006).
8. Turney, P. D.: Thumbs up or thumbs down? semantic orientation applied to unsupervised classification of reviews, *Proceedings of 40th Annual Meeting of the Association for Computational Linguistics (ACL2002)*, pp. 417–424 (2002).
9. Wilson, T., Wiebe, J. and Hoffmann, P.: Recognizing contextual polarity in phrase-level sentiment analysis, *Proceedings of joint conference on Human Language Technology / Conference on Empirical Methods in Nutural Language Processing (HLT/EMNLP'05)*, pp. 347–354 (2005).

Redux^{exp}: An Open-source Justification-based Explanation Support Server

Thomas R. Roth-Berghofer and Florian Mittag

Abstract Trust in any decision depends on many factors. One way of improving trust is by explaining why a certain decision has been made and how certain actions in the context of a decision have been performed. In order to provide such explanations information systems need a mechanism for recording decisions and actions. The open-source server Redux^{exp} is such a system. This paper describes the architecture of Redux^{exp} and first experiences with the system.

1 Motivation

The tendency to have more trust in a particular action, a piece of advice or the decision of another person can be generalized to software systems. If a complex program is able to explain how its output was derived, it can increase trust and gives the user a sense of control over the system (11). To automatically generate explanations the program must record its decisions and actions. In our opinion a justification-based truth maintenance system (JTMS) (1) is the best mechanism for storing such information. Databases, object-oriented repositories, and RDF stores are all too generic for such a task and can not provide the required decision maintenance functionality as will become clear in the following. To our knowledge no other system for storing explanation-relevant knowledge is available.

In 1991, Charles Petrie introduced REDUX (3), which extends traditional problem solver/Truth Maintenance System (TMS) architectures used in heuristic search

Thomas R. Roth-Berghofer · Florian Mittag

Knowledge Management Department, German Research Center for Artificial Intelligence DFKI GmbH, 67663 Kaiserslautern, Germany, and Knowledge-based Systems Group, Department of Computer Science, University of Kaiserslautern,

e-mail: thomas.roth-berghofer|florian.mittag@dfki.de

and hierarchical planning to maintain rationales for decisions and meta-decisions. Later, he extracted a subset of the full REDUX model that led to the Redux' server (5), which does not contain a problem solver, but acts as decision maintenance server taking advantage of a justification-based TMS to represent the problem.

This paper reports on our work on extending the Redux' server with the objective of supporting the generation of explanations using modern software design techniques (2). In the following we briefly introduce the notion of explanation and the general explanation scenario in which Redux^{exp} plays the central role. Section 3 introduces the concept of decision maintenance of the REDUX model and presents an overview of the Redux' server. In Section 4, we extend Redux' and describe the justification-based explanation support server Redux^{exp} in more detail, followed by a brief example of the intended use of Redux^{exp} (Section 5). The last section summarises and concludes the paper with an outlook on future work.

2 Explanation

Explanations, in principle, are answers to questions, whether asked explicitly or only posed implicitly. The term explanation has been widely investigated in different disciplines such as cognitive science, knowledge-based systems, linguistics, philosophy of science, artificial intelligence, and teaching. All these disciplines consider certain aspects of the term and make clear that there is not only one such concept but a variety of concepts. This has as a consequence that there was no common agreement on how this term should be used. One of the reasons is that explanation is some kind of an umbrella term, which covers rather different kinds of explanations. As a consequence, the semantics of this term is ambiguous.

In the early 1980ies research on explanation was conducted in the context of knowledge-based systems, or expert systems as they were called at that time. But with the decline of expert systems research also interest in explanations dwindled. Only recently scientific interest was renewed as the increasing number of publications and workshops shows (cf., for example, (7)).

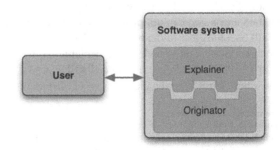

Fig. 1 Participants in explanation scenario (7)

We consider three participants in a general explanation scenario (7): *user*, *originator*, and *explainer* (Figure 1). The originator represents the agent that generates the output that is to be explained, e.g., the solution to a problem, a plan, or a recommendation. The explainer on the other hand is responsible for explaining the output of the originator to the user, which requires knowledge about the process that led to the results. In this scenario, Redux^{exp} plays an important part for the explainer by recording data generated by the originator for later usage in explanation generation.

Explanations play an important role in human understanding and decision-making (8). Their main purpose is to explain a solution and the path that led to the solution. In case of a decision support system their purpose also is to explain how the respective system works as well as how to handle the system.

Spieker (10) (see also (6)) distinguishes several useful kinds of explanations, of which two are of special interest here: Why- and How-explanations.[1] *Why-explanations* justify a decision. *How-explanations* are a special case of why-explanations. They describe the processes that led to a decision.

3 Decision Maintenance with the Redux' Server

The Redux' server (5) is a subset of the REDUX model. REDUX (4) is an architecture for solving constrained decision problems (CDP) in planning and design tasks. The problem itself is represented as goals and decisions with all their dependencies.

We briefly outline the REDUX model in its context of problem solving. We then describe the differences between the full REDUX architecture and the Redux' server, and shift the focus towards explanation support.

3.1 Planning, Design, and Heuristic Search

Although REDUX focuses on AI planning, one of its fundamental methods can be applied in a more generalized way: the *context rationale*. Simply put, the circumstances (context) that justify a choice (rationale) are recorded for later use; this context rationale isn't just restricted to planning problems, but can be applied to any decision a program (or agent) makes.

As an example for a planning problem Petrie takes the task of assigning lectures to university professors. There are constraints that restrict the solution space and heuristics that guide the search: *"One heuristic is to assign initially the courses to the professors that they wish to teach. A second heuristic is to assign courses to the more senior professors first. [...] Suppose that professor Descartes wants to teach PHL305 in the Fall, so we assign him a section of that class, PHL305-1. A less senior professor, Kant, also wants to teach PHL305 in the Fall. But if we assign*

---

[1] Why- and How-explanations have been introduced much earlier. See, for example, (9).

him a second section, PHL305-2, this violates a departmental constraint that there can only be one PHL305 taught per semester. So perhaps we reject this second assignment and instead give Kant a section of PHL380, which he indicated was his alternative choice to PHL305."

Kant probably wants to know *why* he didn't get his preferred course PHL305. The answer to that question is an explanation, more specifically, a *why-explanation*: *"Assigning Kant PHL305-2 would lead to a constraint violation, because Descartes got PHL305 first and there can only be one PHL305 taught per semester. PHL380 was Kant's alternative choice."* This explanation could certainly be more detailed, because Kant may also ask why this constraint exists or why Descartes has priority over PHL305 and not him. Already in (3) the usefulness of REDUX for explanation generation is apparent.

The context of a choice is the set of choices that have already been made. If there would be a third professor, who requires a course assigned to him, the first two choices would be the context of this new choice. The heuristic of assigning teacher preferences first results in a default context and also defines the rationale for this context. The constraint violation is the reason for the rejection of the default context, which in turn is the rationale for the choice of the less preferred course.

Suppose now there is another constraint, which prevents Descartes from teaching PHL305 and the course assignment must be revoked. Suddenly, the reason for the rejection of the default context is invalid, which again invalidates the rationale for choosing the less preferred course for Kant. Given this information, the problem solver of REDUX can now detect an opportunity to improve the solution locally, assuming that the heuristic leads to local optimality.

3.2 Truth Maintenance

In the example above a new constraint was added to the course schedule plan that made it inconsistent. The purpose of a Truth Maintenance System (TMS) is to propagate the effects of such plan changes and thereby maintain the plan's consistency.

REDUX uses a justification-based TMS (JTMS) (1), that can be viewed as a graph or network consisting of *nodes* and *justifications*, which are labeled either IN or OUT.

- A node is labeled IN ⇔ at least one of its supporting justifications is labeled IN.
- A justification is labeled IN ⇔ each element in its IN-list is labeled IN and each one in the OUT-list is labeled OUT.

Figure 2 depicts our example. A circle represents a justification. Nodes connected to the justification through a solid line are in its IN-list, those connected through a dotted line are in its OUT-list. Arrows point to the nodes being justified. Although this TMS network appropriately represents the above example, it reacts overly aggressive to changes. For example, if Descartes became unavailable, the TMS would automatically make the assignment of PHL305 to him invalid, which invalidates the

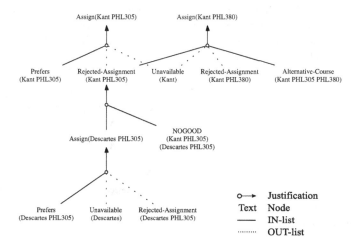

Fig. 2 TMS network of the course scheduling example (extended and adapted from (3))

rejection of PHL380 assigned to Kant and instead assigns PHL305 to him. The opportunity to improve the plan locally causes major changes to the whole plan, which might be worse than keeping a suboptimal decision.

3.3 The REDUX Model

Petrie introduced the REDUX model, which still uses a JTMS, but gives a higher-level view on the problem and allows a more detailed control over changes, as it is a more generalized manner of describing problems, representing them as goals and operators, in which both have the following properties:

1. Only one operator can be applied to a particular goal at one time.
2. Applying an operator can result in new subgoals, new variable assignments, or both, but at least in one of them.

A *goal* represents a task (primitive or complex) such as choosing the color of a new car, planning on where the next vacation will be spent or assigning a course to a professor. While choosing a color is probably a simple task, planning a vacation is most likely to be decomposed into *subgoals*, e.g., choosing an airline and a specific flight, booking a hotel, and organizing someone to take care of the house.

In most cases, there is more than one way to *satisfy* a goal, i.e., there is a set of conflicting operators, from which one must be chosen to *reduce* the goal. This choice is a *decision* with a *rationale*, which results in *subgoals* and *assignments* to be made. A decision may have *admissibility* conditions and it is only valid as long as these hold and it is not *retracted*.

In the course scheduling example, each decision resulted in exactly one assignment and had at least the admissibility condition of the professor being available. In the above mentioned case of planning a vacation, one decision can lead to multiple assignments and subgoals to be made.

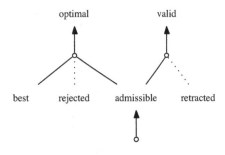

Fig. 3 TMS network of a decision

One of the reasons why a traditional TMS architecture is considered too aggressive is the fact that the sub-optimality of a decision immediately triggers its *rejection* and can thus change the whole plan. To avoid such behavior, the *validity* of a decision is separated from its (local) *optimality* (see Figure 3):

- A decision is *valid* if is admissible and not retracted.
- A decision is *optimal* if it has at least one valid rationale and no valid rejection reason and the goal to which it is applied is valid.

This enables the problem solver to choose whether to keep the sub-optimal decision or to retract it and thereby render it invalid. In case a decision is not admissible, the problem solver has no choice and the decision is automatically invalid. Referring to the example of the conflicting course assignments, the invalidation of the assignment of PHL305 to Descartes does not result in the invalidation of assigning PHL308 to Kant, but in its sub-optimality as Kant can now teach his preferred course, PHL305. It is up to the problem solver to decide whether to retract this decision or not. This separates problem representation and context maintenance from the task of problem solving, which resulted in Redux'.

3.4 The Redux' Server

As stated above, the Redux' server is a subset of the full REDUX architecture without a problem solver. It can serve as a central decision maintenance component. Figure 4 provides an overview of the two different software architectures: REDUX with a monolithic approach and Redux' with its client-server architecture.

The complete theory of Redux' (5) is summarised briefly in the following. Technical details have been adapted to fit more recent programming techniques.

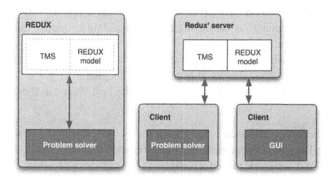

Fig. 4 Architecture of REDUX vs. Redux'

The four main classes used in Redux' are: *Decision, Goal, Reason*, and *Assignment*. Decisions, goals, and assignments are the same as in the full REDUX model, but assignments only have the slot *<variable-value>* with a single value of type *String* and Redux' neither has nor requires knowledge about its meaning. Reasons capture rationales as well as rejections and will be described later. Redux' also maintains a database of facts, which can be seen as assignments made by clients that do not depend upon decisions, e.g., the availability of a resource.

Decisions are the central part of the REDUX model and their state is described using the slots as shown in Table 1.

Table 1 Slots of decisions

Slot Name	Cardinality	Value Type
<name>	single	String
<objective>	single	Goal
<contingency>	multiple	String
<dependent>	multiple	Assignment
<rationale>	multiple	Reason
<rejection>	multiple	Reason
<assertion>	multiple	Assignment
<new-goal>	multiple	Goal
<retracted>	single	boolean
<committed>	single	boolean

Redux' offers commands for the manipulation of objects, such as adding or removing facts from the database, and making or rejecting decisions.

Decisions are described as a choice of an operator from a conflict set, but Redux' only knows the decision itself, and not the alternatives. This has some consequences:

- When the TMS network of a decision is created, the decision is made instantly. To reverse the decision, is must be retracted by adding a premise justification to the retracted node.
- To maintain consistency, a decision can only be made if its objective is unreduced, i.e., there is no other valid decision for this goal.
- When a decision is made, it is assumed to be the best choice in the current context.

The last property mentioned is the reason for the behavior in the course scheduling example: The rationale for making a decision other than the default decision was the rejection of it. To put it more formally:

- If a decision D_2 is made for a goal for which another decision D_1 was previously made but thereafter rejected, the rejection of D_1 will be conjoined to the rationale of D_2. In the case of multiple rejected decisions D_i for this goal, the rejection of each one will contribute to the rationale of D_2.

The last important property regards constraint violations and its solution. Redux' is not a problem solver and has no domain knowledge concerning the data it is maintaining. All assignments, facts, etc. are plain strings. Therefore, if a constraint violation was detected by an outside agent, it must be reported along with a solution in form of three lists (or sets):

1. A list L_c of conflicting assignments,
2. a list L_p of contributing propositions (facts), and
3. a list L_r of assignments, which must be retracted in order to solve the conflict.

Redux' then constructs a rejection reason R consisting of all conflicting assignments that have to be invalidated, together with the contributing propositions, or formally $(L_c \setminus L_r) \cup L_p$. Every decision that asserts an assignment of L_r will be rejected with reason R.

4 Extending Redux': The Justification-based Explanation Support Server Redux^{exp}

While REDUX uses context maintenance as a means to improve problem solving, Redux^{exp} reuses the same information for supporting automatic generation of some basic kinds of explanation, namely why- and how-explanations. Redux' already passes the task of problem solving to external agents; some additional modifications and extensions are needed to improve its capabilities for explanation support: namely provenance support and persistence.

Assuming Redux' was used for maintaining a set of decisions made during the execution of a program, there would already be some data that could explain, what circumstances lead to a decision. This probably is sufficient if there is only one decision making agent, but Redux' was intended for *"federating heterogeneous design agents"* (5). Providing information about the provenance of goals, decisions and facts will most likely increase the amount of trust in and understanding of the explanation. For example, the rationale of a decision made by a program may include some parameter that is a hardcoded default value, but the parameter could also be a user input overriding this default value in some configuration panel.

Every agent (human or computer) that uses the Redux^{exp} component is assigned a string that uniquely identifies it. Every time an ReduxObject is created, the time of creation and the identifier of the creator is stored within the object, allowing to provide information on *who* did *what when* and *why*. The *"how"* is outside the scope of Redux^{exp} and a task of the respective problem solver.

An explanation supporting system is not much use if it forgets the information upon program termination and it is not realistic to assume that the program runs infinitely. The ontology given in (3) and the graph-like structure of the data render RDF a good choice for long term storage. Also, there is no need to store the TMS structure itself, as the structure as well as the labels of the nodes are implicitly defined by the relations between the ReduxObjects.

Redux^{exp} implements a mechanism to serialize the complete model that has been built up during its usage into a single RDF/XML file. This file can later be deserialized and loaded into Redux^{exp} to restore the exact state of the model. It also allows any other implementation of Redux^{exp} to load the model from this file as long as it uses the same RDF schema.

4.1 Redux^{exp} Architecture

The architecture of Redux^{exp} is designed to simplify and centralize access for clients and at the same time prohibit direct manipulation of the model to avoid corruption of the provenance information (see Figure 5). In the following the actual implementation of the most important components is described.

In terms of object-oriented programming, the REDUX model in Redux' is represented by the classes: ReduxAssignment, ReduxDecision, ReduxFact, ReduxGoal, and ReduxReason. The prefix "Redux" is used to distinguish the classes from the actual concepts.

They share some common attributes and methods, so they have an abstract superclass ReduxObject. The original REDUX model by Petrie uses only names in the form of strings to identify and distinguish entities. Redux^{exp} makes use of Uniform Resource Identifiers (URIs) when saving a model to RDF. Also, all ReduxObjects have a validity state, whose meaning depends on the type of the object.

ReduxObjects maintain the relations to other ReduxObjects themselves, but they don't maintain their states, as this is the task of the TMS subsystem. The nodes and justifications in the underlying basic TMS have no semantics, so the REDUX model imposes a structure on them: Each node represents a certain aspect of a specific ReduxObject, such as validity, optimality, and admissibility.

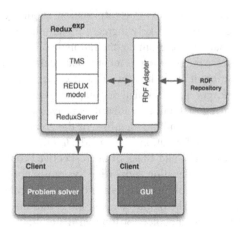

Fig. 5 ReduxExp encapsulates ReduxServer and
RDFAdapter to prohibit direct
model manipulation

The gap between the high-level ReduxObjects and the low-level ReduxTMS is
filled by the ReduxServer class, which connects the java ReduxObjects to their corresponding ReduxTMS subnets and the objects and subnets among each other. It
propagates the effects of actions and keeps the REDUX model consistent, e.g., when
a decision is made or rejected. The ReduxServer translates the high-level commands
of the model into their equivalent changes of the ReduxTMS. There are trivial commands such as the invalidation of a fact, which results in all premise justifications
of the facts validity node being removed, as well as more complex commands, e.g.,
when a new decision is made for a goal which already has a rejected decision, the
ReduxServer will create the right connections through nodes and justifications in
the ReduxTMS.

Another important task is to ensure that commands don't violate any constraints
of the REDUX model before they are executed, such as the identifier or name of a
ReduxObject being unique.

The RDFAdapter is responsible for saving and loading the state to and from an
RDF[2] model, which can be written to or read from a file in an RDF serialisation format, such as RDF/XML. The library used for this is RDF2Go[3] with an underlying
Sesame 2.0 repository[4], which is interchangeable due to the provided abstraction
layer. When saving, the RDFAdapter iterates over the list of all ReduxObjects it obtains from the ReduxServer and constructs RDF statements that describe the objects
and their connections. The unique identifier of a ReduxObject is only the local name
of the complete URI and the namespace is currently hardcoded to make it easier to
later integrate the data from Redux^{exp} with other applications that use RDF.

Loading a saved state of Redux^{exp} is slightly more difficult, because it uses the
same methods for creating the ReduxObject as are used at runtime. When ReduxDe-

---

[2] http://www.w3.org/RDF/

[3] http://ontoworld.org/wiki/RDF2Go

[4] http://www.openrdf.org/

cisions or ReduxReasons are created, all objects they depend on must already exist. This is not a problem during normal program execution, but decisions and reasons can depend on each other in a way that results in a dependency cycle. To resolve this problem, the ReduxObjects are restored according to the following schema:

1. Iterate over all facts, assignments and goals and create the objects.
2. Iterate over all decisions and create the ReduxDecisions with all connections excluding reasons.
3. Iterate over all reasons and create the ReduxReason objects.
4. Iterate over all decisions again and connect them to the rationales and rejection reasons.

Basically, the ReduxServer class is an implementation of the Redux' server with minor modifications while the RDFAdapter offers a persistence layer to the architecture. The ReduxExp class represents a further abstraction of these two services, encapsulating them and restricting external access. In the current implementation, the constructor is public and expects two arguments, the ReduxServer and a string identifying the agent. For a production environment an authentication mechanism needs to be added.

4.2 Behaviour Specifics

As shown above, there are some non-trivial aspects of the behaviour of Redux^{exp} that need to be explained in more detail. The process of loading a saved model became non-trivial because of the same methods used for creating ReduxObjects in different contexts (building and loading the model). A similar situation occurs when a decision is made. Formally, making a decision means changing the validity of a decision from invalid to valid, which happens in three different cases:

- creating a new decision for an objective
- loading a model from file
- making a decision that already exists and was retracted

In Redux', decisions are created at the first time they are made, which also means that a decision cannot be created without being made. But this only accounts for the "working-mode" of Redux^{exp}, i.e. when some agent triggers the creation of a decision. When loading a model from a file, there may be multiple decision for one objective, which means that at most one of this decisions can be valid, the rest has to be invalid. There may also be some decisions that cannot be valid without violating constraints, e.g. a decision with a valid contingency. As a consequence, it is necessary for Redux^{exp} to be able to create decisions without automatically making them.

Another problem is the behavior of Redux^{exp} when a decision is created for an objective that already has decisions, but which are rejected. In this case the rejection of all previously made decisions would add to the rationale for the newly made decision. But when decisions are created while loading a model from a file, adding new relations between ReduxObjects would actively change the model, thus leading to a different model than the one saved to the file.

In the last case, when a retracted decision is made valid again, there should also be no modification to the rationale, because the relations to other decisions have already been established at the time of the creation of the decision.

This leads to three different steps when creating or making a decision:

1. Create the ReduxDecision object with the validity passed as boolean argument.
2. Make the ReduxDecision object valid, if no constraints are violated (such as valid rejection reasons).
3. Add the rejection of existing ReduxDecisions for the objective to the decisions rationale.

When a decision is created during normal operation, all three steps need to be executed, whereas loading a model from a file only executes step 1, and making a decision that was previously retracted only executes step 2.

5 Explanation Support

Redux^{exp} itself does not generate explanations, but it supports this process by providing the necessary information. The example of the course scheduling problem is used again to demonstrate a possible way of doing so. We assume that the process of planning the course assignments was already performed by some agent, here called Administrator. Later, Kant wants to know, if his request to teach PHL305 was granted, so at first he needs to retrieve that information:

```
FOR EACH assignment IN redux.getAllAssignments() {
    IF assignment.getName() == "Kant teaches PHL305"
        RETURN assignment;
}
PRINT assignment.isValid();
```

It is apparent that the above query only succeeds, because there exists some convention about how assignments are named. For now, it is assumed that this problem is somehow solved by the agents. Kant sees that the assignment of PHL305 to him is invalid and asks the question: "Why didn't I get to teach PHL305?"

To answer this question, it is necessary to find the decision that asserts this assignment and then ask for the reason why this decision is invalid.

```
decisions[] = redux.getDecisionsForAssignment(assignment);
```

The result of this query is a list, because there may be multiple decision asserting this assignment, In this case it is only one decision, for which the rationales and rejection reasons can be retrieved.

```
rationales[] = decisions[0].getRationales();
rejections[] = decisions[0].getRejectionReasons();
```

All the information gathered until now are sufficient to construct a simple explanation: "The decision that asserts 'Kant teaches PHL305' was rejected, because there exists a valid rejection reason."

```
ReduxReason rejection = rejections[0];

PRINT "Assignments: ";
FOR EACH a IN rejection.getConditionAssignments {
    PRINT a.getName() + " by " + a.getCreator();
}
PRINT "Facts: ";
FOR EACH f IN rejection.getConditionFacts {
    PRINT f.getName() + " by " + f.getCreator();
}
PRINT "Rejected decisions: ";
FOR EACH d IN rejection.getConditionDecisions {
    PRINT d.getName() + " by " + d.getCreator();
}
```

This code generates the following output, which is a very simple why-explanation:

```
Assignments: "Descartes teaches PHL305" by 'Administrator'
Facts: "At most one teacher per course" by 'Administrator'
Rejected decisions: none
```

6 Summary and Outlook

In this paper we presented an extension of the Redux' server and moved its focus away from problem solving support to explanation generation support. The basic assumption is that the information used by a problem solver to improve a solution can also be used to increase the trust of humans into the output of computer programs. The server-like design promotes scenarios where multiple clients interact and justification is inherent to the problem. Redux^{exp} is seen as an example component of the explainer described in Section 2.

The type of representation of assignments (and facts) has no influence on the functioning of Redux^{exp} because it does not process but only stores them. The example in Section 5 presented such a situation, in which the success of a query highly depended on the correct representation of a specific assignment.

Today, 15 years later, several standardized specifications of how to represent general data exist and are widely used. A promising candidate for a better representation of assignments are RDF statements, as they allow more general statements than simple variable-value assignments, but even complex relations between entities, while being well defined and easily parseable. This allows the usage of query languages, such as SPARQL to search the made assignments or even check for constraint violations of OWL ontologies.

The effort of logging decisions during program execution would be useless without actual explanations generated and presented to the user, which can be textual or visual and may include domain knowledge to enhance comprehensibility. Adapting to the user's level of knowledge is important for a good explanation, which can be supported by a variable level of detail or interactivity of the presentation.

The premises for the generation of good explanations most likely lead to additional requirements for decision logging and these two aspects must be examined in close relation.

Acknowledgements The implementation of Redux^{exp} is loosely based on source code written by Sigrid Goldmann. We also would like to thank Charles J. Petrie, who patiently answered all our questions regarding REDUX and Redux'.

References

[1] Doyle, J.: A truth maintenance system. Artificial Intelligence **12**(3), 231–272 (1979)

[2] Mittag, F.: ReduxExp: A justification-based explanation-support server. Project thesis, University of Kaiserslautern (2008)

[3] Petrie, C.J.: Context maintenance. In: AAAI, pp. 288–295 (1991). URL http://dblp.uni-trier.de/db/conf/aaai/aaai91-1.html#Petrie91

[4] Petrie, C.J.: Constrained decision revision. In: AAAI, pp. 393–400 (1992)

[5] Petrie, C.J.: The Redux' server. In: G. Schlageter, M. Huhns, M. Papazoglou (eds.) Proceedings of the International Conference on Intelligent and Cooperative Information Systems, pp. 134–143. IEEE Computer Society Press, Rotterdam, the Netherlands (1993). URL http://citeseer.ist.psu.edu/petrie93redux.html

[6] Roth-Berghofer, T.R.: Explanations and Case-Based Reasoning: Foundational issues. In: P. Funk, P.A. González-Calero (eds.) Advances in Case-Based Reasoning, pp. 389–403. Springer-Verlag (2004)

[7] Roth-Berghofer, T.R., Richter, M.M.: On explanation. Künstliche Intelligenz **22**(2), 5–7 (2008)

[8] Schank, R.C.: Explanation Patterns: Understanding Mechanically and Creatively. Lawrence Erlbaum Associates, Hillsdale, NJ (1986)

[9] Scott, A.C., Clancey, W.J., Davis, R., Shortliffe, E.: Methods for generating explanations. American Journal of Computational Linguistics, Microfiche 62 (1977). (Revised version in Buchanan, B.G. and Shortlife, E.H. (1984) Rule-based expert systems. Addison Wesley)

[10] Spieker, P.: Natürlichsprachliche Erklärungen in technischen Expertensystemen. Dissertation, University of Kaiserslautern (1991)

[11] Swartout, W.R., Moore, J.D.: Explanation in second generation expert systems. In: J. David, J. Krivine, R. Simmons (eds.) Second Generation Expert Systems, pp. 543–585. Springer Verlag, Berlin (1993)

SHORT PAPERS

Immunity-based hybrid evolutionary algorithm for multi-objective optimization

Eugene Y.C. Wong[1], Henry S.C. Yeung[2], and Henry Y.K. Lau[3]

Abstract The development of evolutionary algorithms for optimization has been a growing research area. A novel immunity-based hybrid evolutionary algorithm known as Hybrid Artificial Immune Systems (HAIS) for solving both unconstrained and constrained multi-objective optimization problems is developed. The algorithm adopts the clonal selection and immune suppression theories, with a sorting scheme featuring uniform crossover, multi-point mutation, non-dominance and crowding distance sorting to attain Pareto optimal in an efficient manner. The algorithm was verified with nine benchmarking functions on its global optimal search ability and compared with four optimization algorithms to assess its diversity and spread. It is found that the immunity-based algorithm provides a useful means for solving optimization problems, and has proved its capability in global optimal search in multi-objective optimization.

1. Introduction

Researches in evolutionary algorithm lie within the realm of bio-inspired computing that concern the use of biological inspired concepts to solve computational and industrial problems. There are many representative evolutionary algorithms for solving optimization problems. One of such algorithms is the artificial immune systems (AIS). Researchers including de Castro and Von Zuben (2000) applied the clonal selection algorithm in immune system to solve traveling salesmen problems (TSP). Endoh et al. (1998) proposed an immunity-based optimization algorithm to solve the nth agent traveling salesman problem called n-TSP. Other researches considered multi-objective optimization and performed computer simulations. Zhang (2007) developed a new

1 Orient Overseas Container Line Limited, Harbour Road, Wanchai, Hong Kong
eugene.wong@oocl.com

2 University of Hong Kong, Pokfulam Road, Hong Kong
h0512964@hkusua.hku.hk

3 University of Hong Kong, Pokfulam Road, Hong Kong
hyklau@hku.hk

dynamical immune optimization algorithm for constrained nonlinear multi-objective optimization problems, and Chen and Mahfouf (2006) proposed a novel population adaptive based immune algorithm (PAIA) for solving multi-objective optimization problems. This paper introduces an immunity-based hybrid evolutionary algorithm known as Hybrid Artificial Immune Systems (HAIS) for solving multi-objective optimization problems. It performs global optimal search through the adoption of the clonal selection and immune suppression theories, and includes key features of uniform crossover and multi-point mutation to efficiently attain the Pareto-front. The developed algorithm is evaluated with benchmarking functions and similar optimization algorithms.

2. Immunity-based Hybrid Evolutionary Algorithm

2.1 Principles and theories

HAIS is characterized by the features of distributed memory, learning, adaptability, self-regulation, and diversity. The effectiveness of the immune response to secondary encountering of antigens is enhanced by the presence of memory cells associated with the first infection. Instead of starting afresh every time, an intrinsic scheme of reinforcement learning strategy is adopted to ensure a fast and accurate immune response after subsequent infection. HAIS also regulates the number of antibodies and increases the diversity of the antibodies in the population through suppression, recruitment, and crossover. The analogies of HAIS with the biological immune system are given in Table 1.

Table 1. Mappings of human immune system entities and HAIS

Immune System	HAIS
Antigen	A Single Objective / Multi-Objective problem
Antibody	Candidate solution
Immune memory	Archive
Memory cell	Archived solution
Clonal selection	Selection of antibodies with respect to their affinity
Suppression	Eliminating antibodies with close affinity values
Identification of effective antibodies	Affinity calculation
Antibody production and recruitment	Crossover and mutation operator

Clonal Selection and Immune Suppression

The concept of domination was adopted for multi-objective optimization search operation where clonal selection (Burnet, 1957) is used for solution exploitation. In the algorithm, two solutions are compared on the basis of whether one has dominated the other. The dominance rating of an antibody is calculated by the affinity value. A high affinity implies a high dominance rating, implying a better solution. The search of optimal solutions is further enhanced by adopting the immune suppression characteristics where similar antibodies in the population are being suppressed and eliminated based on the crowding distance (Deb et al., 2000). This scheme helps the diversified search for global optima.

Uniform crossover operation and Multi-point Mutation Operator
Crossover increases the diversity of the population and enhances the optimal search convergence. Uniform crossover operator produces offspring by cloning the corresponding gene chosen on a randomly generated crossover mask(s). HAIS mutation operator adopts the mechanisms of receptor editing and somatic mutation. The real-valued chromosomes and mutation operators, namely, geometric creep and random replacement are adopted (Beasley et al., 1993). As the gene is altered by a continuous and controlled step, the antibody will be guided towards the local optima.

2.2 Algorithm Design

Based on the mappings described in Table 1, the procedures of HAIS are set up with control parameters including population size, crossover rate ($c\%$), mutation rate ($m\%$), and archive size. The main steps of HAIS are given below:

Initialization: An initial random population of antibodies is created. It simulates innate immunity.

Affinity evaluation: The constraint penalty function and objective function are calculated for each antibody.

Exploitation and exploration: By applying the Pareto-dominance sorting scheme, a constraint penalty function is taken as one of the objectives; with the single objective problem restated as a multi-objective problem based on the Pareto dominance concept.

Proliferation: A number of antibodies are selected and cloned to archive for memory. Excess memory cells with lower affinity are trimmed from the archive.

Receptor editing and Somatic mutation: The $m\%$ of the population with a higher ranking in affinity measure is selected and undergone mutation.

Suppression and recruitment: After the mutation process on the "good" antibodies, $c\%$ of the antibodies with lower affinity ranking is eliminated. New antibodies are produced from the archive by the crossover operator to replenish the population.

Iteration: The above steps are repeated until the stopping condition is met. The conditions are set by the target number of iterations and the target elapse time, and/or by considering the change or improvement in solution of the offspring.

3. Simulations on Optimal Search Performance Benchmarking

3.1 Benchmarking Function Suite

Nine single and multi-objective optimization functions are used to benchmark HAIS. Unconstrained single objective functions include Sphere Function and

Rosenbrock Function (Montiel et al., 2007) and unconstrained multi-objective test functions, namely ZDT1 – 4 and ZDT6 are used (Zitzler et al., 2000). Constrained multi-objective benchmarking tests are also performed using Constr-Ex (Deb, 2001) and BNH (Binh and Korn, 2001). The GA tool Evolver (Laguna, 1997) is used as an implementation platform. Same parameters and configurations are used with 500 generations over 30 trials were performed. The results showed that HAIS outperformed GA in converging to a solution in the first 100 generations.

Table 2. The mean and variance of results from HAIS and GA over 30 trials

Benchmarking Functions	HAIS		GA	
	Mean	Variance	Mean	Variance
Sphere Function	0.000161	3.54E-08	306.7045	3438.832
Rosenbrock Function	2.193986	1.758235	38.84761	1800.696

Figure 1. Convergence of HAIS and GA on Sphere function and Rosenbrock function.

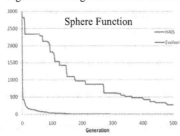 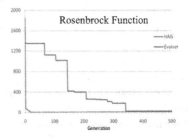

3.2 Multi-objective Functions Benchmarking

Using ZDT1 – 4 and ZDT6, the algorithm is run for 250 generations with over 30 trials, each started with a population size of 100 and archive size of 100. Optimal fronts are obtained as shown in Figure 2.

Figure 2. Pareto plots ZDT1, ZDT2, and ZDT3 function solved by HAIS

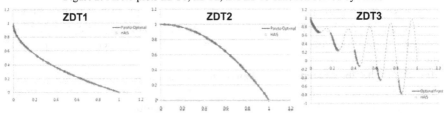

For constrained optimization benchmarking, the algorithm is run with 250 generations over 10 trials. The results show that HAIS solutions fall on the Pareto optimal front for both Constr-Ex and BNH functions. This shows that HAIS can converge to the Pareto optimal even with hard constraints.

Table 3. Generational distance and spread of HAIS over 10 trials

Functions	Generational Distance		Spread	
	Mean	Variance	Mean	Variance
Constr-Ex	0.61929	0.01225	1.20124	0.0018
BNH	2.69605	0.26329	0.61829	0.00391

Figure 3. Pareto plots of Constr-Ex (Left) and BNH (Right) functions solved by HAIS

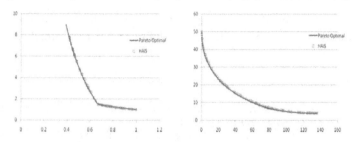

3.3 Comparison with Evolutionary Algorithms

Comparison with other evolutionary algorithms, namely, Pareto Archived Evolutionary Strategy (PAES) (Knowles and Corne, 2000), Strength Pareto Evolutionary Algorithm II (SPEA-II) (Zitzler et al., 2001), Evolutionary Multi-objective Crowding Algorithm (EMOCA) (Rajagopalan et al., 2005), and Non-dominated Sorting Genetic Algorithm (NSGA-II) (Deb et al., 2000) were undertaken. 250 generations over 30 trials were run. Two performance metrics, namely, the (i) generation distance (GD) (Veldhuizen and Lamont, 2000) and (ii) spread metric (Deb et al., 2000) are used to compare their performance.

The results of the mean and variance of GD with 30 trials illustrate that HAIS shows better convergence than NSGA-II in all cases except ZDT2. HAIS performed the best on convergence in ZDT1 and ZDT4 while it fell behind in EMOCA for ZDT2 and ZDT3. The mean and variance of the spread metric over 30 trials are also reviewed. The results indicated that HAIS has not performed as well as other algorithms regarding diversification. The distribution of the solutions of HAIS was concentrated especially in ZDT3. Meanwhile, HAIS outperformed the others in ZDT6. The solutions on the Pareto optimal front of ZDT6 are originally non-uniformly distributed, showing a higher capability of HAIS on tackling non-uniformly distributed problems.

4. Conclusion

A novel immunity-based hybrid evolutionary algorithm known as Hybrid Artificial Immune Systems (HAIS) was developed for solving multi-objective problems. It integrates the distinct characteristics of Clonal selection and genetic theories to search for global optimal fronts. The algorithm has been studied using benchmarking functions and other similar algorithms. Further improvements can be made on the spread of search capability and the ability to solving uniform problem sets. It is encouraged to see the performance of HAIS and its ability to obtain optimal solutions in a timely and efficient manner.

Acknowledgement

The work described in this paper was partly supported by the Research Grant Council of the Hong Kong SAR under the GRF Project No. HKU7142/06E.

References

1. Beasley, D., Bull, D.R., Martin, R.R., 1993. An Overview of Genetic Algorithms: Part 2, Research Topics. *University Computing*, 15 (4): 170-181.
2. Binh, Korn U., 2001. MOBES: A Multi-objective Evolution Strategy for Constrained Optimization Problems. *The Third International Conference on Genetic Algorithm*, pp. 176-182.
3. Burnet, F.M., 1957. A Modification of Jerne's Theory of Antibody Production Using the Concept of Clonal Selection. *The Australian Journal of Science 20*: 67-69.
4. Chen, J., Mahfouf, M., 2006. A Population Adaptive Based Immune Algorithm for Solving Multiobjective Optimization Problems, Bersini, H., and Carneiro (Eds.). *ICARIS 2006*, LNCS 4163, 280-293.
5. de Castro, L.N., Von Zuben, F.J., 2000. The Clonal Selection Algorithm with Engineering Applications. In Workshop Proceedings of GECCO'00, pp. 36-37, *Workshop on Artificial Immune Systems and Their Applications*, Las Vegas, USA.
6. Deb, K., Pratap, A., Agarwal, S., Meyarivan, T., 2000. A fast and elitist multi-objective genetic algorithm: NSGA-II. *Proc. Parallel Problem Solving from Nature VI*, pp. 849-845.
7. Deb, K., 2001. Multi-objective Optimization, *Multi-objective Optimization Using Evolutionary Algorithms*, Wiley, 2001, pp. 13-48.
8. Endoh, S., Toma, N., Yamada, K., 1998. Immune Algorithm for n-TSP. *Proceeding of the IEEE Systems, Man, and Cybernetics Conference*, pp. 3844-3849.
9. Knowles, J.D., Corne, D.W., 2000. Approximating the nondominated front using the Pareto Archived Evolution Strategy, *Evolutionary Computation*, 8(2): 149-172.
10. Laguna, M., 1997. Metaheuristic Optimization with Evolver, Genocop and OptQuest. *Metaheuristic Optimization*.
11. Montiel, O., Castillo, O., Melin, P., Diaz, A.R., Sepulveda, R., 2007. Human evolutionary model: A new approach to optimization. *Information Sciences*, 177: 6-9.
12. Rajagopalan, R., Mohan, C.K., Mehrotra, K.G., Varshney, P.K., 2005. An Evolutionary Multi-Objective Crowding Algorithm (EMOCA): Benchmark Test Function Results. *IICAI 2005*, pp. 1488-1506.
13. Veldhuizen, D.A.V., Lamont, G.B., 2000. On Measuring Multiobjective Evolutionary Algorithm Performance, *Proc. 2000 Congress on Evolutionary Computation*, 1: 204-211.
14. Zhang, Z., 2007. Immune optimization algorithm for constrained nonlinear multiobjective optimization problems. *Applied Soft Computing*, 7: 840-857.
15. Zitzler, E., Deb, K., Thiele, L., 2000. Comparison of Multi-Objective Evolutionary Algorithms: Empirical Results. *Evolutionary Computation Journal*, 8(2): 125-148.
16. Zitzler, E., Laumanns, M., Thiele, L., 2001. SPEA2: Improving the strength pareto evolutionary algorithm, Swiss Federal Institute of Technology, Tech-Rep. TIK-Rep, 103.

Parallel Induction of Modular Classification Rules

Frederic Stahl[1], Max Bramer[1] and Mo Adda[1]

Abstract The Distributed Rule Induction (DRI) project at the University of Portsmouth is concerned with distributed data mining algorithms for automatically generating rules of all kinds. In this paper we present a system architecture and its implementation for inducing modular classification rules in parallel in a local area network using a distributed blackboard system. We present initial results of a prototype implementation based on the Prism algorithm.

1. Introduction

The field of Data Mining from large collections of data has experienced a considerable upsurge of commercial interest and research activity in recent years.

So far relatively little attention has been given to distributing or parallelising data mining algorithms, but as the size of datasets requiring analysis continues to increase it seems inevitable that this will become a major focus of attention. Most data mining algorithms make the implicit assumption that all the training data can be stored and processed in main memory. It is common practice to take a sample of stored data to form a training set for analysis, but as long ago as 1992, Catlett[1] pointed out the loss of predictive accuracy that can result from sampling very large training sets. The datasets considered very large at that time would be considered commonplace by today's standards. In scientific fields such as bioinformatics and cosmology it may be particularly important to process all the data available or risk overlooking valuable relationships in the data.

The Distributed Rule Induction (DRI) project at the University of Portsmouth is concerned with distributed data mining algorithms for automatically generating rules of all kinds. Most rule induction has been for the purpose of classification [2] and the most common approach to classification rule generation is via the intermediate form of a decision tree [2]. Although popular this method suffers from the problem of overfitting and it is generally considered desirable to post-

---

[1] School of Computing, University of Portsmouth, PO1 3HE, UK
{Frederic.Stahl; Max.Bramer; Mo.Adda}@port.ac.uk

prune the trees generated before converting them to rules and then to process the rules further to remove overfitted terms as far as possible [3]. This seems an unnecessarily indirect way to generate rules, especially when there are algorithms that will generate them directly, albeit ones that are less widely known.

The Prism algorithm was developed as an alternative to decision tree generation [4]. For continuous data the algorithm can be summarised as follows, assuming that there are n (>1) possible classes [5].

```
For each class i from 1 to n inclusive:
(a) working dataset W = initial Dataset;
    delete all records that match the rules that have
    been derived so far for class i;
(b) For each attribute A in W
  - sort the data according to A;
    - for each possible split value v of attribute A
      calculate the probability that the class is i
      for both subsets A < v and A ≥ v;
(c) Select the attribute that has the subset S with
    the overall highest probability;
(d) build a rule term describing S;
(e) W = S;
(f) Repeat b to e until the dataset contains only
    records of class i. The induced rule is then
    the conjunction of all the rule terms built at
    step d;
(g) Repeat a to f until all records of class i have
    been removed;
```

Cendrowska's original version of Prism requires the training set to be processed once for each class. It is restored to its original form before each new class is processed. A faster version of Prism has been developed by one of the present authors [6], called PrismTCS (**Prism** with **T**arget **C**lass, **S**mallest first) which maintains a similar level of predictive accuracy. After each rule induced PrismTCS computes the *target class* that covers the fewest instances and induces a new rule for that target class. Thus PrismTCS removes the outermost loop and lowers Prism's complexity. We removed the innermost loop, the multiple sorting of the dataset, by building attribute lists similar to those in the SPRINT algorithm [5, 7] of the structure *<record id, attribute value, class value>*.

Figure 1 shows experimental results with pre-sorting on the *diabetes* dataset [8]. We appended the data to itself either 'vertically' or 'horizontally' to obtain datasets with an increasingly large number of instances or attributes, respectively. We refer to data created by appending in the vertical direction as *portrait data* and to data created by appending in the horizontal direction as *landscape data*.

The speedup factors for all runs were positive, however decreasing for portrait data with increasing number of instances. However for data in landscape format the advantage of pre-sorting is increasingly linear.

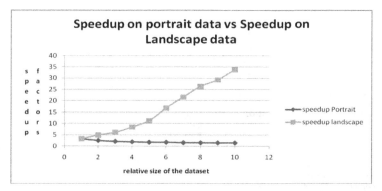

Figure 1 The speedup factors plotted versus the relative dataset size for datasets growing towards landscape and portrait format.

A version of PrismTCS incorporating the pre-sorting technique is currently being implemented. We expect that this will lead to higher speedups.

2. P-Prism: A Parallel Modular Classification Rule Induction Algorithm

There have been several attempts to scale up classification rule induction via parallelisation. In the area of TDIDT we have already mentioned the SPRINT [7] algorithm. Here we focus on parallelising modular classification rule induction using a "shared nothing" or "massively parallel processors" (MPP) system. Our reasoning is that MPP can be represented by a network of workstations and thus is a cheap way of running parallel algorithms. We implemented the parallel Prism (P-Prism) algorithm in a logical master worker fashion by running the basic Prism algorithm on a master machine and outsourcing the computationally expensive tasks, the induction of rule terms, to worker machines in the network. As a communication platform between the Prism algorithm and the worker machines we used a distributed blackboard system architecture based on the DARBS distributed blackboard system [9]. A blackboard system can be imagined as a physical blackboard which is observed by several experts with different knowledge domains, having a common problem to solve. Each expert uses its knowledge domain plus knowledge written on the blackboard to infer new knowledge about the problem and advertise it to the other experts by writing it on the blackboard. In the software model such a blackboard system can be represented by a client-server architecture. The basic architecture of P-Prism is shown in Figure 2.

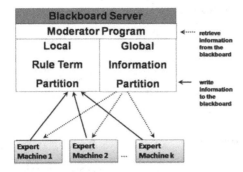

Figure 2. The architecture of the P-Prism algorithm using a distributed blackboard system in order to parallelise the induction of modular rule terms.

The attribute lists are distributed over k expert machines. The moderator program on the blackboard server implements the Prism algorithm, with the difference from the serial version that it delegates the rule term induction to the expert machines. The blackboard system is partitioned into two logical partitions, one to submit local rule term information and one to retrieve global information about the algorithm's status. Every expert is able to induce the rule term that is locally the best one for the attribute lists it holds. It then writes the induced rule term plus its covering probability and how many instances the rule term covers on the local rule term information partition and awaits the global information of how to continue.

The following steps listed below describe how P-Prism induces one rule:

```
Step 1 Moderator (P-Prism) writes on "Global Information Partition"
       the command to induce locally best rule terms.
Step 2 All Experts induce the locally best rule term and write the
       rule terms plus its covering probability and the number of
       list records covered on the "local Rule Term Partition"
Step 3 Moderator (P-Prism) compares all rule terms written on the
       "Local Rule Term Partition"; adds best term to the current
       rule; writes the name of the Expert that induced the best rule
       term on the Global Information Partition
Step 4 Expert retrieves name of winning expert.
       IF Expert is winning expert {
           derive by last induced rule term uncovered ids and write
           them on the "Global Information Partition" and delete
           uncovered list records
       }
       ELSE IF Expert is not winning expert {
           wait for by best rule term uncovered ids being available
           on the "Global Information Partition", download them and
           delete list records matching the retrieved ids.
       }
```

In order to induce the next rule term, P-Prism would loop back to step one. For P-Prism to know when to stop the rule it needs to know when the remaining list records on the expert machines are either empty or consist only of instances of the current target class. This information is communicated between the winning expert and the moderator program using the Global Information Partition.

3. Experimental Results

The first prototype of the P-Prism classifier has been implemented and we have carried out an initial validation in order to identify constraints for future developments. We have carried out experiments with 3 different configurations of P-Prism and serial Prism with attribute lists. We used the *yeast* dataset [8] which comprises 1484 instances, but repeatedly appended the data to itself 'vertically' to achieve datasets with from 5000 to 35000 instances. Both versions of Prism, the serial and the parallel, produce identical rule sets (with 970 terms) on any of the yeast datasets.

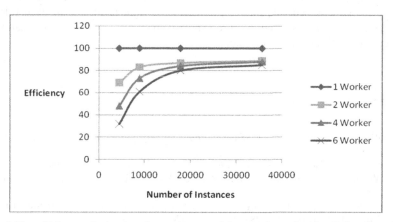

Figure 3 The efficiency calculated as the percentage of the actual speedup factors based on the ideal speedup factors for configurations of P-Prism with one (serial Prism), two, four and six expert machines.

The efficiency is the fraction of the actual speedup factor based on the ideal speedup factor of P-Prism. However achieving an ideal speedup factor is unrealistic as in any MPP environment we have to take overheads in bandwidth and workload balancing into account. The efficiencies for all P-Prism configurations increase with an increasing number of instances up to a workload of about 17000 instances. From then on the efficiency levels off, ranging from 85% to 89%. As already mentioned the discrepancy from 100% efficiency can be explained by communication overheads and workload balancing issues. However further speedup experiments are planned with more instances and more expert machines to examine the breakeven point of possible expert machines.

4. Ongoing and Future Work

Our experiments with P-Prism were based on the assumption that all expert machines have the same computational resources. This is not realistic and so we are currently working on an initial workload balancing strategy. All attribute lists will initially be advertised on a central server. Each expert will take an attribute list from the server, process it by scanning it for covering probabilities, and if there are more attribute lists left, it will take further ones until there are no attribute lists left. This will lead to an initial workload balancing as faster expert machines will retrieve more attribute lists from the scoreboard. A parallel version of PrismTCS based on P-Prism is also in development with which we hope to obtain better scale up results than those for P-Prism.

Our experiments with Prism show the value of the methods we have adopted. Prism has been used as an exemplar of an important class of rule generation algorithms, where each attribute can be processed independently of the others as rule terms are generated. Most rule covering algorithms are of this kind, including those for generalized rule induction (where the right-hand side of each rule can potentially be a conjunction of attribute/value pairs for any combination of categorical attributes) as well as classification.

References

1. Catlett J., *Megainduction: Machine learning on very large databases*. 1991, University of Technology, Sydney.
2. Quinlan J. R., *Induction of decision trees. Machine Learning*. Vol. 1. 1986. 81-106.
3. I.Witten and E.Frank. Data Mining: Practical Machine Learning Tools and Techniques. Elsevier, 2005.
4. Cendrowska J., *PRISM: an Algorithm for Inducing Modular Rules*. International Journal of Man-Machine Studies, 1987. **27**: p. 349-370.
5. Stahl F. and Bramer M., *Towards a Computationally Efficient Approach to Modular Classification Rule Induction*. Twenty-seventh SGAI International Conference on Innovative Techniques and Applications of Artificial Intelligence, 2007.
6. Bramer M., *An Information-Theoretic Approach to the Pre-pruning of Classification Rules*. Proceedings of the IFIP Seventeenth World Computer Congress - TC12 Stream on Intelligent Information Processing. 2002: Kluwer, B.V. 201-212.
7. Shafer J. C., Agrawal R., and Mehta M., *SPRINT: A Scalable Parallel Classifier for Data Mining*. Twenty-second International Conference on Very Large Data Bases, 1996.
8. Blake C. L. and Merz C. J, *UCI repository of machine learning databases*. 1998, University of California, Irvine, Department of Information and Computer Sciences.
9. Nolle L., Wong K. C. P., and Hopgood A., *DARBS: A Distributed Blackboard System*. Twenty-first SGES International Conference on Knowledge Based Systems, 2001.

Transform Ranking: a New Method of Fitness Scaling in Genetic Algorithms

A. A. Hopgood[1] and A. Mierzejewska[2]

Abstract The first systematic evaluation of the effects of six existing forms of fitness scaling in genetic algorithms is presented alongside a new method called transform ranking. Each method has been applied to stochastic universal sampling (SUS) over a fixed number of generations. The test functions chosen were the two-dimensional Schwefel and Griewank functions. The quality of the solution was improved by applying sigma scaling, linear rank scaling, nonlinear rank scaling, probabilistic nonlinear rank scaling, and transform ranking. However, this benefit was always at a computational cost. Generic linear scaling and Boltzmann scaling were each of benefit in one fitness landscape but not the other. A new fitness scaling function, transform ranking, progresses from linear to nonlinear rank scaling during the evolution process according to a transform schedule. This new form of fitness scaling was found to be one of the two methods offering the greatest improvements in the quality of search. It provided the best improvement in the quality of search for the Griewank function, and was second only to probabilistic nonlinear rank scaling for the Schwefel function. Tournament selection, by comparison, was always the computationally cheapest option but did not necessarily find the best solutions.

1   Introduction

Two common forms of selection for reproduction in a genetic algorithm are roulette wheel sampling with replacement and stochastic universal sampling (SUS). Both are forms of fitness-proportional selection, i.e., the probability of an individual being chosen for reproduction is proportional to its fitness. Such approaches are susceptible to both premature convergence and stalled evolution.

[1] Professor Adrian A. Hopgood
Faculty of Technology, De Montfort University, The Gateway, Leicester, LE1 9BH, UK
e-mail: aah@dmu.ac.uk

[2] Ms Aleksandra Mierzejewska
Faculty of Automatic Control, Electronics & Computer Science, Silesian University of Technology, ul. Akademicka 2A, 44-100 Gliwice, Poland
e-mail: aleksandra.mierzejewska@gmail.com

To overcome these problems, fitness scaling methods have been devised to transform the raw fitness, i.e. the objective function, into a scaled selective function used in selecting individuals for reproduction [1]. This paper presents the first systematic analysis and comparison of the performance of a range of six existing fitness scaling methods against two challenging benchmark optimization problems. A new scaling technique called transform ranking is also introduced and evaluated. These seven techniques are also compared with tournament selection, for which the application of fitness scaling would have no effect, since tournament selection is determined by the rank ordering of fitness rather than absolute values.

2 Fitness scaling

Fitness scaling can be applied at the early stages of evolution to weaken selection and thereby encourage exploration of the whole search space. Conversely, at the late stages of evolution, fitness scaling is intended to strengthen the selection pressure in order to converge on the exact optimum. Six existing approaches to fitness scaling are considered here. More detail is available in [1].

Generic linear scaling:
This is a simple linear relationship between the scaled fitness, s_i, and raw fitness f_i. Kreinovich *et al* [2] have demonstrated mathematically that linear scaling is the optimal form of scaling, but only if optimal scaling parameters are known.

Sigma scaling:
Sigma scaling is a variant of linear scaling where an individual's fitness is scaled according to its deviation from the mean fitness of the population, measured in standard deviations (i.e., 'sigma', σ).

Boltzmann scaling:
Boltzmann scaling is a nonlinear method that uses the idea of a "temperature", T, that drops slowly from generation to generation.

Linear rank scaling:
In linear rank scaling, the scaled fitnesses are evenly spread based on the rank ordering of the chromosomes from the fittest to the least fit.

Nonlinear rank scaling:
This is a nonlinear form of rank scaling that increases the selection pressure.

Probabilistic nonlinear rank scaling:
Nolle *et al* [3] have integrated nonlinear rank scaling into roulette wheel selection and SUS, rather than treating it as a separate initial stage.

3   A new scaling algorithm: transform ranking

Linear rank scaling ensures an even spread of scaled fitnesses and hence a lower selection pressure than the nonlinear form. It is therefore suggested that linear rank scaling is well-suited to the early stages of evolution, when exploration of the search space is to be encouraged. It is further suggested that nonlinear rank selection is better suited to the later stages of evolution, when exploitation of the optimum is to be encouraged.

   This paper therefore proposes a new form of rank scaling, transform ranking, that progresses from almost linear to increasingly nonlinear. Its basis is probabilistic nonlinear rank scaling:

$$n_i = roundup\left(\frac{N - Ne^{-cx_i}}{1 - e^{-c}} \right) \tag{1}$$

where n_i is the reverse linear rank of individual i selected by this process for mating, N is the population size, x_i is a set of N random numbers in the range 0–1 (evenly distributed in the case of SUS), c is a constant that controls the degree of nonlinearity, and *roundup* is a function that returns the smallest integer that is not less than its argument.

   Nolle *et al* [3] have already shown that Equation 1 is close to linear rank scaling at $c = 0.2$, but becomes highly nonlinear at $c = 3.0$. So the transition between the two modes can be achieved by a progressive increase in c, analogous to the cooling schedule in Boltzmann scaling. The transition schedule can be either linear or geometric:

$$c_{t+1} = c_t + \Delta \quad \text{or} \quad c_{t+1} = \frac{c_t(100 + k)}{100} \tag{2}$$

where c_t and c_{t+1} are the values of c at successive generations, Δ is the increment added at each generation, and k is a percentage increase at each generation.

4   Experimental method

The two-dimensional Schwefel [4] and Griewank [5] functions were used as fitness landscapes for testing the genetic algorithms. Both are symmetric, separable, continuous and multimodal functions. Each reported result is the highest fitness obtained after 50 generations, which was the termination criterion, averaged over 5000 test runs. Initial experiments were carried out to find optimal parameters, which were then retained for all the scaling experiments. Tournament selection was included in the evaluation for comparison purposes only.

5   Results and Discussion

The comparative results of the selection strategies are shown in Fig. 1. For both test functions, the highest fitness solution has been improved through each of the following scaling methods: sigma scaling, linear rank scaling, nonlinear rank scaling, probabilistic nonlinear rank scaling, and transform ranking. Generic linear scaling and Boltzmann scaling were each of benefit for one fitness landscape but not the other.

The best improvement of all was achieved by probabilistic nonlinear rank scaling for the Schwefel function (Fig. 1(a)) and by transform ranking with a linear transform schedule ($\Delta = 0.1$) for the Griewank function (Fig. 1(b)). The success of transform ranking as a new approach to fitness scaling supports the

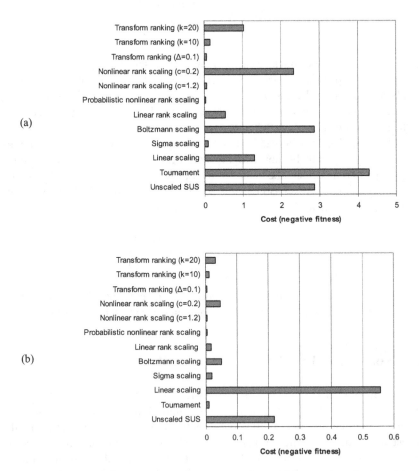

Fig. 1 Best fitness solution using scaled SUS: (a) 2-D Schwefel function, (b) 2-D Griewank function. Tournament selection is included for comparison.

original hypothesis that the transformation from linear to nonlinear rank scaling can lead to improved control of the selection pressure. The improvement is greatest for the linear transform schedule. The geometric transform schedule is highly sensitive to parameter k.

The results show the best fitness obtained, averaged over 5000 test runs. This value was more strongly influenced by the number of times the algorithm failed to reach the global optimum than how effectively the global optimum was exploited. The poor performance of Boltzmann scaling is consistent with the concern expressed by Sadjadi [6] that the method might be susceptible to premature convergence at a local optimum if faced with a complex fitness landscape.

The benefits of fitness scaling always bring a computational cost. Fig. 2 shows the computational costs, normalized with respect to unscaled SUS so that they are machine-independent. The average times for the unscaled SUS were 295s and 299s respectively for the Schwefel and Griewank functions on a 1.5 GHz Inter Pentium computer with 1 GB RAM. The most computationally expensive

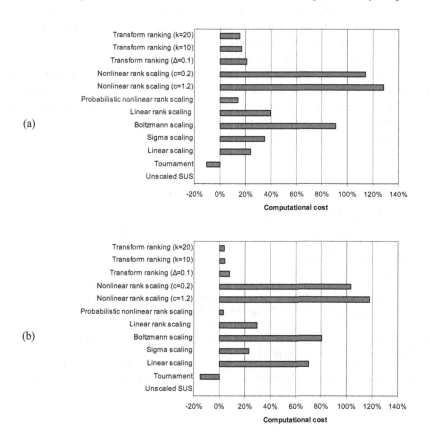

Fig. 2 Computational cost of scaled SUS compared with the unscaled version: (a) 2-D Schwefel function, (b) 2-D Griewank function. Tournament selection is included for comparison.

methods are nonlinear rank and Boltzmann. Encouragingly, the two most effective scaling mechanisms, probabilistic nonlinear rank and transform ranking, are both comparatively inexpensive.

Tournament selection gave poor results for the Schwefel function, but performed much better for the Griewank function. As tournament selection was the computationally cheapest option, it might have found better solutions if the problem had been time bounded rather than bounded by the number of iterations.

6   Conclusions

The benefits of fitness scaling have been demonstrated in searching for the optimum of the two-dimensional Schwefel and Griewank functions. The highest fitness found has been improved through sigma scaling, linear rank scaling, nonlinear rank scaling, probabilistic nonlinear rank scaling, and transform ranking. However, this benefit was always at a computational cost. Although tournament selection performed relatively poorly, particularly against the Schwefel function, it is nevertheless the computationally cheapest option and would therefore have the benefit of additional iterations in time-bounded trials.

A new fitness scaling function, transform ranking, progresses from linear to nonlinear rank scaling during the evolution process, in accordance with a transform schedule. The version with a linear transform schedule provided the best improvement in the quality of search for the Griewank function, and was second only to probabilistic nonlinear rank scaling for the Schwefel function.

References

1. Hopgood, A. A.: *Intelligent Systems for Engineers and Scientists*, second edition, CRC Press, (2001).
2. Kreinovich, V., Quintana, C. and Fuentes, O.: Genetic algorithms: what fitness scaling is optimal? *Cybernetics and Systems*, **24**, pp. 9–26 (1993).
3. Nolle, L., Armstrong, D. A., Hopgood, A. A. and Ware, J. A.: Optimum work roll profile selection in the hot rolling of wide steel strip using computational intelligence, *Lecture Notes in Computer Science*, **1625**, pp 435–452, Springer (1999).
4. Schwefel, H.-P.: *Numerical optimization of Computer models*, John Wiley & Sons (1981).
5. Griewank, A. O.: Generalized Descent for Global Optimization, *Journal of Optimization Theory and Applications*, **34**, pp 11–39 (1981).
6. Sadjadi, F.: Comparison of fitness scaling functions in genetic algorithms with applications to optical processing. In: Javidi, B. and Psaltis, D. (Eds.), *Optical Information Systems II*, Proc. SPIE, **5557**, pp356–364 (2004).

Architecture of Knowledge-based Function Approximator

HASSAB ELGAWI Osman

Abstract This paper proposes a new architecture to build a hybrid value function estimation based on a combination of temporal-different (TD) and on-line variant of Random Forest (RF). We call this implementation Random-TD. The approach iteratively improves its value function by exploiting only relevant parts of action space. We evaluate the potential of the proposed procedure in terms of a reduction in the Bellman error. The results demonstrate that our approach can significantly improve the performance of TD methods and speed up learning process.

1 Introduction

The success of reinforcement learning (RL) method in application to the intelligent control of continuous control systems is turn out to be depend on the ability to combine proper function approximation method with *temporal difference* (TD) [1] methods such as Q-learning and value iteration. This paper proposes the use of behavior-based control architecture and investigates on some techniques inspired by Nature- a combination of reinforcement and supervised learning algorithms to accomplish the sub-goals of a mission. The presented architecture combining *temporal difference* (TD) learning algorithm with on-line variant of random forests (RF) learner that we have developed recently [3]. We call this implementation Random-TD. The approach iteratively improves its value function by exploiting only relevant parts of action space. The approach reaps benefits from both paradigms. From TD-learning we gain the ability to discover behavior that optimizes performance. From supervised learning we gain a flexible way to incorporate domain knowledge.

HASSAB ELGAWI Osman

Computational Intelligence and Systems Science, Tokyo Institute of Technology, e-mail: osman@isl.titech.ac.jp

2 Reinforcement Learning

2.1 A hybrid MDP

In our modeling, we assume a large but limit state space represented by control input matrix Ψ, at any given time step $t = 0, 1, 2, \cdots$, an agent perceives its *state* s_t and selects an *action* a_t. By exploring a state space an agent tries to learn the best control *policy*, $\pi : S \to A$, which maps states to actions by estimating Bellman error. The system responds by given the agent some numerical *reward* $r(s_t)$ and changing into state $s_{t+1} = \delta(s_t, a_t)$. Estimate approximation for reward represented as a vector $R \in \Re^{|s|}$, are incremented by $r_t \phi_t$ and $\phi_t(\phi_t - \gamma\phi_{t+1})$, where ϕ_t, ϕ_{t+1} are control variable vectors at time step t and $t+1$, and the transition probabilities under π can be represented as a matrix $P \in \Re^{|s| \times |s|}$. Given two Markov decision process M_1 and M_2 which share the same state space S but have two different action spaces A_1 and A_1, respectively a new Markov decision process M_{12} can be defined by the composition of M_1 and M_2 such that at each time step the learning agent select one action from A_1 and one from A_2. The transition and cost function of the composite process M_{12} are define by

$$\delta_{12}(s, (a_1, a_2)) = \delta_2(\delta_1(s, a_1), a_2) \text{ and} \tag{1}$$

$$r_{12}(s, (a_1, a_2)) = r_1(s, a_1) + \gamma r_2(\delta_1(s, a_1, a_2)). \tag{2}$$

2.2 TD learning Error

Value-function V^π can be approximated by using proper approximator scheme based on estimating Bellman error or the temporal difference (TD) error. For MDPs, we can define V^π formally as

$$V^\pi(s) = E^\pi \left\{ \sum_{t=0}^{\infty} \gamma^t R_t | s_0 = s \right\} \tag{3}$$

Where $E^\pi\{\}$ denotes the expected value given that the agent follows policy, π, and $0 < \gamma < 1$ is the discount factor. Note that the value of the terminal state, if any, is always zero. A randomized stationary policy can be identified with conditional probabilities $\pi(a|s)$, which specify the probability of choosing action a at state s. From mathematical point of views, value function V^π which can be represented as vector $V \in \Re^{|s|}$, is an approximate solution to Bellman's equation, which is then used to construct near optimal policies.

$$V^{\pi} = \sum_{a \in A(s)} \pi(a|s) \left(R(s,a) + \gamma \sum_{\acute{s} \in S} p(\acute{s}|s,a) V^{\pi}(\acute{s}) \right), \tag{4}$$

2.3 Optimal Control

The *optimal control policy*, π^*, can be defined in many ways, but is typically defined as the policy that maximizes V^{π} for any state s,

$$\pi^* = \arg\max_{\pi} V^{\pi}(s), (\forall s) \tag{5}$$

where $V^{\pi}(s)$ is computed from Eq 3. Alternatively, $V^{\pi}(s)$ could be computed by summing the rewards over a finite horizon h: $\pi^* = \sum_{i=0}^{h} r_{t+i}$. Or uses a discount rate γ to discount rewards over time. The sum is then computed over an infinite horizon: $\pi^* = \sum_{i=0}^{\infty} \gamma^i r_{t+i}$, where r_t is the reward received at time step t.

3 Random Forests in Reinforcement Learning

Learning of RF [2] is refined in this paper to deal with learning control scheme. The state space is partitioned into g disjoint group, in order to transfer a state s from the input space to a vector of input controls (actions), then value function is estimated from control (action) space, $\hat{V} = \vec{\theta}^{\mathrm{T}} \cdot \vec{A_s}$, where $\vec{\theta}$ is the parameter vector and $\vec{A_s}$ is the input controls vector. Represented state as control vectors; for each $s \in S$:

$$\phi_s = [(\phi_s(1), \phi_s(2), \cdots, \phi_s(n))]^T \tag{6}$$

$$V_t(s, \theta_t) = \theta_t^T \phi_s = \sum_{i=1}^{n} \theta_t(i) \phi_s(i) \tag{7}$$

Based on control input ranking we develop a new, conditional permutation scheme for the computation of *action* importance measure [3]. According to control input ranking results, different yet random *action* subsets are used as new *action* spaces for learning a diverse base-learners (decision trees). Individual trees in RF are incrementally generated by specifically selected subsamples from the new *action* spaces. The decision trees consist of two types of nodes: *decision nodes*, corresponding to state variables and *least nodes*, which correspond to all possible actions that can be taken. In a decision node a decision is taken about one of the input. Each least node stores the state values for the corresponding region in the state space, meaning that a leaf node stores a value for each possible action that can be taken. The tree starts out with only one leaf that represents the entire input space. So in a leaf node a decision has to be made whether the node should be split or not. Once a tree is constructed it can be used to map an input vector to a least node, which corresponds to a region in the state space. We will use temporal-difference learning (TD) [1] to associate a value with each region. TD methods are commonly update $V^\pi(s)$ by an amount proportional to the TD error, δ where.

$$\delta = r + \gamma V^\pi(\acute{s}) - V^\pi(s), \qquad (8)$$

and $\gamma \in [0,1]$ is a discount factor.

The forest consist of fully grown trees of a certain depth l. The general performance of the on-line forest depends on the depth of the tree. Thus, we create our on-line forest by iteratively increasing its depth.

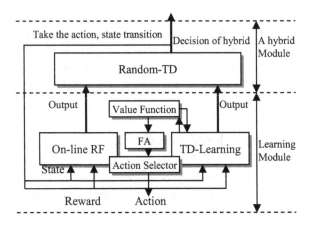

Fig. 1 Random-TD architecture.

4 Random-TD Architecture

One possible way to combine TD with RF is to choose the best combined strategy $\vec{s_i} = \vec{s_i}(s)$ given the expected combined strategy for each learners involved and to represent the value function V^π as combined policy of entire value function, rather than base value of a given state. Figure 1 demonstrates the architecture of the proposed Random-TD. It consists of two modules, a learning module and a hybrid module. These two modules interact with each other. The Random-TD algorithm for value function approximation is shown in Algorithm 1. The function SELECT VARIABLE (s_t, e_t, A, m) uses state s_t as data points and the Bellman error estimate e_t, while the transformation from state space to feature space is done on the previous step. Initially, a single feature which is 1 everywhere is defined and TD is used to compute the parameters of the approximator. On every iteration the Bellman residuals e_t are estimated for each state. In general the model parameters P and R are not be available so the residuals can only be approximated based on an approximate

Algorithm 1 Random-TD Policy Evaluation

1: **Given** the dimensionality d to be used in each projection the number of features to be added in each iteration, m. the desire number of iteration K.
2: Initialize state s
3: Choose action a using policy π and observe reward r and next state $\acute{s}$
4: Update $V(s)$ such that $V(s) \leftarrow V(s) + \alpha[r + (s) - V(s)]$ where α is the learning rate and γ is the discount factor (both between 0 and 1)
5: $s \leftarrow \acute{s}$
6: Repeat steps 2-4 until episode ends
7: $\Phi^0 \leftarrow \overrightarrow{1}$
8: $\Phi^0 \leftarrow TD(s_t, r_t, \Phi^0)$
9: **for** $k = 1, 2, \cdots, K$ **do**
10:     Estimate the Bellman residuals
11:     $e_t \approx R(s_t + \gamma \sum_{s \in S} P_{st,s} \hat{V}_s^{k-1} - \hat{V}_{st}^{k-1})$
12:     $A \leftarrow$ Random-TD (s_t, e_t, d)
13:     $\Psi \leftarrow$ SELECT VARIABLE (s_t, e_t, A, m)
14:     $\Phi^k \leftarrow [\Phi^{k-1}, \Psi]$
15:     $\Phi^k \leftarrow$ Random-TD(s_t, r_t, Φ^k)
16:     $V^k \leftarrow \Phi^k \theta^k)$
17: **end for**
18: **return** $\hat{V}^k$

model, or on sample data. In our experiments SELECT VARIABLES is simply discritizes the state space onto $\Re^2$ into up to m states and returns the combined feature matrix. Random-TD is repeated to obtain a new approximation $\hat{V}^k$.

5 Experimental and Results

Table 1 summarizes the data sets in terms of the size of instance, number of input dimensions (D), the range of the target (predicted) (t_{min}, t_{max}), and the size of training and testing set (N_{trn}, N_{tes}).

In Table 2 we report the results in terms of the mean absolute Bellman error (BE). On another set of experiment, we report a comparison results in Table 3 using Random-TD, TD-learning, and Q-learning (with the discounting factor set to 0.99). The results, are averaged over 20 independent runs. As can be seen in Table 3, the Random-TD always performs significantly better than the standard TD. In Table 4, we report the CPU time in seconds taken by the Random-TD algorithm for function approximation, including the learning in 200 epochs. We have noted that Random-TD converges well before 200 epochs, although we report all the results for 200 epochs. The results indicate we are still very cheap to compute. Our goal in these preliminary experiments is not necessarily to demonstrate the superiority of our approach in terms of sample complexity, but rather its availability as an alternate approach to the reinforcement learning function approximation problem.

Table 1 Description of the Function Approximation Data Sets Obtained from [4]

Dataset	Data size	D	t_{min}	t_{max}	N_{trn}	N_{tes}
Ailerons (AL)	7154	40	-0.0003	-0.00035	1000	6154
Elevator (EV)	8752	18	0.078	0.012	1000	7752
Kinematics (KI)	8192	8	1.458521	0.040165	800	7392
Friedman (FR)	40,768	10	30.522	-1.228	1300	39468

Table 2 Performance of Random-TD on the Function Approximation Data sets in table 1, for different Depths

Dataset	Absolute error				
	Depth=3	Depth=4	Depth=5	Depth=6	Depth=7
Ailerons	0.000111	0.000114	0.000112	0.000117	0.000126
Elevator	0.0702	0.0541	0.0483	0.0298	0.0301
Kinematics	0.1001	0.0672	0.0487	0.0425	0.0521
Friedman	1.1213	0.7322	0.5622	0.6074	0.5628

Table 3 Results showing a comparison using Random-TD, TD, and Q-learning. The units for absolute bellman error. Im denote the improvement of Random-TD over TD-learning

Dataset	Random-TD	TD-learning	Q-learning	Im %
Ailerons	0.000121	0.000125	0.000123	2.9
Elevator	0.0523	0.0543	0.0549	4.4
Kinematics	0.0493	0.0520	0.0507	3.1
Friedman	0.5472	0.7533	0.7512	9.6

Table 4 CPU Time Taken by Random-TD of Different Depths for Different Data Sets

Dataset	CPU Time (seconds)				
	Depth=3	Depth=4	Depth=5	Depth=6	Depth=7
Ailerons	2189	4870	6321	11,602	25,498
Elevator	1100	2000	3723	8,844	22,033
Kinematics	892	1566	3211	6609	15,613
Friedman	3319	7900	14,198	33,928	80,067

References

1. Sutton, R., & Barto, A.: "Reinforcement Learning: An introduction," *Cambring, MA: MIT Press*, 1998.
2. Leo Breiman.: "Random Forests," *Machine Learning*, 45(1):5.32, 2001.
3. Hassab Elgawi Osman.: "Online Random Forests based on CorrFS and CorrBE," *In Proc.IEEE workshop on online classification, CVPR*, 2008.
4. Guvenir, H. A., & Uysal, I.: Bilkent University function approximation repository, 2000. Available online at http://funapp.cs.bilkent.edu.tr/DataSets/.

Applying Planning Algorithms to Argue in Cooperative Work

Ariel Monteserin, Silvia Schiaffino, and Analía Amandi[1]

Abstract Negotiation is typically utilized in cooperative work scenarios for solving conflicts. Anticipating possible arguments in this negotiation step represents a key factor since we can take decisions about our participation in the cooperation process. In this context, we present a novel application of planning algorithms for argument generation, where the actions of a plan represent the arguments that a person might use during the argumentation process. In this way, we can plan how to persuade the other participants in cooperative work for reaching an expected agreement in terms of our interests. This approach allows us to take advantages since we can test anticipated argumentative solutions in advance.

1 Introduction

In a cooperative work context, participants need to interact with one another to achieve their goals. In such a scenario, negotiation is fundamental to reach agreements among participants with conflictive goals. The essence of a negotiation process is the exchange of proposals. Participants make proposals and respond to proposals made to them in order to converge to an agreement. However, not all approaches are restricted to that exchange. One of the approaches is the argumentation-based negotiation [3-5, 7]. In these approaches, participants can exchange additional information as arguments, besides the proposals [5]. Thus, in the context of negotiation, an argument is information that supports a proposal and allows a participant to justify its position in the negotiation, or to influence the position of other participants [7].

Given a situation where it is needed to negotiate, the ability to plan the course of action that it will be executed to solve the conflict allows the negotiator to anticipate the problems that he could find during the interaction, and also, to analyse anticipated solutions to the conflict in order to avoid or minimize its problematic effects. It is worth noticing that this anticipation is also useful to evaluate several plans in advance in order to choose the most profitable one.

In this work, we propose to use Planning to assist a participant with this task. Planning algorithms provide a course of action that, when it is executed on the ini-

---

[1] ISISTAN – UNCPBA, Argentina – Also CONICET
email: {amontese;sschia;amandi}@exa.unicen.edu.ar

tial state, it allows us to achieve an expected final state [2]. An agent assisting a participant in a cooperative work scenario can model the argumentation process as a planning problem and obtain an argumentation-based negotiation plan, which we call *argumentation plans*. In these plans the actions represent the arguments that the participant will utter to persuade his opponents, and hence, to reach an agreement. On the other hand, the arguments must be determined taking into account the participant's beliefs, goals, and preferences. Since most planning algorithms do not consider these issues in the plan conception, we use a planning algorithm based on preferences in which participants' preferences impact on the action selection process and, as a result, on the argument selection mechanism.

It is worth differentiating our work from dialogues for deliberation (e.g. [8]). In deliberation dialogues, agents discuss to make a joint course of action. These models work with argumentation-based dialogues and planning as in our work, but inversely. That is, agents use the argumentation-based dialogues to reach a plan, whereas we use planning to obtain an argumentation plan.

The paper is organized as follows. Section 2 presents an example of a situation where our proposal might be useful. Section 3 shows the argumentation process as a planning problem in order to generate argumentation plans. Then, Section 4 shows a case study. Finally, Section 5 presents our conclusions.

2 Negotiation in cooperative work scenarios

Consider a set of participants *tom*, *mary*, *jane* and *paul* working in a cooperative environment. In this context, suppose that *tom* should reach an agreement in order to perform the action *writereport* (write a report to inform advances of a project). To write this report, the following actions are needed: *writeintroduction*, *writesub1* (describe subproject 1), *writesub2* (describe subproject 2), *writeresults* (describe the results obtained so far), *checkreport*. *tom* can do *writeintroduction* and *checkreport*, but he cannot perform the other tasks. Thus, he has to convince the other participants to work cooperatively so that he can reach his goals. *tom* knows that *jane* can write subproject 1, that *mary* can write subproject 2, and that *paul* is good at reporting results. On the other hand, *tom* knows that *jane* wants to get an overtime payment, and to achieve this *jane* has to send a recommendation letter to the manager. Thus, *tom* can offer *jane* to write the letter on her behalf provided that she does *writesub1* (*tom* offers *jane* a reward as an argument to convince her). Similarly, *tom* can use information about *mary* and *paul* to get the other two tasks done. In addition, *tom* has some preferences regarding the different arguments he can use during negotiation (i.e. he generally prefers to offer rewards instead of threatening participants).

In this scenario, an assistant agent having information about the context of the cooperative work to be done, that is, about the participants' goals, preferences and abilities, could assist *tom* by suggesting an argumentation plan to convince *mary*, *jane* and *paul* to carry out the tasks he needs. The assistant agent should determine the best arguments and with which participants it is better to negotiate in order to fulfil efficiently the participant's goals. In the following sections we show our proposal to generate the argumentation plans.

3 Using planning algorithms in argumentation processes

We define an *argumentation plan* as a partial order sequence of arguments that allows a participant to reach an expected agreement when it is uttered in a conflictive situation. In simpler terms, an argumentation plan will determine how a participant should perform the argumentation process during a given negotiation.

When an agent detects a conflict, it can access to information about this conflict and its context before the negotiation begins. This *negotiation information* includes self-information (participant's beliefs, preferences and goals), information about its opponents and information about the conflict context.

As we introduced earlier, an argumentative agent, in addition to evaluating and generating proposals, must be able to (a) evaluate incoming arguments and update its mental state as a result; (b) generate candidate outgoing arguments; and (c) select an argument from the set of candidate arguments [1]. These actions compose the argumentation process. To achieve this, the agent carry out the argumentation process taking into account the *negotiation information*. Specially, we focus on the generation and selection of arguments. *Argument generation* is related to the generation of candidate arguments to present to a counterpart. To this end, rules for creation of arguments are defined (e.g. [3,5]). Such rules specify conditions. So, if the condition is satisfied in the negotiation context, the argument may be generated and it becomes a candidate. *Argument selection* is concerned with selecting the argument that should be uttered to a counterpart from the set of candidate arguments. The argument selection mechanism must apply some policy over that set, in accordance with the agent's mental state, to select the best argument. A policy can order all arguments by their severity and select: first the weakest [3]; by the trust or reputation of the counterpart [6], among other.

On the other hand, a planning algorithm is used to find a plan of action. A *plan* is a partial order sequence of actions that when it is executed in any world satisfying the initial state description, it will achieve a desired final state [9]. Conceptually, a planning problem is defined as a tree-tuple $<i, f, A>$, where: i (initial state) is a complete description of the world, in which the plan will be executed; f (final state) describes the agent's (participant's) goals; A (actions) is the set of actions (with precondition and effects) to build a plan. For an action to be added to the plan, its preconditions must be satisfied, and with its execution, the world will be modified by their effects. This three-tuple is the input of a planning algorithm. There is one mechanism in a planning algorithm that is important for our proposal: the *action selection* mechanism. This mechanism chooses which action it will be added to the plan in a particular iteration of the algorithm. For instance, [9] defines this mechanism by the non-deterministic *choose* function; nevertheless, it might be redefined in accordance with each planning problem.

Now, we can outline how each input of the planning problem must be defined in order to generate argumentation plans. *Initial state*: the conflict is the beginning point of argumentation, and it is described in the negotiation information. The initial state describes the world where the conflict takes place. *Final state*: the agent's goal in a conflictive situation is to reach an agreement. Thus, the final state represents this agreement. The argumentation plan will support the agreement in the same way as an argument supports a proposal. For instance, if *ag1* needs to execute an action *a* to fulfilling a goal *g1*, but that *a* execution keeps its opponent *ag2* from fulfilling a goal *g2*, the initial state *i* should include information as *isgoal(ag1, g1)*, *isgoal(ag2, g2)*, *believe(ag1, imply(a, g1))* and *believe(ag2, imply(a, not(g2)))*; and the final state *f* should represent the execution of the action *a*. *Actions*: the effect of a rule for argument generation is the argument. So, we can define actions to generate arguments with the same rule patterns, where the action preconditions are the conditions of the rule and the action effect, the argument. Thus, the actions of the plan represent the arguments that the participant can utter to the counterparts. The argument types that the agent can generate are: appeals, rewards and threats [7, 3]. *Appeals* are used to justify a proposal; *rewards* to promise a future recompense; and *threats* to warn of negative consequences if the counterpart does not accept a proposal. For each argument type, we define the actions to generate it, according to the axioms defined in [3]. Moreover, we distinguish two general structures of actions: *create-argument* actions and *accept-argument* actions. The first ones depict the argument generation process as rules, whereas the second represent the counterpart's acceptance of the argument. Let's see an example. **Action**: *createReward(X, Y, ActionR, ActionP, Goal)*; **preconditions**: *iam(X), isparticipant(Y), isgoal(Y, G), believe(Y, imply(ActionR, G)), cando(Y, ActionP), cando(X, ActionR)*; **effects**: *reward(X, Y, do(Y, ActionP), [do(X, ActionR)])*; and **action**: *acceptReward(X, Y, A, B)*; **preconditions**: *reward(X, Y, do(Y, A),do(X, B))*; **effects**: *do(Y, A), do(X, B), cando(X, A)*. This represents the acceptance of rewards. In consequence, *Y* undertakes to execute *A* in exchange for the execution of *B* by *X*. Then, *X* obtains the ability to execute *A*.

Additionally, we must emulate both argument generation and selection mechanisms in the planner. Since the rules to generate arguments can be seen as actions in a plan, when the planner establishes what actions might be added to the plan, checking its preconditions and its effects in view of the current and final state of the world, implicitly, it will be generating the candidate arguments (**argument generation**). Also, for this reason, the action selection mechanism of the planner emulates the **argument selection**. An important consideration to take into account is that the action selection mechanism in a traditional planning algorithm is implemented as a non-deterministic function, and it does not consider the preferences stored in the agent's mental state. In contrast, the selection of arguments is made on the basis of these preferences. Therefore, we use an adapted action selection function in order to consider the agent's preferences about argument selection.

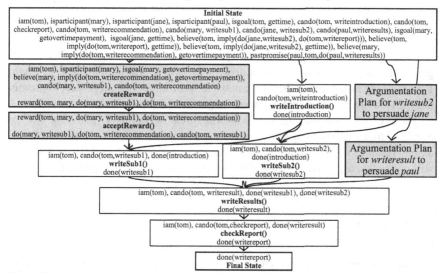

Fig. 1. Plan to write a report

Since our selection function must select the most preferable action, we defined the next format of agent's mental attitude to be used by the planner: *preference(Q, Ac, Ad, level)*; where *Q* represents the goal to achieve, *Ac* is the action that produces *Q*, *Ad* is the action that needs to accomplish *Q*, and *level* determines how preferable is the attitude. For example, with *preference(isparticipant(mary), createReward(tom, mary,_,_,_), acceptReward(mary, tom,_,_),80)* the agent models a preference of 80 (over 100) for the goal *isparticipant(mary)* when this is produced by the action *createReward*, and consumed by the *action acceptReward*. In the context of the argumentation process, this mental attitude represents a high preference level to use a reward, instead of other type of argument, when the opponent is *mary*, maybe, because the trust in her is high.

4 Case study

Consider the cooperative scenario described in Section 2. The information for this scenario is formalised in the initial state (Figure 1). As we said above, there are actions that should be executed to finish the report. Normally, we use planning to find a course of action that allows us to reach our goals. Nevertheless, some actions of that plan may be beyond our control or abilities. So, we have to negotiate with other people their execution. For example, *tom* cannot write the sections about subproject 1 and 2, neither the final results. Therefore, he should persuade *mary, jane* and *paul* respectively. In this context, an assistant agent can integrate the generation of an argumentation plan into the planning of the course of actions needed to write the report. Thus, it can suggest to *tom* the actions to finish the report, and the necessary arguments that he must utter to reach agreements about the actions he cannot perform. Figure 1 shows this idea. We can observe the actions to write the report (in white) and the argumentation plans to agree *writeSub1* (in grey). Similar plans could be generated for *writeSub2* and *writeResults*. In Figure 1, we can see how *tom* can persuade *mary* to write about the subproject 1, promising her to write the letter that she needs to get overtime payment (reward).

The preferences about arguments provide great versatility to planning. For example, if *tom*'s assistant agent increases the preference level of the threat (for example, because it learned that threats were more efficient arguments), the planner will prefer that argument instead of the previous one (reward) to persuade *mary*.

5 Conclusions

We have presented an approach to generate plans to argue during a negotiation process in cooperative work. We explained how the argumentation process may be modelled as a planning problem in order to obtain an *argumentation plan*; and how the planner mechanisms can emulate the generation and selection of arguments. The argumentation plan obtained can be used by an assistant agent to aid the user at achieving his goals.

References

1. Ashri R., Rahwan I. and Luck M. (2003). Architectures for negotiating agents, in *Proc. Multi-Agent Syst. and Applications III*, 136-146.
2. Fikes R. and Nilsson N. (1971). STRIPS: a new approach to the application of theorem proving to problem solving, *Artificial Intelligence* 5(2): 189-208.
3. Kraus S., Sycara K. and Evenchik. A. (1998). Reaching agreements through argumentation: a logical model and implementation, *Artificial. Intelligence* 104(1-2):1-69.
4. Rahwan I., Ramchurn S., Jennings N., McBurney P., Parsons S. and Sonenberg L. (2003). Argumentation-based negotiation, *The Knowledge Engineering Review*, 18(4): 343-375.
5. Ramchurn S., Jennings N. and Sierra C.(2003). Persuasive negotiation for autonomous agents: a rhetorical approach, in *Proc.IJCAI W.on Comp. Models of Nat. Argument*, 9–17.
6. Ramchurn S., Sierra C., Godo L. and Jennings N. (2003). A computational trust model for multi-agent interactions based on confidence and reputation. In *Proc. Workshop on Deception, Fraud and Trust in Agent Societies*, Melbourne, Australia, 69–75.
7. Sierra C., Jennings N. Noriega P., and Parsons S. (1998). A framework for argumentation-based negotiation, in *Proc. 4th Int. Workshop on ATAL*, Rode Island, USA, 177-192.
8. Tang Y. and Parsons S. (2005). Argumentation-based dialogues for deliberation, in *Proc. 4th Int. Conf. on AAMAS*, The Netherlands, 552–559.
9. Weld D. (1994). An introduction to least commitment planning, *AI Magazine*, 15: 27-61.

Universum Inference and Corpus Homogeneity

Carl Vogel,* Gerard Lynch and Jerom Janssen

Abstract. Universum Inference is re-interpreted for assessment of corpus homogeneity in computational stylometry. Recent stylometric research quantifies strength of characterization within dramatic works by assessing the homogeneity of corpora associated with dramatic personas. A methodological advance is suggested to mitigate the potential for the assessment of homogeneity to be achieved by chance. Baseline comparison analysis is constructed for contributions to debates by nonfictional participants: the corpus analyzed consists of transcripts of US Presidential and Vice-Presidential debates from the 2000 election cycle. The corpus is also analyzed in translation to Italian, Spanish and Portuguese. Adding randomized categories makes assessments of homogeneity more conservative.

1 Background & Method

Recent research in text classification has applied the assessment of corpus homogeneity to strength of characterization within fictional work [8]. The idea is that a character within a play is a strong character if the text associated with the character is homogeneous and distinct from other characters—the character is strong if a random sample of text of that character is more like the rest of the text of that character than it is like the text of other characters. Another possibility is that random samples of texts of a character reliably are most similar to its play, at least, if not its character. A playwright whose characters "find their author" in this sense, but not their characters or play, while still highly individual as an author, does not construct strong characters. One goal of this paper is to provide a baseline for comparison in which the contributions of individual characters are not scripted by a single author, but whose contributions have to be understood in light of each other's statements, like dialog: we assess homogeneity of contributions to national election debates.

Another focus of this work is in an attempt to improve the methodology for assessing the homogeneity of corpora. The method is related to inference with the universum in machine learning. Random data drawn from the same probability space as the corpora under consideration are considered among the actual corpora and categories within it. Inference with the universum involves approaching classification

---

Computational Linguistics Group, Intelligent Systems Laboratory, O'Reilly Institute, Trinity College, Dublin 2, Ireland e-mail: vogel,gplynch,janssenj@tcd.ie

* This work is supported by Science Foundation Ireland RFP 05/RF/CMS002.

tasks by supplementing data sets with data points that are not actually part of the categories from which a system is choosing, but which are realistic given the features under consideration [9]. The supplemental data sets, if well chosen, can sharpen the distinction between categories, making it possible to reclassify data points that otherwise fall in between categories. Part of the idea is that clashes with the universum should be maximized. Research in this area includes focus on how best to choose the universum [6]. One can use the same sort of reasoning to quantify the homogeneity of the categories in terms of their propensity to be confused with the universum material. As corpus homogeneity is assessed in part by rank similarity of files within it, the effect of adding random data is to diffuse the homogeneity of texts within a category since it is increasingly likely that randomly constructed data files will be the most similar to some of the actual texts. Thus, a category that is assessed as significantly homogeneous even with the addition of random data can be judged with greater confidence, with a reduction of the possibility of type I error.

In §2 we apply our methods to assess the homogeneity of debate contributions of main the contributors to the US national election debates from 2000.[2] Surprisingly, the transcripts do not reveal Bush or Gore to have provided self-homogeneous contributions (in the sense used here (if they had been characters in a play, they would not have been among the strong characters). Adding fabricated contributions drawn from random sampling from the concatenation of the entirety of the actual data set alters the outcome by weakening some of the rank similarity measures within actual categories. The second experiment individuates the same corpus into a larger number of smaller categories: the categories are individuated by speaker and date, rather than aggregating across the debates. Then universum data is added. Finally, using translations of the debates into Italian, Portuguese and Spanish we turn the problem into one of language classification. On inspecting the texts of Bush vs. those of Gore, one might not think them as distinct from each other as texts of Italian are from those of Spanish. Whatever one's prior expectations about the homogeneity of categories individuated by speaker, there are very clear intuitions about categorization by language (and the effectiveness of letter distribution analysis in underpinning language classification generally [1]). Thus, we are able to use the universum method to enhance the assessment of homogeneity in general instances of text classification problems, as well as in computational stylometry.

The classification method used here involves several stages of analysis. A corpus of text is split into files indexed by categories. Files are balanced by size. In any one sub-experiment, the number of files in each category considered is balanced. Experiments are repeated hundreds of times, and average results analyzed.

The first stage is to compute the pairwise similarity of all of the files in the sub-experiment. Similarity is based on n-gram frequency distributions, for whatever level of tokenization that is settled upon, and for whatever value of n [7]. In the experiments reported here, we use letter unigrams. Their efficacy in linguistic classification tasks is perhaps surprising, but they have repeatedly proven themselves

---

[2] The presidential debates occurred on October 3, 2000, October 11, 2000, and October 17, 2000. The Vice Presidential debate occurred on October 5, 2000. The transcript source was http://www.debates.org/—last verified, June 2008.

[8], and perform well with respect to word-level tokenization [5]. However, other levels of tokenization are obviously also effective. An advantage of letter unigrams is that there is no disputing their individuation, and this renders it very easy to replicate experiments based on letter unigrams. This is important if the text classification task involves authorship attribution for forensic purposes [2]. The similarity metric used is the chi-by-degrees-of-freedom statistic suggested for the calculation of corpus homogeneity in the past by Kilgarriff, using word-level tokenization [3]. This essentially means calculating the χ^2 statistic for each token in the pair of files under consideration, and averaging that over the total number of tokens considered. Normally, χ^2 is used in inferential statistics to assess whether two distributions are significantly different; however, here we are using the value in the other direction, as a measure of similarity. With all of the pairs of files evaluated for their similarity, files within categories can be ranked for their overall similarity. For each file in a category, the Mann-Whitney rank ordering statistic is used to assess the goodness of fit of the file with respect to its own category (its *a priori* category), and with respect to all other categories under consideration on the basis of the ranks of pair-wise similarity scores. The best-fit alternative categories are recorded.

Homogeneity of a category of files is measured with Bernoulli Schema. This is akin to tossing a coin in repeated experiments to assess whether the coin is fair. Here, the coin has c sides, one for each category that could be the best fit for a file. In any one fairness experiment, the c-sided coin is tossed n times, once for each file in the category. With hundreds of n-toss experiments, it is possible to assess whether the coin is fair: when the same side comes up often enough relative to those parameters, it is safe to reject the hypothesis that the coin is fair (that the category of files is randomly self-similar) and to accept that the category is significantly homogeneous.

2 Experiments

The debates from the 2000 US presidential election cycle involved three debates between George Bush and Al Gore, and one Debate between Joseph Lieberman and Dick Cheney. The transcripts were parsed using PlayParser [4] into the contributions of each of the speakers, including a moderator and a member of the audience. The resulting data files were approximately 40K bytes for each of the candidates for each date, and approximately 10K for the moderator. These files were processed using the Unix split command to generate sub-files balanced at approximately 2K each. The data associated with the candidates are indexed in two ways—one is in a broad category which includes all of the speaker's files, and the other uses more categories, treating the different dates for each candidate as a separate category. The files of the moderator are always held within just one category. There was not enough data from members of the audience to consider in the experiments.

The universum data was constructed as follows. The entire data set of the debates was concatenated into a seed file. This was used as a representative distribution of characters to sample from. Depending on the exact configuration of the experiment, a matching number of categories was selected, and those categories were used for a set of files balanced in size and number with the actual data. However, the files were constructed by random sampling from the entire corpus construed as a bag of letters. Thus, the universum is a random data set shaped by the overall distribution of the actual data under consideration. If different levels of tokenization were employed or a different value of n in the n-gram, the seed bag would be shaped accordingly. In the experiments that follow, we first run the experiment with the underlying data that we wish to analyze, and then again with universum categories.

Experiment 1—Speakers Define Categories

In this experiment, the categories were construed from the four candidates and the moderator. The files from all four of the debates were considered together. In each sub-experiment, ten files from each category were considered from the approximately 20 available for each speaker in each debate, and 1000 such experiments were run with independent random samples from the superset in each. In each sub-experiment, we assessed the homogeneity of each category. This meant considering how many of the ten files in the *a priori* category had that category as its best fit in terms of overall similarity. The results are averaged across all 1000 subexperiments. Given these parameters (five categories, ten files each), six out of ten files must be assigned to a category on the basis of similarity for it to be deemed significantly homogeneous.[3] Only the categories associated with Cheney (9.473), Lieberman (7.357) and the Moderator (7.723) are significantly homogeneous. The confusion matrix associated with the assignment of files that did not fit into its *a priori* category is can be summarized as follows: the Cheney and Lieberman categories attract the files associated with the each of other categories (the Moderator is nearly equivalent in homogeneity to Lieberman, but is not an attractor at all).

Next we consider the data associated with another 1000 experiments, but with the additional files generated randomly according to the constraints discussed above (here, five constructed categories with randomly generated files, seeded by the distributions in the concatenated corpus, balanced in size at 2K, with ten files to each category). With ten categories and ten files, five files is the threshold for category homogeneity. The significant homogeneity values are reduced to: Cheney, 8.864; Lieberman, 5.080; Moderator, 7.199. In another universum variation, there is a single large (containing 60 files) randomly generated category, and sampled ten files to any one subexperiment, just like the categories of the actual participants, in each of 1000 random samplings over all of the categories are run. With six categories of ten files each, the critical homogeneity level is six files assigned to the category: Cheney, 9.268; Lieberman, 6.450; Moderator, 7.513. These results suggest that when adding universum categories, it is more conservative to add as many categories as there are categories in the underlying dataset than to draw upon a single large universum.

---

[3] The significance threshold is $p < 0.05$ throughout this article. A longer version of this article, with full tables and confusion matrices is available (http://www.cs.tcd.ie/Carl.Vogel/vlj.sgai2008.pdf).

Experiment 2—Individual Debates

We also considered each debate in isolation. The moderator files are considered as a monolithic category, however. Again, 1000 experiments were constructed each with a sample of ten files from each of the categories. With nine categories and ten files per category, a group of at least five files achieves significant homogeneity. In this experiment, Cheney (9.202), Lieberman (6.230) and the Moderator (7.435) are associated with significantly homogeneous categories as before, as is the Gore category for October 11 (6.275). A confusion matrix of the participants' distribution in similarity to each other across the debates can be summarized thusly: Cheney is an attractor for nearly all the categories; Bush's best alternatives are other Bush files and Cheney; Gore's best alternatives are other Gore files, Cheney and Lieberman.

With an additional nine random categories drawn on the same underlying frequency distribution and containing 20 files each, balanced at 2K in size, and 1000 experiments selecting 10 files from each category. With 18 categories and 10 files per category in each experiment, four files for a category achieves significant homogeneity. The Cheney data from October 5 (8.262), the Moderator data (6.833), and the Gore data from October 11 (5.571) remain significantly homogeneous. The Lieberman data loses significance. None of the individual universum categories are significantly homogeneous. This is because, as before, their files are randomly constructed from an underlying distribution and the files within the categories are often most similar to others of the random categories.

Experiment 3—Translation Filter Added

The debate transcripts are translated into French, German, Italian, Japanese, Portuguese, and Spanish.[4] The source indicates that the translations were constructed using an MT system from the English source data, but does not name which one. The effect of using the translated data is that it introduces noise, presumably uniformly, to each of the natural categories. These languages are sufficiently close to each other that there should be some classification of files to the wrong languages, but equally, the languages should for the most part form clearly separate categories. 1000 experiments were run, with 10 files for each category defined by language. With four categories, seven out of ten is the threshold for significant homogeneity. Each category is homogeneous, as expected (English, 10; Spanish, 9.994; Italian, 9.962; Portuguese, 9.947). The 1000 experiments re-run with four universum category diminishes the homogeneity values, but they retain strong significance (English, 9.949; Spanish, 9.388; Italian, 9.475; Portuguese, 9.788).

---

[4] See http://www.debates.org/pages/trans_trans.html—last verified, June 2008.

3 Final Remarks

These experiments have shown that adding categories of files randomly constructed from the same underlying distributions as the data set under scrutiny has the effect of making judgements of category homogeneity more conservative. Adding the same number of universum categories as underlying categories enhances conservatism. This is certainly the right direction for conclusions associated with positive author-ship attribution in forensic settings in which standards of certainty must be made extremely strict. For other tasks, this may be less advantageous. This work is part of a larger project in extending and validating methods of text classification. We are particularly interested in computational stylometry and the use of these methods to assess the strength in linguistic terms of characters in plays. Here we have applied the same reasoning to contributors to political debates. The results provide some baseline data about expected levels of homogeneity among individuals providing sequences of short monologues in a shared setting which can be used to illuminate the results that emerge when the monologues are all scripted by the same author. We are considering debates from the 2004 and 2008 election cycles as well. With a larger corpus of data, and more temporal calibration to the corpus, it should be possible to expand the analysis of linguistic homogeneity of real players over time.

References

1. W. B. Cavnar and J. M. Trenkle. N-gram-based text categorization. In *Proceedings of Third Annual Symposium on Document Analysis and Information Retrieval*, pages 161–175, 1994. Las Vegas, NV, UNLV Publications/Reprographics.
2. Carole Chaski. Who wrote it? Steps toward a science of authorship identification. *National Institute of Justice Journal*, 233:15–22, 1997.
3. Adam Kilgarriff. Comparing corpora. *International Journal of Corpus Linguistics*, 6(1):97–133, 2001.
4. Gerard Lynch and Carl Vogel. Automatic character assignation. In Max Bramer, editor, *AI-2007 Twenty-seventh SGAI International Conference on Artificial Intelligence*, pages 335–348. Springer, 2007.
5. Cormac O'Brien and Carl Vogel. Spam filters: Bayes vs. chi-squared; letters vs. words. In Markus Alesky et al., editor, *Proceedings of the International Symposium on Information and Communication Technologies*, pages 298–303, 2003.
6. Fabian H. Sinz, Olivier Chapelle, Alekh Agarwal, and Bernhard Schölkopf. An analysis of inference with the universum. In *Proceedings of the 20th Annual Conference on Neural Information Processing Systems (NIPS 2007)*, pages 1–8, 2008.
7. Carl Vogel. N-gram distributions in texts as proxy for textual fingerprints. In Anna Esposito, E. Keller, M. Marinaro, and M. Bratanic, editors, *The Fundamentals of Verbal and Non-Verbal Communication and the Biometrical Issue*, pages 189 – 194. Amsterdam: IOS Press, 2007.
8. Carl Vogel and Gerard Lynch. Computational stylometry: Who's in a play? In A. Esposito, N. Bourbakis, N. Avouris, and I. Hatzilygeroudis, editors, *Verbal and Nonverbal Features of Human-Human and Human-Machine Interaction*. Berlin: Springer, 2008. To Appear.
9. Jason Weston, Ronan Collobert, Fabian Sinz, Léon Bottou, and Vladimir Vapnik. Inference with the universum. In *Proceedings of the 23rd International Conference on Machine Learning*, pages 127–134, 2006.